THE NEW WORLD TRADE ORGANIZATION AGREEMENTS

Globalizing Law Through Services and Intellectual Property

This detailed and insightful book assesses the impact of the WTO through the medium of two new multilateral agreements – the General Agreement on Trade in Services (GATS) and the Agreement on Trade-Related Aspects of Intellectual Property Rights (TRIPs). It explains how these agreements push trade policies 'behind the border', mediating conflicts between contrasting legalities and negotiating political and cultural, as well as economic, issues. Detailed case studies address topics of global significance: competition between different types of legal services, ownership claims to the genetic codes of plants and animals, and access to the content resources and technical facilities of the on-line media. With the Millennium Trade Round in the balance, the book assesses the WTO's potential to move beyond laissez-faire and provide support for independent and alternative producers, providers and users. It takes account of developments up to and including the Seattle ministerial meeting.

CHRISTOPHER ARUP is Head of the School of Law and Legal Studies at La Trobe University, Melbourne. He has held visiting positions at universities in the UK and US, and has provided policy advice to international organizations and governments in Australia. His previous publications include *Innovation, Policy and Law* (Cambridge University Press, 1993), as well as journal articles for *World Competition*, *Prometheus*, *Law and Policy* and the *Journal of World Trade*.

CAMBRIDGE STUDIES IN LAW AND SOCIETY

The broad area of law and society has become a remarkably rich and dynamic field of study. At the same time, the social sciences have increasingly engaged with questions of law. In this process, the borders between legal scholarship and the social, political and cultural sciences have been transcended, and the result is a time of fundamental re-thinking both within and about law. In this vital period, Cambridge Studies in Law and Society provides a significant new book series with an international focus and a concern with the global transformation of the legal arena. The series aims to publish the best scholarly work on legal discourse and practice in social context, combining theoretical insights and empirical research.

Already published:
Anthony Woodiwiss *Globalisation, Human Rights and Labour Law in Pacific Asia*
    0 521 62144 5 hardback 0 521 62883 0 paperback
Mariana Valverde *Diseases of the Will: Alcoholism and the Dilemmas of Freedom*
    0 521 62300 6 hardback 0 521 64469 0 paperback
Alan Hunt *Governing Morals: A Social History of Moral Regulation*
    0 521 64071 7 hardback 0 521 64689 8 paperback
Ronen Shamir *The Colonies of Law: Colonialism, Zionism and Law in Early Mandate Palestine*
    0 521 63183 1 hardback
John Torpey *The Invention of the Passport: Surveillance, Citizenship and the State*
    0 521 63249 8 hardback 0 521 63493 8 paperback
William Walters *Unemployment and Government: Genealogies of the Social*
    0 521 64333 3 hardback

Forthcoming titles:
Heinz Klug *Constituting Democracy: Law, Globalism and South Africa's Political Reconstruction*
    0 521 78113 2 hardback 0 521 78643 6 paperback
Yash Ghai (ed.) *Autonomy and Ethnicity: Negotiating Competing Claims in Multi-ethnic States*
    0 521 78112 4 hardback 0 521 78642 8 paperback

THE NEW WORLD TRADE ORGANIZATION AGREEMENTS

Globalizing Law Through Services and Intellectual Property

Christopher Arup
La Trobe University

CAMBRIDGE
UNIVERSITY PRESS

PUBLISHED BY THE PRESS SYNDICATE OF THE UNIVERSITY OF CAMBRIDGE
The Pitt Building, Trumpington Street, Cambridge, United Kingdom

CAMBRIDGE UNIVERSITY PRESS
The Edinburgh Building, Cambridge, CB2 2RU, UK   http://www.cup.cam.ac.uk
40 West 20th Street, New York, NY 10011–4211, USA   http://www.cup.org
10 Stamford Road, Oakleigh, 3166, Australia   http://www.cup.edu.au
Ruiz de Alarcón 13, 28014 Madrid, España

First published 2000

Printed in Hong Kong by Colorcraft Ltd

Typeface New Baskerville (Adobe) 10/12 pt. *System* QuarkXPress® [PK]

A catalogue record for this book is available from the British Library

National Library of Australia Cataloguing in Publication data
Arup, Christopher, 1949– .
The new World Trade Organization agreements : globalizing
law through services and intellectual property.
Includes index.
ISBN 0 521 77355 5
1. World Trade Organization. 2. General Agreement on Trade in Services (1994).
3. Agreement on Trade-related Aspects of Intellectual Property Rights (1994).
4. Foreign trade regulation. 5. Commercial treaties. I. Title. (Series : Cambridge
studies in law and society).
382.92

ISBN 0 521 77355 5 hardback

CONTENTS

Abbreviations   *x*
Preface and Acknowledgements   *xii*

PART I Globalization, Law and the WTO

1 Trade Law as a Global Mediator   3

2 A Global Context   16
   Convergence and divergence   21
   Legal pluralism   27
   Interfaces   32
   Conclusions   38

3 The World Trade Organization   40
   The ethos of the WTO   42
   The WTO as an institution   44
   The content of the norms   55
   Nullification or impairment   70
   Scope for national regulation   75
   Competition regulation   85
   Conclusions   91

PART II Services

4 The General Agreement on Trade in Services   95
   Status and format of the agreement   100
   Uruguay Round outcomes   106
   The MFN norm   110
   The national treatment norm   113
   The market access norm   117
   The modes of supply   121
   Exceptions   128
   Dispute resolution   132
   Outstanding negotiations   134
   Further developments   138
   Conclusions   142

5 The Case of Legal Services   144
   Styles of service supply   146
   Locations for legal work   151
   National regulation   155
   Impact of the GATS   158
   Country practices   161
   Further developments   167
   Conclusions   172

PART III Intellectual Property

6 The Agreement on Trade-Related Intellectual Property Rights 177
   The Uruguay Round   178
   General provisions and basic principles   183
   TRIPs substantive standards   187
   Other categories   194
   Enforcement provisions   199
   Special and differential treatment   201
   Dispute resolution   203
   Counterbalancing regulation?   206
   Conclusions   211

7 The Case of Genetic Codes   214
   Intellectual property regulation   219
   The concept of invention   224
   Express exceptions   230
   Compulsory licensing   233
   The UPOV Convention   234
   The TRIPs agreement   238
   Recognition for indigenous property rights?   242
   Conclusions   248

PART IV Convergence

8 The Case of Communications Media   253
   Industry-specific regulation   259
   Impact of the GATS   260
   Intellectual property regulation   263
   The TRIPs agreement   272
   WIPO treaties   274
   Competition regulation   280
   Conclusions   301

9 Conclusions and Prospects   304

Notes   *312*
Index   *337*

ABBREVIATIONS

APEC	Asia-Pacific Economic Cooperation Organization
ASEAN	Association of South-East Asian Nations
CIS	Commonwealth of Independent States
DSB	Dispute Settlement Body
FAO	Food and Agricultural Organization
GATS	General Agreement on Trade in Services
GATT	General Agreement on Tariffs and Trade
ILO	International Labour Organization
IMF	International Monetary Fund
ISO	International Standards Organization
ITO	International Trade Organization
ITU	International Telecommunications Union
JFBA	Japanese Federation of Bar Associations
MAI	Multilateral Agreement on Investment
MFN	Most favoured nation treatment
NAFTA	North American Free Trade Association
NGOs	Non-governmental organizations
NICs	Newly industrialising countries
NIH	National Institutes for Health (USA)
NT	National treatment
OECD	Organization for Economic Cooperation and Development
PBR	Plant breeder's right
QUAD countries	United States, European Union, Japan and Canada
SPS	Agreement on the Application of Sanitary and Phytosanitary Measures
Triad countries	Japan, European Union and United States
TRIMs	Agreement on Trade-Related Investment Measures
TRIPs	Agreement on Trade-Related Aspects of Intellectual Property Rights
UNCITRAL	United Nations Commission on International Trade Law

UNCTAD	United Nations Conference on Trade and Development
UNEP	United Nations Environment Program
UNESCO	United Nations Educational, Scientific and Cultural Organization
UNIDO	United Nations Industrial Development Organization
UPOV	International Convention for the Protection of New Varieties of Plants
WIPO	World Intellectual Property Organization
WTO	World Trade Organization

PREFACE AND ACKNOWLEDGEMENTS

The completion of this book has provided me with a challenge in life. My earlier work in these fields made me realise that their international dimensions were becoming ever more important. Internationalisation grew into globalization, which is a general and grand phenomenon, yet one which we must try to represent in an open minded and nuanced way. This effect is even harder to achieve when the focus is on law for, traditionally, we are obliged to treat law with great precision. Consequently, the approach I have taken might seem cautious. But I should like to think that the book will grow on readers, revealing depths as well as breadth. My objective has been to analyse the agreements closely and study their impacts in selected fields. But it is not a blow by blow account of their origins or progress. It aims to be forward looking, conceptualising and evaluating their role in the globalization of law.

Some thanks are overdue. Even if my research has been a solitary pursuit, unwittingly others have provided inspiration. Probably, the greatest assistance came from the opportunity to take part in international gatherings of the law and society movement, particularly conferences in Amsterdam, Onati and Tokyo, and meetings of CONGLASS in Glasgow and New York. The work of Michael Blakeney, John Braithwaite, Peter Drahos, Walter Goode, Sol Picciotto and Sam Ricketson I have found especially helpful to my thinking. I should also thank the readers of the manuscript for having enough faith in me to be critical and demanding. My editors at Cambridge, Phillipa McGuinness, Sharon Mullins and Heather Jamieson, were the most positive influence of them all. I was grateful for an Australian Research Council grant at the start of the project. Peter Quinlivian and Ian Yorke were intelligent assistants at a time when it was just taking shape. I should acknowledge that an early version of chapter five appeared in the journal *World Competition*, of chapter six in the *Australian Intellectual Property Journal*, and chapter eight in a report published by the La Trobe Online Media Program. My thanks in each instance to the editors.

Closer to home, while I had teaching and administrative work to do during the time of the book's writing, my University was kind enough to allow me study leave in 1995. On a daily basis, my colleagues in the School and Faculty created a very cheerful and helpful environment. I thank members of my family, Jenny, Tom, Henni, Janet and Jo, as well as Simone Gardiner, for putting up with the odd hours and the fact that the project hung around for so long. Finally, I am grateful to David Parsons and Chris Nathan for lending me their holiday house at a key moment. I am looking forward to a carefree summer in that vicinity some day soon.

PART I

GLOBALIZATION, LAW AND THE WTO

CHAPTER 1

TRADE LAW AS A GLOBAL MEDIATOR

This first chapter identifies the subject matter of the book and charts its course. As the book is situated in a large and often hazardous field, I am sure it would be useful to make clear what it hopes to achieve. Here, I introduce the ideas which I wish to pursue and indicate the purposes which the book might serve.

My primary objective is to examine the texts and assess the impacts of the World Trade Organization (WTO), largely through the medium of two of its new multilateral agreements. The agreements in focus here are the General Agreement on Trade in Services (GATS) and the Agreement on Trade-Related Aspects of Intellectual Property Rights (TRIPs).[1] In so doing, I should like the book to serve as a useful resource for any student of the WTO. Therefore, a solid component of the book is given over to what I hope will be regarded as a careful analysis of the norms and processes of the organization, using these two most innovative agreements to illustrate how its reach has been extended significantly. It seemed clear from the outset that the agreements would be significant landmarks in the development of international trade law overall. They remain so today. The shambles which was the Third Ministerial Conference late 1999 in Seattle has highlighted the difficulties confronting those who wish to broaden the WTO's agenda. For the time being at least, work on the WTO will concentrate on a better understanding of the architecture which has so far been established, and a cautious development of agreements like the GATS and TRIPs which have an 'in-built' agenda. No new agenda can be expected before the next Ministerial Conference, which is not likely to be held until the year 2001. Yet this experience with the established agreements might point up ways in which other topics, such as competition policy, can sensibly be pursued in the future.

The two agreements were struck when the Uruguay Round reached a conclusion late in 1993.[2] Naturally, they have already attracted their share of expert commentary. Much of this early analysis has been provided by specialists in trade policy, working within the context of the transition from the General Agreement on Tariffs and Trade (GATT) to the WTO. Their perspective is often one of neo-classical economics and consumer welfare.[3] Another established approach, found for example in international relations, has begun to focus on the WTO and its new regimes, thinking particularly in terms of their impact on state power and specifically of national sovereignty.[4] Sourced in political science and policy studies, a related approach has begun to consider where the WTO fits into theories of regulation.[5] Public choice and game theories have figured among the theories which have been brought to bear on the explanation of the WTO agreements. Here, a focus has been the international dynamics of regulatory competition and cooperation. More critical stances are drawing on the long-standing resources of political economy,[6] while post-colonial studies has developed a concern about the impact of the agreements on cultural diversity.[7]

Globalization and law

In this book, I have decided to look at the provisions and implications of the WTO agreements from a different angle again. Our understanding can be advanced if we consider the roles they are playing in the globalization of law. To do so, we shall need to draw on the assistance of theoretical concepts from the field of socio-legal studies. A discussion of those concepts precedes the analysis of the texts. While I appreciate that the concepts will be foreign to some readers, they will allow us to avoid the traps of more technical legal terms. As well, I thought that an understanding would be aided by an empirically minded identification of the operation and impact of the agreements. Thus the analysis is succeeded by case studies of the roles which the agreements play in the provision of legal services, the appropriation of genetic codes and the organization of the on-line media. These case studies have been chosen because their areas of interest also contribute greatly to the process of globalization. They are what I shall call 'global carriers'.

The book then has a specific contribution to make, but I would like to think it might also offer something of general value to the current discussion around globalization and law. It will be my contention that these two agreements are much more than a logical extension of the GATT and the agreements which its parties have made to trade industrial goods over national borders. Because the agreements deal with personal services and intellectual endeavours, they reach 'behind the border' into social fields that were not regarded on the whole as related to trade.[8] In extending the notion of trade, they press for domestic laws and legal practices to be adjusted in distinctive ways to the expectations of foreign suppliers. Furthermore, we shall see that they use law themselves in interesting ways in order to achieve these ends. Consequently, we shall find that many more matters – at the core of economics, politics, cultures, and law – become subject to the influence of trade norms and processes.

In favouring this perspective, I appreciate that a choice has been made that others would not have made, especially those who work within one of the more established approaches to trade or who are concerned with the urgent matters of policy to hand. Nonetheless, I believe this focus on law will prove to be a perspective that can accommodate some of the nuances of the complex, fluid character of globalization. Yet, at the same time, it need not render us entirely dispassionate about the outcomes of this high-stake transformation of society.

Legal pluralism and inter-legality

The perspective employs several conceptual tools familiar to socio-legal scholars. They shall be noted here and discussed more fully in the next chapter. The first is the concept of legal pluralism, the idea that social fields are likely to incorporate a multiplicity and diversity of legalities. We shall identify several varieties of 'legality' in a moment. Under conditions of globalization, such legal diversity often comes to be regarded as difference. From the viewpoint of some traders, this difference gives rise to 'systems friction'. They would like to see such friction eliminated. But for others it represents alternative sources of expression and ordering that ought to be preserved and promoted. We shall be suggesting that the subsuming phenomenon is one of inter-legality. Inter-legality is an uncommon term which Bonaventura da Sousa Santos derived from postmodernism's literary interests in inter-textuality.[9] But the concept of inter-legality nicely conveys the sense that the plural legalities of the world encounter and interact with each other. They clash on occasions but they can also inter-mingle and create new hybrid legalities. Hence, while it seems unfamiliar, inter-legality proves a more accommodating notion than, for instance, the traditional notion of conflict of laws.

Globalization can be expected to widen and deepen the phenomenon of inter-legality. Such inter-legality is spreading wider across the world as many more countries open up to the global flows of goods, persons, money, information and services. Inter-legality is also extending deeper down into the layers of each locality as foreign suppliers seek not only to ship finished goods but also to provide services and make investments. In keeping, we shall see that the two WTO agreements are still concerned with cross-border supply of personal services and intellectual resources. This supply is taking on added dimensions, greatly enhanced by techno-logical innovations. But, additionally, the agreements are concerned with the inter-legalities involved in the establishment of a commercial pres-ence or the presence of natural persons within the locality. In establish-ing this presence, the foreigner encounters a rich variety of legal arrangements which have been made for domestic production and pro-vision, indeed for socially significant activities such as legal services, farm-ing and communications media. These local legal arrangements involve not only legislative measures but also judicial and administrative norms and all manner of unofficial customs and practices.

Why might it be useful to talk here of legalities as well as laws? In such an analysis, we shall need to speak with some precision about particular laws, such as rules for the constitution of the legal profession, national patent laws and telecommunications access codes. We shall need to do the same for the second order laws which govern the relationships between these different laws, such as the bodies of private and public international law. But the concept of legality assists the discussion by pro-viding a more accommodating notion. It allows us to acknowledge a greater variety of normative ordering and certainly more varieties than the official laws of the nation state. It is also accommodating enough to show how the law reflects the colours of economics, politics and cultures. We can anticipate for instance that some legalities will be largely consti-tutive, others regulatory in an instrumentally or strategically minded way, while others again embody custom and tradition. Perhaps the reader will allow a relaxed sense of the possibilities, so that we do not become too caught up in definitional debates. I suggest we shall find that the WTO agreements themselves have a feel for these broader legalities.

To trace the fields in which these agreements operate, it is necessary to identify the patterns or matrices of inter-legality. We shall see that, pri-marily, the agreements address relationships between legalities that are distinguished by their geo-political origins or attachments. Essentially, they see things in terms of foreign and local legalities. A common focus for international and comparative law has been nation-to-nation legali-ties. Along these lines, the foreign legality is founded in another national legality, that of the home rather than host country. Our subject, the for-eign supplier of services, finds that the host country's legality conflicts with the home country legality. This conflict becomes more complicated when some suppliers are able to engage in comparisons between legali-ties and possibly manipulate choice of laws so that they can connect with the most sympathetic 'home country' legality they can find. The sugges-tion is that globalization makes this strategy accessible to a wider range of persons. In the process, national jurisdictions cut across each other because of the multiple points of attachment which global carriers, such as the on-line media, make available to the suppliers and receivers. Yet, the various countries which are implicated will not necessarily accept the suppliers' private choices of law. They may engage in competition over conflict-of-laws criteria as well as over substantive regulatory standards.

At the same time, the foreign legality need not be centred on one nation state or another. The studies of globalization are finding that certain emerging legalities are much more free floating and self-referential. There is interest for instance in the re-emergence of a supra-national *lex mercatoria* in the business field.[10] Built on transnational contracts, model codes and private arbitration, it gives its own legal character to financial transactions, licensing agreements, strategic alliances and corporate mergers. Through the media of electronic commerce, these legal arrangements might assume even more ethereal and transitory manifestations.

So, too, the local legalities which the foreigner encounters need not be grounded in the official public laws of the nation state. We need not treat local legalities as entirely synonymous with national sovereignty. Local legalities might be said to embrace a host of private as well as public legalities. When the laws in the statute books converge, the foreigner only encounters further layers of normative ordering. This ordering can run to the closed cooperative relationships which are forged between local businesses when they organize the production or distribution of services. Alternatively, it might be founded in the customary arrangements which indigenous peoples make to manage and share native resources. These private and unofficial legalities receive various degrees of recognition and support from the nation state.

So supply across the border or the establishment of a presence within a territory may encounter a variety of adverse local legalities. The foreign supplier's dealings with the locals will not be confined to a small elite group which shares common perspectives and interests. It will not be possible to settle on a single legality simply as a matter of consensus. The further 'trade' reaches, the more likely it is to make contact with strangers, in large numbers, whose value systems diverge. These strangers do not always respect the foreigner's legal claims, yet the foreigner increasingly comes to rely on them either for resources or for consumption.

No doubt I am already saying that I do not think that globalization produces convergence or homogeneity in law. While, certainly, that tendency is present within globalization, we should see through the studies why difference remains sustainable. For a variety of reasons, global suppliers find that they still have to negotiate the richness of local diversity. They need to call on the legal support, primarily of the nation state, to open a path for them and safeguard their passage. But, perversely, the same process of globalization has the effect of undermining the competence of the national jurisdictions to which they turn for support.

The WTO interface between legalities

These features of globalization stimulate the efforts being made to formulate agreements such as the WTO agreements. I shall argue that, if we are to understand the agreements and their role in the globalization of law, we need to add the less familiar concept of an interface to our array of conceptual tools.[11] Like a software interface in computer technology, our interface operates to connect legalities, to make them work together, but it does not need to suggest a full integration of the legalities which are interacting or even an ordering of them in a strictly hierarchical fashion. As well as disciplining legalities, the interface provides a kind of mediation. Mediation is meant in its common sense of connecting or creating a link between two positions which initially seem strange or hostile to each other. Mediation is a process of connection which should involve some give and take. The main outcome of the book, I hope, is a better appreciation of the nature of the interface constructed by the WTO and its two 'behind the border' agreements. Perhaps it will also help to make the concept deployable in other contexts. There will of course be many further attempts to mediate legalities as globalization gains in intensity.

While the concept of the interface is drawn from the field of computers and communications technology, I do not want to give the impression that the interface will operate in a neutral, machine-like way. Even when we are dealing with the interfaces between technologies, we find that some are more open, less proprietary, than others. Any attempt to manage inter-legality will put its own particular stamp on the legalities involved. So, at this early stage, it would be unwise to overstate the accommodating nature of the WTO agreements. Indeed, they may turn out to be among the most emphatic of the interfacings in the global legal field. On this basis, another purpose of the book is to characterise the agreements, to point up their biases as it were, and make suggestions for opening out the values and interests they can accommodate.

What might the WTO interface look like? We would naturally expect the interface to favour those legalities which support trade. However the interface is operating with a much more expansive notion of the legalities which relate to trade and which, specifically, act as barriers to trade. To think of intellectual endeavours and personal services as objects of trade is to place them squarely within the realm of the international marketplace and, to trust their fate to the forces and values which operate in that marketplace. More subtly, this exposure has a tendency to abstract or decontextualise these endeavours or services or, more precisely, to extract them from the milieus in which their meanings and values are derived primarily from their local and particular resonances. We might expect some to make the shift and go from strength to strength, while others will find it difficult to compete.

We might also expect the WTO interface to favour global legalities over local. We need to gauge the implications of looking at certain traditional ways of dealing with these endeavours and services (certain legalities) as barriers to trade. The onus is placed on national governments to refashion their regulations as trade-neutral measures or as legitimate exceptions to the norms of trade law. This means that, at the least, local legalities must be mindful of and receptive to the legalities which foreigners bring with them. They must become more cosmopolitan. But we cannot expect all the legalities to survive in a harmonious coexistence. The WTO is pushing in a particular direction.

Put at its strongest, the WTO agreements can be linked to a neo-liberal agenda of regulatory reform. The objective is not just to ease conflicts between foreign and local legalities but to promote 'efficient regulation' around the world.[12] This agenda extends beyond free trade in the sense of breaking down barriers at the border. Its program for reform behind the border seeks to achieve two more ambitious goals. It aims to ensure that markets are accessible to foreign, commercial suppliers while at the same time they are secure for their investments. There are different ways of characterising this package of reforms. They can be seen as a blend between access and security, liberalisation and control, free and fair trade, or deregulation and re-regulation.

Such a program requires a re-orientation, not just of legalities which were designed to protect local industries from foreign competition, but ultimately of a wide range of legalities with preoccupations other than trade, such as professional conduct, natural heritage and media diversity. One immediate target of the agreements is the kind of nationally based, industry-specific legislation which limits foreign participation, guarantees space for local and less powerful producers, and insists on meeting public service obligations. We can expect the agreements to challenge these regulatory legalities and enlarge the scope for more generic bodies of business law, such as private property and contractual rights, to operate in their place. But the new agreements go further than this, as they begin to prescribe the content of that business law directly. Intellectual property and competition law provide two early tests of the prescriptive nature of that content.

However, we should appreciate that, in keeping with the nature of mediation, the agreements remain tentative in their approach to industry-specific regulation. Similarly, their specifications of business law remain incomplete. Moreover, it is not their view to treat intellectual property or even competition law solely as business law. Therefore, we should not be too ready to portray the agreements as single minded. In particular, we should see whether they lend support to independent and alternative producers, those producers, we might say, who cannot make use of the same powers of capital and technology as the largest operators in a laissez-faire global market. So we are asking after the breadth of the access which the agreements give to the rules and resources of globalization.

Non-discrimination

To answer these questions, we examine the norms and processes of the agreements. The examination requires me to provide some background on the WTO as an institution, specifically on the processes established for the conduct of negotiations, the setting of agendas and the settlement of disputes. A particular interest here is how law is used to enhance the WTO's own capacity to mediate as well as to discipline the relationships between legalities. The agreements do not decide which national jurisdiction is to apply in the way that traditional conflict-of-laws doctrine does – we shall see that this kind of choice is becoming increasingly problematic. Instead, the agreements proceed from a principle of non-discrimination. This principle has two component norms, called most favoured nation treatment and national treatment. The essence of non-discrimination is that national legalities treat foreigners no less favourably, the point of comparison for most favoured nation treatment being the treatment of other foreigners, the point of comparison for national treatment being the treatment of locals.

The liberal norms of non-discrimination may seem innocuous and unobjectionable to apply. It is said in particular that both most favoured nation treatment and national treatment do not prescribe the content of a host country's regulatory standards – they only need to apply the standards they choose to adopt equally among foreigners and locals. We shall see that it is becoming rather simplistic to characterise the norms in this way. When the norms are applied in the fields of personal services and intellectual endeavours, being required to treat foreigners no less favourably tends to narrow the regulatory legalities or 'modalities' which are available to national governments when they pursue their preferred policies. A key task for this book is to gauge the reach of these norms in those fields where the foreigner is importing legalities associated with certain types of production process, forms of business organization and modes of service supply (see chapters three and four particularly).

One instance we shall see is that most favoured nation treatment means that foreigners cannot be treated less favourably because a host country disapproves of the policies of their home country, for example in the way they treat the host country's nationals or the spillover effects they produce internationally. So the norm restricts its ability to influence the home legalities of another country. National treatment is significant because countries do wish to apply restrictions to foreigners – they have sought to treat foreigners differently. They wish for instance to protect local industries from foreign inroads or to assert regulatory competence over foreign operators. National treatment may say that formally identical treatment can actually constitute less favourable treatment, for example, if the foreigner finds it more onerous to meet the same requirement as the local. Such a standard means that foreigners cannot be treated simply according to local legalities. It requires the local legality to make concessions to the foreigner's legality. These implications will be explored in subsequent chapters.

Our analyses will show that the agreements work on the content of legalities in a number of ways. For example, the agreements make exceptions for certain non-conforming regulatory measures, but the measures must nonetheless satisfy disciplines which the agreements prescribe. So too the treatment of the foreigner may be deemed satisfactory, if it is part of a formal procedure for the recognition of the home country legality, or if it is in line with an agreed international standard.

Market access and intellectual property protection

Eventually, we shall see that, as influential as they may be, these norms of non-discrimination do not convey all the character of the WTO interface today. While still deregulatory in its inclination, the norm of market access begins to push the reform agenda further. It pushes against the non-discriminatory controls which national regulatory measures have placed on entry and participation within domestic markets generally. It starts to point in the direction of economic 'liberalisation' across the board. So it greatly increases the range of activities we are meant to regard as trade related and the legalities which may be questioned for getting in the way of trade.

I have noted that these activities now include supplying services personally, investing in new or existing establishments, and licensing the use of technology or the arts. Those protective of local ways have made the argument that such activities are not a proper part of trade. But this argument seems largely to have been lost; it might retain some staying power in respect of direct investment. Yet, the critics are right to see that the new 'trade' agenda reaches much further behind the border. The aim is really to open up markets. At its most fundamental, market access means permitting things to be bought and sold. A contrasting approach keeps some sensitive activities out of the field of commerce altogether, so that they are, for example, accessible as part of a public commons or reserved for domestic use. Then, liberalising market access involves lifting restrictions on participation, such as controls on numbers or requirements of fitness to trade. Standard setting is eschewed: sales take place on the terms which the participants themselves determine.

At the same time, a liberalised market is not necessarily a libertarian one. If intellectual property protection prevents a rival from using existing work in a derivative way, with the purpose of offering a cheaper or otherwise more attractive product, the market is being structured by government controls. An alternative might be to let the speed of innovation or quality of performance determine success. Government controls would also be involved if competition policy actually required incumbent producers to provide all comers with access to essential facilities on reasonable and non-discriminatory terms. This style of regulation can be contrasted with the more traditional way of dealing with imbalances in the private power of capital and technology, which is to apply selective licensing to market entry, coupled with performance requirements for those who obtain licences.[13]

In the tradition of the GATT, the focus of the WTO is on government measures that place barriers in the way of access to markets. Our analyses will reveal how the definition of government 'measures' is broadening out. However, as these government measures fall away, the WTO seems to be asking for more again. It begins to expect that member countries regulate to remove 'private' obstacles to market access. The agreements start to question whether government inaction is good enough. The WTO's tests for nullification or impairment of the benefits of an agreement are explored for potential here (see chapter three). Another focus is the regulation of exclusive suppliers, such as telecommunications carriers. The argument is that if government measures have afforded suppliers the power to operate in a discriminatory way, then government should be responsible for applying disciplines to the supplier.

The regulation of intellectual property protection has found a place within the WTO. We have already suggested that the interface expects member countries to provide security to suppliers as well as freedom to trade. Again, if we were to think in conventional terms, the interface would be signalling to governments that they must not disrespect the private property rights of foreigners. In this regard, the draft MAI (Multilateral Agreement on Investment) has sought to prohibit government from 'expropriating' foreign investments.[14] The discussion around the MAI showed how far reaching might be the impact of that negative constraint. However it is worth appreciating that the WTO interface already goes further. It expects governments to provide foreigners with legal protection against the threats to their intellectual property which stem from the unauthorised activities or measures of other private persons (see chapter six particularly). If trade agreements traditionally signalled a deregulatory response, this intellectual property protection indicates there is at the same time a strong re-regulatory dimension to the interface. Such a standardisation of legalities is a clear way to overcome the conflict between laws, even the arguments about discrimination. Foreigners can expect the same legality to be observed around the world.

The WTO's norms of intellectual property protection also reach far behind the border. The initial target of trade-related intellectual property rights was cross-border traffic in pirated and counterfeited goods. But the TRIPs (Agreement on Trade-Related Aspects of Intellectual Property Rights) agenda broadened considerably to address the legalities of domestic production in areas such as agriculture, health, culture and human life itself. A main task of this book is to consider the circumstances in which the WTO requires a national legality to recognise a foreigner's entitlement to intellectual property. Crucial too are the control rights which the members must provide over the uses of the intellectual resource. On the whole, we can say that the WTO favours the liberal legality of the private property right. Yet, as emphatic as the norms are in translating clashes of legalities into issues of private property, it is not surprising that the WTO has left room for other national and international legalities to interact. These legalities for instance recognise alternative bases for building entitlements and make allowance for competing uses of the resource.

Competition policy

These allowances are evidence of an appreciation that the interface should not become too one-sided. Economic liberalism provides opportunities for market power to be strengthened, here now on a global scale. Accordingly, accommodation must be made for measures that seek to counteract abuses of this market power. Otherwise, liberalisation might simply end in laissez-faire. Already, we are seeing evidence of second thoughts about the virtues of untrammelled financial freedom. There are a number of critical regulatory legalities which the WTO is being asked to bring within the contemplation of the interface. They include regulation for tax collection, the prudential supervision of financial institutions, core labour standards, and the protection of the natural environment. But for the time being at least, the WTO's position is to keep these issues of regulation at bay. The most it seems to do is make a minor allowance for certain approved national measures, when they risk cutting across the liberal trade norms themselves. As we shall see, the WTO is being prevented from moving on these urgent concerns by its own conceptual and political limitations.

So, without in any way underestimating the importance of these issues, my work here will focus on another regulatory legality. The focus is competition policy. My judgement is that competition policy represents the re-regulatory initiative most likely to be brought within the interface of the WTO. It is the approach which a neo-liberal regulatory reform agenda is most likely to offer us as a safeguard against abuses of market power. However the content of the competition policy which the WTO will support is very much unresolved at this stage. The WTO may expect competition policy to override those remaining national legalities which afforded domestic industry immunities and impeded the access of foreigners to domestic markets. But, as competition policy is drawn into the WTO interface, we can also ask whether it will offer a means to question the legality of the restrictive trade practices in which some transnational suppliers engage. Simply leaving a space within the trade norms for national governments to regulate will not necessarily make this happen. Without some impetus being provided from within the interface, globalization will mean that many national governments do not enjoy the legal jurisdiction or the political power needed to apply such disciplines. The commitment is not only important in its own right. If the WTO was prepared to forge a re-regulatory code of conduct here, it could serve as the experimental model for the fashioning of codes in other areas too (such as labour). We shall return to the question of the WTO's competition policy after we have sought to evaluate the contribution it is making to the liberalisation of markets.

Global carriers

These types of inquiry inevitably give the book a somewhat dry flavour. I wish to give the treatment more life by looking at the ways in which the WTO agreements, using the kind of conceptual and procedural approaches we have begun to describe, mediate the inter-legality of certain global 'carriers'. The carriers selected for study are those of legal services, genetic codes and on-line communications media.

The carriers are worthy of study because of their role in the circulation of knowledges, technologies and signs around the globe. Along with money, they are among the most physically mobile, indeed the most symbolically conveyed of all the global currencies. Furthermore, by enhancing the power of calculation and critique, they promote the capacity of persons and firms to operate in a socially reflexive fashion.[15] For whoever enjoys access to their rules and resources, they provide means to monitor, circumvent and exploit many of the different conditions to be found around the world. These differences range through physical conditions, production factors, financial charges and regulatory requirements to cultural mores and social practices. Not only do the carriers afford capacity to cut loose from the imperatives of the locality in this way, they help to construct new global networks of social relations. We should see how legal services provide means to fashion commercial transactions and business associations globally. Genetic codes of the living organism help promote global systems for the production of food and medicines. So too, the on-line media can project popular entertainment content and specialist informative services within all corners of the globe.

Yet the studies reveal how the ties to the locality can still be strong. If the carriers themselves offer ways to undermine locally based regulation, the legalities associated with these carriers continue to reflect a diversity of established approaches. More proactively, they represent efforts to position particular groups advantageously within an expanding global competition. Those seeking to make use of the carriers, in extreme circumstances to obtain control of them, are interested in mediation of the relationships between their favoured legalities and those of others. If the WTO is asked to mediate, what impact does it have on the relationships between these legalities? In particular, we ask whether it can offer assistance to various sorts of independent and alternative producers, providers and users who seek to override the control points of the past and make globalization work for them too. Thus, the case studies can help us to 'ground', where it matters, the kind of general observations we are making about the WTO's norms and processes.

Chapter two provides a global context for the WTO, exploring the basic phenomena I have characterised as legal pluralism, inter-legality and interface. Chapter three gives essential information about the WTO. Chapter four analyses the provisions of the GATS, while chapter five, still focussing on the GATS, makes the first of the case studies – the study of legal services. Chapter six analyses the provisions of TRIPs. Chapter seven follows up with a case study of genetic codes. Chapter eight's case study, on-line media, enables the impacts of the GATS and TRIPs to be considered within the same field. For those readers intending to pick and choose, you will find that each chapter commences with a summary of its contents.

CHAPTER 2

A GLOBAL CONTEXT

Chapter two provides the global framework for the analysis of the two new WTO agreements and the impact they are having on the inter-legalities of legal services, genetic codes and on-line media. It gives some definition to the three key concepts we shall be carrying with us through the studies. It begins by suggesting why globalization is both something new and something old. It spends time considering how globalization reconfigures the plural legalities of the world. Sources of convergence are identified in the ways economies work but also in the role of cultures. The chapter notes, too, the influence of politics and the complex processes of regulatory competition and cooperation.

The contention here is that diversity remains sustainable, even if that diversity increasingly comes to be treated as difference. Convergence theory tends to suggest that nation states must offer the same regulatory regime if they are to meet the expectations of global suppliers. However it appears that localities retain some leeway to vary their approaches and, indeed, globalization provides opportunities for the expression of new differences. It is necessary for us to be prepared to 'deconstruct' the content of global legalities and here we can appreciate that they do not push simply in the direction of some kind of standardised regulation. So within globalization, we are likely to be exposed to currents which are running opposite ways, towards destruction and creation, deregulation and re-regulation, disconnection and re-attachment, exclusion and access.

Chapter two, then, identifies the capacities of law specifically to promote both convergence and divergence. On the one hand, law abstracts and generalises. These capacities are enlisted by those who would disconnect the networks of social relations from their ties in space and time. But of course law can also display rich, localised textures. The navigation of these legalities depends on familiarity with detailed, even tacit knowledge which can only be acquired through an enduring presence deep within the layers of the locality. The chapter relates the examples of intellectual property and competition law in order to indicate why, when economic, political, cultural and legal fields interact, conflicts of laws are likely to continue.

The chapter goes on to acknowledge the interest which socio-legal scholars have shown in the phenomenon of inter-legality. It begins to outline ways in which this interest can be translated into the contemporary global scene. If inter-legalities seem predominantly to be nation-to-nation (that is inter-national) legalities, globalization adds more complexity to the grid of relationships. It constructs relationships between transnational, national and sub-national legalities. It leads on, indeed, to relationships between different international legalities. This matrix of inter-legalities is complicated today by the participation of a greater number of nation states, the operation of many more non-government organizations, and the increasingly multi-polar arrangement of international institutions.

Finally, to see if it can assist us in understanding how these inter-legalities might be mediated, the chapter adds in the concept of an interface. The concept is defined and its role expounded. The interface under scrutiny here is operated by the WTO. This leads the chapter into a consideration of the way such multilateral institutions proceed. We shall ask what sort of legal arrangements provide one such institution with the rules and resources to mediate successfully. In particular, we shall be interested to know whether the indeterminacy of law, as much as its capacity to order and discipline relationships, assists in the task of mediation. We find this condition of indeterminacy in the norms and processes of the successful institution. Chapter two stresses the point that we should measure the success of an institution by the capacity of the interface to accommodate perspectives. Success is not to be marked by a single-minded insistence on a narrow agenda.

Yet the interface is far from being a neutral conduit. While the concept of inter-legality rejects the more extreme ideas abroad about the incommensurability of legal traditions, it is not meant to imply that the different legalities meet on equal terms. Certainly, the widening and deepening of the contacts between legalities make it more difficult to impose a strict hierarchy or uniformity on law. We might observe that, in many instances, the past methods of imposition are becoming less effective. The use of military force or even economic sanctions meets greater resistance, and less deference is shown to the superiority of Western models of universality. A more subtle approach is sought. But, inevitably perhaps, the mediating device puts its own twist on the relationship between the legalities. It may very well skew the relationship in favour of certain kinds of legality. Moreover, we might discover that it is successful in doing so precisely because it proceeds by way of mediation.

Research

The idea that law is moving more and more to engagement across international and transnational fields has become a major topic for research in studies of law and society. The identification of such fields for law emerges from the pursuit of varied research interests. The interests have included the changing nature of legal practice and the legal profession, the relationship between lawyers and business, international business regulation, human rights, the rights of indigenous peoples, trans-border health and environmental hazards, and population and migration movements. The research may start as subject-specific work, good examples being the regulation of international business taxation and international securities markets. However it assumes more general significance as it identifies new regulatory norms and processes at work, such as regulatory competition and cooperation, and even the globalization of legal phenomena.[1]

Whenever the concept of globalization is invoked, we are reminded of the lengthy and weighty pedigree of comparative and international law scholarship. Not surprisingly, much of the recent interest is still organized around such established headings and it moves only gradually to a more holistic view of the world. Such organization reflects a naturally cautious response to the sweeping claims made for globalization. However, we should not be too ready to let go of the idea that something profound is represented by the proliferating multi-polarity, yet essential interconnectedness, of legal fields. Much of the recent work could be said to be striving for an approach that recognises the scale of the issues at stake, while remaining positive about the degree of diversity and contingency in the world.

Here, my inclination is to agree with Handler that 'something big is happening', at least to the extent that some commentators envisage the globalization of free trade and a borderless capitalist economy.[2] Nonetheless, Dezalay is right to counsel us not to confuse practices with the discourses which 'orchestrate' them.[3] We should appreciate that globalization is as much an idea or perspective as its competitors, such as the seeming naturalness of local legal traditions. There is nothing inevitable about globalization. For the time being at least, we should be inclined to expect that 'there will be more cognitive orientation, more decentralised norm creation, more autonomy of political arenas, more cultural competition, hence less stability and less transparency of the normative order'.[4] After making a valiant attempt to plot the matrix of international securities regulation, Trachtman makes a similar point:

'This article has indicated the overlapping, interacting, and generally chaotic nature of international deference and cooperation in the single sector of securities regulation. Multiple reasons, multiple methods, and multiple scopes interact to form a complex and often indistinct matrix.'[5] This recalls the idea, from globalization theory, of there being 'unity in diversity'.

Outlooks

It follows that one way we might 'cope' with the very demanding task of conceptualising globalization is to think of it as a construct. Globalization may be invested with various meanings and enlisted to different causes. Thus, the conceptualisations of globalization produce contrasting attitudes. In particular, these attitudes may contrast activism with fatalism, or hope with despair. We appreciate that the most confident global outlook is usually associated with the new economic liberalism. The 'end of history', the collapse of communist regimes in Eastern Europe, and the transition to market economies in Latin America and Asia, have led many to conclude that it is the dominant fact of world life. In recent times, there have of course been different versions of this formulation. We might say that the modernisation movement aimed to educate 'backward' societies in the virtues of Western liberal institutions.

The more contemporary and powerful version has proved to be the idea of an inevitable search for greater economic efficiency on a global scale. The search includes the most efficient set of regulatory arrangements on offer.[6] Open trade and free markets are said to enable that search to take place. The 'neo-liberalism' of open trade and free markets has attracted a great deal of attention in business, government, university and international circles since the 1980s. This conjuncture provides an opening for the widespread acceptance of global markets in agricultural commodities, manufactured goods, the delivery of services, investment flows and transfers of information. Finally, it might be possible to make full use of comparative advantages, so raising the level of consumer welfare across the world.

An approach which is allied in many ways is that of 'big science' and high technology.[7] Our drive to control nature is exemplified by the ambitious plans to mobilise nature's genetic codes. Genetic research and biotechnology will transform food production and health care, perhaps human reproduction as well. As we shall see from the case studies, communications and professional services may also hold out the promise of more technical mastery over the forces of nature and human society

On the other hand, globalization has fostered a somewhat more pessimistic view, harking back to the political economy of world systems theory. Today, there is understandable concern about the global power of corporate conglomerates and technocratic elites. Globalization may produce the conditions for a new economic order, accentuating divisions, even to the extent of a new kind of feudalism which is based on control over abstract values and social capital such as information resources. In this world view, the division between centre and periphery may have lost much of its spatial specificity. But it takes on new form in the polarisation of the working conditions of skilled and unskilled workers, or the gap between the information rich and the information poor.

Globalization can produce such divisive effects because it undermines what has been one of the main lines of defence for social welfare. Democratic forms of government have been centred on the nation state or, in some instances, the local community. For those concerned about global overshadowing, the struggle to maintain the viability of domestic regulation is vital. This regulation has been important to the efficacy of a number of local protections. For instance, it has provided the means to ensure a local revenue return, build up indigenous capability, maintain political authority, preserve cultural traditions and safeguard physical and social environments. Hence, in the process of globalization, the local, the spatial, becomes the rallying point for a considerable range of distributional concerns, communitarian sentiments and non-economic values. For some, of course, this orientation points to the need to preserve existing state institutions, public instrumentalities and statutory requirements. But we should appreciate that it also runs to the defence of a whole host of informal, 'private' regulatory spaces.

As important as these concerns are, the discussion rarely ends there. A notable addition to the debate is the cautious optimism about the value of looking outward and making the global shift work for various 'social' groups. Among these groups are represented consumer, labour, feminist and environmental perspectives. As we have suggested, the main themes of globalization often stress the power of such 'players' as financial dealers, multinational corporations, big science, media conglomerates, and elite technocrats. They may do so in a positive or negative light. But globalization becomes a source of hope for others who have experienced disenchantment with the policies of their nation state. As Baxi reminds us, this orientation is not new.[8] Indeed, he argues that the new narrative of economic globalization is a challenge to an older culture of globalism, of universal humankind, human rights and self-determination. The new social movements are the successors to this tradition of globalism for which the main international institutional field has been the United Nations. Professor Baxi is not as optimistic as others about the prospects for the two streams to be reconciled. He detects a reluctance in both self-confident economic liberalism and relativising postmodernism to maintain this culture.

Axford casts this issue in sociology's terms of the structure–agency distinction.[9] To some degree, we can accept that individuals are scripted by institutional orders and cultural accounts. However, globalization undermines existing institutions and offers new ones which compete. It may thus provide individuals with opportunities to adopt fresh perspectives and practices. It erodes the physical and temporal barriers which once protected local interests and identities, so that it appears a welcome opportunity in some cases to escape local intolerances and insularities. At the same time, it exposes individuals to a wider range of knowledges and experiences. Global economics and technologies do not engender a feeling of certainty and safety, rather they increase the sense of risk and contingency in people's lives. Yet, as more informed and critical – albeit anxious and insecure – agents, they might enjoy greater scope for self-realisation and collective development. They gain the capacity to interpret, act upon and perhaps transform the institutions which are in the making. Thus the process of global 'structuration' that is now gradually taking shape is to be seen as a negotiated and contingent one.

CONVERGENCE AND DIVERGENCE

How might these broad orientations and aspirations contribute to both the multi-polarity and interconnectedness of globalization? Perhaps the most sensitive and nuanced representations of globalization characterise it as a fluid process, riven by cross-currents of economic, cultural and political flows. These representations put the metaphor of water to good use. In assigning some direction to the flows, the uncertainties and ambivalences surrounding the potentialities of globalization may be revealed in the force which people are prepared to attribute to the currents of economies, polities and cultures. Thus, a common view presents a mismatch between the strong tides of a global economy, on the one hand and, on the other, the backwaters of fragmented political power, which is still – at least formally speaking – assigned to the nation state. In addition, the rich diversity of cultural experience may be viewed as a source of harbour-like relief or respite from the reduction of the 'life world' to either market exchanges or power relations.[10]

It would be convenient, schematically, if the various sources of legalities could be compartmentalised like this. But we should acknowledge that the compelling issues of identity cannot be so neatly separated from those which are connected with material interests or wills to power, that is, with desire or reason. Such a separation is especially artificial in the fields where the WTO agreements are reaching, such as intellectual and artistic endeavours, the provision of services with a high personal or social quotient, and the construction of law itself. In any integrated analysis, the economies of culture have to be related to the cultural and political contexts of the market. A ready example comes from the field of tourism. From personal experience maybe, we understand how global tourism both trades on culture and aestheticises economics, while at the same time it may attract intense political attention. For a current illustration, we might point to the case of tourism in Egypt.

This kind of interactivity has implications for law. In keeping with the mismatch analysis, it has been suggested that material exchanges which take place on a global scale have dispensed with the need for normative integration. If there is integration of systems, it will be 'behind the backs' of the participants. So, as we noted, Gessner foresees a greater cognitive and instrumental orientation to social relations with, accordingly, less political solidarity and less effective cultural ties. But it has long been understood that markets are never pre-social: there are as many markets as there are possible legal rules to define them. Furthermore, when markets are structured by rules, such rules are not taken up in merely an instrumental fashion. They form part of the politics and cultures that afford meaning and legitimacy to claims of interest, for example by building up the necessary respect and goodwill for them. So, while they certainly include the laws promulgated by nation states, the conventional site of legal authority, they are also comprised of all kinds of informal normative knowledges and observances. We could say that this has been the lesson for those societies which have endeavoured to embrace the free market and expose their economy to open trade, without building up the value systems and community networks of civil society which are needed to glue it all together. In truth, the onset of open trade and free markets only revives the competition to claim the economic, political and cultural content of the law. We have resolved to see how the WTO agreements entail a struggle over those associations. In particular, we seek to identify the support which they give to competing perspectives and interests.

The economic sphere

While doing its best to be interdisciplinary, a work like this cannot expect to convey all the richness and complexity of globalization; the present remarks are intended merely to give a feel for the essential duality of globalization. Globalization breaks down the boundaries of time and space, while at the same time underscoring the continuing ties of the locality. Such a broad brush approach is meant to provide a backdrop to the subject matter of the case studies. With this in mind, we can start considering the economic sphere by acknowledging the tendency of globalization to give a worldwide organization to economic processes. It is notable for feeding lines of investment, transfers of information and travel of personnel into the flow channels, along of course with the more established trade in finished goods and primary commodities. Such services support the global coordination of production in which the transnational corporation emerges as the key actor and many of the flows are not only intra-industry but also intra-firm. Increasingly, they also involve the supply of intellectual and personal services across borders into end-consumer markets.

Yet, paradoxically perhaps, the same process of coordination takes advantage of local specialisation. It reveals the national base of many corporations, the varying industrial organizations of national cultures, the shifting pattern of strategic alliances and contracting out, the contribution made by small firms, the use of flexible modes of production and feedback from sophisticated users. However, these developments should not be treated simply as evidence of disintegration or even disorganization. Rather, we should appreciate that they give rise to the complex organism of the network. Place still has a role to play in these global networks. Participants draw on their historical and geographical strengths. For example, recent work has detected clusterings of industry in webs of researchers, suppliers, producers, distributors and users. Even the management, financing and design functions of global operators tend to be grouped in certain city centres.[11] But globalization reveals all sorts of strengths and dependencies. The current thirst of science and industry – for fresh supplies of natural genetic materials and original forms of artistic expression – provides a poignant example.

Furthermore, we know that much production continues to be for home markets. Producers often need to be near to their customers if they are to meet their demands responsively. This need to maintain a local presence makes the movements of natural persons and the flows of direct investment both more crucial and more sensitive issues. In this configuration, connections also need to be made with indigenous producers, say through strategic alliances with local firms and the employment of workers with skills specific to the local context. Of course, any capacity to abstract and standardise supply modes works in the other direction, but we should keep in mind that standardisation is not fail-safe. For example, supply from a distance often exposes the services to the risk of unauthorised access and competition from copying technology.

The political sphere

A strong theme in the writing about globalization is of economic processes that undermine the nation state's capacity to exercise regulatory choice and competence. For example, free flows of capital enable financial markets and business corporations to pass judgement on national policies and to obtain favourable concessions by playing states

23

off in rounds of 'regulatory arbitrage'. States feel pressed to adopt the kind of policies which attract and reassure investors. The ethos and practices of the private international business world may be introduced into the national realm more directly through the corporatisation and privatisation of public sector instrumentalities.

The resulting cross-investments, intra-group transfers and transnational linkages make it increasingly difficult for nation states to apply regulation effectively, either to capture the benefits of globalization or control its costs. Taxation is proving to be a case in point. Tax competition through transfer pricing is replacing competition through trade in finished goods. If, at an earlier stage, the flows had materialised in a particular location, then states at least knew where to apply disciplines to the competition they experienced. Now a transactional cyberspace conveys the notion that markets need not have any geographic location or time zone at all. They could almost be regarded as existing somewhere in the ether.[12] In Ruggie's imaginative conceptualisation, a 'space' of flows floats free above the space of places.[13] Such flows create enormous uncertainties for national governments. They enable further detachment of formal abstract relations from the physical sites of production and delivery, throwing conflict-of-laws criteria into confusion and making the applicable regulatory regime an option for greater numbers of ordinary people.

Yet the same process of globalization provokes many domestic groups (including business groups) to look to the nation state for protection. These constituencies may vary with the issue. Indeed, it is important to understand that the very same people may find themselves shifting between roles – in one capacity the beneficiary, in another the victim, of globalization. We shall use intellectual property as an example of this. Many producers are also borrowers and copyists. As a consequence, nation states continue to address the use of market freedoms and powers in a range of regulatory policies. So, when intellectual products and personal services reach behind the border, they encounter sensitive regulatory domains, designed to assert economic independence, political sovereignty and cultural integrity.

At the same time, we should accept that the attitudes of global suppliers to state policy are not single minded. Certainly, we can say that they do not produce simply a demand for deregulation. Much of the deregulation appears to be occurring unilaterally, as local elites invoke globalization as a rationale for their domestic agendas. Instead, global suppliers often seek a mixture of flexibility and security. This mix involves a relaxation of restrictions on flows at the same time as protection from unfair or excessive competition. Dezalay wryly comments: 'Not only does the logic of the market, of which they are the agents, gradually submerge the national cultures of which they are the inheritors; but, to construct an international market, they rely on the very state structures they are undermining.'[14]

If state regulation is still an issue, there seems to be no singular desire to standardise that regulation. The cost of complying with differential national requirements is a consideration for global operators but they may themselves see convenience in the maintenance of differences. Even if the search is for efficiency, there is no single set of 'efficient' regulatory arrangements.[15] What is efficient will depend in part on one's standpoint. The recent vagaries of the international financial markets highlight this observation. The message to be derived from this is that we should be prepared to 'deconstruct' the demands of the global, just as we expect to find diversity among local aspirations. Thus, for nation states, the lesson of new growth and strategic trade theories is (to adopt economic terminology) the imperfect nature of competition in global markets. Advantages are to be gained by practising selective support, brokerage and organizational policies. While no longer necessarily inward looking – that is, based on defensive measures which aim to shelter domestic production and further import substitution – the national stance may be a neo-mercantilist one rather than one which is receptive to free trade.

For activists, this suggests that the pressures of globalization are refracted through the prism of national policies. It is sometimes said that standardisation is more likely to emerge in the regulation of areas like private property, market transactions and business association – the basic building blocks of a liberal market economy.[16] Any serious comparison, however, reveals differences in these respects as well as the more predictable areas of industry assistance and social regulation. Furthermore, while regulatory competition analysis often suggests a laddering down of standards – a race to the bottom – it may be possible for localities to engage in a global economy on the strength of high standards. Success may be found in a compromise between competition and cooperation, private freedoms and public policy, consumption and production.[17] However, before we get too hopeful, we should enter a note of caution. This strategy may have its limits. As the global actors become even more mobile and reflexive, the viability of social regulation may depend on the control of regulatory competition through the introduction of international standards.[18]

The cultural sphere

While it accommodates a richer pattern of economics and politics, this kind of analysis is still too materially and instrumentally oriented ever to begin to encapsulate the nature of globalization. We shall benefit by taking to heart the renewed interest in culture. Certainly, it can be said that the regulation of intellectual products and personal services

assumes cultural significance. But culture too has contradictory tendencies. Cultural flows may be treated as the ultimate carriers of universalis-
ing global messages. In Waters' handy formulation: 'material exchanges
localize; political exchanges inter-nationalize; and symbolic exchanges
globalize'.[19] It is not hard to see how products and services which are
largely symbolic in nature can detach identity from place. Submersion
within some of the contemporary media may also encourage people to
lose track of time. Living in an ever transient present, diverted by imagi-
nary futures, they are tempted to forget the lessons of history and the
value of traditions. My own children seem reluctant to read anything but
contemporary literature, if they are not immersed in audiovisual media.

However, globalization can also be seen to sharpen a sense of cultural
difference. While that sense can be highly defensive, in its positive manifestations, it points up the strength of long-standing cultural practices.
These practices include non-market and non-industrial means of meeting material needs. In other words, disjuncture does not simply arise out
of modernisations not taking readily in developing countries. Various
localities show resistance to the wholesale commodification of culturally
significant activities, such as agriculture, health care, education, artistic
expression and professional service. Of course, it is readily appreciated
that, across the world, the range of cultures is great. So too, many locations contain a variety of religious and ethnic groups within them. But,
even from within the organization of thoroughly capitalist societies, differences are significant. Contrasts can be made, for example, in the levels
of commitment capitalists make to long-term relationships with suppliers, workers, customers and communities.[20] Such levels of commitment
vary, not only from country to country, but also from sector to sector and
period to period. In fields like legal services, the use of genetic resources
and the Internet, such cross-cultural divides can frustrate attempts to
gain market access for services or to win local respect for claims to intellectual property.

Yet, scepticism remains. In some quarters, there is doubt whether all
the cultural profusion and traffic associated with 'postmodernity' are
anything more than the surface phenomena of another highly adaptive
phase in capitalism's development.[21] And it is true that the hyper-reality
of media cyberspace or science eugenics provides no substitute for the
authentic identities and personal relations which are rooted in local
communities. Yet we should retain some optimism about the prospects
for cultural pluralism at the global level. The most obvious candidates for
a third culture are the business elites and symbolic analysts. But globalization may enable new (and not so new) social movements to connect
up across the world and bring influence to bear on transnational fields.
'Destructuration' at the national level is especially evident in the growth

of non-class movements, some seeking definition and association through their choice of expressive or aesthetic lifestyles, rather than their rational and material outlooks.[22]

LEGAL PLURALISM

Horizontal private business justice

Where do we begin to place law within this loose frame of reference? Of course we have already touched on law in the discussion of the economic, political and cultural spheres. For law is 'imbricated' within these spheres and displays all the fluidity and contrariness of their flows. So, we can begin by claiming that law works for globalization, most obviously where its symbolic and abstract qualities are enlisted to disconnect relations from their spatial and temporal reference points. Certain kinds of laws (and lawyers) become the carriers of worldly ideas and practices. For Dezalay, it is precisely law which fills the void left by the withdrawal of coercion – the symbolic production of law playing an active role in the construction of a transnational field of business justice.[23] We can think of this justice being built on offshore incorporation, transnational contracts, commercial arbitration and model commercial codes, leading to the crystallisation of a new supra-national, and possibly a-national, *lex mercatoria.*[24]

It is important to note that the facilities lent by this kind of law do not just guide traders and investors in their selection of physical location. The legal media of contracts and corporations provide opportunities to manipulate the matrix of jurisdictions. Components of a total legal package may take different transactional forms and be routed between entities with a variety of jurisdictional links.[25] We know that sophisticated legal and other business services play an important part in designing these packages and fitting them to the circumstances of the clients. The enhanced mobility and reflexivity make it difficult for nation states to fix their sights on the traders and investors, rendering their regulation 'competent'. Indeed, as we noted in our discussion of politics, they may feel compelled to offer up these regulations if they are to compete for business. In this process, more and more areas of national law, previously regarded as domestic concerns, become the subject of international economic policy considerations. Eventually, it is suggested, business will find a home in a self-contained and self-referential field of justice that floats free above the claims of the nation state altogether.

Yet our understanding of the role of law in globalization needs to be given greater nuance. First, we should acknowledge that business law is not developing merely out of immediate material self-interest. Studies capture the dualism of business lawyers, torn between competition and ideals. They often evince a desire to affirm the legitimacy of their vocation

27

through a contribution to international public service. Certainly, such lawyers have been involved with national governments in advising on changes to local legislation or agreement to bilateral treaties which are meant to accommodate the needs of business, for example in the tax area. But they may place their role on a higher plane. They make a contribution to world growth by building systems of cross-cultural communication, peaceful dispute resolution and private justice. One could acknowledge for instance the public-spirited work done by lawyers towards the codification of business law through such international organizations as UNCITRAL, the Sale of Goods Convention, the Hague Convention and Unidroit. Their peculiar skills may fit them to this task. Law lends legitimacy to specific economic practices by translating them into law's specialist discourse of abstract principles and equality of treatment.

Richly textured local law

If law were to be involved in the construction of a transnational field of business justice, we would most likely expect it to be sourced in freedom of contract. Its autonomy would derive primarily from the consent and cooperation of the parties. However, if this kind of cohesion comes apart, a more likely prospect as the field widens and deepens, the participants will continue to look to national legal systems for support. National jurisdictions may take this opportunity to question the content of the international contracts. The controversies over the validity of exemption and penalty clauses, indeed over choice-of-law clauses, provide evidence of this remaining oversight. But such an interest is reflected not only in differential national contract law. It is also manifested in a range of what are more conventionally called regulatory laws such as fair trading, consumer protection, prudential supervision, access and equity, taxation, employment protection, and environment management laws.[26] One consequence of this is that countries do not simply accept private choice-of-law manoeuvres. They clash over conflict-of-laws criteria as well as substantive standards of conduct. A pertinent example is their unwillingness to accept commercial arbitration where it encompasses regulatory questions such as competition law.[27]

In this process of differentiation, the locality need not always be inward looking. Globalization provides an opening for a variety of national and other legal bases to orient outwards, inserting their own models into international fields and exporting them to other places. The usual suspect is the West. But, given the different organizational forms which capitalism assumes, we might expect to see more self-confident assertions of transnational legal links across non-Western cultures. A case in point might be the operation of Singapore lawyers in Hong Kong, Vietnam and China. Greater consciousness of the culturally specific origins of legal universals and greater acceptance of cultural relativism have tempered the force with which legal liberalism is recommended as the sole model for adoption by modernising and internationalising countries.

Such abiding national law displays, to use Olgiati's descriptive terminology, rich or thick localised characteristics.[28] Knowledge and practice of this law are enhanced by presence, proximity and temporality. A whole range of economic advantages, political privileges, cultural traditions and legal peculiarities provide reasons for continuing legal differentiation and the failure of universalist models to take at the local level. Certainly, this is observable when one looks beyond the layers of law represented by the law in the statute books and judicial decisions. So the location of law making still matters. When laws converge on the surface, they merely give way to further layers of institutional and cultural resistance to external influences.[29] The simile sometimes employed is one of 'peeling an onion'. Ultimately, such resistance turns not so much on overt formal rules as on deep informal, private understandings and customs. Thus, law continues to assume specific cultural and social forms. Just as transnational business constructs its own regulatory systems, law at the local level is made by private practices. Even where jurisdictions are attracted to international trade and investment, for example through corporate mergers and acquisitions or public sector privatisation, the local legal culture will still end up displaying its own peculiarities.

Intellectual property and related laws

To underscore this basic point, we shall now consider the main subject matter of the book. Again, as well as illustrating these basic points, the discussion should help set the scene for our case studies. We might begin by observing that dealings in intellectual property are quite often not confined to small elite groups which share common understandings and interests. If we think about the circumstances in which the seeds of plants are produced and then utilised, or how snatches and samples of music, text and images are deployed in the on-line media, the practices involve widely dispersed strangers and divergent value systems. Divergence characterises views, for example, about what is invented or authored, or what is entitled to attract remuneration rather than be open to free access and use.[30] The problems producers face controlling the infringements of their putative property rights present the obvious case. It is unlikely a consensus mechanism like a contract can be used very often.

Of course, such problems do not stem just from differences in attitudes. Logistically, enforcement can be daunting. Aided by communications and copying technologies, these strangers take advantage of the public nature of many intellectual resources. The producers need to be able to call on legal regulation, if there is to be an effective social relation of exclusion and control. Yet the multi-party, multi-national way in which these resources are often produced and distributed places in considerable confusion the law which is to apply.[31]

For instance, a phenomenon like the new on-line media allows many possible points of attachment to jurisdictions. Among these points might be the site of the origin of the work, the site of an assignment or licence, the site of the emission or reception of the transmission, the nationality or residence of the producer, or the nationality or residence of the infringer. Thus the media can readily be seen to generate permutations with a vast potential for a clash of laws. Indeed, the operation of the media may make it hard to decide just where those sites of attachment happen to be, even if agreement has been reached on which site is to provide the locus for the law. Messages can be switched from point to point, from server to server for instance, travelling around the world in thin air and at great speed. They are often received within the privacy of domestic households. In a sense, such problems are inherent in the notion of intellectual property, for it is property in something intangible and as such much more a relation between people than command over a material object which can be physically and temporally connected with a location. Could intangible ideas know no bounds whatsoever? The picture is further complicated where the law concedes that the many people who are involved in these activities may operate as juridical entities rather than as natural persons. Location can then be manipulated through the abstract forms in which they appear as well.

The traditional way of resolving these problems is through conflict-of-laws criteria. Very broadly, we can suggest that private international law involves the resolution of three issues: governing law, judicial forum and recognition of judgements. Another way to characterise this conundrum is to think in terms of locating three functions: legislation, adjudication and enforcement. The necessary determinations interact in a very, very complex manner.[32] Practical as well as doctrinal reasons lead property holders to litigate in a host jurisdiction, where a real purchase can be obtained on the infringing activity or entity. But this necessity may affect the governing law; the forum may well be disposed to apply its own local law rather than a foreign law. Application of the foreign law would be regarded as having an extra-territorial reach.

How does intellectual property sit within this approach? Except perhaps in the matters that can be characterised as purely contractual, intellectual property is a body of law very much characterised as territorially based. Recognition from local law must be obtained in each territory in which protection is desired. Consequently, if the territorial locus of the law is to be where the subject matter is exploited or infringed, rather than the nationality of the holder or the site of the invention, origination or publication of the subject matter, we may have to concede that the holder is at the mercy of the host country. Producers cannot manipulate location as a strategy to obtain the best protection, unless the host country sees it as serving its interests or consistent with its values to offer protection. We might anticipate that some countries will see an advantage in withholding protection, either to support local producers and users, or even to act in transnational commerce as an intellectual property 'haven'. They might resent attempts by the home countries to assert their own laws extra-territorially. At the same time, agreement may not be reached on common choice-of-law criteria. And these positions will not simply be strategically driven. They may be rooted in alternative cultures, for instance of agricultural or media production.

For our discussions below, we should recognise that competition law presents similar conundrums. Of course, there are many instances in which the practices in question, such as collusive agreements, exclusionary dealing, or mergers and acquisitions, are locally situated. But as markets are opened to global flows, it is equally clear that practices and persons which are situated abroad can have effects at home. Again, the presumption of territoriality is likely to operate. Yet, it is far from easy to establish a satisfactory territorial connection when the very object of the competition regulation is a trade in symbolic forms such as contracts and corporations. For example, we know that the corporate form can be multiplied many times, until it assumes complex patterns of associated and related companies, parents and subsidiaries, and holding and operational companies. If responsibility is to be effectively sheeted home, not only must the veil of the corporation be pierced, but regulatory regimes must be prepared to see through the formal legal structures of corporate groups and networks into the realities of their technical and economic connections. In his perspicacious way, Teubner argues that this insightfulness must extend to piercing the 'contractual veil'.[33]

The task is complicated by the fact that the corporate group or network may be distributed among foreign and local companies. Jurisdiction over corporations has traditionally turned on nationality. If the separate entity approach to corporate regulation is employed, nationality will be defined on the basis of the country where the particular company is incorporated, or maybe the location of its seat or head office. But if enterprise principles are applied, so that the regulators can strike at those who exercise real decision-making authority or financial power, the regulations may need to extend to foreign affiliates and become involved in what conventionally looks like extra-territorial application.[34] However, increasingly, we may not be able to centre functional control as neatly as this approach requires.

Of course, these regulatory challenges range much wider than competition law, but the field of competition law has seen some countries

31

endeavour to assert an extra-territorial jurisdiction. Here, the United States has been active in its roles both as a host and home country. Yet few countries, even the United States, may be able to carry off such a policy unilaterally. The linking of enterprise concepts of corporate responsibility with extra-territorial application may render host countries unattractive to mobile investors who are making strategic locational decisions. At the same time, home country corporations may resist being told what to do abroad. The extra-territorial extension may clash with laws in other overlapping jurisdictions; the United States reach for instance has met with blocking statutes. Yet, at the same time, the coordination of competition regulation continues to face hurdles. The bilateral cooperation agreements are hesitant. One suspects that most countries wish to retain the opportunity to maintain differences and exercise discretion, so that they can, for instance, protect their own industries domestically and bolster them externally.

INTERFACES

Under these conditions of pluralism, we have to think about how the encounters between legalities might be resolved, for it is a feature of globalization that they will be brought into relation in one way or another. They will not, as it were, continue to live in splendid isolation. We can quickly acknowledge that the intersections and interactions of these many different legalities have become a theme of the writing on legal pluralism.[35] Here, the focus has been at the national and local levels, though, given that it has often concerned inter-legality in the colonial situation, it has also involved a world dimension – the relations between the old and new worlds, the North and South.

Unilateral and bilateral initiatives

The colonial situation was one in which we might expect military force to be used to impose a hierarchical order on legalities, but the picture often proved to be more complex. The research has identified areas where the indigenous and local orders continued to operate. Conceding that the legalities inter-mingle, the interest turned to the avenues which opened up for two-way flows between state and other sources of normative ordering. Rather than putting the question endlessly as an opposition between European and other law, it has looked for possibilities for mutually constructive and transformative relations. Now the resonances of such pioneering work are to be heard in post-colonial studies when they speak of 'hybridities'.[36]

However, when writing on legal pluralism, Merry sounded a cautionary note. It was evident that the legalities could vary greatly in their access to power, that is to say in their coercive potential or their strength symbolically. Thus, inter-legality could present an opportunity to express asymmetrical relations of power, subjecting people to structures of dominance from far outside their immediate worlds. Subtly, Santos suggested that world legalities tend to be good at abstraction and standardisation, but they tend to achieve this effect at the expense of the particularity and embeddedness of local legalities.[37] This observation is in keeping with our remarks above about law's contrary capacities.

In a post-colonial world, we have to think flexibly and with versatility once again about the processes whereby inter-legalities are resolved. In our discussion of pluralism, we began to identify how the legalities might relate in a global way. We have already seen that much of the relating takes place in the absence of official international law-making institutions. For instance, private international law is a domestic attempt to choose between existing legalities. We saw, in relation to intellectual property, that it is becoming increasingly difficult to pursue. Instead, inter-legalities might be resolved by adapting laws. Nimmer and Krauthaus highlight the use of modelling as a way to bring laws closer together.[38] To some extent, this process is a variation on the transplantation phenomenon which Alan Watson pursued so insistently in his research.[39] However, Nimmer and Krauthaus suggest that the production of models is a much more concerted and purposeful activity today. Here, we can identify the work of professional and expert bodies in formulating and promulgating suitable models for adoption by countries which are seeking to bring their legal systems into line with international expectations. We might also note the weight which national governments, philanthropic trusts and multinational corporations are putting behind the provision of 'technical' legal assistance to countries in transition from centralised to market economies. For countries which are hungry for foreign trade and investment, the phenomenon of regulatory competition can give a real urgency to this search for suitable models. For some countries, an additional pressure has been the IMF and World Bank policies of conditioning aid on internal reforms, such as 'good governance', a concept that has included the adoption of intellectual property laws.[40]

Where national governments weigh in to support their exporters and investors, we have seen not only the power of persuasion but the threat of economic sanctions being deployed to bring about favourable changes in law. A steadily mounting catalogue of bilateral agreements have demarcated the parties' respective jurisdictions, addressed conflicting requirements, and promised fair treatment within each other's territories. Among the subject matter of those agreements are investments, intellectual property and services. Yet, the bilateral approach is increasingly being seen as deficient. Not only does it demand the devotion of considerable resources when more countries are interacting, but the nature of the global flows makes it difficult to tie the benefits to the nation states which choose to become involved.

Of course, bilateral agreements have been supplemented for some time now with multi-party conventions. However, on the whole, the ambitions of these conventions have been limited. For example, they have often been content to lay down broad principles of non-discrimination such as national treatment or to coordinate bargaining within a procedural framework. Important as they can be, multilateral principles of non-discrimination do not deal squarely with the conflict-of-laws question. They simply say that, where a country's law does apply, it should be applied without discrimination to foreigners. Nor do they deal with the question of disparities between substantive standards. They leave countries free to set their own levels of access and security, provided they offer the same levels to foreigners as they do to locals. We shall have more to say about this in chapter three.

Multilateral institutions

Under conditions of globalization, the attractions of a legislative institution may begin to brighten. Most obviously, the multilateral institution becomes a reference point for those seeking to escape the industry–government bargaining or the popular political controversies which occur at the national level. It may also seem a way to escape the worst of the power relations involved in bilateral approaches. Both those seeking benefits from globalization, and those feeling threatened, may be prepared to support harmonisation or, given the rather nebulous content of this concept, to seek standardisation at the multilateral level.

Yet, it is well understood that standardisation encounters obstacles at this level too. When a large number of countries are involved, each possibly carrying different configurations of domestic interests and global aspirations, it is not surprising that it proves difficult to develop multilateral norms. In terms of making headway, a key consideration is whether any countries enjoy enough power to insist on a strong line being followed. Latterly, this inquiry has centred on the 'hegemonic' power of the United States to promote its preferences for multilateral standards. Some analysts insist on the strength of the power inequalities between nations as a way of explaining the pattern of international regime formation. However, in the post-colonial era, it seems that more states are gaining the confidence to play an assertive role in institutional affairs, their power bolstered by new regional and cultural alignments. Not only do the ex-colonial states become less deferential, but the national unities of the once powerful nations are fractured by globalization. Allegiances are forged across national lines, especially through the transnational non-governmental organizations such as the business and industry associations and the new social and aesthetic movements. These non-government organizations also seek representation in supra-national forums.

Paradoxically, observers are able to discern within these developments the potential for new kinds of coalitions. A general theme is the part which knowledge seems to play in promoting acceptance of new conceptual linkages and institutional arrangements.[41] Yet, while these developments create potential for regime formation on an issue-by-issue basis, greater contingency also accompanies the kind of regime which emerges. The emerging forms of global governance are quite fragile. Thus plurality and interaction are likely to be features of the configuration of regulatory fields at the global level too. For example, the multi-polar pattern of international agreements provides scope for forum shopping. There is movement back and forward between organizations in a search of access to the most sympathetic rules and resources.

Such a situation suggests rivalry between the organizations and at times a clash of norms. But it also points up the interconnectedness, the complex interdependencies, which increase the chances of hybrid regimes being fashioned. As part of this process, we might expect the international organizations to create their own linkages, exchanging information, joining committees, and taking part in each other's deliberations. They may go further to acknowledge and assign each other respective spheres of operation, even being prepared to apply each other's existing standards or standard-setting processes. But would we still expect any one regime to have a greater impact on the global field than others? What then are the conditions for institutional success at the international level?

At this juncture, it is useful to identify some markers to guide the ensuing analysis. A particular interest once again is in the role of law. In this respect, Garrett takes the view that a legal system is the strongest indication of supra-nationalism.[42] In gauging the likely success of a legalised system, the inquiry concerns the reasons why the parties might be prepared to abide by a ruling or countenance a sanction, even if it means that a domestic constituency must be sacrificed to do so. In spite of the short-term sacrifice, support for the decision may be necessary if the long-term benefits of a viable system are to be obtained. Such an attitude relies on there being recognition and acceptance that the system can produce benefits overall. It calls for a certain cognitive convergence as well as a normative consensus. Many judgements are bound up in that attitude, though one may well be that the alternatives are not workable. For example, the more powerful participants may no longer think it feasible to operate the system as an old boys club where informal manoeuvrings and corridor deals suffice. The weaker participants may think

35

that a rule-based system will extend benefits to them which they could not obtain by bilateral bargaining or unilateral action.

The role of law

In this approach, the nature of law itself may be invested with capacity to give the system efficacy and legitimacy. Other regimes will suffer by comparison if they are not legalised or their law is considered to be 'soft' law. On the other hand, 'hard' law helps set up the system in such a way that it is difficult to alter or avoid. We can think here in terms of the constitution of the regime, such as the voting rights on key issues or the freedom to resile from commitments. The substance, specificity and compulsion given to its norms will be important too. Beyond the text of the norms, the authority of the dispute settlement process can be crucial. The system gains purchase if this process has a measure of automaticity and enforceability to it. But the role of the dispute settlement process includes the legitimacy which it can afford the kind of decisions needed to advance the system. Thus, assessing the European Court of Justice, where some experience is available, Mattli and Slaughter point to the way in which its decisions are couched in apparently technical and apolitical terms, though inevitably they must carry profound social implications.[43] Likewise, Davies suggests that the Court has avoided an overt, articulate balancing of the competing policies which the issues of market integration put into contention.[44] The appeal to principle and precedent, the insistence that the decisions are only interpreting and applying rather than creating and choosing, the requirement that political and social claims be framed as legal arguments, and the exclusion of controversial points as non-justiciable, all build up a highly specialised way of treating issues.

Garrett is right however to warn us against attributing any magical properties to law. In the light of the observations we have made about the nature of interfaces, one is entitled to suspect that the norms will continue to provide space within the bounds of their prescriptions for the operation of national differences and indeed for the retention of national sovereignty over which differences to pursue. The norms will allow the national members a certain modicum of discretion regarding implementation, as well as freedom not to implement them in certain respects. Furthermore, they will leave open opportunities for other international institutions to fill out the norms along certain lines. Much of this may be done by express provision. Nonetheless, the general features of the norms, such as their novelty, ambiguity, generality and subjectivity, will create further conditions of indeterminacy.

Rather than insisting on compliance, the procedures will also provide space for the national members to return to negotiation and agreement, should gaps appear or interpretations diverge. Such proceduralism may be better suited to deal with the issues, especially if the gains and losses which flow from the competing stances are difficult to balance. In other words, the institution is likely to find ways to mediate differences, rather than to legislate or arbitrate them out of existence. There are also other softer procedures available to encourage compliance, such as reporting, monitoring and reviewing procedures. Law plays a different kind of role in facilitating this kind of proceduralism.

Most appropriately of all, legitimacy may turn on the opportunities which are provided for democratic participation and social accountability in the decision making of the institution. While some hope that the trade organizations can avoid 'politicisation',[45] others do not expect such a modus operandi to be sustainable indefinitely.[46] The democratisation of the multilateral trade institution may depend, not just on the accommodation of a wider range of nation states, but also on the access which is offered to non-governmental institutions and the links which are forged with other complementary international institutions. In keeping with this approach, it will be our contention throughout the book that the ultimate 'success' of an institution should be measured by the values it recognises, the world views and interests which it accommodates, not just by its strength and single mindedness.

The role of the interface

So, at this point, we should stress that such institutions serve to mediate as well as to order and discipline. In characterising mediation, we can talk of them providing an 'interface' between legalities. Can we see the WTO agreements acting in this way? As one might suspect, the concept of an interface is borrowed from the world of computing and communications media. To dwell in this world for a moment, we know that people use the media to send each other messages. The reach and depth of their particular messages will be enhanced by the capacities of the carriers they can employ. However we should appreciate that the carriers are not just a matter of powerful hardware; the senders need software to enhance their connectivity with the receivers. To be effective, the software must do more than provide a channel for incoming signals, even do more than translate the language of the server into the language of the browser. It must connect systems, so that they can operate together.

In this regard, we should note as well that reception is not just a passive, one-directional process. The receivers put up resistance to the messages, interpret them from their own standpoint and provide feedback to the sources. Lury calls this 'reactivation'.[47] So we should not think of the local as merely an empty vessel through which global messages will flow. Global flows can be localised and played back on their originators. In fact, the global network allows for many-to-many communications which criss-cross in all sorts of directions. Furthermore, the interface does not act merely as a conduit, linking the various terminals. It begins to take on a life of its own. In the spirit of metaphors, it is easy to stray over to the biological world for further inspiration here. Picking up this connection, it might be said that through their many interactions, the senders and receivers begin to lose their individual identities and merge into new hybrid forms.

However, we know enough to treat biological metaphors with caution and there is a warning here for the study in hand. The replacement of long-standing local means of sustenance carries a risk to biodiversity. Likewise, in the communications field, some remain sceptical about the emancipatory powers of the Internet. In particular, they question whether its interfaces produce truly open systems. Could they institute proprietary standards which require independent producers and users to fit the mould of dominant suppliers? Clearly, we have the WTO in mind when we ask such questions. On this rather suggestive note, we leave chapter two.

CONCLUSIONS

In endeavouring to establish a context for the examination of the WTO agreements, this chapter has attempted to convey a balanced view of globalization. Such a view should be mindful of the fact that something big is happening, yet remain positive about the degree of diversity and contingency in the world. The strongest, certainly the most self-confident, global view carries the economic prescription of neo-liberalism for open trade and free markets. But it need not be overwhelming. A more nuanced view may lack the elegant simplicity of more linear projections. However it finds reasons, in the ways economies, polities and cultures work, why differences are still maintainable, indeed, why alternatives can be injected into the global circuits.

Such pluralism is also an attribute of law. Where its powers of abstraction and symbolism can be employed, law works for a certain kind of convergent and ordered globalization. It detaches our social relations from their spatial and temporal reference points. But law continues to display rich localised characteristics. Knowledge and practice of this law are enhanced by the power of presence, proximity and time. Such a feeling for the cross-currents in law is to be obtained by observing the conflicts within intellectual property law and related laws such as competition law.

The persistence, and even the proliferation of these conflicts give rise to demand for mediation by an inter-governmental institution. The most interesting feature of globalization is the relationships between the legalities and the way we might conceptualise the interfaces which begin to mediate them. The notion of an interface suggests that the relationships should amount to more than a one-way transmission of messages from dominant to subordinate actors. They should comprise a many-to-many round of communications which carries with it possibilities for transformative outcomes. The chapter began to apply that concept to the appraisal of a multilateral institution like the WTO. A particular interest is the role of law within such institutions. The discussion ended by stressing that the 'success' of an interface should be measured by the values it promotes, the world visions and conditions it accommodates, not simply by its strength and single mindedness.

THE WORLD TRADE ORGANIZATION

Chapter three provides an introduction to the norms and processes of the WTO and its two agreements. Such an introduction seeks to highlight the aspects of the agreements which reveal most about their role in mediating inter-legalities around the world, but necessarily the chapter commences with essential background on the agreements' institutional housing, the WTO. We shall note that the WTO reveals both continuities and discontinuities with its predecessor, the GATT (General Agreement on Tariffs and Trade). Looking forward, there are general features of the WTO which are important to the impact of the agreements. The chapter identifies the WTO's constitutional bodies for making decisions about obligations, the place for bargaining over specific commitments, the procedures for monitoring compliance by members, and especially the scope and force of the dispute settlement process. A particular interest lies with the role which law plays in structuring these processes. We should see that both order and indeterminacy are evident here. While the agreements impose disciplines, in many respects they are best regarded as 'unfinished stories'. They are providing further opportunities for mediation through successive rounds of agenda setting and negotiations over commitments, as well as the progressive output of the dispute settlement process in particular cases.

The measures of order and indeterminacy in the agreements depend also on the styling of the norms which they advance. Chapter three offers some initial characterisation of these norms, drawing on the jurisprudence which is relevant to such norms. The norms start with the principles of non-discrimination, that is, the principles of most favoured nation treatment and national treatment. We begin to see how the WTO interface requires the inter-legality to be resolved. The focus here is how national legalities are meant to deal with foreign legalities in a non-discriminatory way. The analysis moves on to the potentially more demanding norms of providing market access and protecting intellectual property. At this point, the main interest becomes their potential to advance the neo-liberal agenda for regulatory reform, which we can broadly characterise as a combination of liberalisation and protection, more specifically as access and security. We move from an interest in legalities as they are distinguished by their geo-political origins into a prescription of the contents and, to a lesser extent, the forms which legalities should adopt. Yet, at the same time, we see that the scrutiny of the norms remains contained by the WTO's long-standing preoccupation with the role of 'government measures'. In these new agreements, we note an effort to extend the notion of government measures and to come to grips with the blurring of the boundaries between public and private measures. The GATT concept of 'nullification or impairment' might also be seen as grounds for extension of the reach of the WTO's disciplines, particularly in relation to government 'inaction' on impediments to market access sourced in the domestic private sector.

If the traditional preoccupation is with deregulation at the national level, we begin to see how the norms also allow, authorise and even prescribe different kinds of legalities. If the 'silences' of the agreements leave some space for member nations to maintain their regulatory autonomy, the chapter also identifies the tendency of the agreements to make explicit exceptions for non-conforming regulation, provided this regulation is linked to certain specified objectives. But, in another instance of mediation, the agreements apply strictures to these kinds of regulation, demanding that they adopt the most trade-friendly approaches to the fulfilment of their objectives. While, on the one hand, they give some support to mutual recognition and harmonisation of regulatory standards, on the other they limit the capacity of members to express their regulatory concerns on a unilateral basis. A key example is their concerns with the negative spillovers of policies adopted in other countries, such as the destructive tendencies towards regulatory competition.

Finally, if the tendency of the agreements is to enhance global market power, we look for indications that they might counterbalance this power. The chapter starts to search within the agreements for the international impetus to advance, and not simply tolerate, the regulatory concerns of the members. It entertains the doubt whether the WTO is ready to promote the broader concerns of international 'social regulation'. Consequently, it suggests that the focus for the time being should be on the contribution the WTO might make to the regulation of business practices – competition policy is the most likely candidate. The chapter notes how trade law can treat competition regulation either in a deregulatory fashion, that is as a conventional barrier to trade, or in a re-regulatory fashion, as a device for opening market access. Could it then transcend this preoccupation with national government measures and turn its attention to the restrictive business practices of transnational corporations? But how far would this turn in competition policy advance the cause of international regulation?

If the WTO proves unable to accommodate perspectives that fall outside the interest in free trade and commerce, then the book should ask whether it has the capacity to coordinate its efforts with other international organizations which might be more sympathetic to social causes. We begin to see how the agreements not only cut across the provisions made by other international organizations but, in some instances, defer to or actively support them. However, on the evidence here, we have to question whether the WTO is serious about this project of 'complementarity'.

THE ETHOS OF THE WTO

The representatives and supporters of the Organization convey a strong sense of a mission to promote open trade across the world and free markets in every locality. There is a touch of evangelism to this mission, for open trade and free markets are seen as the natural concomitants of globalization. 'Globalization is more than the liberalisation of trade, capital movements, communications, technology. It is about the gradual convergence of our interests, our goals and aspirations, and our perceptions of the world.'[1] The Director-General goes on to argue that such a development, such an idea really, is blurring all the old divisions, the divide between the North and the South, the gap between the developed and the developing economies, and the debate over the roles of the state and the market. Globalization means greater economic prosperity for all and a true community of nations.

The optimism of the Director-General echoes several of the themes we have identified within the general discourse around globalization, the blurring of boundaries, the role of carriers, and the new opportunities opening up. However it does not subject to scrutiny the particular twist which the pursuit of an open trade and free market agenda might place on the shape of globalization. Perhaps a more detached appraisal can help ascertain which perspectives, aspirations and interests may find room within this vision of our future. We begin that appraisal here with an overview of the norms and processes characteristic of the WTO. We link them to the two selected agreements. In the subsequent chapters, we investigate their application within the specifics of these agreements.

In working through the norms and processes of the WTO agreements, it is helpful to think in terms of the consequences of building a frame of reference for globalization around trade. Nowhere is this framing device more significant than in its acceptance that intellectual endeavours and personal services are primarily objects of world trade. To regard these endeavours and services as objects of trade is to trust their fate to the forces and values which operate in a global marketplace. More subtly, their exposure to the global marketplace has the tendency to lift them out of the milieus in which their meanings and values are derived largely from their local and particular resonances. Instead, it is to measure their worth and stake their benefits on their treatment in a far larger and possibly less sympathetic environment. We might expect some to make the shift and go from strength to strength, while others will find it difficult to compete.

Secondly, the appraisal needs to gauge the implications of looking on certain traditional ways of dealing with these endeavours and services, such as certain legalities, as barriers to trade. This means that at the very least local legalities must be receptive to the different legalities foreigners bring with them (which may be local legalities in their place of origin). They must become more cosmopolitan. But, as we have suggested, it does not necessarily mean that all legalities survive in a harmonious co-existence. The norms of open trade and free markets place a range of 'behind the border' legalities on the defensive, such as industry-specific regulation, corporatist industry–government relationships and public sector instrumentalities. The onus is placed on national governments to refashion their legalities as trade-neutral measures or as legitimate exceptions to the norms of trade.

This onus starts with the requirement that national legalities treat foreigners no less favourably than they do locals. National treatment, a seemingly simple principle of non-discrimination, has far-reaching implications. National legalities have sought to treat foreigners differently. As we shall see, they have sought to restrict the participation of foreigners in certain sensitive sectors in order to preserve a space for locals. They have sought to apply conditions to foreign participation in order to ensure a return to the locality from that participation. But it may not be enough for non-discrimination simply to subject the foreigner to the same legality as the locals. Non-discrimination may require the local legality to make allowance for the foreign legality. Furthermore, we shall see that the norms of trade law move beyond non-discrimination. Norms of market access and intellectual property protection signify a broad-based agenda of regulatory reform. The objective is not merely to ease conflicts between foreigners and local legalities, but to promote 'efficient regulation' across the world. These norms challenge non-discriminatory local legalities. Do they promote a particular kind of economic liberalism, with a preference for legalities such as property, contract and business association? If so, local legalities must adjust to a particular kind of transnational legality which those with mobility in such a marketplace can carry with them and deploy on a world stage.

If the norms of trade are vital to our understanding of the WTO, the processes which it deploys to further those norms are also worthy of our attention. A multilateral, rule-based regime is said to provide an opportunity to impose order on the processes of globalization. For example, it provides legal definition to the norms and it 'juridifies' the resolution of disputes about complying with them. Legalisation promotes the norms, but it also provides an opportunity to limit the scope of such change, perhaps to develop a new space in which alternative views can also find voice. It is not altogether surprising, then, that the WTO agreements display a certain hesitancy in pursuing such profound changes; they tend to act in some respects as mediating as well as disciplining devices. They may even provide a focal point for initiatives to apply correctives to the abuses of global market power. The core of this chapter concerns the norms of the two agreements. But let us first say something about the nature of the institution which backs the agreements and the ways its processes promote adherence to the norms.

THE WTO AS AN INSTITUTION

Chapter two nominated certain institutional features which were likely to give the necessary support to a program of trade liberalisation. Of course, the success of the program depends essentially on how compliance with its norms suits different perspectives and interests. In any one case, there may be costs associated with bringing national measures into line with the norms. However we should understand that adherence to the norms comes as part of a package. Compliance is not a choice to be made in isolation in the individual case. Member governments are asked to sign up to the WTO agreements as a system for the conduct of trade relations or, in our terms, for the resolution of inter-legalities. They are being asked to support an institution.

The manner in which the WTO norms are to be embodied and observed is a feature uppermost in the minds of those who represent the Organization. In 1995, the Director-General, Renato Ruggiero, made enthusiastic claims for this organizational form.[2] He argued that without a firm framework of rules and disciplines, openness of trade would degenerate into anarchy. Open trade must therefore be trade within the rule of law, which is why the WTO is so important, for it is the only body of agreed trade rules whose coverage approaches the global. Indeed, the aspirations of the Organization extend further. Identifying the WTO with globalization, the Director-General recently advanced the proposition that the universal, rule-based, multilateral trading system is rapidly becoming a central pillar of a new international order, a key link between the North and the South, an indispensable foundation for an ever more interdependent world.[3]

In such prescriptions, we can discern a hint of the reasons why such regimes might receive support. It is true that many countries are opening markets to trade individually. Domestic reform programs tend to free demand for foreign goods, investment and expertise, together with access to export markets for the local counterparts. But it is also true that some countries stand to gain more than others, at least in the short term. All countries choose to maintain selective controls, especially in those sectors which they regard as sensitive. Such a regime offers a further means to overcome resistance, a more legitimate means perhaps than other means such as the threat of military or economic sanctions.

A multilateral, rule-based approach may also appeal to those who hold reservations about open trade. The rules are meant to provide the smaller nations with a defence against the demands of the larger nations or the transnational corporations which might otherwise play them off against each other. Multilateralism is said to generalise the benefits of open trade to those who would not have the power to obtain them through bilateral bargaining. And, from our point of view, it is interesting that law is given a major role in providing this order to the global trading system. We would be wise to retain our doubts about the capacity of such regimes to override imbalances in power relations. However we can look for evidence of order in the presence of clear rules and a centralised design. Constitutional procedures for making policy and resolving disputes provide another useful indicator. Let us begin with the constitution of the WTO.

The WTO constitution

The WTO has grown out of a contractual arrangement known as the GATT, the General Agreement on Tariffs and Trade. The GATT began its life modestly, following the failure of the attempt after World War 2 to implement a broad compact, the Havana Charter. That Charter would have established a major institution, the International Trade Organization. But it foundered on the reservations of several countries, finally being killed off when the United States Congress declined to accept it in the early 1950s.[4]

For most of its life, the GATT has been concerned with standardising and, to some extent, reducing tariff barriers which are imposed on the import of manufactured goods at the border. Of course this trade was a significant enough phenomenon and over the years the GATT consolidated its position considerably. Through a succession of rounds, the text of its agreement was elaborated, supplemented by the construction of national schedules of commitment to tariff reductions and the process-ing of disputes over compliance between the parties. But it continued to style itself as a contract between national parties and it minimised its institutional features.

This position began to alter when the GATT felt compelled to turn its attention to the use of non-tariff barriers to trade. The proliferation of these national measures led its trade-related interest to reach behind the border, beyond control on imports such as voluntary export restraints and other 'grey measures', to a variety of local support measures such as differential technical standards, financial subsidies for local industry, and the preferential use of government procurement powers.[5] The GATT also examined more closely the measures of retaliation against unfair trade, such as countervailing duties and anti-dumping procedures, which it had allowed the contracting parties. Its panel process began to exam-ine the use of the exceptions to its norms which it had been obliged to concede to doubtful parties.

While this interest generated a great deal more trade regulation, it was largely on the basis of 'side codes' to the main agreement. Adherence to these codes was optional. So too, with infringing parties holding effective veto power, the GATT's dispute resolution processes remained essen-tially voluntary. Furthermore, great swathes of world trade such as trade in agricultural commodities and trade in services were still left largely outside its purview. From the perspective of this book, the most signifi-cant result of the Uruguay Round was the expansion in the sectors and consequently the measures which were brought within the GATT frame of reference and ensemble of norms. But the institutional arrangements were also strengthened considerably.

In contrast to the GATT, the WTO is notable first for being styled as an organization with members rather than an agreement between con-tracting parties. Here, the message is that it has more of a life of its own which transcends the desires and manoeuvres of its national con-stituents. In many ways, it can still be regarded as a collection of special-ist agreements. But now the agreements are presented as a package with associated legal instruments. The price of membership of the WTO is submission to the Agreement Establishing the World Trade Organiza-tion, together with the Multilateral Agreements on Trade in Goods, updated versions of the Tokyo side codes, the Agreement on Trade-Related Investment Measures, the GATS, the TRIPs, the Trade Policy Review Mechanism, and the Understanding on Rules and Procedures Governing the Settlement of Disputes (see articles II:2 and XI:1 of the WTO Agreement).[6] Only four plurilateral trade agreements, which include the Agreement on Government Procurement, remain optional (article II:3). The price of membership also extends to the making of commitments under the GATT and the GATS (article XI:1).[7]

Representatives of the governments involved in the negotiations met at Marrakesh in April 1994. There they signed the Final Act Embodying the Results of the Uruguay Round of Multilateral Trade Negotiations, whereby they agreed to submit the WTO Agreement for the consideration of their respective competent authorities, with a view to seeking approval of it in accordance with their procedures.[8] They also agreed on the desirability of acceptance of the WTO Agreement by all participants in the Uruguay Round with a view to its entry into force by 1 January 1995. They further agreed to adopt a raft of ministerial declarations and decisions, some of which as we shall see relate to implementation of the GATS (General Agreement on Trade in Services) and TRIPs (Agreement on Trade-Related Aspects of Intellectual Property Rights).[9] The WTO Agreement has subsequently come into force. Article XIV was to keep the Agreement open for acceptance by the participants for a period of two years following that date.

Interestingly, it is not so clear that the package has to be taken by those countries which are subsequently seeking accession to the Agreement (presently some twenty-nine countries). Article II has to be read with article XII which says that other countries may accede on terms agreed between them and the WTO. Article XIII also seems to envisage that a particular agreement would not need to apply between the acceding member and any other particular member.

The agreements come with a common institutional framework for the conduct of trade relations (article II). The WTO Agreement establishes a constitution for decision making such as setting agendas, conducting deliberations, shaping policy, reviewing compliance and settling disputes. The WTO is headed up by a Ministerial Conference composed of representatives of all the members (article IV:1). It is to meet at least once every two years, and has already met three times – in Singapore in December 1996, in Geneva in May 1998 and in late 1999 in Seattle. In the intervals between the meetings of the Conference, the functions of the WTO are to be conducted by a General Council, which again is made up of representatives of all the members (article IV:2). The Council establishes its own rules of procedure.

The General Council also convenes two specialist bodies designed to give the system greater follow-through, the Trade Policy Review Body and the Dispute Settlement Body (article IV:3 and 4). These two bodies also establish their own rules of procedure. Picking up on specifications in the individual trade agreements, the WTO Agreement provides for a Council for Trade in Goods, a Council for Trade in Services and a Council for

Trade-Related Aspects of Intellectual Property (article IV:5). Again, they have carriage of their own procedures. Membership of these Councils is to be open to representatives of all members. The Ministerial Conference is charged to establish a Committee on Trade and Development; it has also created a Committee on Trade and Environment.

The Agreement says the WTO shall continue the practice of decision making by consensus followed under the GATT 1947 (article IX:1). Nonetheless it contains brakes on ready alterations to the framework of norms and disciplines. The most notable are the requirements for large majority votes among members. Each member is to have one vote and decisions of the Conference and the General Council are to be taken by a majority of the votes cast (article IX:1). However, a decision to adopt an interpretation of the agreements requires a three-fourths majority, so too any decision to waive an obligation imposed on a member by an agreement (article IX:2 and 3). A waiver can only be granted in exceptional circumstances and it is subject to a procedure. Amendments to the agreements may only be made by two-thirds majority of members; while those amendments which would alter the rights and obligations of members shall only affect those members which accept them (article X). Alteration to certain constitutional provisions, including the MFN (most favoured nation) obligation contained within the GATS, requires acceptance by all members. It is possible to withdraw from the Agreement (article XV).

Bargaining procedures

Of course, a formal specification like this does not fully disclose the nature of decision making. To a large extent the appraisal must wait on empirical evidence. For the time being, it is useful to note that the agreements themselves build bargaining into the WTO processes. The GATS was in fact already structuring the conduct of negotiations over the schedules of national commitments during the Uruguay Round. Negotiations often began between two major trading partners and then expanded to take in some other countries.[10] Negotiations over commitments were extended in several key sectors beyond the Round and have only now been finalised. In addition, several aspects proved too difficult to resolve at this early stage and they are set down to be revived; these aspects include subsidies and government procurement. More fundamentally, the GATS programs members to enter into successive rounds of negotiations generally 'with a view to achieving a progressively higher level of liberalisation' (article XX:1). The next round is due to start up towards the end of 1999. The approach which the GATS takes to the negotiation of specific commitments is worthy of detailed analysis. We undertake that analysis in chapter four.

In relation to TRIPs, the Uruguay Round involved informal country-to-country negotiations on both framework and single issues, together with the construction of coalitions, until the outstanding issues were finalised and the form of the agreement reached.[11] The TRIPs did not, however, schedule another round of negotiations and it remains to be seen if it will be reopened to consider emerging issues. However, the agreement did schedule the review of several of its provisions, the most notable being the requirement to revisit the exception allowed to the patentability of plants and animals within four years of the WTO Agreement coming into force (article 27:3(b)).

Monitoring implementation

As foreshadowed above, monitoring is one of several ways compliance may be furthered. The Uruguay Round established a Trade Policy Review Mechanism. In particular the Trade Policy Review Body is charged to examine the impact of the members' trade policies and practices on the multilateral trading system and to report to the General Council. Its work is lent assistance by the procedures imposed on members to notify and report various measures. Obligations of transparency contained within the individual agreements give support by seeking to make the members' measures accessible to scrutiny, though, as we shall be saying, a number of ways in which the obligations and commitments are expressed makes the measure of compliance problematic. The dispute settlement process may be invoked.

The monitoring mechanism is preoccupied with the extent to which the measures of the members at the national level comply with the agreements. Critics have argued that the WTO ought to feel obliged to monitor the impact of the multilateral norms and disciplines in a much broader sense, given the ambitiousness of the claims being made for them and the changes being compelled. Since the Round concluded, some developing countries have been saying to the Trade Policy Review Body that the implementation of the agreements is proving contentious and onerous domestically, causing problems for their industries.[12] The WTO response is largely one of providing training programs to national officials to assist with implementation. Several of the northern countries have provided the WTO with generous support for technical assistance and it has also been the subject of cooperation agreements with other international bodies such as WIPO (World Intellectual Property Organization).

The dispute settlement process

In our consideration of the prospects for consolidation of an international regime, significance was attached to the role of dispute settlement. One of the most emphatic outcomes of the Uruguay Round was a strengthening of the GATT processes. As we have foreshadowed, the Round produced the Understanding on Rules and Procedures Governing the Settlement of Disputes. The process for dispute resolution still has much in common with the GATT, but it is clear from the nature of the personnel, procedures, the sources on which it should draw, and the action which it must take, that the process has the incipient traits of a court.[13] Further, an element of compulsion has been introduced into the overall process. While it remains extremely cautious and elongated, the complaining country is effectively in a position to move it through to the point of enforcement.

Its primary objective is to achieve agreement between the complaining and responding parties. The process starts with consultations between the members involved in the dispute (article 4 of the Understanding). The Director-General of the WTO lends his or her good offices and seeks to conciliate and mediate, if need be (article 5). However, if consultations fail to resolve the dispute, the complaining party may request the General Council, sitting as the Dispute Settlement Body (DSB), to establish a panel (article 4). Thus the WTO continues with the panel system which the GATT introduced. Now, however, a panel must be established unless the DSB decides by consensus not to do so (article 6). In other words, a negative consensus is now required to block a panel, whereas previously a positive one was needed to establish a panel.

Panels are to be drawn from the pool which member countries have nominated. For a particular dispute, the WTO Secretariat nominates the individuals from this indicative list. If there is no agreement on the panellists, the Director-General selects. The panellists must be well qualified individuals, whether they come from governmental or non-governmental backgrounds (article 8). Article 8 is also concerned with their independence. They must serve in their individual capacities and not as government representatives or representatives of any organization. In particular, the panellists for a specific dispute must not be citizens of the member countries involved.

What sources may the panels draw upon in making their decisions? The Understanding stresses that panels are to preserve the rights and obligations of the members under the covered agreements (article 3:2). In other words, the basic prescription is to uphold the rules. As we have said already, much will depend on how rule-like the obligations and commitments really are. In the event of uncertainty and ambiguity, the Understanding points to the general sources on which they may draw. The provisions of the agreements may be clarified in accordance with the customary rules of interpretation of public international law (article 3:2). We should also recall article XVI:1 of the WTO Agreement, which provides more substantive guidance. It states that the WTO should be guided by the decisions, procedures and the customary practices followed by the contracting parties to the GATT 1947 and the bodies established under it. We should note that this jurisprudence is gathered together in an official publication, the *Analytical Index*, which was last updated in 1994.[14]

Nonetheless, as we have been suggesting, the WTO agreements break new ground. It is to be anticipated that the jurisprudence will take new turns. New subject matter and new text will mean that the GATT jurisprudence is inadequate. The negotiations leading up to the conclusion of the agreements are one available source of enlightenment; a number of 'legislative histories' have already been prepared.[15] The GATS and, to a lesser extent, TRIPs have taken the trouble to elaborate statements of objectives, provide definitions and notes of interpretation, and particularise norms in specific annexes. In addition, we have seen that the Marrakesh Meeting of Ministers reached a number of decisions which bear on the implementation of the agreements. Reference will be made to these sources as we work our way through the agreements.

The panels may of course wish to take evidence and argument in the individual case. The Understanding says that the panels are to meet in closed session with deliberations to be confidential (article 14). The members involved in the dispute make written submissions (article 12). They can be invited to make oral submissions, which must then be made in the presence of the other members involved in the dispute. Appendix 3 to the Understanding elaborates these working procedures. At the same time, other members having a substantial interest in a matter before a panel are also to have an opportunity to be heard (article 10). In addition, each panel shall have the right to seek information and technical advice from any individual or body it deems appropriate (article 13). It may also seek information from any relevant source and may consult experts to obtain their opinion on certain aspects of the matter. The Understanding does not give the members the right to examine this information, advice and opinion, but in general terms the members have a right to respond at the time the panel issues its interim report (article 15). All this relates significantly to expectations about procedural legalities.

Under the GATT, the panel could end its deliberations with a recommendation. Because the recommendation had to be accepted by the GATT Council, which operated according to consensus among the contracting partners, the infringing country could effectively veto any action. There was also 'fudging' in the way the Council adopted the panel reports. Now the panels report to the DSB. The DSB must adopt the report unless there is consensus against doing so (article 16:4). At the same time, provision has been made for members to appeal against a panel report (article 17). The Appellate Body is a standing body made up of persons of recognised authority, with demonstrated expertise in law, international trade and the subject matter of the covered agreements generally (article 17:3). But any appeal is to be confined to the issues of 'law' covered in the panel report and legal interpretations developed by the panel (article 17:6).[16]

The DSB is charged to decide how to implement the panel report. It makes recommendations and rulings. The Understanding says a solution mutually acceptable to the parties and consistent with the covered agreements is to be preferred (article 3:4). Otherwise, if the measure is inconsistent with the agreement in question, the prime objective should be to secure its withdrawal. In the case of TRIPs, we should note that it will sometimes be more accurate to say that a party should introduce a measure consistent. In any case, in the event that it fails to conform to the agreement, the responding party must negotiate the payment of compensation to the complaining party (article 22).

If no satisfactory compensation is agreed, then, as a last resort, the DSB can authorise suspension of concessions or other obligations. In other words, the complaining party can be authorised to impose trade sanctions. Such retaliatory action is to start with concessions or other obligations in the same sector and under the cover of the same agreement as the infringement. But, if this action is not practicable or effective, it can move to cross-retaliation within another sector covered by the same agreement. If the circumstances are serious enough, it can extend to other agreements. Nevertheless, the level of suspension must remain equivalent to the injury which the infringement has caused to the complaining country, that is the level of the nullification or impairment (article 22:4). We discuss the concept of nullification or impairment below. Also below, we shall see that the Understanding distinguishes violation and non-violation complaints of nullification or impairment. It should be kept in mind that the programmed response to a non-violation complaint is more mild (article 26). The responding country is not under an obligation to withdraw its measure. Rather, it is required to find a mutually satisfactory adjustment with the complaining country.

Attitudes to the dispute settlement process

The greater access and impetus given to the dispute settlement process are likely to make its proceedings much more authoritative. Since the Agreement and the Understanding came into force at the beginning of 1995, the take-up rate has been high. By the middle of 1998, some 139 disputes had been notified to the DSB.[17] It is evident that many of these disputes still related to the core GATT component of the WTO agreements. However, several have concerned compliance with the TRIPs requirements, including its enforcement provisions. A number of disputes have been settled. Again, most of the panel reports have concerned disputes relating to trade in goods; a sizeable number have dealt with measures relating to trade in food products. At the same time, the new Appellate Body has made several legal rulings. One of its reports examined the key provisions of the new WTO Agreement on the Application of Sanitary and Phytosanitary Measures.[18] Another concerned India's compliance with the patent protection provisions of TRIPs for pharmaceuticals and agricultural chemical products.[19] We shall discuss both these reports below.

Once a pattern emerges, it will be extremely interesting to see which countries make most use of the dispute settlement process. We can surmise that a favourable finding is likely to give moral support to a complaining country. However, in those situations where trade sanctions need to be a genuine threat, then the process may appeal most to those countries with lucrative markets to close, that is where retaliation hits the hardest.[20] But, equally so, countries with the most attractive markets may be the main target of complaints. The figures from the WTO web site suggest that developed countries have made three to four times as many complaints as the developing countries, with the United States the most active single user. Still, this means that a range of countries have notified disputes and requested consultations. Developed countries have been the targets of complaints as well as the initiators. For example, the United States has received challenges to its health and environmental measures from South American and Asian exporting countries; its own intellectual property protections are beginning to be challenged as well. The European Union has raised the question whether the United States' own schemes for unilateral trade sanctions are compatible with the WTO's dispute settlement processes.[21] It is too early to say which countries will be most able to see disputes through to a favourable conclusion.

Of course, another vital consideration will be whether the disputes settlement process favours those who seek the most liberal interpretation of the agreements or those who seek to preserve measures against them. Again, the way in which the agreements cast the norms will be central, including the measure of the injury needed to invoke the process, which the WTO characterises as a matter of nullification or impairment (see discussion below). However, we know enough about how ordinary courts work to say that the dispute settlement process must inevitably involve the panels in the eminently arguable issues of fact-finding and legal interpretation. As independent as they may be, the panellists will still be drawn from trade circles. Already, reformists have begun to focus their energies on opening the process to a wider range of views, including those which represent non-trade perspectives and values. The NGOs are not content to channel their arguments through the national delegations. There has been a suggestion that at times national representatives run 'dead in the water' in their defence, for example, of their own environmental protection measures.[22]

The legalities of the process

Many early proposals for reform have favoured a further legalisation of the process. One significant strand seems to be recommending the model employed in the United States for public interest litigation of administrative decision making. This model involves an opportunity for NGOs to assess the cases argued by national representatives, to file amicus briefs, and to comment on the panels' interim reports. A broader claim is for the dispute settlement process to go public. Interestingly, this claim has received mainstream support from the President of the United States, who recently declared: 'I propose that all hearings by the WTO be open to the public, and all briefs by the parties be made publicly available.'[23] Such a reform might counter the impression that the WTO is making important decisions in secret and without proper accountability.

All the same, further legalisation of the process will bring its own problems. We know how uneven legal resources can influence the outcome of domestic cases. It is already appreciated that the smaller member countries may lack the resources to contest WTO disputes effectively. It was significant that a GATT panel once refused a small African country permission to have private legal representation as a way of overcoming its deficiency in trade law expertise.[24] But the Appellate Body recently let private lawyers appear in the hearing of the dispute between the United States and India over compliance with TRIPs. It is fair to say that NGOs, such as environmental groups and indigenous peoples, will have to call on all their collective resources if they are to match those available to major governments. Such a process might also place pressure on the WTO itself to provide facilities for the weaker parties.

If the process were remodelled in such a way, standing would also be given to those who were injured by WTO-inconsistent measures. There is already a lobby for this kind of access.[25] It is clear that the ultimate beneficiaries of the responsibilities which are placed on governments are meant to be foreign traders, suppliers and property holders. But presently these private individuals are not provided with access to a process by which they can insist that the governments implement and observe the provisions. We should note that the OECD draft for an MAI (Multilateral Agreement on Investment) has sought to submit governments to binding international arbitration where private investors claimed they had contravened their obligations under the agreement. Thus, there would be investor–state procedures as well as state–state procedures. If a case were proved, the investors would be entitled to the full range of remedies, including declarations, compensation and restitution. The draft also charges governments to make their own courts and tribunals available to aggrieved investors.

In all this, it is possible to see the dispute settlement process itself producing encounters between legalities. The process would not just mediate the relationship between the legalities of foreign and local regulatory measures. In fashioning its own internal modus operandi, it would have to deal with the interactions, sometimes clashes, between the procedural legalities which the various participants sought to bring to the forum.

THE CONTENT OF THE NORMS

Most favoured nation treatment

Most favoured nation treatment, known as MFN, is a principle of non-discrimination. It is well known to the GATT, where it applies to the treatment of goods or products from other countries, particularly for the purposes of applying tariffs.[26] It has become a general obligation within both the GATS and TRIPs agreements. In this ground-laying chapter, we should note first that the MFN has a direct concern with the conditions of trade. It requires a country to accord to the products, services or nationals of any other country no less favourable treatment than it accords to the counterparts of any other country. The concept of no less favourable treatment is a complex one. It is shared with national treatment and we shall deal with it in most detail in the sections given over to national treatment, both in this chapter and in chapter four. But basically we can say that it requires that a member country's measures must not place foreigners at a competitive disadvantage when they seek to trade. In the case of MFN, the point of comparison is the treatment of other foreigners; in the case of national treatment, the point of comparison is the treatment of the member's own nationals.

MFN is claimed to take a neutral stance on the content of a member's local measures, provided that they do not discriminate between the nationals of different countries. It should also be noted that MFN is not a choice-of-law rule. It does not determine which country's law is to apply. It says that if a host country's law does apply, it should not be discriminatory. So it does not resolve the problem of differences in substantive standards. Nor does it promote the liberalisation of markets as such by favouring certain types of measures over others. Another way of putting this point is to say that the obligation takes on more force when it is coupled with the neo-liberal reform agenda of secure access to markets.

However, the obligation is crucial to the ways in which conditions of treatment may be obtained by home countries and, correspondingly, may be conferred by host countries. If MFN is unconditional, then treatment cannot be based on material reciprocity, that is to say it cannot take the form of favours granted to the nationals of those countries which are prepared to respond in kind. So treatment obtained say in bilateral bargaining must be extended to the nationals of other countries. Furthermore, countries that are subject to the obligation cannot give preferential treatment to selected other countries as part of a regional agreement.

GATS and TRIPs MFN treatment

The WTO aims to promote multilateralism broadly. The obligation is taken to the point where it applies to all the measures of the member within the purview of the relevant agreement. It is not confined to the minimum protections required by the TRIPs (article 4) or the actual commitments obtained under the GATS (article II). So it could encompass concessions made to countries that are not part of the WTO. Nonetheless, in order to reinforce the incentives to join the WTO, MFN is made conditional in the sense that the obligation to multilateralise only relates to the treatment of the nationals of the other members of the WTO.

During the life of the Uruguay Round, countries such as the United States very actively deployed the threat of closing off their large home markets in order to prise concessions from targeted countries towards intellectual property protection and access to services markets. A framework of MFN is meant to give more powerful countries less scope to press unilaterally for extra concessions. It affords less powerful countries the benefit of concessions they would not otherwise be able to obtain. In this vein, it will be important to the integrity of the WTO that it deals sensibly with unilateral initiatives, such as the use of the United States special trade legislation.

Both the GATS and TRIPs allow certain exceptions to their MFN obligations. For example, they provide space for some pre-existing reciprocal agreements. In a concession most significantly to the European Union, the GATS also permits preferential regional agreements to be maintained under certain conditions (article V). But perhaps the biggest qualification to the multilateralism of the WTO agreements is how they seek to reconcile the obligation with the demand of the more powerful countries that the agreements achieve a balance between rights and obligations or commitments. We should appreciate that the way the TRIPs takes care of this demand is to impose the same substantive standards on all members. The GATS response, however, was less clear-cut.

As we already know, the GATS permitted countries to vary their level of commitments to national treatment and market access. This bargaining structure threatened to undermine the multilateral character of the WTO. The provision for MFN exemptions played a special role here (article II:2). The agreement placed no legal restrictions on the circumstances in which the exemptions could be taken. As we shall see, the United States in particular employed the threat of an exemption for the purpose of gaining leverage in the negotiations. Most spectacularly, it threatened to take wholesale exemptions in the basic telecommunications and financial services sectors and leave itself free to operate exclusively on a bilateral and regional basis. It argued that, unless many members were more forthcoming in their offers, it would be obliged to extend its commitments to countries that were not reciprocating materially. In order to placate the United States, the negotiations in these sectors were extended beyond the conclusion of the Round. But it was by no means clear that the GATS required negotiations to produce a 'balance of commitments'. We return to this issue in chapter four.

At this point, we should note two other dimensions. The MFN obligation is breached if a country imposes trade sanctions to single out another country for special treatment. If that other country is itself in violation of the trade agreement, the agreement may authorise the suspension of the first country's obligations or commitments by way of retaliation. We saw that the WTO's own dispute settlement processes envisage this step being taken. In the case of goods, such trade-based remedies have extended to the protection of local producers from the 'dumping' of foreign products. Anti-dumping procedures and remedies have become a very substantial part of the practice of trade law, but they have not yet been authorised in the case of trade in services or intellectual property.

At this juncture, we should note too that trade sanctions may be imposed because a country takes objection to the political, social or environmental policies of the country in which the trade originates. It may be concerned for instance with the spillover effects of those policies. Again, unless exceptions are made, we shall see that such trade sanctions contravene the MFN obligation. Sanctions might be permitted if the objective is to protect an interest which is recognised by the trade agreement or if it is to support compliance with agreed international standards. However, the discussion of exceptions below will indicate that these let-outs remain tightly restricted.

National treatment

As a long-standing principle of liberal internationalism, national treatment is the other main norm of non-discrimination. It requires countries not to take measures that discriminate against, again depending on the subject matter of the agreement, foreign products, services or nationals such as service suppliers or property right holders. Again, the norm is very much concerned with trade. Its point of comparison is the treatment given to local counterparts. It is concerned with the conditions under which foreigners can expect to compete with locals. In the GATT, it was concerned with taxes and other measures that sought to discriminate against foreign products once the barriers at the border had been lowered and access to the local market obtained.[27] We argue that, through the GATS and TRIPs, its implications will be more far reaching.

In identifying the reach of such a norm, we should start by saying what it does not purport to do. It is not a choice-of-law rule. It comes into operation where the host country's measures apply. So it does not help international traders, or national governments for that matter, with conflict-of-laws issues. For example, it does not resolve the kind of issue presented when trade in cyberspace creates points of attachment to a number of jurisdictions, and maybe facilitates rapid switching between jurisdictions according to the balance of legal convenience. Therefore, it does not deal with a threat to national sovereignty which is arguably as big as any requirement that foreigners be treated like locals.[28]

It follows that national treatment is in some respects a very old-fashioned principle. Yet it remains a significant mediating device in the sense that it manages how local legalities should respond to foreign legalities, once the two have necessarily come into contact. To what extent does it constrain the scope of the local legality? National treatment has been said to take a neutral stance on the question of the content of local legalities. When governed by the norm, a country remains free to strike its regulatory standards at any level it sees fit. The proviso is that it does the same in effect for foreigners as it does for locals.

Constraints on local legalities

The advocates of national treatment say that it is in truth a very simple and unobjectionable principle. Countries can maintain any regulatory policy they wish to pursue. For instance, they can limit the extent to which the supply of certain services is opened up to private competition; they can control the number, concentration and market share of individual participants; or they can restrict the business forms in which they may operate. The proviso is that these kinds of measure do not discriminate against foreigners. To use an example, it follows that a country can still choose not to privatise a public service. However, if it does decide to do so, it must allow foreign private operators competitive opportunities equivalent to those allowed to locals. Depending on the type of trade to which the norm applies, we may be talking about the purchase of shares in a privatised corporation, the obtaining of licences to operate as a service supplier in a market open to private competition, or the receipt of contracts, subsidies or other concessions to provide services.

In truth, the norm can have profound implications for the content of local regulatory legalities. Many countries continue to see good reasons for protecting local industries from foreign competition or bolstering them with assistance in order to meet that competition. For example, national governments have identified sensitive sectors in which they restrict foreign ownership or limit the participation of foreign providers. As we shall see, professional services are among such sectors, so too are audiovisual and basic telecommunications services. The motive has not only been to shore up local economic interests. Providing a space for local voices may be designed to safeguard political independence or cultural identity. The case studies are intended to give life to these legalities.

Another reason for discrimination has been regulatory competence. While they allow foreigners to compete, national authorities may wish to apply different kinds of requirements to them because those differential requirements are needed to ensure that the regulations can be effective. If effective decision-making power or financial resources are located offshore, special requirements may be imposed to create an attachment to the local jurisdiction and thus to give some purchase to the regulatory regime. For example, in the financial services sector, the supplier might be required to incorporate locally rather than simply operate as a branch of the head office overseas. In this way, it acquires a local legal persona. A stronger requirement would be to meet a prescribed level of capitalisation locally. These requirements tend to restrict the foreigner's choice of mode of service supply.

Requirements may be applied not so much to provide redress against harm as to extract a positive return from the foreign supplier to the locality. For example, withholding tax may be imposed so as to hold some of the revenue from the foreigner's operation within the country. Regulations may require that local and offshore companies from within the international group conduct transfer pricing at arm's length. Conditions may be attached to approvals or grants that technology be licensed out or supplies sourced locally. These kinds of performance requirements are designed to ensure that benefits flow back to locals from the access which the country has allowed the foreign operators.

What scope does the norm allow to a neo-liberal agenda for regulatory reform? We can see that, strictly speaking, it does not require a country to liberalise market access for services or secure investments in intellectual resources. It can continue to deny both locals and foreigners these privileges alike. Member countries may maintain non-discriminatory regulation. However, if a country decides to liberalise unilaterally, as many countries are currently doing, then it must extend the opportunities and facilities to foreigners. In many sectors, especially when we add in personal services and intellectual resources, the result may be to let in not just a greater number of competitors, but competitors who are far better resourced and more experienced than the locals. And, in the absence of material reciprocity, or multilateral content standards, a country may find that it is offering more to foreigners as a host country than its nationals enjoy in the foreigners' home countries.

Allowances for foreign legalities

More scope is being created because trade law is saying that formally identical treatment may be less favourable treatment. On this basis, it is not enough for the local legality to make the same requirement of foreigners as it does of locals. The foreigner's peculiar circumstances may make the same requirements harder to meet. These circumstances might include the foreigner's own home legality. In terms of mediation between two legalities, the consequence is that the local legality must make allowances for the foreign legality. The foreigner's disadvantage may lie in its need to satisfy two sets of conflicting requirements, one at home and one in the host country. This view may push the host country into accepting the regulatory standards which the foreigner has met at home.

The host country's ability to maintain what it sees as appropriate standards is undermined by this kind of allowance. For instance, a country's regulatory policy may say that nationality or citizenship is not a precondition for admission to the legal profession – foreigners are free to apply. However, admission may be offered on the condition that the applicant has obtained a local educational qualification and acquired local practical experience. A country may take the view that the quality of services available to its citizens is enhanced or indeed the legal system is supported, if lawyers are steeped in such locally specific knowledge. The foreigner may argue that it is easier for the local competitor to meet these requirements. If the norm applies, then the host country may have to take the foreigners as they are or at least give them credit for the requirements they have met back home. We shall also see that in some situations the norm creates an impetus for regulatory coordination to reconcile the disparities between the two legalities. A process for mutual recognition is the most common response. But occasionally it leads to standardisation which is, after all, the surest way to overcome conflict-of-laws problems. We shall discuss this potential later in the chapter.

Under the GATT, no less favourable treatment has conventionally been limited to products which are 'like'. Thus, on the basis that two products are not alike, some differential treatment is permitted, provided it is not discriminatory. But obviously a crucial question is what is regarded as like. The GATT dispute settlement process has had to grapple with this issue. In the case of products, the subject matter of the GATT, it has been possible to look to the physical qualities of the goods in question. A more general approach considers whether the consumers of the products regard them as substitutable.[29] Yet we know, from the common law practice of reasoning by analogy, that similarities only exist alongside differences. For instance, if a country places a tax on the sale of trucks but not on the sale of cars, and trucks are all imported while cars are largely locally produced, has the country failed to accord no less favourable treatment to a like product? The national authorities may say that the tax is imposed differentially because trucks pollute the air more and do greater damage to the roads than cars. They are not like products. In the field of services, a zoning policy might ban standardised fast food outlets from residential neighbourhoods but permit independently owned and operated cafes or street stalls to establish.

Under the GATT, the scope for argument encouraged a tendency for the panels to defer to the categorisations made by the national authorities.[30] Those in favour of freer trade are now advancing an argument that the likeness limitation on the norm should be dropped. The idea has been raised by officials from the WTO;[31] it also had its supporters at the negotiations over the text of the MAI. Instead, members would be required to justify their differential treatment according to one of the legitimate purposes for which the trade agreements concede that non-conforming measures may be maintained. But, as we shall see, the scope of these exceptional purposes is drawn quite narrowly.

GATS and TRIPs national treatment

Both the GATS (article XVII) and TRIPs (article 3) embody the principle of national treatment. Despite the significance of the field, the principle seems arguably of less import in the case of TRIPs because it at the same time requires members to provide quite substantive levels of protection to the nationals of other members. These foreigners can demand the same substantive protections as the locals and of course they can expect to find them within all the countries of the WTO. However, the principle retains some import, for (with certain exceptions) it extends to any protections that members offer above and beyond the minima prescribed by the agreement, for example in those respects in which they are granted a discretion to legislate or in those respects in which they are left entirely free to do so, given the gaps in the agreement's coverage. Thus it has an important role to play in managing the residual diversity of regulation.

The principle of national treatment is one of the main thrusts of the GATS. A potentially large and increasingly significant global field has thus been subjected to this kind of mediation on the strength of the argument that the regulation of supply of services is trade related.[32] As we shall see in chapter four, the GATS took an expansive view of the range of service sectors that could be exposed to the norms. Furthermore, it encompassed all possible modes of service supply, not just the cross-border mode of supply, which is most clearly trade related, but also supply through the presence of national persons and through a commercial presence in the territory of another member country. Only the scope of supply through a national presence was limited categorically, the agreement being declared not to apply to measures affecting access to employment markets or regarding citizenship or residence. The wide scope of commercial presence was particularly portentous. In extending to the acquisition or maintenance of a juridical person, it introduced the issue of foreign direct investment into a truly multilateral framework.

The impact also depends upon the scope read into the principle itself. For example, we shall see that the GATS gives broad scope to the principle by adopting a realist test of discrimination (article XVII:2). At the same time, the agreement's decentralised, discretionary approach to the making of commitments provides a means to manage its impact. National treatment (and market access) is referable to a broad swathe of national measures, but it ultimately only applies in those service sectors which members actually list or 'inscribe' in their individual schedules of commitments. In these listed sectors, they have a further option to limit their commitments by listing or 'entering' non-conforming measures. The case studies will reveal that all members chose not to inscribe certain sectors at all. In the sectors they did inscribe, they entered both across the board (horizontal) limitations on certain modes of supply and sector-specific limitations. Economic protection might often have been a reason for these reservations, but the limitations also represented a view that certain types of services were not to be treated simply as economic transactions. Professional services and communications services were among these services.

Therefore, national treatment is more accurately to be described as a goal of the agreement rather than an obligation. All the same, one can anticipate situations in which measures will be subjected to the scrutiny of the principle, perhaps through the dispute settlement process. For instance, a member might have failed to enter a measure as a limitation on national treatment in a sector it has nonetheless inscribed.

Market access for services

Perhaps the most profound norm, certainly of the GATS, will turn out to be that of market access (article XVI), but its full implications also remain to be explored. If it operates narrowly within the GATT tradition, it will be concerned with restrictions that are placed at the border on the passage of foreign services into domestic markets. Such restrictions inevitably single out foreigners for discriminatory treatment. Thus, market access has much in common with national treatment, but the concept of market access can also be read in a broader sense. If foreigners are to enjoy effective access to domestic markets, non-discriminatory restrictions will also have to be lifted.

There are indications that the GATS norm proposes reductions in this kind of domestic regulation. Some regulation restricts the opportunities for both foreigners and locals to enter markets and engage in market activities. As we shall see, the language of the GATS is by no means conclusive. In relation to the negotiation of specific commitments, it speaks of 'effective market access', for instance, but also of submitting restrictions on 'trade' to the scrutiny of this norm (article XIX). Insight into its intent is offered by the article enumerating measures that cannot be maintained, once a sector is inscribed and exposed to the disciplines of the agreement (article XVI:2). The list includes measures that discriminate against foreigners, placing limits on levels of foreign investment. It extends to measures that may or may not discriminate, restricting the type of entity which may be used to supply the service. It adds measures that clearly affect both local and foreign suppliers, that limit the number, for instance, of suppliers permitted to operate in a services market.

If this wider ambit is the objective of the agreement, then market access has the potential to further the neo-liberal program of privatisation and competition. It requires existing markets to be liberalised where regulatory schemes have restricted participation, say by licensing a fixed number of entrants or by drawing lines around the participants' spheres of activity. If it applies to non-discriminatory qualitative limitations, then it requires markets to be created where they have not been permitted, say because a country places a ban on the sale of certain services or it chooses to provide them by way of a public monopoly supplier. It is concerned with the scope of market activities as well as the conditions of entry into existing markets.

In rolling back these types of controls, the GATS appears to clear the way for private 'regulation' to operate more freely. But, despite its focus on certain types of public regulation, the norm of market access may not remain entirely compatible with the kinds of regulatory relationships which are constructed by the 'private' sector. It begins to challenge the way governments employ various kinds of regulatory schemes, including competition law, to foster and guide internal domestic arrangements such as export cartels, producer–distributor alliances, merger rationalisations and research and development consortia. It begins to insist on non-discriminatory enforcement of the law already on the books.[33] It should, then, begin to open up the field to the possibility that the restrictive business practices of the powerful transnational suppliers can be regarded as restrictions on market access. Our analysis will look for any hints that this constructive re-regulatory approach is supported by the GATS and TRIPs.

Protection for intellectual property

The WTO TRIPs agreement is the clearest indication that the catalogue of norms includes security for certain kinds of investment as well as the freedom to trade. This strand of the agreements might also be characterised as regulatory protection from excessive or unfair competition. To further this norm, the WTO must demonstrably do more than insist that its member states relax and remove measures that affect trade: it requires them to impose regulatory measures on the kinds of private sector/free market activities which threaten the traders' property. Thus it goes further than the investment treaties which have included intellectual property among the investments they protected from discriminatory or expropriatory government incursions.

To advance this protection, the TRIPs ranges wide across the world. It applies its frame of reference to the regulation of the knowledges, techniques and signs which circulate around the member countries. It also reaches deep behind the border. The Uruguay Round's connection with intellectual property began with a concern on the part of several producer nations that counterfeited or pirated goods, such as clothing, videos, disks and games, were being traded across borders. But, as we shall see, the agenda strengthened considerably when it embraced the view that inadequate treatment and enforcement of intellectual property rights generally caused distortions to trade. This view implicated dealings with products meant for domestic markets such as generic drugs, processes internal to industrial production such as chemical processes, and localised practices such as the sowing of crops or treatment of the sick.

This view chose to regard lack of protection as the barrier to trade. In the short term at least, intellectual property rights might be seen to exclude others from the use of resources that seem naturally to be public goods. The justification for such restrictions on access to critical resources is the contribution intellectual property makes in the longer term to productive or dynamic efficiency. On this basis, security encourages investment in innovation. So, in the long run, protection benefits users and consumers as well as producers. However, this call for heavy regulatory intervention has a certain irony. It is difficult to see why these regulatory restrictions can be justified in the case of knowledge capital, if industrial workers are not entitled to protections that safeguard their investment in their 'human capital' or indigenous peoples in their cultural capital. Protection, it has to be said, is partly a function of value preferences. Protection is justified where competition is 'unfair'.[34]

The TRIPs agreement also ranges extremely widely because it binds countries that clearly import far more of the protected goods and services than they export. It implicates economic practices which, as end users and secondary producers, they might not regard as unfair. In certain countries, the case for protection encounters a deeper layer of cultural or social resistance. Where they commodify intellectual endeavours or at least tie them to instrumental uses, intellectual property rights may become associated with inroads into the domains of sociality, spirituality and the natural environment. Thus certain social movements may act to maintain limits on appropriation. Their objective might be to allow local producers free access to essential facilities, to keep resources in the public domain as part of a common heritage, to encourage freedom of expression and learning, or to assert non-market values such as moral or ethical concerns.

On the other hand, just as fragmentation at the national level reveals secondary producers and end users who question the benefits of strengthening protection, even in the exporting states, the global operators do not always find themselves in favour of blanket and exclusive rights. The property interests of authors, artists and publishers may diverge from those of the industrial firms which seek freely to acquire, reconstitute and distribute content in packages and services. Likewise, some producer groups have become attracted to the idea of using intellectual property to assist indigenous peoples to assert their claims to genetic materials or to cultural artefacts. We shall use the studies below to test this potential.

We should note that the TRIPs agreement is by no means the first international instrument for the protection of intellectual property. Indeed, in the Paris and Berne Conventions, intellectual property provided one of the earliest occasions for multilateral agreement. Still, we shall see in chapter six that TRIPs is significant for the range of subject matter which it subsumes within intellectual property protection. It brings fresh categories, such as confidential information, to the international level, as well as enveloping core categories such as patents, copyright and trademarks (see articles 9–39). In categories such as patents and trademarks, it is more wide ranging than many national systems and more prescriptive than the existing international conventions.

However, its role in this respect is not all radical. In the copyright field, where those conventions were already more substantive, its main function is to incorporate their existing provisions and give them the backing of a large trade organization. At the same time, it omitted to address the issue of intellectual property in the realm of the on-line media. In other categories too, it left spaces for national variations to run or for other international conventions to re-enter the field. For this book, another case in point is the ownership of generic materials. Such tentativeness also provides scope for the WTO dispute settlement process to supervene in an interpretive role.

Measures affecting trade

The norms of the WTO agreements must be considered against the backdrop of the kinds of measures or effects which they will subject to such scrutiny. Conventionally, the target of trade norms has been the measures taken by national governments who are the parties to the agreement or the members of the organization. Thus the dominant perception has been that governments are the source of the barriers to free trade and open markets. The goal, then, has been negative or deregulatory, to lift those government measures which act as barriers. Consistent with this view has been a disinclination to require governments to intervene in the marketplace to discipline non-government or private sector 'barriers to trade'.

All the same, the GATT itself was mindful that government measures were not confined to the formal legislative measures of the national government. The GATT applied its norms of non-discrimination to laws, regulations and requirements. We appreciate that governments employ a range of measures to further protection of local industries or to extract concessions from foreign suppliers. Some of the most effective of these measures may be buried in the administrative practices of the operating agencies. They often extend to the provision of assistance or the granting of favours. We should note that the ability of the GATT to comprehend measures like this was tested in a dispute over conditions expressed in contracts let to foreign suppliers by the Canadian government.[35] The GATT was to take the view that such purchase undertakings could be regarded as requirements. The government's patronage was conditional on the foreigner meeting the conditions which were attached. Of course, certain types of measure have attracted the attention of specialist agreements; subsidies are the most notable example.

In keeping with this approach, the GATS defines the measures to which its norms apply to include any law, regulation, rule, procedure, decision, administrative action or any other form (article XXVIII(a)). We can already see that this definition goes wider again than the GATT. It is likely to catch various kinds of administrative guidance which government gives to the private sector, provided of course that it transgresses the substantive norms of the agreement. Consideration of the question of subsidies has however been postponed to the year 2000.

The TRIPs approach is more traditional, primarily applying its norms to national legislation. Nonetheless, its provisions for effective enforcement recognise that administrative practices can substantially determine the real strength of protections. So again it reveals the tendency to extend the scrutiny of the norms deeper into legal cultures of the locality well beyond the surface layer of legislative enactments.

The GATS also realises that the obstacles and expectations which foreign suppliers encounter may be located at the regional or local government level (article I:3). Indeed, as national measures are disciplined, they may be displaced to these levels. The evidence is that globalization tends to pick and choose certain regions and certain cities over others, distributing its benefits across national lines. So 'sub-national' legalities find themselves drawn into a mediated relationship with foreign legalities. Compliance, however, is rendered more problematic if the parties to the trade agreement are not the same as the targets of the norms. The agreements continue to rely on the nation state members for their implementation. Thus the GATS obliges the member nations to use their best endeavours to ensure these sub-national legalities conform.

The GATS definition extends to measures taken by non-government bodies in the exercise of powers delegated by central, regional and local governments (article I:3). Such an ambit brings into contention the relationship between member government measures and the private sector practices which are seen as impeding market access by foreign suppliers. To what extent will trade agreements place the onus on government members to remove private barriers to trade? The GATS extension is cautious. It envisages a situation in which the non-government body is acting on behalf of the government. In that sense, the government remains the source of the non-conforming measure. Responsibility is extended out through the obligations concerning monopoly and exclusive service suppliers. The GATS says that where governments formally or in effect create monopolies or oligopolies, the governments are bound to ensure that they do not act in a manner inconsistent with the commitments which the governments have made to national treatment or market access (article VIII). Generally, it should be ensured that they do not abuse their monopoly rights. In the case of basic telecommunications carriers, the obligations imposed by the GATS are more specific. Members must ensure that foreign suppliers are given access to and use of their services on reasonable and non-discriminatory terms.

We shall suggest in chapter eight that the telecommunications access obligation is spreading responsibility further afield. It obliges member governments to regulate the practices of those carriers which they require to offer services to the public generally. The carrier need not be a state owned or controlled corporation and it seems that a government measure would not have to be the source of the carrier's power to control access for the obligation to regulate to apply. I think this kind of provision is mindful that the trend to corporatisation and privatisation is blurring the public/private sector divide, but it might still be possible to think in terms of purely private domestic arrangements and relationships which exclude foreign suppliers from access. If these 'measures' were to be challenged, the trade norms would be calling governments to account for inaction. As we shall soon see, government failure to enforce competition laws may be what the regulatory reform agenda has in mind. However the agenda need no longer be confined to that legality. It is important to remember that such a re-regulatory demand would not be novel. In essence, the TRIPs agreement is demanding that members take action against private practices, such as free copying, that are considered deleterious to foreign traders. In most countries, governments are not the main sources of disrespect for intellectual property – it is the conduct of local users, distributors and producers which so worries the foreign suppliers.

Transparency and form

The WTO agreements also make certain demands on members regarding the form in which they embody and administer these measures. It would be tempting to say that the WTO is promoting the Western concept of the rule of law, a claim made by President Clinton when the United States reached agreement with the People's Republic of China on accession. However, it remains to be seen whether trade norms such as non-discrimination, market access and intellectual property are compatible with a variety of national legal institutions and practices.[36]

The way the core norms are expressed lends credence to this view. The GATS sets up standards by which government measures can be appraised. The standards are for the benefit of foreign nationals but they are not written as individual personal rights or freedoms to the same extent, for example, that they are in the Treaty of Rome. The way the individual national commitments to these norms are to be expressed also leaves much scope for ambiguity. It would be difficult for the national legislatures and courts to determine how individuals could invoke them directly if the member state had failed to translate them into local law. TRIPs pushes harder in this direction by requiring members to afford rights to foreign nationals. But it is still an obligation imposed on the state; one might still argue that the TRIPs prescriptions are not written with sufficient precision for it to be self-evident how they would translate into private law.

On this view, the primary objective of both agreements is to establish public law or government-to-government obligations. The initiative to achieve compliance lies with these national units, the member countries, through the WTO's own dispute settlement processes. In this vein, the agreements do not create transnational legal institutions for the assertion of private rights and obligations, despite the increasing difficulties that globalization creates for the identification of the appropriate national jurisdiction in which laws are to be legislated, adjudged and enforced. Again, a contrast might be made with the draft MAI which has proposed to give aggrieved investors rights of access to international arbitration tribunals as well as the courts of the countries with which they are disputing.

It is perhaps in their prescriptions of the form which national implementation should take that the agreements are most rule-of-law or rights-like. For example, both agreements require members to provide transparency by documenting, translating and publishing the measures they are either required or permitted to maintain.

TRIPs is most prescriptive in specifying that members must institute procedures and remedies for the effective enforcement of protections it advances (articles 41–61). Several of the prescriptions require government agencies to act to provide protection directly, but others are designed to afford private property holders access to administrative and judicial avenues at the national level so that they can enforce the protections which the member states have had to institute. If the GATS is primarily intended to eliminate various national measures, it also lays down certain requirements for the domestic regulation which members may choose to retain. These requirements include an obligation to maintain judicial, arbitral or administrative procedures which provide service suppliers with avenues of review and remedy of administrative decisions affecting trade in services (article VI:2). Reviews are meant to be objective and impartial.

At the same time, both agreements contain concessions to differing legal traditions. GATS article VI on domestic regulation says that members are not required to institute procedures inconsistent with their constitutional structures or the nature of their legal systems. Arguably, TRIPs is less forgiving of different traditions, but, within the provisions regarding enforcement of intellectual property, it does say that members do not have to put in place judicial systems distinct from those for the enforcement of law in general (article 41:5). This article goes on to say, rather obliquely, that nothing in these provisions creates any obligation with respect to the distribution of resources as between the enforcement of intellectual property rights and the enforcement of law in general.

TRIPs is also requiring members to institute substantive measures of protection. The form in which the member state should institute them may be part of the issue of compliance. The WTO's decision on the complaint by the United States against India certainly suggests so. In part, the United States complaint concerned the way India had complied with the provisions of TRIPs requiring a 'mail-box' system to be set up for the filing of patent applications (article 70:8).[37] As a developing country, India enjoyed a period of grace of four years before it was required to implement the substantive protections of the agreement (article 65:2). The mail-box system was to ensure that applications made during this transitional period preserved their eligibility for patents until the time came for India to apply for substantive protections. In the jargon, this was called 'pipeline protection'.

The panel held that the administrative arrangements which India had made for the mail-box system did not meet its obligations under TRIPs. It was true that article 1 of the TRIPs agreement said members were free to determine the appropriate method of implementing the provisions within their own legal system and practice. But the arrangements created legal insecurity and unpredictability about the treatment which the patent applications would receive when the time came for India to decide on the substantive issue of patentability. They had failed to provide a sound legal basis. Instead, legislative measures were required if compliance was to be adequate. Otherwise, the administrative regime could be challenged for inconsistency with India's patent statute.[38] Article XVI:4 of the WTO Agreement requires each member to 'ensure the conformity of its laws, regulations and administrative procedures with its obligations as provided in the annexed Agreements'. The panel also held that the arrangements did not meet the obligation of transparency. Thus, the panel made significant statements about the nature of the rights to be enjoyed under TRIPs and the form of law which the member countries would have to adopt. On this score, the Appellate Body has since upheld the panel's report.[39]

NULLIFICATION OR IMPAIRMENT

The basis of complaints

Issues concerning the reach of the norms may find expression in the peculiar GATT concept of nullification or impairment. We should take the trouble to identify this concept. Nullification or impairment is a test of a member's compliance with the agreements which surface in the dispute resolution process. To use the language of the law, it links breach with damage.

The Understanding on Rules and Procedures Concerning Dispute Settlement derives the concept of nullification or impairment from the GATT. Under the GATT, nullification or impairment of the benefits of an agreement could come about in three ways: through violations, non-violations and situations. The most clear-cut is a violation of the provisions of an agreement. Article XXIII of the GATT 1994 first enables members to bring a complaint where another member takes a measure that violates an obligation or commitment under an agreement and this violation results in a benefit accruing under the agreement being nullified or impaired. In the GATT context, a clear example would be a measure imposing a tariff at a level higher than the level conceded in a member's schedule.

Such a concept can be translated into the context of the GATS or TRIPS. We shall see that both the agreements give recognition to such complaints. Under the GATS, for instance, a member might have made a commitment to allow foreign lawyers to give advice to local clients on their home country law. Subsequently, the government decides to reserve that activity for local lawyers. Under the TRIPS, a member is obliged to provide copyright protection for computer programs. Now the government decides that locals should be free to make copies of foreign computer programs for certain purposes, such as inter-operability, whether the rightful owner of the copyright authorises the copying or not.

We can readily accept that the text of the agreement will not always identify violations clearly. The meaning of the text can be argued in the dispute settlement process. But the GATT also envisaged a second category of complaints, called non-violation complaints. Members may complain of measures that nullify or impair benefits without cutting across the text of the agreement. The GATT had in mind measures that thwart or counteract the benefits of the agreement. For example, a member offsets the value of a tariff concession to a foreign trader by providing a subsidy to a local producer. The relevant jurisprudence speaks of unanticipated measures that undermine the legitimate expectations of the foreign trader by upsetting the competitive relationship with the local producer.[40]

In the jurisprudence of the GATT, the principle of legitimate or reasonable expectations helps determine the benefits of the agreement. The principle has been explored by a number of GATT panels.[41] We can readily see that the expectations of the complaining party will have been frustrated if the provisions of the agreement are directly contravened by a government measure. The principle could also arguably be of assistance as an aid to the interpretation of the provisions where their requirements are not entirely clear. Interestingly, the panel in the dispute between the United States and India over patents applied it to the resolution of a violation complaint under the TRIPs agreement. However, the Appellate Body was at pains to say that it was to have a very limited role in relation to violation complaints under TRIPs. Violation was essentially a question of India's conformity with the express obligations of the agreement.[42]

Non-violation complaints

Thus the principle has most relevance to determining whether the benefits – some would say the 'balance' of rights and obligations or commitments and concessions under the agreement – have been undermined by a measure that does not violate the text of the agreement. Not every measure will frustrate such expectations. It should be a measure that was not reasonably foreseeable at the time the expectation arose. That time normally is the time the agreement was reached. Interestingly, the source of such expectations need not be the text of the agreement. It can run to the statements made during the negotiations, for instance, or the prior conduct of the respondent party. Much of this approach is familiar to those of us who are interested in the construction of contracts.

Under the GATT, the expectation has largely been of the benefit of a tariff concession. Now it could be the benefit of a certain level of intellectual property protection or a degree of liberalisation of market access for services supply. However, it is important to reiterate that the agreements are not promising that the foreign traders will achieve sales. Rather, the expectation goes to the conditions of competition within a national market, specifically the competitive relationship with the traders from other countries and with the local traders.

On its face, a non-violation complaint would seem more difficult to substantiate than a violation complaint, which after all is a breach of the letter of the agreement rather than the spirit. The photographic film and paper dispute between the United States and Japan (discussed below) indicates that the onus of proof will also have an influence over the outcome in such cases. Where there is an 'infringement of the obligations assumed under a covered agreement', the Understanding says there is prima facie a nullification or impairment (article 3:8). It places the onus on the infringing party to rebut the presumption that the breach of the rules has an adverse impact on the complaining party. Because of the difficulties involved in establishing the impact of a violation on trade in a factual way, the GATT panels tended to treat the presumption as conclusive.[43] Where a non-violation complaint was laid, the onus was cast on the complaining country to establish the effect. The new WTO Understanding requires the complaining party to present a detailed justification in support of any complaint relating to a measure which does not conflict with the relevant covered agreement (article 26:1). The onus of proof will create a substantial burden for those who complain that lack of competitiveness is the result of the government measure in question.

The most recent jurisprudence we have is the contribution of the panel report in the dispute between the United States and Japan over Japanese measures affecting consumer photographic film and paper.[44] The panel considered a non-violation complaint of nullification or impairment of a benefit under the GATT agreement, namely a tariff concession for imported film and paper. But the complaint was not against something as directly related as a subsidy given to the local competitor. Instead, the United States complained of a number of measures the Japanese Government had taken in relation to local distribution systems. Specifically, it targeted measures taken to rationalise distribution structures and processes, the provisions and administration of the Japanese

Large Retail Stores Law, and the regulation of promotional activities such as prizes and discounts. For this reason, it is worth noting the panel's ruling.

The panel ruled against the United States complaint. The report was significant in several respects. First, it continued the trend to take an expansive view of the concept of 'government measures'. The complaint challenged the acts of executive and administrative bodies that ranged from the Japanese Cabinet, MITI (the Ministry for International Trade and Industry) and the Fair Trading Council through to government–industry bodies such as the Manufacturers' Council and the Retailers' Council. In each case, the panel was prepared to regard the acts as government measures. While the measures were, legally or formally speaking, non-mandatory, the panel found that the government had held out sufficient incentives or advantages for them to take effect.

The measures spanned a number of years. So a real obstacle to the success of the complaint was the fact that American importers were on notice about the measures when they began to trade. In other words, their expectations were conditioned by the presence of the measures or, in some cases, an anticipation that they would be introduced. But the most important issue in the end was that of causality. The panel was not convinced that uncompetitiveness of the imported film was attributable to these measures rather than to a range of other factors. Impact or effect was the issue here, not the intent which lay behind the measures. Still, the onus of proof was a heavy one. Being an exceptional remedy, the burden lay with the complainant to provide a detailed justification in support of its contention. This the United States failed to do.

In relation to the rationalisation measures, the panel placed store on the fact that the measures were directed equally at domestic and foreign products. They sought order in the market for all. Of course, it was possible to say that a policy which was formally neutral could still be applied in a way that upset the competitive relationship between foreign and local products. But the United States failed on the basis of causality: it had not shown that the private distribution system would break down in the absence of the government measures. Similar arrangements for distribution were evident in the United States itself.

Japan's Large Retail Store Law has long been a target of United States bilateral initiatives.[45] The Law places restrictions on the establishment of shops beyond a certain size in city neighbourhoods, including conditions that agreement must be reached with local councils, existing small shop owners, and consumer groups. It also regulates the hours such shops can open and the holidays they must take. Again, the panel noted that the policy was on its face neutral as to products and their origins. However, the United States argued that large stores carried more

imported products and were less susceptible to pressure from local manufacturers. The panel held that the policy carried no explicit or implicit
disadvantage. The panel was of the view that there is 'nothing intrinsic
in the nature of imports that renders them less capable of competing in
a marketplace where a diversity of retailing outlets is promoted'.[46]

Such a decision puts a dampener on non-violation complaints. The
record shows that some ninety per cent of complaints in the past have
been violation complaints. Overall, there have been fourteen non-violation complaints considered, with four proving successful.[47] But if the
non-violation complaint still targets governments' measures, the GATT
also conceived of countries bringing 'situation complaints'. Under this
head, they may allege that benefits are nullified or impaired by a
member allowing the existence of any other situation (which may not be
the result of government actions). Thus, depending on how it is interpreted, the concept provides potential for members to be required to act
on private barriers to trade. It seems no complaints so far have sought to
invoke this ground.

Nonetheless, it is further worth noting that the members can also
bring any of these three types of complaint under the GATT where a
measure impedes the attainment of any objective under the relevant
agreement. GATS and TRIPs contain a number of aspirational or indicative statements that range beyond the specific obligations they impose
on members.

Complaints under GATS and TRIPs

The negotiators appreciated that the non-violation and situation complaints would have somewhat different and uncertain implications for
compliance with the TRIPs and GATS agreements. After debate, it was
resolved not to allow these complaints to be taken under TRIPs (see article 64). Reconsideration is scheduled for the year 2000. It might be
argued that non-violation and situation complaints were not really relevant to TRIPs. The agreement requires governments to provide substantive levels of protection for intellectual property and backs them up with
procedures for enforcement against infringements. The real question is
whether national legislation matches up to these standards. However, we
might still envisage circumstances in which delay or obfuscation on the
part of government authorities might undermine the protections which
were promised in the national legislation.[48] Again we should note, however, that TRIPs is meant to protect against acts of misappropriation,
such as unauthorised copying of the works. It is not the role of TRIPs to
guarantee the success of any intellectual property in the sense of market
access and the level of sales and other custom which it attracts.

Some countries also thought the GATS was not ready for such complaints. In the end, these complaints were allowed (article XXIII:3) in relation to the general obligations and the specific commitments (national treatment and market access) made under the agreement. At least one of the several disputes relating to the GATS which has been notified to the WTO involves a non-violation complaint; we shall mention this dispute in chapter four.

Non-violation and situation complaints really expand the range of injuries for which members can seek remedies. Before leaving this issue, it is worth noting that the WTO remedies for breach do not work like injunctive relief in the equity jurisdictions of the common law. An infringing party is not permitted to argue that the impact on its economy or its wider society of removing a measure would be more serious than the nullification or impairment of benefits experienced by the complaining country. However, it is true that the infringing party can choose to pay compensation rather than withdraw or modify its measure.

SCOPE FOR NATIONAL REGULATION

If the WTO agreements concede space to variations in national regulation by restraining the scope, specificity and compulsion of their norms, another, explicit concession is that certain legitimate regulatory purposes justify exceptions being made to compliance with those norms. Regulations which on their face would seem to cut across the norms can be maintained if they are attributable to these purposes.

The biggest concession the GATS makes is in its listing approach. It may be to further certain particular regulatory purposes or, as proposed above, to preserve a general regulatory competence, that members have listed non-conforming measures or decided in fact to withhold sectors from the disciplines of the agreement altogether. But, in addition, the GATS enumerates a number of exceptional purposes itself, sending signals about the local economic, political and cultural concerns which are to be regarded as remaining legitimate. For the GATS, these purposes include public order, the orderly movement of persons over borders, the prevention of deceptive or fraudulent practices, the quality of professional services, prudential supervision of financial institutions, and the collection of services taxes (article XIV). This provision is notable both for the purposes it includes and, of course, the purposes it leaves out.

TRIPs is much less explicit about the nature of the purposes which it considers legitimate when it allows members (through their national legislation) to provide for conditions, limitations, exceptions and reservations to the rights it prescribes. Only national security receives direct recognition (article 73). There are indications that the agreement expects members to draw on the relevant norms of the existing intellectual property conventions, but their take-up of this option is likely to provide a fertile ground for disputes. For many countries, once committed to property rights, the key question is the scope to insist on non-voluntary licensing. Such licences authorise people to deal with intellectual property in ways that would otherwise amount to an infringement of the property holder's rights if the holder's permission to do so was not obtained. Licences may be legislated for such purposes as criticism and review, the reporting of news, research, instruction and study, technology transfer, the local working of an invention, and the opportunity to supply derivative or related products and services.

Disciplines applied to the use of exceptions

When recognising the need of members to maintain such regulation, the trade agreement will often impose disciplines upon their use of the exceptions. Strictures are applied so that the regulation is exposed to scrutiny to determine whether it is a bona fide exercise of the exception and whether it involves the least interference with trade. In this vein, the disciplines recurringly demand that the measures not be a disguised barrier to trade, do not act as an arbitrary or discriminatory restriction on trade, can be objectively and technically justified by the purpose, adopt the least trade disruptive solution, and be in proportion to the purpose being served.

Together with the nature of the norms of trade themselves, the use of such open-ended and value-laden disciplinary criteria creates a lot of scope for mediation. It affords the dispute resolution bodies in particular influence over the 'balance' which is to be struck between free trade and national regulation, such as regulation for the protection of consumers and the natural environment. Even if the decision makers do accept a place for local regulation, they can begin to mould the kind of regulatory modalities from which the national governments may choose if they are to further a regulatory purpose. The ethos of such agreements lends support to the view that national governments will plump for those modalities which the neo-liberal philosophy finds most compatible with the market. For example, we might expect disclosure of information to consumers about the sources and contents of products and services to be favoured over outright prohibitions or even substantive specification or performance standards which these products and services should meet.[49] Once again, tax measures may be preferred to regulatory directives.

The GATS provision which concedes that members will maintain domestic regulation in the spaces beyond their schedules of commitments installs requirements of this nature (article VI); so too do the provisions for general heads of exception to the norms of the agreement (article XIV). The TRIPs provisions for exceptions to be taken are couched in a more specialist terminology, which may become a friction point for disputes. A common theme of these provisions is a requirement that they do not conflict with a normal exploitation of the subject matter and that they do not undermine the legitimate interests of the right holder (see for example article 13). It is also worth noting that the overall WTO package included substantial disciplines regarding measures that apply to trade generally; these disciplines are to be found for instance in the Agreement on Technical Barriers to Trade and the Agreement on the Application of Sanitary and Phytosanitary Measures.

Regulation and international concerns

One issue regarding the legitimacy of regulation illustrates the tendency of the agreements to favour free trade over what might be seen as equally valid international concerns. Conventionally, a country seeks to apply its regulatory legality to a foreign supplier on its home ground. But, as we recognised in chapter two, it is in the nature of globalization that activities which are conducted in a location offshore nevertheless have effects on conditions at home. For example, a country may want to say that products reaching its shores are being manufactured or harvested in ways that conflict with the standards which it applies at home.

We have noted that this particular inter-legality results in a clash with the other countries whose own laws are meant to apply to the activities in question and which are inconsistent with the first country's standards. They may refuse to cooperate with the policy the first country is seeking to promote. Even if the importing country can find a point of attachment to the activity among its own nationals, say as operators of businesses offshore or consumers of products from outside, it may encounter resistance. Its nationals may not be willing parties to what they see as their government's attempt to further a foreign policy. Yet, at the same time, it is possible that the offshore practices are creating 'unfair' competition for local producers who have to meet more exacting standards. Pressure is thereby generated to relax local standards. More directly, they may be causing spillover effects such as the despoliation of a common social or natural environment.

We should acknowledge the complexity of these issues, in terms both of how these processes operate in practice and what are the appropriate policies to adopt. In the context of this book, we confine our inquiry to whether such regulatory legalities run counter to the norms of the agreements. One such way is for a country to make the point of attachment to its regulation the entry of the products into its territory. Thus, it might place an embargo on such goods. Of course, it is not my intention to underestimate the practical problems of doing so. For instance, globalization provides more opportunities to hide or confuse the origins of goods. When it comes to services, such as those provided over the Internet, it becomes increasingly difficult even to establish the fact that they are entering the country in some way at all.

These kinds of trade sanctions have received the attention of the GATT panels. In two cases, the panels heard the complaints against a United States conservation policy which banned the import of tuna products. The policy was aimed at tuna which had been harvested with the use of driftnets. This harvesting method caught and killed everything in its path, including the blue nose dolphins which shared the sea with the tuna fish. The complaining parties alleged that the ban discriminated against imports from Mexico. As we have noted, the relevant articles of the GATT required MFN and national treatment to be extended to 'like products'. Despite the particular way the tuna was fished, the panels thought the tuna in the can was like any other tuna product.

If the ban breached the norms of non-discrimination, it had to be founded in one of the explicit exceptions.[50] On a broad reading of the GATT, it was referable to a legitimate objective – protection of the life and health of the dolphins or their conservation as a natural resource – so long as it was not to be considered an arbitrary or unjustifiable discrimination between countries where the same conditions prevailed, or a disguised restriction on international trade (GATT 1947, article XX). However, the ban was seen to be employing a strategy that sought to influence activities beyond the United States' territorial jurisdiction. Significantly, both panels thought that it was not clear from the text of the GATT that the exceptions were confined to measures operating within a country's territory. So there might conceivably be situations where extra-territorial reach was tolerated. However, in this case, the United States had gone further. It had let it be known that the embargo would be lifted if the Mexican Government outlawed driftnet fishing within its waters. Both panels held that the measures were not allowable under the GATT. They read the disciplines which applied to non-conforming measures very strictly. The 1991 panel was of the opinion that other options had not been exhausted and it was preferable for the United States to pursue its environmental objective through the medium of an international agreement.[51] The 1994 panel thought that the United States was trying to force another country to change its policy with respect to the conduct of persons within that country's own internal jurisdiction. To single out a country in this way was to upset the balance of the multilateral framework for market access.[52]

A recent WTO panel report has adopted this GATT jurisprudence.[53] The panel examined a United States measure against imports of shrimp products where the shrimp had been harvested in a manner harmful to sea turtles. The panel found against the measure, seeing it as a threat to the multilateral trading system. The security and predictability of trade relations would be undermined if members were allowed such measures. The measures conditioned market access on the adoption of certain policies by the exporting nation, such as conservation policies. Other countries would follow suit with their own bans and exporters would be faced with multiple conflicting requirements. Interestingly, the panel made special note that the United States was not taking the measure in order to apply a multilateral environmental agreement to which it was party. The subsequent Appellate Body report was much more legalistic in its approach, but it too condemned the unilateralism of the United States.[54]

We know that the United States has employed this strategy of trade sanctions to further other sorts of policy too. It has applied sanctions to products from countries whose political systems it abhors, including Cuba, and other countries have been involved in trade boycotts and embargoes too, such as the campaign against apartheid in South Africa. Most pertinently, we should also recall that the United States has actively threatened to apply trade sanctions to those countries which do not provide appropriate intellectual property protection within their own borders.

Regulatory competition and coordination

In formal terms, it remains true that the content and strategy of a country's regulatory policy are only called into question if they involve measures that cut across the trade norms. Thus countries are free to adopt their own regulatory standards so long as they remain consistent with those norms. This makes regulatory autonomy – or national sovereignty as some characterise it – a matter of the construction and interpretation of those norms. But we should appreciate that this formal approach belies the secondary or indirect effect which trade agreements have on regulatory competence. They smooth the path for those forces which can undermine the competence of national regulation and they set countries on a course of regulatory competition.

In such circumstances, governments increasingly have to rely on global 'markets for regulation' to produce the necessary demands for high standards. As we noted in chapter two, there is some optimism that competing up is a viable unilateral strategy.[55] Certain jurisdictions may be able to attract and sustain economic activities on the strength of high quality regulatory regimes. Among these standards are sound prudential supervision for investments placed in the financial sector, fair dealing and quality control for the consumers of professional services, and physically safe and social amenable conditions for tourists and business visitors. But we should understand that regulatory competition also transmits incentives to countries to consider skimping on local standards, while at the same time off-loading the responsibility onto others to provide relief if things go wrong. The fall-out from the failures of financial institutions such as the Banco Ambrosiano has pointed up this problem.[56]

The dynamics of regulatory competition are very complex and it is stressed again that the aim is not to try to capture them here. Many variables are at work in locational decisions. For instance, in chapter two we argued that suppliers are not simply free to chop and change location as they wish. Various factors endogenous to the regulatory regime influence their decisions. Here, we are confining ourselves to noting ways in which the trade agreement might itself mediate the competition. Thus, the trade agreement's legitimation of exceptional social measures provides a little space for those countries which feel they can regulate unilaterally. But, for many countries, regulatory coordination will be required if they wish to control such competition.

In this regard, chapter two has suggested that competition could occur broadly in relation to three basic legal functions: legislation, adjudication and enforcement. Such competition is most directly expressed through comparisons made between substantive standards, but we have said that it may also be pursued by means of competitive conflict-of-laws criteria. Such criteria signal that the country's own standards will be applied in preference to others'. Along these lines, regulatory coordination may begin with cooperation that is designed to ensure that each country's enforcement measures are effective. Countries cooperate on the investigation of breaches or the execution of judgements. But such cooperation may need to involve acceptance of the other country's right to adjudicate. Partly, this cooperation is a matter of resolving jurisdiction. But it may lead back to the question of legislation, that is, to the choice of the law which is to govern the conduct or the person targeted by the regulation.

We can identify mutual recognition as a formalised government-to-government choice of law principle that mediates differences between national legalities. At the same time, it reduces the costs for international operators of multi-country compliance where requirements conflict. Some trade agreements adopt such a principle of mutual recognition. We shall see some limited support for this approach in the GATS. It is most common for this approach to allow foreigners access to host markets on the strength of their compliance with home country requirements. Yet we should entertain the possibility that mutual recognition does not eliminate regulatory competition. Indeed, it can become a channel for transmitting incentives to differentiate, especially for those operators who do have the ability to manipulate their 'location' between home and host countries. To obviate such tensions, the parties to the mutual recognition arrangements find that they must reach agreement on a core of minimum standards. These standards establish bands of individual national discretion, drawing boundaries round the tolerance to difference. They thus endeavour to combine the cohesion of a core with the freedom to individualise and localise.[57]

So we shall see that the GATS allows for recognition of standards to be achieved through harmonisation between countries or to be based on multilaterally agreed criteria (article VII). We might also see a preference for multilateralism in the GATT panel reports we discussed above. They seem to be recommending that members seek international agreement on environmental standards. Thus, the trade agreement would be prepared to allow the observance of accepted international standards to act as an exception to its norms. Several of the existing international environmental agreements go so far as to call on their signatories to invoke trade sanctions in order to ensure that protection is made effective; a ban on trade in rare and endangered species comes to mind. Such an allowance is helpful to the extent that it would signal that the trade agreement will not get in the way if the members manage the difficult task of settling on standards.[58]

However, some observers fear that the same approach will produce a pressure to reduce standards to a lowest common denominator. Members will not be able to insist on more exacting requirements for fear of transgressing the trade norms. Such a concern has been expressed about the WTO's new Agreement on Sanitary and Phytosanitary Measures (SPS agreement). The agreement nominates the Codex Alimentarius Commission as a reference point for international standards. Critics accuse the Commission of being unduly influenced by industry interests. It has been suggested that some fifty per cent of the standards which it recommends are below the present levels adopted in the United States.[59] Therefore, there was much interest when the WTO Appellate Body ruled on the United States complaint against the restrictions the European Union has been placing on meat products derived from animals administered genetically engineered growth hormones.

The Appellate Body upheld the right of members to establish a higher level of sanitary protection in matters relating to human health.[60] That right was an important and autonomous right of governments, and not merely an exception to the general SPS obligation to base measures on prevailing international standards. We should note, however, that the Appellate Body ultimately ruled against the measures the European Union was applying.[61] The Body took the view that the measures did not satisfy the disciplines imposed in the SPS agreement on allowable national measures. In particular, the Union did not satisfy the Body that the measures were justifiable against an objective and scientifically assessed standard. Such disciplines are imposed to prevent members

deploying arbitrary sanitary and phytosanitary measures as a trade barrier in disguise, but they have a very discouraging effect in cases like
growth hormones and genetically modified substances generally. These
substances are new and not all the evidence is available regarding their
hazards. Such disciplines place the onus on those seeking to regulate
rather than those seeking to trade. Specifically, the regulators carry the
'burden of uncertainty' regarding the indirect and long-term hazards of
such substances. The 'precautionary principle' may not be applied. Furthermore, we should appreciate that risk assessment is not properly just
a technical exercise. Inevitably, the assessment will involve elements of
what is socially and subjectively acceptable as a risk. Objectification tends
to give prominence to what is acceptable to a particular type of expert.
The nature of risk assessment is a complex issue, and one we cannot take
on here. However it is clear that, as genetically modified organisms come
onto the market, a huge issue is looming for trade law.

If, within such strict limits, members retain some freedom to apply
their own preferred standards at home, what of their concern about the
standards being observed among their trading partners? We know that, at
times, trade produces its own dynamics for standardisation. The minimi-
sation of conflicting requirements may appeal to some traders. More substantially, core social standards may be seen as a means of controlling the
excesses of competition. Some competition is characterised as unfair in
the sense that countries give producers who locate with them an unfair
advantage by enabling them to 'under cut' on social or environmental
standards.[62] The terminology of 'social dumping' has been used in an
attempt to create a link with the established anti-dumping provisions. On
this basis, trade sanctions would be permissible if the goods or services
were produced under conditions that did not respect the social standards.

Just as there is dissatisfaction with the use of traditional anti-dumping
remedies, some see such moves for a 'social clause' as a new form of protection. Rather than getting into arguments about why countries vary
standards, the Organization might legislate a benchmark set of core standards, the way, after all, it has been prepared to do for intellectual property protection. Vogel sees the trade agreement as giving impetus to
countries with high standards to persuade other countries to agree to take
them on board too, and expects them to seek multilateral agreement to
their higher standards.[63] But, already, the experience with labour regulation suggests that it is not going to be easy to obtain agreement on such
standards in the social fields. The proposal to put the WTO's weight
behind core labour standards has been unable to obtain a consensus.

Another example is a case in point, the difficulties being encountered
by a treaty to ensure safe trade in genetically modified organisms. At the
conference in Cartagena, Colombia, conducted under the aegis of the

Biodiversity Convention, the United States lobbied hard to exclude two staple foodstuffs, soya bean and corn, from the deliberations.[64] As is known from the beef hormone dispute, countries that apply controls unilaterally run the risk of contravening the trade norms. They may not be able to satisfy the stringent criteria for their regulation to be regarded as a legitimate exception to the operation of these norms. A major concern for importing nations is to protect their plant and animal species, as well as their human populations, from physical contamination by the genetically modified counterparts when they are released into the environment. In addition, a number of countries, such as India, also fear that the use of genetically modified organisms will economically undermine their traditional agricultural practices. Such a concern is unlikely to be recognised in the exceptions trade agreements traditionally allow. We shall discuss this fear in chapter seven when we consider the patenting of these organisms. Not surprisingly, patentability helps create a powerfully motivated lobby for the acceptance of these organisms.

Institutional structures

If progress is to be made on social standards, some see reform of the constitution of the WTO as the answer. Reform of the dispute settlement process broadens out into a campaign to make the WTO more democratic. Here, democracy is being conceptualised in a cosmopolitan, participatory sense consistent with an optimistic reading of globalization.[65] The WTO's 'democratic deficit' is indeed a significant query for a body that aspires to a central place in a new international order. Democratisation seems essential if trade values are to be reconciled with non-trade values. For instance, new processes need to be devised to ensure that the most powerful member countries (such as the QUAD countries) cannot simply foist deals on the bulk of the membership. There also needs to be accommodation for those organizations which increasingly cut across the perspectives of the nation states, such as the associations of indigenous peoples and the environmental movements. Environmentalists are especially suspicious that the current WTO carries no real sympathy for their cause.

The WTO Agreement picks up a clause in the original ITO (International Trade Organization) charter that enables it to make 'appropriate arrangements for consultation and cooperation with non-governmental organizations concerned with matters related to those of the WTO' (article V:2). The WTO Secretariat has been making moves in this direction already, such as the timely provision of documents.[66] But the workings of the General Council and the Committees are a closed book and the NGOs do not sit at the conference table unless they are incorporated, as certain industry associations have been, within national delegations.

At the Singapore Meeting of Ministers, some NGOs were given official observer status, but many felt they were shut out of the informal negotiations which determined the outcomes of the meeting.[67]

If the WTO were opened up to the NGOs, there would be a risk that they were being co-opted, lending credence to the decisions of a body that remained fundamentally inimical to their world views. In such a fluid and uncertain situation, the greatest potential may lie in an open interface with other international institutions. If it is not made for this kind of social responsibility, it might be better for the WTO to coordinate standard setting with the more experienced and dedicated institutions of the United Nations, such as the ILO (International Labour Organization). In this vein, article V:1 of the WTO Agreement directs the General Council to 'make appropriate arrangements for effective cooperation with other intergovernmental organizations that have responsibilities related to those of the WTO'.

Of course, the international landscape is already dotted with organizations that provide a contrast with the WTO in terms of their underlying ethos, their special expertise and their particular constituencies. The GATT itself developed quite distinctly from the United Nations organizations after World War 2. The WTO's assumption of the new trade issues clearly carries the potential for it to act as a rival to these organizations. Some read the TRIPs agreement as a successful strategy to shift the focus for intellectual property away from WIPO.[68] Likewise, the GATS could be said to take quite a different set on issues which have preoccupied bodies like UNCTAD (United Nations Conference on Trade and Development) for many years. Yet the studies below will reveal that the relationships are not simply rivalrous. TRIPs has already applied many of the provisions from the Berne and Paris Conventions. TRIPs makes use of the learning and legitimacy of these conventions, while in return providing powerful new sanctions for their non-observance. We explore these connections in chapter six. Now it is mooted that the WTO consider applying the provisions of two new WIPO Treaties through amendments to TRIPs (see chapter eight).

At the same time, we can say that cooperation has a long way to go. We should see that the WTO is hesitant to link TRIPs further afield, for instance with the UPOV Convention (International Convention for the Protection of New Varieties of Plants) or the United Nations Convention on Biodiversity (see chapter seven). We should also note that the GATS has very little to say about linkages, though it does occasionally point the members in the direction of multilateral standard setting organizations such as the ISO (International Standards Organization) and ITU (International Telecommunications Union) (see chapter four). Though clearly of relevance, neither TRIPs nor GATS gives any support to the codes of conduct on technology transfer and restrictive business practices which have been developed in the United Nations. We shall argue that the WTO has acquired a responsibility to give material support to these kinds of codes.

COMPETITION REGULATION

The question of international social regulation is becoming more critical and urgent. It is not for lack of concern that the discussion will be curtailed here. But, to concentrate resources, the book will plump for the issue of international competition regulation. It seems to me that competition regulation is the next item on the neo-liberal regulatory reform agenda. Certainly, it is receiving a good deal of intellectual support from trade policy experts, some of whom are officials or consultants to international organizations such as the OECD (Organization for Economic Cooperation and Development) and the WTO itself, others who are more academically detached. Now the Singapore Meeting of Ministers has agreed to study issues relating to the interaction between trade and competition policy, including anti-competitive practices, in order to identify any areas that may merit further consideration in the WTO framework.[69] This book will consider the ways in which the WTO might shape the international competition regulation agenda.

Of course, part of the purpose of this inquiry is to gauge the positive potential in such an emerging policy for a range of independent and alternative producers to gain access to the rules and resources of globalization. If this competition policy is unable to provide such potential, it will leave us with the conclusion that we are in need of other kinds of international regulatory reform, other kinds of international legality. If globalization does reduce the capacity of national governments to regulate independently, it would be naive not to expect that some business operators would misuse their market power. Already, our analysis reveals that countries are being pressed to lift their traditional controls on the exercise of market freedoms, such as their industry-specific regulation and foreign investment regulation. At the same time, they are being asked to strengthen the security of the global operator, in particular through the provision of intellectual property protection.

National treatment and competition policy

At the end of chapter eight, we return to the WTO agenda for competition policy. At this point, we need to indicate how competition policy sits with the more established norms of international trade law. We begin by observing that the advocates of free trade often say that it leads to greater competition. It exposes domestic producers, suppliers, investors and workers to competition from their foreign counterparts. So trade regulation is concerned in its own way to eliminate the impediments which national legalities create for foreigners when they seek to compete with locals. In particular, we have seen how the norm of national treatment translates into a requirement that national legalities maintain equivalence in the opportunities to compete.

The focus of this trade norm has been government regulation at the national level. On this basis, a national competition law should not be cast in such a way that it accords less favourable treatment to foreigners. Competition laws must satisfy the norm like any other national measures. A concern here might be that the national authorities deny like foreign firms the advantages allowed to domestic firms such as restrictive trade practices, mergers and acquisitions, or participation in consortia and cartels. Or they may make demands on foreigners, such as that they license out intellectual property, which are not made on locals. Of course, the very purpose of the authorities may be to bolster the position of domestic firms because they are encountering rivalry from better endowed foreign firms within the sphere of import markets. In addition, certain firms may be looked upon as national champions abroad on export markets.

Nonetheless, the motives behind competition regulation can be hard to discern. For example, the even-handed application of competition criteria may lead to a similar conclusion as a protectionist policy. Import competition increases the number of market players, making mergers among locals less likely to result in a dominant position. In any case, economies of scale and scope may be regarded by authorities as pro-competitive. As a leading expert concedes, the national systems vary in their characterisations of competitive behaviour.[70] Economic theory fluctuates: the attitude taken to the uses of intellectual property is a case in point. Such arguable interpretations make the task difficult for any trade agreement that seeks to discern the motive behind national regulation.

In the application of competition law, the favouritism shown to local firms may not be reflected so much in the explicit criteria of the system, such as its carve-out of block immunities or the nomination of the benefits which may be taken into account when deciding whether to tolerate a restriction on competition. It may instead be buried in the administrative practices of the responsible authorities. Not only do the legislative criteria leave themselves open to varying interpretations, but the authorities develop working policies for prioritising offences, granting clearances and accepting undertakings. We have seen in this chapter how the trade agreements are extending their scrutiny to these kinds of regulatory legalities by broadening their definitions of the government measures which are subject to their norms.

Moreover, even if the rationale of this informal regulatory legality is not to disguise favouritism, another trade norm – transparency – militates against the maintenance of administrative flexibility. It first demands that the authorities publish their policies. If it goes further, and requires them to embody their policies in legal rules, then it constrains dramatically the ways in which competition policy is often pursued. Competition policy may call for situation-specific judgements about the merits of the conduct, as well as experiments with compliance strategies in order to fit them to the characteristics of the firms which are being regulated. Transparency may also insist that an administrative scheme allow foreigners access to a review of its decisions.

If the national competition law transgresses the norms of the trade agreement in any of these respects, then it must be brought within one of the explicit exceptions which the agreement allows. Even then, it must meet the disciplines which are applied to the measures which take these exceptions. In our detailed analyses of the agreements, we shall find that the GATS and TRIPs both make some allowance for government measures which are aimed to deal with practices that restrain competition and hence restrict trade.

Competition policy and market access

Here we see a hint that competition law will be assigned a role in expanding market access. The agenda is not content to see equal treatment for foreign-sourced products, investments and services. As we have recognised, the norm of market access places pressures on members to make commitments to roll back their non-discriminatory regulation of markets. It applies to regulation that specifically limits foreign participation within sensitive sectors. But it goes further by targeting regulation that, for foreigners and locals alike, places restrictions on market entry and limits the form participation may take.

We might see why free trade enthusiasts feel that competition law complements this approach. When industry-specific regulation is phased out, the disciplines of competition policy are applied to sectors that once enjoyed immunities. For instance, public sector instrumentalities are exposed to competition from private firms; professions lose their monopolies over certain types of service; and controls on the number of market participants are lifted. On this approach, the pressure is kept on governments to roll back their own measures which provide a protective space for local producers.

Yet we might also see that the trade agreement's concern with market access generates a demand that governments act to open out the private relationships which domestic producers, financiers, distributors and users have struck. Complainants perceive an unwillingness on the part of the member government to take action to break up long-standing exclusive dealing relationships between local producers, distributors and retailers. Here we see how foreign suppliers become frustrated with the resilience of the local private relationships, styled by some as a contrasting relational form of capitalism or even as a cultural cohesion which appears beyond the reach of the market.

When the government's role is placed under scrutiny in such situations, the finding might be that it is using its various administrative, commercial and personal influences with the industry to foster these relationships. In the dispute over the distribution of Kodak film and paper products in Japan (discussed above), it seems the main subject of the United States complaint was the role it saw that the Japanese government agencies played in strengthening vertical distribution and single-brand distribution channels to the advantage of local producer Fuji.

However, it is possible to conceive of a situation where inaction might be the only government contribution to the barriers. A direct attack on these embedded relationships would generate a demand that national authorities enforce the competition laws which they have placed on their books. In its structural impediments initiative, the United States has made such a claim on Japan. But, in this regard, Professor Malaguti has argued that a mere omission to enforce legislation would not be enough to ground a complaint under the current provisions of the GATT.[71] A simple failure to act on private barriers to trade would not seem to be sufficient, except where the agreement in question had placed the member under a positive obligation to take measures against such barriers. As many countries do not have competition laws at all,[72] the agenda is likely to turn to the institution of such laws. Thus, the further reaches of the norm of market access and, more explicitly, requirements that competition policy prescriptions be applied, can be seen as part of a neo-liberal regulatory reform project.

The implications could be far reaching. Apart from any interest in shielding or bolstering their domestic industries, national authorities have of course a whole host of other political and cultural reasons for placing regulatory controls on market activity. Competition law may contain some recognition of the value of these controls, but it has to be said that its focus is essentially economistic. Thus we should appreciate that this agenda is not only pushing harder at the kind of support government might give local industry. The depth of this complaint is further evidence of how trade norms are challenging the political, social and cultural foundations of the regulatory controls placed on certain types of market activities. Thus, while the Japanese Large Retail Stores Law is used for protectionist purposes, it also reflects powerful cultural and environmental attitudes. Undermining the law will affect the way urban areas are configured and lead to changes in social relationships too.

At this juncture, we should note also that trade law has produced its own counterbalance to out-and-out competition in international markets. Commonly, the agreements provided for members to apply trade sanctions to counter the dumping of goods. These procedures have been well used by the developed nations, in part to placate their domestic producer constituencies. But their use has caused friction with the other countries which seek to export into these markets. Our new WTO agreements have been hesitant to build in these trade remedies. At the same time, it has been suggested that these trade-specific measures should be replaced with generalist competition regulation, which of course would be accessible to foreigners as well as locals. Instead of dumping, for instance, we would consider predatory pricing. However the standards of competition law do not coincide squarely with those of anti-dumping and countervail. On the whole, competition law is more difficult for the injured party to invoke.

Competition policy and transnational business practices

Breaking down national regulatory barriers certainly extends the breadth of markets beyond the confines of the national jurisdictions. It enhances the opportunities for transnational corporations and alliances to implement globally coordinated strategies of production and distribution. Decisions taken offshore can more readily produce effects within national segments of what have become global markets. Simply rolling back national government impediments to market access does not ensure that real competition will occur. Indeed, a laissez-faire approach to liberalisation and privatisation may result in further concentrations of market power. Paradoxically, liberalisation may encourage and spread cartelisation. For example, Scherer warns that informal understandings, strategic alliances and mergers between multilateral firms may attempt to divide up world markets into spheres of influence and to place restraints on international diffusion of technological know-how.[73] Thus, it has been said that: 'Competition policy complements liberalisation where the market has an oligopolistic or monopolistic structure.'[74]

Now that national controls are under challenge from free trade regulation, some of its more thoughtful advocates are calling for a more balanced and comprehensive approach to multilateral disciplines.[75] The calls are reminiscent of the concerns which were expressed by third world critics of freer trade and which led to the moves within the United Nations for codes of conduct that would apply to the restrictive business practices of transnational corporations. Looking ahead to the WTO,

Raghavan counselled: 'Equal attention must be paid to those aspects of the behaviour of the TNC's [transnational corporations] – restrictive trade practices, restrictions on the free flow of technology, market-sharing agreements, etc. … Any equitable multilateral arrangements must then also include acceptance by TNC's and the governments of the developed countries of their own responsibilities.'[76]

The early proposals for international codes of conduct were informed by the sense that many smaller countries lacked the legal jurisdiction and the political power to apply controls to the transnationals on their home ground.[77] Even if trade agreements left them space for industry-specific regulation and foreign investment regulation, they were not in a position to effect performance requirements. They would require the cooperation and reinforcement of larger countries where the corporations made their home bases or enjoyed their biggest markets. However globalization has stepped up the competition between countries to offer inducements that attract and retain the transnationals. Global mobility and reflexivity also allow the corporations far greater opportunities to circumvent the bilateral agreements which have been struck between countries that do wish to cooperate.

In this more complex and interdependent world, some countries have crafted sophisticated criteria by which they attach their jurisdictions to these restrictive practices. They use multiple aspects of the conduct in question or the 'persons' involved as the way to establish a nexus with their territory. In particular, they do not accept the separate entity conceptualisation of the corporation. But the idea that the effects or impacts of corporate activity are sufficient to attract jurisdiction, an idea with currency in the United States for instance, continues to meet resistance. Where the more powerful countries did endeavour to give 'extra-territorial' reach to their own unilateral policies, they encountered, as we have noted, resentment among the private firms which were asked to carry the responsibility abroad. Extra-territoriality also provoked clashes with other governments which were concerned to guard their own sovereignty over competition policy. It produced blocking statutes. Furthermore, as we sought to show in chapter two, this kind of regulation often needs practical support from other jurisdictions if it is actually to enforce the judgements it thinks are appropriate to make. However, it will not attract support unless its regulatory standards are respected by these other countries.[78]

So a different argument for the international standardisation of competition regulation – an international code – is the need to override these constraints on the efficacy of national regulation. In the succeeding chapters, we must look for signs that the two WTO agreements give support to this internationalisation. We shall also ask whether the WTO is prepared to take on a new responsibility for coordination. Before the Singapore Meeting of Ministers, there were signs of acceptance in the remarks of the Director-General: 'If the international community seeks to negotiate agreements that require countries to give rights to foreign companies, it is almost inevitable that the issue of international co-operation to deal with possible abuses of those rights will also arise.'[79]

Yet, as the study will reveal, many member nations and NGOs remain sceptical about the WTO's preparedness to tackle problems associated with the restrictive business practices of transnational corporations. Moreover, we should appreciate that the issues go much wider than the concerns of competition regulation. Venda Shiva argues that the global debate is not simply about technology transfer from the North to the South, it is about inter-cultural dialogue and respect.[80] In her view, rather than dwell on competition policy, the WTO will have to give its support to more appropriate codes of conduct. It should match the new rights of global traders with the obligations of their global citizenship. But we should now see if the analysis bears out these projections. We shall turn first to the GATS.

CONCLUSIONS

The role of this chapter was to identify the basic institutional and normative elements of the WTO agreements. Analysis of the specifics of the GATS and TRIPs agreements is to follow, supplemented by the assessment of their impact in the three case studies. Overall, it seems as if the WTO is advancing a neo-liberal regulatory reform agenda that has already gained considerable momentum around the world, but it is doing so within a particular institutional and normative framework. This chapter identified its firming framework for decision making, including the processes for the negotiation of commitments and the settlement of disputes. It also began to identify the potential reach of its norms. The apparently innocuous principles of MFN and national treatment are given fresh meaning when they are related to the supply of services and the conduct of intellectual endeavours. However, the agreements extend their prescriptions further into the substance of local regulatory measures. The norm of market access places the onus on quantitative limitations which do not discriminate against foreign suppliers. Protection for intellectual property moves to the other side of the equation by requiring governments to re-regulate and provide suppliers with security from 'unfair' private competition. This re-regulatory trend would be afforded a more general momentum if the traditional GATT concepts of 'measures affecting trade' and 'nullification or impairment' were expanded again. But we saw in the photographic film and paper case that the

WTO's Appellate Body pulled back from the brink of giving the concept of 'nullification or impairment' a very volatile potential.

It remains to be seen how accommodating this re-regulatory approach might be to different perspectives. For those concerned about the risks associated with open trade and free markets, it raises the issue whether the WTO should be pressed into becoming more politically accountable and take positive responsibility for 'social' regulation. The chapter indicates that such agreements make allowance for certain national regulatory objectives, but their disciplines restrict the members' choice of regulatory strategy. A notable instance is their attitude to regulation that expresses international concerns, such as concerns about the environment. The WTO suggests that such regulation has to be supported by multilateral agreements if it is to gain exemption from its trade norms, but at this stage the WTO does not feel itself competent to promote such agreements. To give this discussion further particularity, the chapter focussed on the case of competition regulation. Depending on how it is conceived, competition law is the kind of regulation which can cut across the norms, which may be seen to further the norms, or which might effectively express some of the international concerns abroad about abuses of power in a globalized economic sphere. While the first is now commonplace, and the second is being discussed, it appears the WTO is yet to show the resolve to make the third potential real.

PART II

SERVICES

THE GENERAL AGREEMENT ON TRADE IN SERVICES

Chapter four's immediate aim is to lay out informatively the provisions of the GATS agreement. The GATS provides both a set of norms for trade liberalisation and a structure for successive rounds of negotiations over commitments to such norms. The first of these negotiations took place within the Uruguay Round; another round is scheduled for commencement in the year 2000.

A theme of this analysis is the significance for globalization of a multilateral services agreement. Services have the potential to carry globalizing messages far into the reaches of a locality, challenging domestic arrangements for supply and undermining competence to regulate for social purposes. The GATS mediates relationships between the local legalities of supply and those of foreign suppliers, which are often more favourable to them. In addition it takes a position on content, challenging industry-specific regulation and promoting market-oriented regulatory 'modalities' such as contract law and possibly competition law.

The first concerns of this chapter are the status and format of the GATS. We recognise that the structure of the negotiations over commitments has been a key factor in mediation. Central to this is the listings approach of the GATS: the way national governments have been permitted to control the exposure of their regulatory measures for services sector by sector. In examining the course of these negotiations and the outcome of the Uruguay Round, we demonstrate how the listing process has given expression to a range of reservations about liberalisation. This chapter also reports the outcome of the negotiations in the financial services sector, which were carried over after the conclusion of the Uruguay Round. Negotiations and commitments in several other key sectors are assessed in chapters five and eight.

The main task of chapter four is to assess the strength and substance of the GATS norms. It starts with the familiar principle that government measures should not discriminate against foreign services and service suppliers. To promote the GATS as a multilateral compact, one component of this principle, most favoured nation treatment, is a general obligation. It means that commitments could not be conditioned on reciprocity. But the chapter highlights how provision was made for members to take exceptions and the use they made of this allowance. The other component of non-discrimination is national treatment. In the GATS, members must make specific commitments to national treatment; it is not a general obligation. Nonetheless, because the agreement takes an expansive view of services and embraces all possible modes of supply, including commercial or natural presence within the territory of a member, it has power as a norm. The chapter considers the extent to which commitment to the norm allows a member to treat foreigners differently; the foreign services must be 'like services' for the norm to be applicable. A twist in the tail is the specification that formally identical treatment of locals and foreigners may amount to less favourable treatment.

The chapter goes on to highlight the implications of the norm of market access for regulation in services sectors and particularly its potential to advance the neo-liberal agenda of regulatory reform. It remains consistent with national treatment for members to restrict the free play of markets, provided they do so for locals as well as foreigners. We gauge the extent to which the norm of market access is intended to put pressure on the non-discriminatory regulation of services markets. The chapter then appraises the scope of the agreement's recognition of regulatory objectives. Certain objectives enjoy the status of limited, legitimate exceptions to these norms. But the space explicitly conceded by the GATS comes at a price. The chapter notes that the disciplines which the agreement applies to this regulation tend to narrow the members' choice of regulatory instrument.

The main thrust of the GATS is deregulatory; it attacks non-conforming national government measures. Finally, we look for indications that the agreement will provide support for re-regulation. As government measures are rolled back, trade norms increasingly focus on private barriers to market access. The trade norms begin to develop a more demanding notion of how private barriers receive government support, including the support of government inaction. But the current norms carry limited potential for this agenda. Instead, it could be that competition law will be enlisted as a means to break down (what foreign suppliers tend to see as) collusive and closed domestic producer relationships. Does such an agenda open up the possibility that competition law will play a positive role for small and independent producers in disciplining the restrictive business practices of transnational suppliers? The GATS acknowledges national competition law, but we find little evidence at this point that the GATS is meeting the challenge of promoting high standards of business regulation across the world, either through competition law or otherwise.

A trade agreement for services?

The General Agreement on Trade in Services (GATS) might turn out to be the most significant of the WTO agreements. Not only do services comprise a growing proportion of international trade overall, but the ways in which services are supplied provide potential to undermine the economic sufficiency, political sovereignty and cultural identity of the locality. Services, particularly those with intellectual content, carry far deeper messages than goods. They traverse fields clearly connected with social relations – professional, financial and communications fields that are likely to shape the structure of a global society. Services provide means to introduce fresh, foreign perspectives, construct cross-border transactions and affiliations, question the value of parochial knowledge and custom, and undermine the competence of local regulation.

Yet many services retain distinctive geographical, temporal and personal features. While international suppliers will use various strategies to try to overcome these particularities, the provision of services is likely to remain tied into their local contexts. In many services sectors, effective supply still depends on being able to establish a presence in the locality, to be there at the right time, and to demonstrate familiarity with the local ways of doing things. But the suppliers who seek to obtain competitive conditions of access behind the border encounter a host of regulatory legalities that run counter to their own legalities of operation. As a consequence, both the suppliers and the locals become involved in attempts to reconcile these legalities.

Trade in services has already been mediated by a web of bilateral, regional and sectoral arrangements.[1] However, the GATS is the first fully fledged multilateral agreement on services. Services was to be a new field for the GATT which, as we have seen, was previously occupied with barriers to trade in goods. Furthermore, the essential approach taken by the GATT was to assimilate those trade barriers to a common measure of tariffs and then to seek reductions in these quantitative impositions on trade in goods. Services can be incorporated in goods, but often the real action on the supply of services is expressed through personal relationships between providers and users. It can be more difficult to keep track of services supply than it is trade in goods. Certainly, a wider range of domestic measures might be implicated by the application of trade norms to the supply of services. This lack of comparability between trade in goods and trade in services provided an argument for not making a trade agreement for services. It was also to raise questions about the suitability of extending many of the GATT concepts to the GATS; one such example is the provision for anti-dumping procedures and remedies.

Yet the objections to a services agreement were not just technically minded. The GATS produced a broad framework for negotiations over the liberalisation of trade in services. The agreement embraces all but a narrow category of services and actually leaves the definition of services at large. It comprehends all possible modes of service supply, not just cross-border supply but also supply through a commercial presence or presence in person within the territory of another country. It then subjects the regulation of these supply activities and modes to the norms of national treatment and market access. Regulatory arrangements, operating deep behind the border and representing all sorts of economic, political and cultural concerns, may become barriers to trade. For one practised commentator, such inclusiveness dramatically changed the political economy of multilateral trade liberalisation.[2]

In these circumstances, we should ask why countries were prepared to expose their services sectors to the norms of a multilateral trade agreement. In gauging the scope of the agreement, it is handy to note some suggestions as to why they did so, before identifying ways in which the agreement allowed them to limit its scrutiny. We might begin by saying that all countries reveal strengths and weaknesses, confidences and sensitivities if you like, when they contemplate exposing their services sectors to the competition of international trade. As a general rule, we might expect the developed countries of the North to be favoured by liberalisation. But this bias depends a great deal on which sectors are included. Would they include those sectors which are labour intensive or culturally diverse, as well as those which are capital intensive and technology based?

The liberalisation of trade in services?

Certainly, countries such as the United States that have been losing their advantages in the trade of manufactured goods see knowledge-based services as an opportunity to redress trade balances. What is more, the range of countries which identify prospects in services is broadening: India's strength in computer software provides an example. So too the enhanced transportability of services allows labour factors to come into play. For example, new technology enables services such as information processing and call centres to be provided offshore. A broad multilateral agreement provides an opportunity for concessions in one services sector to be traded off against advances in another. Of course, within the compass of the Uruguay Round overall, the negotiations involved the extra leverage of linking access to services markets with access to markets for various types of goods.

While the negotiations were often specific and hard-headed, it is important to remember that the GATS was made possible because the idea that services are a commercial activity amenable to international trade has gained legitimacy. Perhaps the receptivity of many countries was enhanced by their own domestic programs of liberalisation. The stimulus for these programs is to be found within the countries themselves, as well as in the initiatives of their trading partners and, in some instances, the prescriptions of international organizations such as the World Bank and the International Monetary Fund. Latterly, such national reform programs have shifted their attention directly to the service sectors, advocating the privatisation of public monopolies, the removal of statutory immunities and the application of competition requirements. From this perspective, services are seen as major cost items for the operation of domestic industry; they are also increasingly regarded as a source of export growth in their own right.

Yet we might expect many countries to retain reservations about wholesale liberalisation. For example, they might see that concessions could be made on home territory without any real guarantee of access being obtained to markets overseas. Even where government restrictions are rolled back, the close relationships between local businesses or the cohesion of local cultural practices can act as effective barriers. At the same time, concessions surrender controls at home that are not so much concerned with economic protection as with aspects of political autonomy and cultural integrity. Furthermore, even where countries do decide to afford access to foreign suppliers, they may wish to retain the freedom to apply regulatory measures to them. They remain concerned to safeguard local conditions or to obtain benefits locally from the foreign participation.

The GATS contains features to accommodate this natural caution about concessions and commitments. We shall see that the agreement's own norms lack a certain specificity. While GATT jurisprudence helps to cast light on the norms, it is perhaps only when they are applied to specific services measures that their implications will be properly appreciated. Moreover, the agreement's particular approach to the making of commitments allows considerable scope for restrictions to be maintained. This listings approach allows member countries to nominate (inscribe) the services sectors in which they will participate and to withhold sectors from the scrutiny of the norms. In the sectors which they do inscribe, they may enter non-conforming measures as limitations on national treatment and market access. In the Uruguay Round itself, countries were to take advantage of both these options.

Yet the same process enables countries to bargain hard with other countries for commitments. They have opportunities to hold out, if they do not think the balance of commitments is right – if they think for instance that they are offering more than they are being conceded in return from the other members. Once countries have submitted sectors, it is true to say that the agreement is multilateral and they must take what each other country has been prepared to commit. But it is notable that certain countries, such as the United States, pursued the opportunity to take exemptions from the agreement's MFN obligation as a way of pushing along other countries which it thought were not sufficiently forthcoming. The United States had some success with this strategy. Negotiations in several key sectors were extended on beyond the end of the Round and further commitments to liberalisation resulted.

Furthermore, we should appreciate that the agreement has an in-built momentum towards liberalisation. The members undertook to engage in successive rounds of negotiations, the first of which was scheduled to commence in the year 2000 (article XIX). In the meantime, the dispute settlement process has afforded an opening for a well resourced country to argue an expansionist interpretation of the norms, for example in relation to the kind of government measures (or possibly non-measures) that fall foul of them. We foreshadowed this possibility in chapter three, and we shall pursue it again here as we work through the agreement.

STATUS AND FORMAT OF THE AGREEMENT

This introduction begins to indicate how the particular structure of the agreement has exerted an influence over the negotiations. In analysing the structure of the agreement, we need first to clear some formalities. The GATS is styled as a multilateral trade agreement in its own right. However, unlike the side codes which were formulated in the Tokyo Round, which were the first of the GATT moves behind the border, it is not a voluntary optional agreement. As Annex 1B, it is an integral part of the WTO Agreement and hence, like other such multilateral agreements and their associated legal instruments, it is binding on all members of the WTO. That is to say, it is a condition of membership of the WTO. Thus membership of the WTO requires acceptance of the general obligations which are set down in the GATS.

Membership also depends on annexing a schedule of commitments to the GATS itself. Those countries which took part in the Uruguay Round and signed up for membership of the WTO have already submitted such schedules. Article XX of the GATS provides for each member to set out in a schedule the specific commitments it undertakes under Part III of the GATS. After the last minute adjustments to offers, the close of the

Round was succeeded by a period of ratification and verification, leading up to the meeting of government representatives at Marrakesh to sign the Final Act. This procedure permits us to treat the annexed schedules as an authoritative record of these commitments. The members' commitments are to be found in the schedules of specific commitments which have now been collected in volumes 28–30 of the *Legal Instruments Embodying the Results of the Uruguay Round of Multilateral Trade Negotiations*.[3]

We should also note that, now it is in force, the GATS has become difficult to alter. Generally, amendments to the GATS take effect on acceptance by two-thirds of the members, with amendments to Part II and III and the respective annexes taking effect only for those who do accept the amendments. Amendments to article II:1, dealing with the MFN obligation, must be agreed by all members. It is also worth noting that it is difficult to resile from the individual national commitments which have been made under the GATS. Schedules of commitments may only be modified after three years and, on giving notice of modification, members may be required to make compensatory adjustments to other members (article XXI). These adjustments should maintain the general level of mutually advantageous commitments which pertained prior to the modifications. Such adjustments must also be made on a most favoured nation basis.

Scope and definition

The GATS is divided into six parts. It also has a preamble that may assist with the interpretation of the directive provisions. The preamble contains aspirational statements which emphasise the goal of progressive liberalisation of trade in services, while acknowledging the right of members to regulate in order to meet their national policy objectives. The particular needs of developing countries are recognised, though, in keeping with the outlook of the agreement, it is suggested that these needs include increasing participation in trade and expansion of exports through the strengthening of the capacity, efficiency and competitiveness of their various service sectors.

The first substantive part deals with the agreement's scope and definition. This contains important indications of the services, the modes of supply of services, and the measures by members which fall within the scope of the agreement. Article I:1 states that the agreement applies to measures by members affecting trade in services. The agreement encompasses all services except services supplied in the exercise of governmental authority (article I:3(b)). While many kinds of services may be linked to government, for instance the practice of law, the delineation of this exclusion is a minimalist one: 'services supplied in the exercise of governmental authority' means any service which is supplied neither on a commercial basis, nor in competition with one or more service suppliers.

Interestingly, the base point concept of 'services' is not otherwise defined. This really leaves the actual scope of the agreement at large. For instance, with the WTO joining the enthusiasm for e-commerce, it has been considering whether to place electronic transmissions under the cover of the GATS rather than the GATT, say. Nonetheless, for most practical purposes, the course of the negotiations and the discussion of schedules of commitments were largely to determine which sectors were exposed to the agreement (bearing in mind that the key national treatment and market access norms only apply in those sectors which members inscribe in their schedules). The GATT's own sector classification list helped to mark out these sectors within the national schedules of commitments.[4] The list also received recognition in the Dispute Settlement Understanding, where it deals with cross-sector retaliation for non-compliance (article 22:3(f)).

For the purposes of the agreement, trade in services is defined as the supply of a service by one or other of four modes of service supply (article I:2). The modes are: (a) supply from the territory of one member into the territory of another member; (b) supply in the territory of one member to the service consumer of any other member; (c) supply by a service supplier of one member, through commercial presence in the territory of any other member; and (d) supply by a service supplier of one member, through the presence of natural persons of a member in the territory of any other member. We shall consider below the ways in which the agreement elaborated or confined these modes of supply.

The agreement applies its standards to measures by members affecting trade in services. Measures by members means measures taken by central, regional or local governments and authorities; but also by non-governmental bodies in the exercise of powers delegated by central, regional or local governments or authorities (article I:3). As we have already begun to appreciate, the concept of measures is an expanding one. Article XXVIII defines it to mean any measure by a member, whether in the form of a law, regulation, rule, procedure, decision, administrative action, or any other form. Again, we should see how this expansive approach increases the significance of the prescriptive provisions.

Substantive and procedural requirements

The second part of the GATS lays down the agreement's general obligations and disciplines. The most significant of these is the requirement of most favoured nation treatment (MFN) in article II. As we have acknowledged, MFN treatment is an obligation with a GATT pedigree. We identified the content of the norm in chapter three; here we must consider its application to measures which affect trade in services. We must also consider what it means to say that the obligation is a general one, given the discretion which members enjoy to decide whether to make commitments to national treatment and market access. Part of the consideration is the allowance made for the listing of exemptions from the MFN obligation (article II).

Part II follows up with an obligation that measures be made transparent (article III). The remainder of Part II is largely concerned with recognising exceptions to the norms of the agreement and placing disciplines upon the non-conforming measures which members maintain. We shall also examine these exceptions and disciplines below.

At the heart of the agreement, in Part III, lies a structure for the process by which members are to make specific commitments to national treatment and market access. At the same time, the agreement provides definitions or, more precisely, indicators of the standards of national treatment and market access which the members are to meet in making their commitments. Unlike NAFTA or the European Treaty, for instance, the agreement does not however impose obligations of a general nature to provide national treatment or market access. Legally, it is within the individual member's discretion to decide in the negotiating process the extent of its commitments. The less prescriptive concept of 'norm' can best capture this approach.

Nevertheless, there is an interplay between the normative structure of the agreement and the process of commitment. While the commitments can be described as essentially voluntary or discretionary, as we shall attempt to illustrate below, the agreement has a thrust to it. Where a member decides to submit a services sector, its measures become subject to the requirements of the agreement. Its range of non-conforming measures must be listed. These requirements bear on all service sectors which are inscribed, but they are augmented in respect of certain key sectors by the elaboration of special annexes to the agreement.

The tenor of the agreement

This brief outline begins to reveal the dualistic nature of the GATS. It has appealed to some countries because it has appeared to place liberalisation within the framework of a multilateral rule-based system. All members must respect the obligation of most favoured nation treatment and work towards the liberalisation of national treatment and market access. On this basis, the smaller countries could expect to enjoy the benefits which had been offered and obtained by the major players in the negotiations. The commitments would be specific and binding. They could look forward to an orderly process of implementation. Even where liberalisations were not forthcoming, they could gain valuable intelligence about the extent of restrictive measures in other countries. At the same time, they could in a sense legitimise their own restrictive measures.

However, the degree to which the agreement 'juridifies' the process of liberalisation is yet to be determined. As we shall see, its approach to the making of commitments, its decentralised negotiation process, and indeed the inherent specificities of the various service sectors, work against the development of a jurisprudence. Such flexibility and proce-duralism may have been important to the acceptance of any framework at all; they are certainly in keeping with the style of the GATT in the past. They allow members room to move, so that much of the real substance of the interface is constructed, sector by sector, in a fluid and ongoing process. Nevertheless, the potential for further juridification might be detected in several quarters – the tentative attempts at elaboration of norms within the GATS itself, the availability of prototypes from the experience with other agreements such as the European Treaty, the insti-tution at the WTO of a more emphatic disputes settlement procedure, and ultimately the successive rounds of GATS negotiations which have been foreshadowed.

GATS listings approach

Before considering the content of the norms, some observations on the process of making commitments to them is appropriate. The agree-ment's approach to the listing of commitments has been characterised as a hybrid one. Members first choose which sectors to list positively (or inscribe) in their schedule of commitments. Within the sectors they have inscribed, they must then decide which limitations or exceptions to place on national treatment and market access. The agreement is at its most voluntary, formally speaking, at the initial point of deciding whether to list a sector positively (i.e. nominate it) in a schedule of specific commit-ments. In contrast to other agreements such as NAFTA and CER, there is no automatic inclusion of sectors. Thus the onus is cast on countries taking part to delineate restrictions on the scope of the sectors they wish to reserve from the scrutiny of the agreement.[5] In other words, sectors are not included by default, by failing to make an express exclusion. Such an approach would cast the onus upon the members to delineate very carefully the sectors they wish not to expose and countries might there-fore be inclined to 'carve out' broad reservations in order to keep their regulatory options open.

Of course, a positive listing approach may encourage caution in its own way; the scope of the sectors which are committed might be cir-cumscribed in a conservative way. For once a sector is inscribed, the member country is meant to be held to the limitations which it actually lists. The Guide to the schedules states that:

When making a commitment a government therefore binds the specified level of market access and national treatment and undertakes not to impose any new measures that would restrict access into the market or the operation of the service. Specific commitments thus have an effect similar to a tariff binding – they are a guarantee to economic operators in other countries that the conditions of entry and operation in the market will not be changed to their disadvantage.[6]

It follows that, even if a country was prepared to go to the trouble of listing all its existing limitations, that is to make a 'stand-still commitment', it might prefer to keep its regulatory options open for the future. A decision not to inscribe a sector would express a preference to remain free to make changes in the sector with new regulations. One reason is that the global carriers may well afford suppliers the capacity to bypass the technology and industry-specific controls which the members have had in place.

Such a concern is evident from an inspection of the individual country schedules. Certain sectors such as legal services were withheld from the listings entirely. In some nominations of sectors, we find that the description of the sector is used to limit the scope of the activities in which the foreign suppliers may engage. A column for 'additional commitments' sometimes elaborates on this circumscription. The columns for national treatment and market access then list the specific limitations on the availability of some or all of the four different modes of supply with this sector's scope. Hence, a commitment might say that foreign lawyers can advise on their home law, but then require that they do so by establishing a presence in the member's territory.

Once a sector is inscribed, the listing becomes more of a formal obligation. Article XX prescribes that each member set out in a schedule specific commitments it undertakes to market access and national treatment. With respect to sectors where such commitments are undertaken, each schedule shall specify: (a) terms, limitations, and conditions on market access; (b) conditions and qualifications on national treatment, (c) undertakings relating to additional commitments; (d) where appropriate, the time frame for implementation of such commitments; and (e) the date of entry into force of such commitments. Thus, in listing a sector, a member attracts an onus to provide intelligence about its remaining regulations. It should also have to determine which of those regulations it wished to retain as a matter of policy.

Notwithstanding this onus, it is evident that members availed themselves of the negative listing option. Certain entries are cast as horizontal limitations, that is, limitations across all of the sectors inscribed in the schedule. For example, a member might reserve a review and conditioning procedure for any direct foreign investment in its country. Other entries represent sector-specific limitations. In many cases, member countries listed their existing limitations, that is, they made stand-still commitments. The actual format of the schedules allowed the members further leeway. Instead of being required to itemise all the limitations they wished to retain, the Guide suggests that members were permitted to choose to indicate a limited commitment by describing what they were offering rather than the limitations they were listing. This option was combined with an entry that commitments were otherwise 'unbound', that is to say, 'the member wishes to remain free in a given sector and mode of supply to introduce or main-tain measures inconsistent with market access or national treatment'.[7] While often employed in relation only to a particular mode of supply, and especially to supply through the presence of natural persons, this approach tempered the force of the process. It blunted the pressure that would have been generated by a 'list it or lose it' requirement.

URUGUAY ROUND OUTCOMES

Level of commitments

By the end of the Round, members had completed their schedules for all but a couple of sectors. It is difficult to assess the commitments made. A proper judgement would require information about the level of the restrictions which have been lifted when compared with those remaining. We would also have to think in terms of the economic and social values of the service activities affected. Assessment of the commitments has tended to be somewhat formalistic. We know that some ninety-seven schedules were submitted, involving 106 member countries.[8] The number of sectors inscribed ranges from one or two up to the whole of the 155 sectors on the GATT's own sector classification list.[9] For the developing countries overall, slightly less than one fifth of all these sectors were inscribed while, for the developed countries, the proportion rose to around two-thirds. Goode estimates that, in economic terms, these listings comprised fifteen per cent and fifty-three per cent of all services respectively.[10] There were to be significant omissions, even in the case of the largest developed coun-tries. Perhaps the greatest reservations about the benefits of participation were to be seen in the schedules of the dynamic, emerging economies, the newly industrialising countries, especially those of South-East Asia.

Where commitments were made, they largely represented what has been called a stand-still position. Members undertook to keep measures at their present level though, occasionally, they would leave these com-mitments 'unbound'. Making distinctions between modes of supply, the limitations were both horizontal and sector-specific. Altinger and Endes found that limitations were placed on the presence of natural persons in ninety-two per cent of the entries and on commercial presence in seventy per cent. Limitations were less prevalent in the case of cross-border supply and consumption abroad, but then again these modes were more likely to be ruled out altogether. The combinations reflected the developing countries' interest in foreign direct investment. They sought local establishment but wished at the same time to place controls on the form which the establishment took. Developed countries were freer with the form of investment but wanted to retain the right to give local firms subsidies, for instance for research and development. Developed countries were comfortable with intra-corporate transferees but all countries restricted access by natural persons and especially by self-employed service providers.

The MFN exemptions were also significant, running to 350 entries.[11] Some represented the fact that bilateral arrangements had already been made, but in important sectors they were to represent a challenge to the multilateral rule-based ethos of the agreement.[12] They were efforts to gain leverage in the negotiations and insist on material reciprocity.

Ultimately, any assessment of the commitments depends on whether we support liberalisation or not. From the free-trade standpoint, the responsibilities of participation in the agreement had the appeal of providing national governments with a rationale for making commitments that would counter domestic opposition and lock in liberalisation initiatives at home. Nonetheless, this perspective is inclined to say that the positive listing approach allowed an opening for the expression of divisions at the national level. Such an approach boosted the importance of domestic political factors. Negotiating positions were to be influenced by the perception of sector-specific gains and losses, perceptions shaped by the particular configurations of the communities or networks of industry representatives, public officials and government ministers.

Supporters of free trade portray this process as giving expression to national interest group politics, at considerable expense to those constituencies who would benefit by generalised or principled liberalisation. Free traders tend to point to the aggregate benefits of liberalisation, especially for the consumers of services. Nonetheless, if we are to understand how the process operated, we should appreciate that liberalisation is criticised for having negative consequences for local populations. It has been argued that small business suppliers, workers in both public and private sectors, and those dependent for services on nation states and local communities, can all lose out to foreign competition.[13]

Sources of reservations

If this perspective carries weight, then one reason why certain sectors were not inscribed was a desire to nurture a local service industry. Countries might see little benefit in liberalisation, if their own suppliers were not yet able to compete effectively, either in the domestic market or on export markets. Such a sensitivity is most readily attributable to the developing countries, though we have made the point that all countries have service industries which they wish to protect.

Across the board, the Uruguay Round revealed less willingness on the part of the developed countries to afford the developing countries the special and differential treatment which has been associated with the GATT in the past. In the case of the GATS, the listings approach provided scope to maintain protections on a case-by-case rather than a categorical basis. Recognition of this outlet is to be found in article XIX, which foreshadows the successive rounds of negotiations to obtain specific commitments. It allows for the process of liberalisation to take place with 'due respect for national policy objectives and the level of development of individual members, both overall and in individual sectors' (article XIX:2). Embodying a form of words that was proffered by Canada and the Nordic countries,[14] it envisages that 'there shall be appropriate flexibility for individual developing country members for opening fewer sectors, liberalizing fewer types of transactions, progressively extending market access in line with their development situation and, when making access to their markets available to foreign service suppliers, attaching to such access conditions aimed at achieving the objectives referred to in article IV'.

This final clause refers to article IV which urges members to negotiate specific commitments to increase the participation of developing countries. Here, the agreement has in mind participation in an international economy for services. Their industries can be strengthened by access to technology, through access which is on a commercial basis. Access to distribution channels and information networks will also enhance participation, together with liberalisation of access in sectors and modes of supply of export interest to them. So, the ways in which developed countries fashion their own commitments are meant to lend assistance. These countries are also meant to provide technical cooperation such as information about their own markets. However, it has to be said that these provisions are essentially declarations of good intentions on the part of the members. Article IV recognises that the developing countries need more than open access to export markets. They need access to resources that are in private hands. Here, as we have identified, a key issue is the attitude of the developed countries to the restrictive business practices of the service suppliers themselves.

Beyond economics, cultural and social reservations can also be read into the schedules. Other agreements such as NAFTA and the OECD Codes have provided explicitly for such reservations. The GATS contains no provision for such a 'cultural exception', despite the suggestions made early in the Round to include one from countries as diverse as India, Canada, Egypt and members of the European Union. Cultural sensitivities are evident in the omission of whole sectors from the schedules, such as the audiovisual and legal services sectors. Such sensitivities are also registered in the horizontal or across-the-board limitations which many countries applied to the sectors which they did list, especially the limitations they placed upon the entry of natural persons or direct foreign investment. Of course, they might also appear in the sector-specific limitations and the case studies in following chapters are designed to elicit such information. In other words, the desire to retain freedom to impose restrictions or requirements was not simply a desire to protect the economic interests of local industry. Sensitivities are perhaps most readily recognised in the concerns expressed within certain Middle-Eastern and Asian countries. In extremis, this perspective sees liberalisation as a new, cultural form of imperialism or as neo-colonialism. However, even Western countries like France, Canada and Australia expressed concern about the potential for the United States media industries to dominate their local markets.

Another reservation about liberalisation stems from the desire to maintain regulatory competence. As the European Union appreciated in opposing the early United States initiative for a negative listing approach, disaggregation enabled the negotiations to attend to the divergent specificities of each sector. On this view, each sector was seen to represent different issues. The special annexes which were produced for sectors such as financial and telecommunications services represent the high point of this approach, though it should be noted that arguments for special annexes in some sectors, notably audiovisual and legal services, were resisted. But we should appreciate that the concern with competence runs beyond the integrity of the sectors themselves. It is apprehensive that liberalisation of services flows will undermine the effectiveness of regulation across a broad range of national objectives. The impact of freer financial and professional services on the capacity to collect taxes is a good example.

Some of those commentators who support greater liberalisation have expressed regret about the way the commitments were permitted to be listed. In particular, they identify the decision to permit the schedules to split commitments among the four modes of supply. In part, this criticism is based on the observation that the modes are complementary rather than alternative for some service suppliers; it can even be difficult to distinguish factually between the modes being adopted. Moreover, they sensed that this format made it easier for members to pick and choose between modes of supply. In the extreme, a member could choose to restrict that mode which seemed to suit the foreign supplier over the local supplier. From the standpoint of trade liberalisation, a more purposeful approach would have been for service suppliers to seek guarantees of the combination of modes which best met their needs.

Yet we should realise that member governments wanted to maintain distinctions between supply modes out of a concern for regulatory competence. Of course, the presence of natural persons often emerged as a sensitive mode but, interestingly, it was cross-border supply as much as commercial presence and thus foreign direct investment, that encountered limitations. Sauve suggests that some countries saw *requirements* of establishment as affording greater regulatory oversight and strategic bargaining power.[15] So, while the listings approach means that the agreement provides no right of establishment, equally, suppliers enjoy no right of non-establishment, that is, to choose to supply services across borders from home bases.

THE MFN NORM

Article II:1 states 'with respect to any measure covered by this agreement, each member shall accord immediately and unconditionally to services and service suppliers of any other member treatment no less favourable than it accords to like services and services suppliers of any other country'. The discussion in chapter three considered the broad nature of the norm. It also indicated that its coverage can vary. Here, we should appreciate that it is for the benefit of the services and service suppliers of the member countries only. But, at the same time, the obligation is not confined to treatment under measures pertaining to the sectors or modes of supply which countries choose to list in their schedules or to which they make specific commitments. The obligation is a general one in the sense that members must multilateralise all measures of which the agreement has cognisance, that is measures affecting trade in services – which is to be read as measures affecting the supply of service (article I:2). So it differs in this way from the agreement's 'obligations' regarding national treatment and market access.

Nonetheless, this general obligation has sat uncomfortably with the actual process of negotiations over national treatment and market access. While in spirit a multilateral and multi-sectoral process, the settling of specific commitments was still to be, in Broadman's words, a function of 'iterative bilateral request and offer negotiations conducted seriatim on a country by country basis'.[16] We might also say on a sector by sector basis. Countries displayed reluctance to make offers without knowing the value of concessions forthcoming from other countries. Unless a way was found to involve them, there was a temptation for countries to hold out in negotiations, only to 'free ride' on the commitments made by others. Yet many countries had legitimate reasons for being cautious about exposing their service sectors to foreign competition.

MFN exemptions

At the same time, provision was made for member countries to take exemptions from the MFN obligation (article II:2). There was an obvious reason for this provision. Prior to negotiations, countries might have already arranged special reciprocal rights with other countries that they wished to honour. An elaborate pattern of air traffic landing rights was expressly conceded in the Annex on Air Transport Services. A more ad hoc instance comprises the arrangements which have been made for co-production of films in the audiovisual services sector.

Provision for MFN exemptions was, however, to have a more profound impact on the pattern of commitments. Legally speaking, members were permitted to maintain measures inconsistent with the MFN obligation simply by listing them. Again, there were some limits bound up with the decision to make commitments under the agreement. The MFN exemption was not meant to detract from the commitments which a member did make in its schedule. The Guide states:

> Where commitments are entered, therefore, the effect of an MFN exemption can only be to permit more favourable treatment to be given to the country to which the exemption applies than is given to all other Members. Where there are no commitments, however, an MFN exemption may also permit less favourable treatment to be given.[17]

Thus, where the entry of some commitments is considered worthwhile, the MFN exemption provides scope to reward another country on the basis of material reciprocity by making further concessions to it. The result can be characterised as a baseline of MFN with a top-up of material reciprocity. Yet, while the MFN obligation is meant to be a general one, this approach to exemptions allows a member, by choosing to make no commitments, to continue to operate exclusively on a bilateral or regional basis.

Feeling that its commitments would be generous compared to others, the United States in particular expressed concern about lack of reciprocity, though some, uncharitably perhaps, attributed its reservations to doubts about the competitiveness of some of its own services sectors. Specifically, it threatened to withhold commitments and take a broad MFN exemption in both the basic telecommunications and financial services sectors. Its argument was that the GATS negotiations were not giving it enough in return for the multilateralisation of the commitments it was being asked to make in its own markets. It had certain countries in mind.

Yet Trebilcock and Howse argue that, so long as they are taking steps in the right direction, article XIX:2 concedes that the developing countries may offer less than the developed countries.[18] A lesser level of commitment would not be a justification for an MFN exemption. At the same time, article XIX speaks of a process of negotiations taking place with a view to promoting the interest of all participants on a mutually advantageous basis and to securing an overall balance of rights and obligations.

Whatever might have been the legitimate scope for exemptions, the threat of a wholesale MFN exemption was to become a form of leverage. It was used to extract further commitments from recalcitrant members. Coping with the threat of an MFN exemption was a key reason why negotiations were extended on after the conclusion of the Round in several key sectors. Later in this chapter, we shall use the example of financial sectors to indicate how the WTO sought to manage the uses made of the exemption.

A GATS Annex on Article II Exemptions laid down some formal conditions for the taking of exemptions. Measures of the member countries which were inconsistent with the MFN obligation had to be entered into lists. These lists were attached to the Annex in the treaty copy of the GATS agreement, which was settled at the Marrakesh Meeting of Ministers. The GATS allowed members to apply for new exemptions after the WTO agreements had entered into force. But these exemptions would need to attract the support of three-fourths of all the member countries. Special provisions were made for the taking of exemptions in the sectors in which negotiations were outstanding at the end of the Uruguay Round and we shall note those provisions below.

The provisions of the Annex were also concerned with the review and termination of the exemptions. Each exemption was to have a terminating date and, in principle, no exemption was to run for more than ten years. The Council for Trade in Services was charged to review all exemptions that were granted for a period of more than five years. This review was scheduled to take place in the year 2000. In addition, the exemptions were meant to be subject to renegotiation when the next round of negotiations over liberalisation started up, again in the year 2000.

Accommodation of regional agreements

In this context, we should also note the explicit provision made in relation to economic integration and labour markets integration agreements. These regional agreements may involve a compromise of broader MFN obligations. In article V, the GATS sets standards for the kind of agreement it will accommodate. Generally, the agreement must be an agreement liberalising trade in services among its parties. It must have substantial sectoral coverage in terms of the number of sectors, the volume of trade affected and the modes of supply. It must provide for the absence or elimination of substantially all discrimination in the sense of national treatment. The regional agreement must also extend its benefits to those suppliers from third countries who are established as juridical persons under the laws of a party to the agreement and who engage in substantial business operations in the territory of the party to the agreement.

In supporting its norm of MFN, the condition of the GATS is that the regional agreement does not raise the overall level of barriers to trade in services for members of the WTO who are outside such an agreement, when it is compared to the level applicable prior to such an agreement. This condition suggests that greater access can be given to parties to the agreement in the sense of preferential rather than non-discriminatory treatment but only so long as it is not at the expense of the access which members outside already enjoy. Of course the article had in mind such agreements as the European Union and NAFTA, but it is a potential constraint on new regional agreements such as APEC, which are grappling with this issue of treatment of insiders and outsiders. Article V is more tolerant of agreements to which developing countries are party. Provision is also made to keep a check on the progress of such agreements and a member's commitment to them.

THE NATIONAL TREATMENT NORM

National treatment is a norm well within the ken of international trade law, including the GATT, but it carries distinctive implications for the services sectors. Article XV:1 states that:

> in the sectors inscribed in its schedule, and subject to any conditions and qualifications set out therein, each member shall accord to services and service suppliers of any other member, in respect of all measures affecting the supply of services, treatment no less favourable than that it accords to its own like services and service suppliers.

We can start by saying that this norm creates both a goal and an obligation. It is a goal in the sense that each round of negotiations is meant to work towards commitments to national treatment. But it is also an obligation in the sense that members must accord national treatment in respect of all measures affecting the supply of services in the sectors inscribed in their schedules and subject to any conditions or qualifications set out therein. Members can thus prevent the operation of the norm by declining to inscribe sectors. But where a sector is inscribed, all such measures are caught by the norm unless and to the extent that conditions and qualifications have been listed.

So in identifying the scope of the norm, we need to think first in terms of measures affecting the supply of services. Later, we shall note how 'measures' were defined broadly by the agreement. We should also note that 'the supply of a service' is defined to include the production, distribution, marketing, sale and delivery of a service (article XXVIII:(b)). We should further recall that the agreement enumerates four possible modes of supply of a service. The agreement's prescriptions for these modes of supply were examined above. At this point it is worth saying that the inclusion of all such modes was designed to enhance the foreign supplier's freedom to choose the supply modes which suit its particular style and purpose. But ultimately of course that freedom is dependent on the schedule of commitments each member was prepared to make.

Less favourable treatment

If we know which measures we must keep in mind, we must then try to establish which of these measures is not going to conform to national treatment. What does the norm of national treatment demand? It demands that foreign services and service suppliers be accorded no less favourable treatment than is accorded to local counterparts. We have a general sense of this standard from our discussion in chapter three. To translate it now into the specifics of the GATS, we should note first that article XVII:2 indicates that a member may meet this requirement by according to foreign services and service suppliers either formally identical or formally different treatment to that which it accords to its own like services or service suppliers. Such formally identical or formally different treatment shall be considered to be less favourable if it modifies the conditions of competition in favour of services or service suppliers of the member compared to like services or service suppliers of any other member (article XVII:3). In opting for such a test, the agreement has made connections with the jurisprudence of the European Union and of course the earlier jurisprudence of the GATT itself.

The test is said to be a practical or realistic one. It is not necessarily whether foreigners and locals are given formal equality, or what some commentators term facially non-discriminatory treatment, but what the treatment means effectively for the competitive relationship between them. The foreigner should enjoy equivalent opportunities to compete. At the same time, the member is not under an obligation to ensure that the foreigner enjoys success in the marketplace. It is only the opportunity to compete which should be equivalent, so far as it is affected by government measures. Foreign suppliers meet all sorts of 'natural' obstacles to successful supply. They face difficulties, for example, in storing certain services. They meet resistance from business and household consumers for a variety of private, market-based reasons. Accessibility, familiarity, prejudice, loyalty, come-back, are all factors that can influence consumers to favour local services. Such factors are usually beyond the influence of the host government's own measures. In this respect, a footnote to article XVII cautions that: 'specific commitments assumed under this article shall not be construed to require any member to compensate for any inherent competitive disadvantages which result from the foreign character of the relevant services or service suppliers'.

Still, as it is specified, the norm has a broad catchment. First of all, we should realise that countries do set out to treat foreign suppliers less favourably in an overt way. They have reasons for wanting to afford locals opportunities which are not available to foreigners. We shall find examples in each of the sectors we examine. The measures may involve limits being placed on foreign participation by all or any one of the four modes of service supply. Thus, foreigners might be barred from supplying a particular service at all. They might be prevented from supplying it from an offshore location or by way of investment in a local business. The measures may involve impositions or demands being placed on foreigners exclusively when they supply services. They may involve favours or subsidies being granted to locals exclusively. The case studies are the best way to illustrate the many variations on this theme.

It follows that identical treatment, that is treatment which is not overtly or 'facially' discriminatory, may constitute less favourable treatment. The measures may make the same demands of foreigners, but put the foreigners at a competitive disadvantage because they create a more onerous burden for them.[19] Such complaints extend the reach of the norm and require the member to accommodate the legality of the foreigner. It seems clear from the footnote that the foreigner cannot simply argue that the disadvantage lies in being unfamiliar with the local requirements. But instead the argument might be that the requirements come on top of requirements met at home. The foreigner may have met technical requirements at home and must now convert or embellish the service in such a way that it meets the requirements of the host country. For example, it must convert the service to another computer language or interface standard. The foreigner might have established a certain business structure at home and not want to have to duplicate it abroad. For example, it might have to meet a requirement of capitalisation, establish a separate office or a local company, or take residence and deliver the service in person. Finally, the foreigner might be grounded in a home culture but now must become versed in the host country's knowledges and practices. For example, the foreigner may have to acquire a local educational qualification, perhaps in another language.

Like services

However, the host country may have very good, non-trade related reasons for imposing these requirements on foreigners and locals alike. Indeed, in some cases, it may have good reasons for insisting that it is only foreigners who must meet such requirements. There may be greater concern about the foreigner's ability to satisfy the regulatory objectives. So, extra measures are needed to assert regulatory competence over the foreigner. It is important to appreciate that differential treatment is not necessarily less favourable treatment. The norm only requires the comparison to be made with the treatment accorded 'like' local services or service suppliers. In chapter three, we first identified this issue and saw briefly how the GATT panels decided that products were like. Where products are involved, the physical qualities can be compared. But is this approach applicable to services? Another approach could be applied to services which looks to see whether consumers think the services are competing for the same market, whether, most liberally, they are substitutable. But if we recall the unwillingness of the GATT panels to allow the measure to discriminate on the basis of the way the product was manufactured or harvested, we shall need to ask where a service ends and the nature of its inputs and its style of operation begin. In the case of services, the distinctions are not likely to be so clear-cut. Furthermore, the norm also calls for comparison of the treatment of like service suppliers.

In chapter three we also saw that this distinction is under pressure. Notably, an official from the WTO's Trade in Services Division has argued that a different approach be taken.[20] He suggests that, even if the national measure does not class the services as like, the onus should remain with the member country to justify its unfavourable treatment. It would do so by demonstrating that the measure was intended to further one of the regulatory objectives for which the agreement allows an exception. This approach would enable the WTO to query the motive behind the distinction. It would also require the member to demonstrate the necessity of the treatment and choose the least trade restrictive way to achieve its regulatory objective. Such an approach would further narrow the members' regulatory options. We shall see that the list of exceptions is short and the disciplines tend to narrow the choice of instrument.

Yet we should not forget that the GATS listings approach ultimately affords the member discretion. It may retain those measures it thinks are essential to its regulatory objectives. The agreement permits the members, for instance, to distinguish between modes of services supply when making specific commitments. Earlier, we noted the argument that this discrimination be disallowed. It means that a member may put a foreign service at a disadvantage by refraining from making commitments to national treatment for that mode which particularly suits the foreigner.

But we should appreciate that the member might distinguish between modes in order to assure regulatory competence.

Government procurement

Governments are also large consumers of services. A good example is their demand for information and communications services. Sometimes, they do not operate as private consumers are meant to act, in an 'economically rational' way. They deploy their procurement powers to give preference to local suppliers or to extract concessions from foreign suppliers in the furtherance of a range of legitimate policies. These include industry and employment promotion policies. In the Tokyo Round, government procurement became the subject of a voluntary side code. Many countries guard these powers jealously and the code had limited success. The Uruguay Round has constructed, as a plurilateral trade agreement, an agreement on government procurement. This agreement remains optional. However, the GATS is more abstentionist again. In article XIII, it declares that its MFN, national treatment and market access articles shall *not* apply to laws, regulations or requirements governing the procurement by government agencies of services purchased for governmental purposes, and not with the view to commercial resale or with the view to use in the supply of services for commercial sale. At the same time, it promises multilateral negotiations on government procurement in services within two years of the date of entry into force of the WTO agreement.

THE MARKET ACCESS NORM

Article XV:2 states that 'with respect to market access through the modes of supply identified in article I, each member shall accord services and service suppliers of any other member treatment no less favourable than that provided for under the terms, limitations and conditions agreed and specified in its schedule'. In what ways can we talk about market access as a norm of the agreement? Like national treatment, it is recognised expressly as a goal in the sense that article XVI envisages specific commitments being made with respect to market access through the modes of supply identified in article I. Furthermore, article XIX:1 foreshadows successive rounds of negotiations over commitments 'to be directed to the reduction or elimination of the adverse effects on trade in services of measures as a means of providing effective market access'.

We also need to give the norm some content. The question remains as to whether the agreement gives any obligatory content to the norm, certainly as a norm distinct from non-discrimination such as national treatment. Another way of putting this question is to ask whether the purview of market access is confined to measures preventing entry into national markets from abroad – measures which clearly discriminate against foreigners. In this division of functions, national treatment has a limited role too. Its domain of operation is to be found behind the border, that is in relation to measures that apply post-entry and post-establishment. Its purpose is to prevent measures being applied here that would frustrate the benefit of the concessions made on tariffs and other restrictions on market access in the traditional GATT sense of this norm.

The proscribed measures

The norm of market access is not defined in the GATS agreement. The clearest indication of the intention of the agreement is to be found in its identification of measures that are considered to obstruct market access. Article XVI:2 contains a list of measures which a member shall not maintain or adopt in sectors where market access commitments are undertaken, unless they are otherwise specified in a schedule. From this wording, it can be seen again that the agreement does not mandate the avoidance of these measures; rather it casts the onus upon members to take up one of three options: withhold a sector from its schedule, specify limitations on the commitments which are made, or satisfy explicit exceptions.

In article XVI, the 'proscribed' measures include limitations on the participation of foreign capital in terms of the maximum percentage limit on foreign shareholding or the total value of individual or aggregate foreign investment. Countries place limitations on foreign ownership as a way of bolstering commitment to the locality and providing opportunities for local earnings and local voices. Such a measure, which is still very common, is clearly a discrimination against foreign supply which uses direct investment as a means to acquire a commercial presence. It is a very significant inclusion because it is arguable that the acquisition of equity in a local enterprise is not really a mode of service supply as such. We would want to know what followed from that acquisition. Indeed, it could have the opposite effect if the investor were then to restrict the enterprise's supply activities.

The proscribed measures also include measures which restrict or require specific types of legal entity or joint venture through which a service supplier may supply a service. Such measures may be directed at foreigners, for example to make effective regulation of those suppliers whose 'loyalties' lie outside the jurisdiction. To this end, the regulation might require local incorporation, allowing subsidiaries to operate but not branches. But choice of legal form is also regulated for various non-trade reasons. A good example is the requirement placed on legal professionals to practise either singularly as natural persons or in partnerships, denying them permission to operate in the guise of a corporation. The proscription of such measures begins to suggest that the norm of market access does not equate – four square – with norms of non-discrimination such as national treatment. But it also suggests that, as they apply to services, the domains of market access and national treatment overlap. Our earlier discussion of national treatment provisions tends to back this interpretation.

The other proscriptions advance this interpretation. Their concern is quantitative limitations. Article XVI:2 specifies limitations on the value of service transactions or assets, and service operations or service output, together with limitations on the number of natural persons that may be employed in a service sector or by a service supplier, where any such limitations take the form of numerical quotas or the requirement of an economic needs test. Perhaps the major proscription concerns restrictions on the number of service suppliers who may operate. In this respect, article XVI:2(a) specifies 'limitations on the number of service suppliers whether in the form of numerical quotas, monopolies, exclusive service suppliers or the requirement of an economic needs test'. If this proscription was truly obligatory, then members would need to remove measures that gave support to monopolistic or exclusive arrangements. Such arrangements might favour a local supplier, perhaps one owned or controlled by the state. But the norm is also reaching beyond non-discrimination. It would not be discriminatory to restrict the number of licensees operating in a sector, provided foreigners were accorded equivalent conditions under which to compete for the licences which were available.

The reach of the norm

In his appraisal of the agreement, Hoekman suggests that: 'The GATS is the first multilateral trade agreement to recognize that non-discriminatory regulatory regimes may nonetheless act to restrict access to markets.'[21] The norm of market access begins to insist that markets must be exposed to private competition across the board. Liberalisation increases the commercial opportunities available to foreigners as well as locals. Members should remove barriers to entry into markets and restrictions on the scope of activities within those markets. If this interpretation is accepted, it is clear that market access carries profound implications for domestic industry structures and economic relationships overall. Thus, market access, as a norm of trade relations, reinforces the process of liberalisation of domestic markets. While this process is occurring unilaterally in many countries around the world, the presence of such a norm within a trade agreement will condition the capacity of each country to control the course of liberalisation according to its own national circumstances.

We should see that the scope given to the norm will affect the kinds of legalities which a member may maintain. A range of measures can be hypothesised to test its implications. Some measures would appear to be clear transgressions, certainly in terms of article XVI:2. The norm challenges the kind of industry-specific regulation we identified in earlier chapters. A clear case would be the rationing of the number of licences available for the broadcasting of television programs. Please note that we are not considering here whether the member has legitimate non-trade reasons for applying such a limitation, which it might well do. But what if a member imposes restrictions of lines of business or geographical spheres of operation? Here, the member might bar a supplier which operates in one sector from participation in another, while allowing other suppliers free access to this second market.

Thus the characterisation of the measure as a limitation on market access may be arguable. A member might reserve the provision of certain legal services to accredited practitioners. Anyone who qualifies may practise in this sector, but the professional association administers an admission examination which is very difficult to pass. The numbers who enter practice are thus controlled. Another example involves a securities or futures exchange that limits the number of seats available to brokers. Exchange trading may be serviced from other locations, but a seat at the exchange makes supply much more effective.

Quantitative and qualitative limitations

Once we move away from the focus on quantitative limitations, the implications of the norm are even less determinate. At the outer limits of scrutiny might be a ban which a member places on the commercial supply of certain services such as sexual or gaming services. After all, every jurisdiction sets boundaries to the scope of markets – that is, what is to be appropriable and tradeable at all, even if those boundaries are not always effective in practice. Such a ban would not allow access by any supplier, whether as a monopoly or otherwise. Is market access denied if no market is allowed to exist? In any case, such a ban would not seem to be encompassed by article XVI:2. A milder version would be a government's bar on the advertising of a service, which is a restriction on the way certain commodities may be marketed, as well as the closure of an immediate market in advertising services. Consider here too the status of a public fund which is to be the sole source of insurance cover against liability to pay compensation for work or transport injuries.

In this kind of speculation, we also need to take into account our point from chapter three that the concept of nullification or impairment can embrace non-violation and situation complaints. Thus, it has been argued that the absence of basic legal infrastructure might frustrate effective market access. We have mentioned competition law. A similar point has been made about decisions to withhold the legal support necessary to establish or enforce property and contract rights, so that business must rely upon its capacity to resort to extra-legal measures if it is to secure its commercial interests against those who will not pay for its services.[22] The implications for the kinds of legal approach which members have observed are potentially far reaching. However the text of the agreement does not really let us say how far this potential will reach. Article XIX talks of 'effective market access'. Eeckhout describes this language of article XIX as a compromise. It moves the multilateral negotiations beyond national treatment but still talks of the reduction or elimination of the adverse effects of measures, on *trade* in services, as the means of providing effective market access. Perhaps, the ultimate impact of the norm is bound up with the scope of that linkage to trade. The question becomes the nature of trade in services and the measures which affect it adversely.

Of course, the greatest inhibition on speculation about the normative import of the agreement is the listings approach. Members can avoid the scrutiny of the norm by deciding not to inscribe sectors. In the sectors which they do inscribe, they may list limitations. Here, the role of article XVI:2 is intriguing. In sectors where market access commitments are undertaken, it requires the member to specify any measure that falls into the categories it has proscribed. Does this mean that members are not obliged to list any measures that limit market access other than those which article XVI:2 has identified? The Guide's comment is suggestive: 'Article XVI:2 of the GATS lists six categories of restriction which may not be adopted or maintained unless they are specified in the schedule. All limitations in schedules therefore fall into one of these categories.'[23] It could be just that the language is infelicitous. But the WTO official, Mattoo, seems to accept this reading when he observes: 'a Member could maintain, without being obliged to schedule, a high non-discriminatory tax on a particular service which severely limits market access'.[24] Such a tax does not fit any of the article XVI:2 categories. We can take this reading further: the GATS only intended the norm to apply to quantitative limitations, though the members could still enter additional commitments if they really wished. Certainly, the kind of measures envisaged by article XIV, the article on domestic regulation, could be kept out of negotiations, at least until the next round started up in 2000.

THE MODES OF SUPPLY

The agreement comprehends all four major modes of service supply. It is important to appreciate that the agreement is doing so largely in a descriptive fashion. Most of the time, its impact on service modes depends on the extent of the commitments which the members are prepared to make. Yet such inclusiveness has both symbolic and procedural significance. Where a sector is being entered into negotiations, it requires the member to give consideration to the measures which affect each mode of supply. But we should also note that, occasionally, the agreement becomes prescriptive about modes. In order to ensure that commitments are effective, it requires that certain conditions of supply are met.

Cross-border supply

The agreement starts with perhaps the most obvious mode, cross-border supply. In article I:2(a), the GATS describes this mode as supply of a service from the territory of one member into the territory of any other member. Transfers across border lines may carry services directly to the consumer or provide the resources needed to support other modes of supply such as a personal or commercial presence. Often, the different modes operate in tandem rather than as alternatives. Services may be carried in a range of mobile media such as goods, paper or money transactions. A notable development is their abstraction in the symbolic medium of information which can be transmitted electronically. Data processing is of course a major services industry in its own right; insurance and airline companies, for example, now have data processed in overseas offices and sent back home. But lawyers and other professionals construct transactions between metropolitan headquarters and offshore financial centres and tax havens, which have broad consequences for national regulatory policies.

It follows that a key objective for international suppliers is to obtain conditions of freedom and security for their private trans-border data flows. Seeing them as crucial conduits for the supply of all manner of services, the GATS is notable for imposing obligations on members to facilitate these flows. For instance, its Annex on Telecommunications requires members to ensure that service suppliers may use public transport networks and services for the movement of information within and across borders. This includes movement for the conduct of intra-corporate communications of such service suppliers and for access to information contained in databases or otherwise stored in machine-readable form in the territory of any member.[25] Another significant example of the agreement's promotion of cross-border supply is the Understanding on Commitments in Financial Services.[26] Its provisions disavow measures that prevent transfers of information, including transfers by electronic means, where such transfers are necessary for the conduct of the ordinary business of the financial services supplier.

At the same time, the GATS is called on to support the security of these private flows. There is a general allowance for members to impose measures for the protection of privacy of individuals in relation to the processing and dissemination of personal data and the protection of confidentiality of individual records and accounts (article XIV(c)). The Annex on Telecommunications permits members to take such measures as are necessary to ensure the security and confidentiality of messages. But how are these allowances to be squared with the legitimate regulatory objectives of the members? The Annex on Financial Services reveals the GATS confusion. It allows members to attach measures to financial services for prudential reasons. However it goes on to say that nothing in the agreement shall be construed to require a member to disclose information relating to the affairs and accounts of individual customers or any confidential or proprietary information in the possession of public entities.

Discussion of data flows already brings in financial flows. Transnational transfers of funds and movements of capital are often another support facility for the supply of various kinds of services. However, they also represent a major international sector in their own right, which has huge ramifications for national economic and social policies. They represent portfolio investments and speculative transactions in financial instruments such as securities and derivatives; they also comprise longer-term foreign direct investment in business enterprises. We shall argue that the GATS is not an investment agreement as such. It deals with foreign direct investment so far as that investment is concerned to obtain a commercial presence and that presence is a mode of supplying a service (see below). It does not deal with speculative transactions, except in the sense that the structure of the financial services sector itself, and in particular the openings provided for access by foreign services suppliers, influences the patterns of such activity. We shall note the negotiation of commitments in this sector later in this chapter.

Here, the GATS deals with those transfers and movements which are conducted in support of trade in services to which commitments have been made. In article XI, the GATS prevents members from applying restrictions on international transfers and payments which are for the purpose of current transactions relating to its specific commitments in any service sector. Article XII elaborates an exception for restrictions to safeguard the balance of payments. Likewise, a member is under an obligation not to impose restrictions on any capital transactions inconsistently with its specific commitments regarding such transactions, except under the balance of payments exception or at the request of the International Monetary Fund.

Another very significant facilitative provision is contained in a footnote to the article which deals with market access (article XVI:1). It states that, if a member undertakes a market access commitment in relation to cross-border supply, and if the cross-border movement of capital is an essential part of this service itself, that member is thereby committed to allow such movement of capital. Similarly, if a member undertakes a market access commitment in relation to supply of a service through a commercial presence (see below), it is thereby committed to allow related transfers of capital into its territory.

Consumption abroad

Article I:2(b) describes this mode as supply of a service in the territory of one member to the service consumer of any other member. The preferred mode of supply of many services is in person, and international trade in services thus involves the movement of foreign persons into national spaces. One high volume flow of people is the movement of consumers to the site of delivery of the service. This mode is commonly associated with tourism, though it is also part of the delivery of such services as medical treatment, health care and formal education. This movement is generally treated favourably by host countries because of the economic benefits it provides. Nevertheless, movements of this kind are sometimes regulated as a result of a concern that they will have a deleterious impact on the locality in terms, for instance, of culture, safety or environment. Some countries place limits on the purposes for which their own nationals may consume services elsewhere. For example, financial, legal and other business services may be 'consumed' offshore in an effort to escape the application of regulatory controls 'at home', though often this consumption is combined with cross-border supply. Again, I do not think we should try to elaborate all the possible cases. The sheer range is indicated by the recent attempts in some countries to limit their nationals' consumption of sex or gambling 'services' abroad.

Presence of natural persons

The reverse flow is the movement of the service supplier to the site of the consumer. The movement of natural persons supplying services activates sector-specific host country concerns, for example about their competition with locals for business and employment. It may also touch on general or 'horizontal' migration policy concerns. It is likely to encounter a national regulatory domain of temporary visas, work permits, grants of residence and programs of settlement. It is also the subject of bilateral and sometimes regional arrangements. In the main, of course, such regulation is restrictive. However, we should note that, for the supply of certain services such as legal services, the national regulation may actually require presence in person, that is, if supply by foreigners is permitted at all (see chapter five).

Article 1:2(d) recognises the supply of a service 'by a service supplier of one member, through presence of natural persons of a member in the territory of any other member'. However, the liberalisation of measures affecting this mode of supply was to prove sensitive, really to all countries. To assuage concerns, a special annex to the agreement was devoted to movement of natural persons supplying services under the agreement. Essentially, it sought to limit the agreement's impetus to movements temporary and specific in nature. Proposals had been made by developed countries to confine the scope of liberalisation to movements of business visitors, the senior personnel of multinational corporations, and technical and professional experts on assignment, many of whom provide services in person as an adjunct to a commercial presence. Such a restriction was opposed by developing countries like India, Mexico, Thailand, Argentina, and Egypt. They saw it as favouring suppliers of capital-intensive and knowledge-based services over such service suppliers as construction, tourist, hospitality and domestic workers.[27] Why, conceptually, could any distinction be made between the different groups of service workers, or, for that matter, between free markets for labour and free markets for other services?[28]

The annex states that members may negotiate specific commitments that apply to the movement of all categories of natural persons supplying services under the agreement. It goes on to say that natural persons who are covered by a specific commitment shall be allowed to supply the service in accordance with the terms of that commitment. But, within their schedules, many countries were to apply limitations, both across-the-board and sector-specific, to the entry of natural persons into their territory. Horizontal entries often merely listed the exceptions to general controls on entry; sector-specific entries declared that this mode of supply was unbound.

The agreement recognises the members' interest in screening those who enter its territory. In this regard, the annex declares that the agreement is not to prevent a member from applying measures to regulate the entry of natural persons into its territory, or their temporary stay in it. This includes those measures necessary to protect the integrity of its borders, and to ensure the orderly movement of natural persons across them. The Group of Ten were able to obtain a proviso that such measures not be applied in such a manner as to nullify or impair the benefits accruing to any member under the terms of a specific commitment. However, a footnote made it clear that the sole factor for requiring a visa for natural persons of certain members and not for those of others should not be regarded as nullifying or impairing benefits under a specific commitment.

The bigger issue was the movement of people to find work. There have been large-scale migrations for economic reasons. Migrant workers have been attractive to employers in the agricultural, manufacturing and service sectors of the developed world. But recession, changes in modes of production and the movement of capital offshore have latterly reduced this demand for migrant workers. As we shall see in chapter five, the movement of professionals such as lawyers, especially if they are seeking permanent work, also meets resistance in a range of countries. The annex seeks to keep this issue out of the negotiations by stating that the agreement would not apply to measures affecting natural persons seeking access to the employment market of a member. Nor would it apply to measures regarding citizenship, residence or employment on a permanent basis. The annex is said to apply only to measures affecting natural persons who are service suppliers of a member, and natural persons of a member who are employed by a service supplier of a member, in respect of the supply of a service.

Some developing countries were unhappy about the exclusion of the question of migration for work from the ambit of the GATS, though problems surrounding intra-regional movements of workers between these countries suggest just how sensitive the issue can be. A developing country lobby, which included India and the Philippines, also sought to keep the migration issue on the agenda as a counter to the calls by certain developed countries such as the United States and members of the European Union for a social clause. The social clause would require a commitment to core labour standards at home as the quid pro quo for market access abroad. Comparative labour standards seem most in contention where manufactured goods are traded, but they can also become a factor when services are tradeable. We mentioned earlier that services like data processing are now being provided across borders. Where service workers, such as construction workers, travel to the site of the consumers, an issue may be whether home or host labour standards are to apply.[29]

The migration issue was also to provide a counterweight to the negotiations over financial and telecommunications services which were carrying over beyond the end of the Round. At Marrakesh, a decision was taken to extend the negotiations over measures affecting the movement of natural persons too.[30] The preamble to this decision seems to acknowledge the interests of the developing countries in augmenting their exports of labour-intensive services. A group was established to negotiate further liberalisation of movements with a view to achieving higher levels of commitment. It was to conclude its work and produce a final report no later than six months after the entry into force of the WTO Agreement. The developed countries dug in their heels, and in 1995 the negotiations produced few further commitments to entry. Only Australia, Canada, the European Union, India, Norway and Switzerland extended their commitments.[31]

Commercial presence

The other mode of supply which engages national regulation deep behind the border is the mode envisaged by article I:2(c), supply by a service supplier of one member, through commercial presence in the territory of any other member. Here, the agreement broaches the issue of direct foreign investment. We appreciate that foreign investment is regulated for a variety of reasons. Some government measures are designed to protect local industry from foreign penetration and control. As more countries adopt an outward looking economic strategy, seeking to attract capital and expertise from abroad and to connect into international networks, the remaining prohibitions on foreign direct investment are likely to represent broader economic, political and cultural concerns. For example, the preservation of national sovereignty and identity is a strong concern in industries such as the media, agriculture and defence.

Whatever the objective, many countries retain regulatory schemes that enable them to screen investment proposals. The services sectors are among the sectors where these measures are applied. They may limit the level of foreign investment in certain sectors. More generally, they impose performance conditions which are intended to derive some benefit from the foreign presence for the host country. The benefits they commonly have in mind are commercial sales, technology transfer and taxation revenue. In some situations, to ensure that foreign suppliers can be regulated effectively, they may insist on a local presence and go on to prescribe the form that presence must take.

In such a context, how much impetus does the GATS give to the liberalisation of investment? We start by saying that the GATS deals with direct foreign investment in a roundabout way. It gives recognition to foreign investment in its role as a facet of one of its modes of service supply, the mode of commercial presence. Article XXVIII(d) defines commercial presence to mean any type of business or professional establishment within the territory of a member so long as it is for the purpose of supplying a service. It includes the constitution, acquisition or maintenance of a juridical person or the creation or maintenance of a branch or representative office. In turn, a juridical person is defined to mean any legal entity duly constituted or otherwise organized under applicable law, whether for profit or otherwise, whether privately owned or government owned, including any corporation, trust, partnership, joint venture, sole proprietorship or association.

Many countries would regard each of these means of obtaining a commercial presence as a foreign investment. The foreigner might constitute a legal entity through which to run a business and hold shares or some kind of non-equity interest in it. The foreigner might be joined by other investors, including some of local origin. Significantly, the agreement recognises that the foreigner might acquire an existing legal entity. It might then take over a local corporation. Now we know that corporations are constituted and acquired for a variety of reasons; some we might regard as primarily financial. In this light, the scope of the GATS might be read down. It contemplates investment where the foreigner's object is to supply a service and the foreigner's target is a business or professional establishment. Nonetheless, this definition provides a major opening, especially in relation to the forms of foreign participation which are envisaged.

At the same time, we should stress once again that the GATS listings approach provides no guarantees regarding the liberalisation of this mode of supply. A contrast might be made with the NAFTA treaty. An exception to this voluntarist approach was the Understanding on Commitments in Financial Services. But, as we shall see in a moment, the Understanding was to have very little influence over the commitments which the members made in this sector. We know from the discussion of market access above that the measures proscribed by article XVI relate very much to commercial presence. But we also know that the effect is not to ban them but to create an onus on members to list such limitations if they apply in a sector for which the members have made market access commitments.

EXCEPTIONS

Legitimate regulatory objectives

The agreement explicitly recognises certain regulatory objectives. These objectives may justify non-conforming measures, that is, they act as exceptions where conformity to the norms is required. The exceptions which the agreement specifies separately are for emergency safeguard measures, restrictions to safeguard the balance of payments, and security exceptions (articles X, XII and XIVbis). Each of these objectives is a well recognised and explored category within the GATT. Here, in the GATS, its availability is carefully circumscribed. In particular, the security exception is defined narrowly. National security has of course been the rationale for a range of regulatory measures, such as sponsorship of local industry, limits on foreign investment, and controls on exports. Even countries which do not readily admit to a policy of national economic planning or industry support invoke national security for these purposes.

The GATS also includes a list of general exceptions which enjoy a GATT pedigree (article XIV). To begin, the agreement permits the adoption or enforcement of measures necessary to protect public morals, to maintain public order, or to protect human, animal or plant life or health (article XIV(a) and (b)). A Decision on Trade in Services and the Environment has charged a new committee to examine and report on the relationship between services trade and the environment, including the issue of sustainable development, in order to determine whether these exceptions should be modified to take account of measures necessary to protect the environment. The Committee provided its first report in time for the Singapore Meeting of Ministers.[32] In chapter three, we learnt that the relationship would benefit from a more sophisticated interface. When applied to imports of products, environment protection measures have fallen foul of the GATT on several occasions because they extend beyond what the panels think is legitimate to the protection.

If environmental hazards increasingly fail to respect national borders, the other general exceptions begin to recognise the challenges to national regulatory competence of physically mobile or electronically dematerialised economic flows. A legitimate regulatory objective concerns assurance of the quality of services supplied. The GATS exceptions allow measures that are necessary to ensure compliance with rules or regulations relating to the prevention of deceptive and fraudulent practices or to deal with the effects of a default on services contracts (article XIV(c)). There is also recognition of legitimate exceptions in the article on domestic regulation of measures relating to qualification requirements and procedures, technical standards and licensing requirements (see below).

The freer flow of services internationally enhances opportunities to engage in tax avoidance. The GATS allows measures inconsistent with the article on national treatment, provided the difference in treatment is aimed at ensuring the equitable or effective imposition or collection of direct taxes in respect of services or service suppliers of other members (article XIV(d)). In acknowledging examples of the measures which members have taken to protect their tax bases, a footnote to this exception provides an insight into the complexity of the arrangements in the field. However, it must be appreciated that the exception only applies to the collection of taxes which are imposed on the services themselves or their suppliers. It does not acknowledge the broader role service suppliers such as professionals play in constructing tax avoidance schemes and the need to regulate services supply on this basis.

The agreement also recognises measures inconsistent with the MFN obligation, provided the differences in treatment are the result of an agreement on the avoidance of double taxation (article XIV(e)). The integrity of double taxation agreements is also protected by a later provision that prevents national treatment objections to a measure that falls within the scope of an international agreement relating to the avoidance of double taxation. But the double taxation agreements were forged largely to obviate the conflicting requirements which were experienced by those operating in more than one country. It is clear that globalization is intensifying tax competition between countries.

Again, the GATS gives limited recognition to a regulatory problem with huge international spillovers. The Annex on Financial Services recognises the need for members to take measures for prudential reasons, including the protection of investors, depositors, policy holders or persons to whom a financial duty is owed, or to ensure the integrity and stability of the financial system. Again, this provision is essentially permissive. Later, we shall see that there is some mild support for regulatory cooperation between members.

Disciplines applied to the exceptions

At the same time as it allows these exceptions, the agreement applies disciplines. When members take up the exceptions, they must keep within the limits allowed. The GATS disciplines carry over tests of acceptability from the GATT which appear to represent a mixture of concerns. One concern is to ascertain the genuineness of the motives behind the taking of the measures. Another is to limit the effect of the genuine measure on trade.

Thus the article of the GATS which provides the general exceptions, article XIV, requires that the member's measures are not applied in a manner which would constitute a means of arbitrary or unjustifiable discrimination between countries where like conditions prevail. As well, they should not be a disguised restriction on trade in services. In keeping, a footnote to the paragraph that allows non-conforming measures to protect public order states that the exception can be invoked only where a genuine and sufficiently serious threat is posed to one of the fundamental interests of society. Furthermore, each one of these general exceptions requires that the measure be necessary to the attainment of the objective. We noted some of the GATT/WTO jurisprudence on exceptions like this in chapter three.

The listings approach of the GATS means that each member is able to maintain measures that do not have to conform with the norms of the agreement and hence do not have to fit within one of these exceptions. At the same time, in an expansive mood, the GATS article on domestic regulation, article VI, develops rationales and mechanisms for attaching disciplines to these measures too. A particular concern of article VI is that measures 'relating to qualifications requirements and procedures, technical standards and licensing requirements' do not constitute unnecessary barriers to trade in services. The Council for Trade in Services is charged to develop disciplines that aim to ensure such requirements are: (a) based on objective and transparent criteria, such as competence and the ability to supply the service; (b) not more burdensome than necessary to ensure the quality of the service; and (c) in the case of licensing procedures, not in themselves a restriction on the supply of the service (article VI:4). We shall look at the Council's work in chapter five. However, we should note here that in sectors where it has undertaken specific commitments, the member's obligation is immediate. If their requirements nullify or impair the commitments they have made, they must ensure that the requirements comply with the three criteria (article VI:5).

The GATS also seeks to promote international coordination of these regulatory requirements. A small step in this direction comes again from article VI. It states that in determining whether a member is meeting the three criteria, account shall be taken of international standards of relevant international organizations which are applied by the member. A major step is article VII, which allows members to recognise the education or experience obtained, requirements met, or licence or certifications granted in another country. It applies a discipline to that process of recognition. Recognition should not be accorded in a manner which would constitute a means of discrimination between countries or a disguised restriction on trade in services. But the article is also concerned to promote the multilateralisation of recognition agreements and arrangements. Members are to afford adequate opportunity for other interested members to take part.

In article VI, the agreement signals that recognition may be achieved through harmonisation or otherwise. So the article concedes that recognition might defer to the other country's standards and so standards would remain disparate. However, the article also states that where appropriate recognition should be based on multilaterally agreed criteria. In appropriate cases, members are to work in cooperation with relevant inter-governmental and non-governmental organizations towards the establishment and adoption of common international standards and criteria for recognition, also of common international standards for the practice of relevant services trades and professions.

The sector-specific Annex on Financial Services allows a member to recognise the prudential measures of any other member in determining how its measures relating to financial services are to be applied. Again there is provision for this recognition to be multilateralised. But the Annex gives no support to the international standards which, for example, the Basle Committee has established for capital adequacy requirements under the aegis of the International Bank for Settlements. The Annex on Telecommunications is a little braver in declaring that members undertake to promote international standards of inter-operability through the work of such bodies as the ITU (International Telecommunications Union) and ISO (International Standards Organization). Even Mattoo regards these prescriptions as extremely weak. Really, as we shall see from the case studies, the GATS is skirting around serious issues of international regulation that are inextricably bound up with its push to free up the flow of services. Its support is irresponsibly timid.

The GATS article on domestic regulation contains another potentially significant discipline. Article VI requires members to ensure that measures of general application affecting trade in services are administered in a reasonable, objective and impartial manner. To bring this about, the agreement reaches beyond the layer of law to be found in the statute books and deeper into the disparate legal cultures of the member countries. It requires each member to maintain or institute as soon as practicable judicial, arbitral or administrative tribunals or procedures which provide, at the request of an affected service supplier, for the prompt review of, and where justified, appropriate remedies for, administrative decisions affecting trade in services. It goes on to say that, where such procedures are not independent of the agency entrusted with the administrative decision concerned, members must ensure that the procedures in fact provide for an objective and impartial review. Another provision calls for decision making and notification of decisions within a reasonable period of time.

This provision is backed up by the agreement's general provision for transparency. To further transparency, article III assigns an obligation to each member to publish all relevant measures of general application. They must also inform the Council for Trade in Services of any changes to existing laws, regulations or administrative guidelines which significantly affect trade in the services covered by their specific commitments.

As chapter six indicates, such legal infrastructure demands on members are also a concern of the TRIPs agreement. Service suppliers may complain that legal informality provides an opportunity for economic protectionism and political patronage, even corruption, to be practised under cover. But informalism is regarded as a strength of the government–industry relations which operate within certain organizational forms of capitalism. Such demands may consequently be characterised as a peculiar American form of administrative and private legality. This legality is largely incompatible with political styles of decision making and cultural processes of conflict resolution which are in evidence elsewhere in the world.

However, it should be noted that article VI does allow for administrative or arbitral rather than judicial tribunals and procedures. Moreover, it states that the provisions for review should not be construed to require a member to institute such procedures or tribunals where this would be inconsistent with its constitutional structure or the nature of its legal system (article VI:2(b)). In any case, the disciplines may only apply in sectors where specific commitments are undertaken.

DISPUTE RESOLUTION

What processes are established to ensure compliance with obligations and commitments under the GATS? The benefits of its obligations and commitments are extended to the services and service suppliers of other members and these beneficiaries are identified in the definitions within article XXVIII. But the agreement is of course addressed to the national governments of the member countries. While article VI seeks to afford suppliers 'standing' to obtain review where they are affected by an administrative decision, it does not say whether they may invoke directly the obligations of the agreement or the commitments made under it in such proceedings. No provision is made for access to an international tribunal. As a source of rights to private persons, the agreement depends on how national legislators translate the terms of this inter-governmental public law into domestic law. In some countries, it is possible to talk of treaties as being self-executing. In others, domestic courts may choose to draw on international standards which have not been legislated into local law, if they see them as capable of constituting individual rights. Largely, however, compliance with the GATS agreement is likely to be a function of the WTO's own government-to-government dispute settlement process.

We have noted that the Uruguay Round produced an intensive effort to bolster the sanctioning power of the WTO. The new Understanding on Rules and Procedures Governing the Settlement of Disputes staggers the process of dispute settlement and builds in various checks and balances. However, the essential change from the GATT is the introduction of an element of compulsion into the procedure for consideration of a dispute and the provision of remedies for non-compliance. The new process was described in chapter three.

Articles XXII and XXIII link the GATS to the Understanding. Specifically, article XXII:1 provides support for consultations over matters arising under the agreement. Article XXIII:1 provides that any member which considers that another member has failed to carry out its obligations or specific commitments under the GATS may have recourse to the Understanding with a view to reaching a mutually satisfactory solution. Article XXIII:2 empowers the Dispute Settlement Body to suspend the application of a member's obligations or specific commitments if it considers the circumstances are serious enough to justify such action.

The GATS allows non-violation complaints. Article XXIII:3 allows recourse to the Understanding if a member considers any benefit it could reasonably have expected to accrue is nullified or impaired by the application of a measure which does not conflict with the provisions of the agreement. The article specifies that, if there is nullification or impairment, the member will be entitled to a mutually satisfactory adjustment which may include the modification or withdrawal of the offending measure. In the event an agreement cannot be reached, suspension can be authorised. In chapter three, we mentioned that the Understanding envisages the possibility of cross-retaliation, that is, the suspension of concessions or other obligations pertaining to other sectors within the same agreement, or to other covered agreements, and not just to the sector in which the nullification or impairment has been experienced. In the case of the GATS, the developing countries argued against cross-retaliation. For non-compliance with the GATS, the Understanding confines retaliation to sectors within the GATS itself (see article 23:3(g)(ii)).

OUTSTANDING NEGOTIATIONS

Negotiations were extended beyond the end of the Round in relation to three sectors – maritime transport services, basic telecommunications, and financial services – as well as one mode of supply – movement of natural persons. These negotiations were the subject of decisions at Marrakesh. We shall not deal with maritime transport services where, in any case, the negotiations broke down and were suspended until the year 2000.[33] The results of the negotiations over the movement of natural persons were noted earlier in this chapter and the results for basic telecommunications are to be examined in chapter eight. Here we mention briefly the negotiations in the globally significant sector of financial services.

It is perhaps unnecessary to say that the financial services sector represents activities which have a huge impact upon the conduct of national monetary, fiscal, industrial and social policies. A phenomenon that has gathered pace globally – the liberalisation of financial flows, such as flows across borders – raises issues far greater than the practices of its supporting services sectors. But it is a two-way process: the complexion of financial services – who for instance may deal in different instruments and markets – has an effect on the pattern of capital movements, the placement of funds for investment, the effectiveness of controls over volatility and risk in the financial markets, even the structures of industries in general and the capacity of national economies to pursue a variety of regulatory purposes such as taxation or the control of crime. A good example is control over the investment decisions for the huge pension and superannuation funds; hedge funds are another case currently provoking anxiety.

Measures regulating choice of intermediary – whether for instance foreign or local, bank or other institution, including the choice of disintermediation – affect access to different kinds of financial instruments and markets. Indeed, in many cases, these services are so closely bound up with the financial activities themselves that measures are common to them both. Notwithstanding that most governments around the world have decided not to try to control financial flows, either inwards or outwards, they still regard the control of services supply as highly sensitive.

Countries are concerned to regulate aspects such as ownership and control, the forms of participation in the sector, the modes of supply, and the range of activities in which various types of supplier may engage. Some such measures target foreign suppliers; others have the effect of impeding market access by foreign suppliers.

Scope of the financial services negotiations

The GATS provides broad coverage of the sector. The Annex on Financial Services included within its definition of financial services all insurance and insurance-related services and all banking and other financial services. The list of banking and other financial services extended to 'trading for own account or for account of customers, whether on an exchange, in an over-the-counter market or otherwise'. The objects of such trade included the new financial instruments such as money market instruments, foreign exchange, derivative products and transferable securities. The list of services also included participation in issues of all kinds of securities, money broking and asset management.

The agreement's only containment was to translate the general exclusion on services supplied in the exercise of governmental authority into the specifics of this sector so as to mean:

i) activities conducted by a central bank or monetary authority or by any other public entity in pursuit of monetary or exchange rate policies;

ii) activities forming part of a statutory system of social security or public retirement plans; and

iii) other activities conducted by a public entity for the account or with the guarantee or using the financial resources of the government.

The second and third activities, however, were brought back within purview if they were conducted competitively.

In the course of the Uruguay Round, the negotiation of sector-specific commitments met resistance from many countries. In chapter three, we recognised how the United States threatened to take an MFN exemption, saying it was not prepared to multilateralise its commitments to liberalisation unless other countries were willing to make more commitments. It would rather pursue bilateral arrangements. We should also note that the financial services sector in the United States has been the subject of intricate regulation and that the Federal Government was facing a major domestic reform task if it chose to be party to the liberalisation of access.

A Decision on Financial Services was taken to extend negotiations beyond the close of the Round. The Decision sought to accommodate the United States position. Despite the deadlines written into the agreement, it was allowed to continue negotiating without prejudice to its right to take an MFN exemption. During the extension, members remained free to improve, modify or withdraw all or part of the specific commitments they had made without offering compensation. They also remained free to list measures inconsistent with the MFN obligation when the period allowed for the extension had expired. However, in an attempt to control the leverage which the exemption gave, the Decision said that, during the negotiations, members were not to apply any exemptions they had already listed which had been made conditional upon the level of commitments undertaken by other participants or upon exemptions by other participants.

A second Annex on Financial Services was added to the agreement. Then, at Marrakesh, the ministers adopted an Understanding on Commitments in Financial Services, which was an attempt to give substance and specificity to the commitments to liberalise the sector. In particular, it prescribed commitments relevant to market access, including commitments on monopoly rights, cross-border trade, commercial presence, new financial services, temporary entry of personnel and non-discriminatory measures. It did likewise for national treatment. Interested members were to inscribe in their schedules specific commitments conforming to the approach set out; any conditions, limitations and qualifications to these commitments were to be limited to existing non-conforming measures. While in several of these respects the approach was circumspect, the Understanding pushed countries on commercial presence, entry of personnel and the cross-border purchase of services in another country. Furthermore, the provisions on national treatment began to elaborate the kind of issues we raised above. National treatment was to extend to membership of or participation in or access to a self-regulatory body, securities or futures exchange or market, where it was requisite to supply on an equal basis or where privileges and advantages attached. According to this Understanding, the significant adverse effects of non-discriminatory measures were also to be avoided.

Outcome of the negotiations

It seems the Understanding was all but abandoned by the key countries within the OECD when the negotiations became earnest.[34] Understandably, a number of developing and newly industrialised countries saw the sector as strategically sensitive. They sought to retain their existing measures, even, in some instances, to retain the freedom to strengthen measures controlling foreign investment in local suppliers and measures restricting entry by foreign suppliers into certain markets. Countries in South-East Asia were a notable source of resistance, though many of these countries were to be parties to the agreement which was eventually struck.

Permission was obtained to keep the negotiations open beyond the original deadline with all improved offers left on the table. Ultimately, in July 1995, an agreement was reached with the United States remaining outside. Of the seventy-six countries who made commitments at the close of the Round, around thirty were party to this subsequent agreement. These countries included members of the European Union, Japan, Australia and Canada, together with a number of countries from Asia. The WTO's reading of the results was upbeat.[35] It reported increases in the number of licences being made available to foreign suppliers, the levels of foreign equity which would be permitted, and the participation of foreign-owned banks in cheque clearing and settlement systems. Nationality or residence requirements for members of boards were also being liberalised. The agreement would lead to more foreign banks, securities firms and insurance companies, a greater availability of banking, securities and insurance services sold across borders by companies overseas, and the provision of asset management and other financial services by wholly or partially foreign-owned companies. However, the WTO itself conceded that limitations on foreign equity and exclusions from certain financial services activities were still very much in evidence.

This 1995 financial services agreement was to be implemented for an initial period running to 1 November 1997. At this point, members were again able, for sixty days, to modify or increase their offers and to take MFN exemptions. The Protocol to which these new schedules of commitments are annexed was laid open for acceptance until 30 June 1996 and it was to come into force thirty days after the last of the parties has accepted it.[36] The new commitments were embodied in supplements to the relevant members' schedules, designed to replace their initial entries for the financial services sector.

The United States was to withdraw most of its initial offer and take an MFN exemption in respect of all financial services and all countries. Its exemption maintained: 'Differential treatment of countries due to application of reciprocity measures or through international agreements guaranteeing market access or national treatment'. It contended that this reservation was needed 'to protect existing activities of US service suppliers abroad and to ensure substantially full market access and national treatment in international financial markets'.[37] In the spirit of multilateralism, the countries which were parties to the agreement agreed nonetheless to extend to the other parties any commitments they may make with the United States bilaterally. In late 1994 and early 1995, Japan had made commitments to the United States in both insurance and other financial services sub-sectors. They included commitments relating to trade in derivatives and management of pension funds.[38] The United States has also worked out a reciprocal accord with the European Union.[39] The

WTO leadership hailed the progress made by the deal, but expressed regret about the withdrawal by the United States. It also recorded concern about the effect of this withdrawal upon the outstanding negotiations over basic telecommunications.[40] The United States had signalled a similar approach to this sector late in the Round (see chapter eight).

However, in April 1997, the WTO restarted the negotiations, with the aim of extending the commitments further and bringing the United States back into the agreement. A further agreement was concluded on 12 December 1997. The agreement was laid open to acceptance until 20 January 1999. It is to become the fifth Protocol to the GATS.[41] This time seventy countries made commitments.[42] Expressing support for multilateralism, the United States came into the agreement late in the piece. The commitments related to foreign investment, the liberalisation of modes of supply including cross-border fund raising, forms of participation such as permission to operate as branches rather than as subsidiaries, and allowance for other suppliers to enter markets previously reserved for banks. It has been suggested that a number of countries in Asia and Latin America were now experiencing a great deal of pressure from the IMF to liberalise their financial services sector and let in foreign suppliers.

FURTHER DEVELOPMENTS

The measures under scrutiny

In this last section, we consider how the scope of the GATS may be extended in the future. Of course, the biggest development would occur if the next round of negotiations, scheduled to commence in the year 2000, pushed liberalisation beyond the stand-still positions. For example, pressure may be brought to bear on the qualitative limitations which many countries place on market access in various sectors.[43] We have not yet seen an agenda for this round. At the same time, the scope may be extended by a broader conceptualisation of the measures which must meet the scrutiny of the norms.

Earlier analysis has indicated how the GATS conceived measures broadly to encompass laws, regulations, rules, procedures, decisions, administrative action or any other form (article XXVIII(a)). We appreciate a government's measures can be manifested subtly in informal coordination and administrative guidance. They can work through the medium of providing facilities in kind or financial assistance to industry. We should note here that the GATS stopped short of disciplining the use of subsidies by members. Instead, it required them to enter into negotiations with a view to developing the necessary multilateral disciplines to avoid trade distortive effects (article XV). Those negotiations must commence by the year 2000. They will also address the appropriateness of members being empowered to take measures of countervail against the dumping of services.

In chapter three we also noted that the GATS extended its scrutiny to other levels of government by identifying measures taken by regional or local governments or authorities (article I:3). The Uruguay Round schedules identify some measures operating at this level, but it is possible the next round will devote greater attention to them as the negotiations over national measures are exhausted. Of equal potential is the cognisance the GATS takes of non-government measures that cut across national treatment and market access. We noted that the definition extends to measures taken by non-governmental bodies in the exercise of powers delegated by government. In the services sectors, a relevant example might be the power delegated to a professional association to regulate admission. Corporatist government–industry relationships produce many varieties of these hybrid public–private arrangements. Paradoxically, the movement of functions out from the core of government, for example through outsourcing and privatisation, seems to spin off more varieties.

In this regard, the most substantive obligation relates to monopolies and exclusive service suppliers. Article VIII requires members to ensure that monopoly service suppliers do not act in a manner inconsistent with the commitments members have made to national treatment and market access under the agreement. To this end, members are also to ensure, when a monopoly supplier competes outside the scope of its monopoly rights, that the supplier does not abuse its monopoly position. This language is reminiscent of the traditional competition policy approach to the use of intellectual property rights. But the concept of monopoly rights is not defined by the agreement.

However, the responsibilities extend to exclusive service suppliers. For the purposes of the article, the GATS identifies a service supplier to be an exclusive supplier, where a member formally or in effect authorises or establishes a small number of suppliers and substantially prevents competition between them (article VIII:5). One imagines that these provisions had publicly owned or controlled suppliers in mind, especially in the case of monopoly suppliers. But, for a variety of reasons, a member government may seek to limit the number of private suppliers which may operate in a particular sector.

As we shall see from the study in chapter eight, this possibility is clearly envisaged by the GATS Annex on Telecommunications. It requires members to ensure that foreign service suppliers are afforded access to and use of public telecommunications transport networks and services on reasonable and non-discriminatory terms. Public services are defined as any service required explicitly or in effect by a member to be offered to the public generally. We know that it is the tradition in certain countries for the 'common carriers' to be in private hands. Privatisation of public instrumentalities is spreading that phenomenon. At the same time, a greater understanding of how these markets work is expanding the sense of what a common carrier might be. Though its first application is to various telecommunications carriers, we shall see in chapter eight that it has been suggested that Microsoft's control over the computer platform makes it a common carrier for Internet services, a provider of essential facilities.

It is clear that such provisions of the GATS are helping to expand the notion of the government measures which might contribute to trade barriers. Liberal interpretations by WTO panels also contribute. As we noted in chapter three, the panel report in the photographic film and paper dispute took a very liberal view of the Japanese measures which fell within this ambit. In this dispute under the GATT, the complaint of the United States targeted the Japanese Large Retail Stores Law. A dispute notified to the WTO under the GATS has done so too.[44] But the photographic film and paper dispute indicates how difficult it is to prove a non-violation complaint of nullification or impairment, even where the government is actively involved in encouraging the exclusionary private practices. Mere failure to act on such practices is less likely again to ground a complaint, unless the agreement in question has placed the member under a positive obligation to take measures against such practices.

Competition regulation?

It is unlikely that the GATS will provide much succour here. Article IX:1 of the GATS embodies a recognition by members that certain business practices of service suppliers may restrain competition and thereby restrict trade in services. Thus, it envisages that members may wish to take measure against those practices – without, however, making it clear what level of exemption those measures should enjoy themselves from the demands of the trade norms. We noted in chapter three that competition laws count as government measures just like any other laws. If it contains an implicit exemption for competition laws, nevertheless, article IX is doing little positively to promote the application of competition laws. Its tenor is permissive and it does not require members to take measures. We know that members rely on the cooperation of other members to act effectively against restrictive business practices. The GATS merely obliges members, at the request of other members, to enter into consultations with a view to eliminating such practices (article IX:2).

The United States initiative is an attempt to break down domestic industry relationships which impede market access by its exporters. If it were to be supported by the WTO, it would have destabilising implications for a variety of sectors. It is understandable that members did not want the GATS to be promoting competition law in such a way that it undermined the remaining immunities which their industries had been allowed by virtue of the looseness of the norms themselves or the leeway in the listings approach. However, as we foreshadowed in chapter three, there is a further potential in the WTO agenda for competition law. It may provide assistance to those countries which wish to discipline the restrictive business practices of the transnational suppliers. Writing in 1990, Grey anticipated that the GATS was not likely to compel private controllers of services to supply those services, should the competitive disciplines of the global market provide insufficient incentive for them to do so.[45] Now, a broader view of WTO responsibilities would confront the restrictions which foreign suppliers place on access to their services, especially on the producer services which local enterprises need if they are to be genuinely competitive. Competition law concepts such as abuse of dominant position and the denial of access to essential facilities might be put to good use here.

When the GATS Annex on Telecommunications actually imposed obligations on members to regulate service suppliers, those members who participated in the carry-over negotiations decided to tackle issues of regulatory design together. The reference paper which the negotiations produced begins to adopt the competition law approach, though it remains very general and permissive in its approach. We shall give this issue detailed attention in chapter eight as the book is brought to a close. The formulation of the broad WTO competition policy agenda is also discussed at the end of chapter eight. It is possible that competition law cannot afford the necessary comprehension of these restrictive practices or the effective means to promote good corporate citizenship worldwide. If this proves to be the case, then the WTO must consider giving positive backing to the kind of codes of conduct that can 'civilise' global capitalism.

Other business regulation

Chapter three began to acknowledge the case being made to marshal international support for other kinds of business regulation. The difficulties which global markets present to governments which want to tax effectively are slowly being appreciated.[46] Likewise, the failures among financial institutions in a number of countries seem finally to be moving world leaders to take the coordination of prudential supervision seriously. One would be right in saying these issues are not new, but freer access to internationalised services is boosting the capacity to avoid regulatory controls. Cross-border facilities of financial intermediation are drawing funds into unregulated areas, including those which are so hard to locate in cyberspace.

We saw above that the GATS most openly acknowledges these concerns by conceding spaces for national regulatory measures, provided they represent certain legitimate objectives. Thus, its general exceptions provide concessions to members that wish to regulate. The specialist annexes also give hints that the negotiating parties had started to think about the stresses on regulation when services flow more freely across national borders. But simply allowing exceptions to the norms does little for regulatory competence. Ultimately, the WTO must be pressed to take more responsibility than this. It is not hard to see that the GATS is adding considerably to the strain being placed on this competence. In its present state, the GATS does very little directly to require any coordination or standardisation of regulation in the service sectors. Its small steps in the right direction only indicate how much ground there is to make up if liberalisation is not simply to end with laissez-faire or libertarianism. Perhaps the round scheduled for the year 2000 will be used as an opportunity to do so.

CONCLUSIONS

This chapter has offered a detailed analysis of the first multilateral and multi-sector agreement on services. But the study has also been interested in the significance of the GATS for the globalization of law. In terms of its definition of the field, the range of the GATS is wide indeed. It subjects to the norms of open trade and free markets a wide range of activities carrying messages about economies, politics, culture and social life. As the discussion suggests, financial, professional and media services can transmit powerful intellectual, organizational and personal content. The GATS draws all but a very narrow category of services within its ambit and it applies its scrutiny to each of the major routes of service supply. Cross-border supply, the consumption abroad, the movement of persons and commercial presence, are all embraced.

Through its norms of MFN, national treatment and market access, the GATS proposes a neo-liberal agenda for services supply. However, it is clear that, in order to attract the participation of a broad variety of countries, it had to provide leeway. We might say it had to mediate as well as discipline. So, on the one hand, the GATS offers a multilateral framework for the regulation of services trade. An attraction for those countries whose service sectors are not powerful is that they receive the benefits of access to other countries without necessarily providing full material reciprocity. But the GATS has also allowed the opportunity to enter MFN exemptions. We have noted the difficulties which the WTO has experienced, especially in the context of the negotiations which extended past the Round, disciplining the strategic use of this avenue.

Likewise, the chapter explores the broad scope of the national treatment norm in this field. It challenges measures that discriminate against foreigners, whether the measures be taken to protect local suppliers or to further a country's general regulatory competence over those who supply from a base offshore. Furthermore, it says that the measures need not be overtly discriminatory. It is their effect which matters. In questioning formally identical treatment of foreigners, it will require local regulators to make certain concessions to foreign standards. But, in any case, the agreement goes further. Its norm of market access places on the defensive non-discriminatory controls on participation in markets. At this stage, the focus seems to be on quantitative limitations. In successive rounds, it is likely to turn its attention to the more sensitive question of qualitative limitations.

Nonetheless, the analysis reveals the tendency of the GATS to leave the full impact of the norms to the process of implementation. The definitions show some hesitation, particularly in respect of free participation in labour markets. The norms are expressed in largely general terms and they are likely to attract interpretation through the dispute settlement process. But the main site for mediation is the GATS two-fold listings approach. It turns the spotlight on the process of negotiations between members, first within the Uruguay Round, and now in the succeeding rounds which are to start up in 2000. The listings approach has allowed a space for countries to hold back whole sectors from the scrutiny of the agreement, as well as to preserve non-conforming measures in those sectors which they do expose. In various sectors, and across all countries, this opportunity has been utilised. The GATS also provides explicit recognition to certain national regulatory objectives.

In liberalising supply in sectors like finance, law and communications, together with modes such as the movement of people and direct foreign investment, the WTO is altering the balance in favour of transnational businesses. A question mark hangs over its preparedness to support the kind of re-regulation needed to ensure that these businesses do not close off access to services privately. This chapter has used competition law standards as a litmus test for this commitment and this example will be taken up again in the case studies below. It remains very much to be seen just who will have access to that regulatory potential. At present, the GATS makes only a weak gesture in the direction of support for such regulation.

CHAPTER 5

THE CASE OF LEGAL SERVICES

Chapter five is the first of the case studies. Its subject is a notable global carrier, the supply of legal services internationally. The object of this first case study is to examine the evidence of the impact of the WTO, and specifically of the GATS, on the inter-legalities which arise out of the provision of legal services internationally. The chapter is the first field test of the interpretations which we have placed on the WTO's relationship between globalization and law. In this case, the test material is law itself, articulated at the very particular level of the activity which we might call 'lawyering' or, more familiarly perhaps, the work of lawyers. With the book's interest in globalization and law, a good starting point is the identification of a new international, possibly transnational, style of lawyers' work. The chapter suggests how this kind of lawyers' work may project around the world a distinctive brand of transaction-based and market-oriented legality (based on private contract and commercial arbitration). This legal service has the potential to cut global relations loose from the regulatory specifications and cultural ties of the locality. Its style is reflected in the ways these lawyers conduct themselves in their relationships with their clients, third persons and other lawyers, including the ways they site and organize their work.

The chapter argues, however, that these lawyers' own legalities fail fully to negotiate the rich texture of local legal rules and practices. The inevitability of inter-legality bolsters the need to provide services locally, giving attention to the time and place of law. Effective provision of legal services requires relationships to be formed, not just with commercial partners, but also with government bodies and local communities. Chapter five recognises that the demands of the lawyers' own 'product markets' – or, in the terms of the book, the nature of the economic, political and cultural milieus in which they operate – contribute to this reliance. But they are reinforced by the extensive direct local regulation of the supply of legal services. The foreign suppliers of legal services encounter legalities of supply modes which diverge from their home country legalities and, if they are becoming truly transnational, their own preferred 'private' ways of organizing and operating.

Thus a consideration of trade in legal services provides insights into the broad phenomenon of the globalization of law. But the relation which the competition between lawyers bears to the broader competition between types and locations of law is not a straightforward one. The supply of legal services exhibits its own economic, political, cultural – and legal – features. There are inter-legalities peculiar to the supply of legal services which provoke attempts at mediation. The chapter describes the detailed and prescriptive ways this regulation controls the modes of supply of foreign legal services and the purposes which lie behind such controls. The modes which are subject to control range from disembodied provision across borders to supply by natural presence in the jurisdiction, either temporarily or on a continuing basis. It also includes supply via a commercial presence. Commercial presence may be established through a local office, employment and partnership with locals or, conceivably, financial acquisition of existing local firms. Local regulation still limits the choice of supply mode. A particular feature of the interaction between service supply and local regulation in this sector is the basis on which foreigners may gain admission to the profession and thereby access to the work which is reserved exclusively for the profession. Increasingly, the nature of educational qualifications is the key to this admission. Failing admission, the issue becomes the scope of activities permitted outside this monopoly, say as a foreign consultant.

Returning to the WTO, the chapter identifies the impact of the GATS. It notes the implications of the agreement's norms for local regulation, then proceeds to assess the outcome of the negotiations over commitments within the Uruguay Round. In particular, it examines the commitments which Japan, the United States, and the members of the European Union were prepared to make to liberalisation of their regulation in order to further national treatment and market access. The impact of the Round on developing countries, especially in Asia, is also noted.

The chapter indicates that the outcome of the Round was a very guarded and tentative move in the direction of liberalisation. Even in the North, the bulk of the local profession remains apprehensive about foreign competition and governments too have reservations about opening up. But successive rounds of commitments have already been scheduled. Further deregulation of traditional controls on competition may have a radical effect on professional practices and the GATS may be challenged to provide a new basis for observance of standards in this globalizing field. Protocols for mutual recognition of qualifications do not necessarily resolve the issue of substance. Will the answer be found in an international competition law, or will positive codes of conduct be required if cross-cultural understandings are to be fostered, and ethical practices which are respectful of local conditions are to be observed?

STYLES OF SERVICE SUPPLY

Demands of international clients

While not a major trade sector in terms of volume or revenue, legal services form part of the business or producer services which are so important to the internationalisation of trade in goods, finance, knowledge, investment and other trade flows. As we have noted, such flows contribute to the breakdown of national economic, political and cultural differences, widening and deepening the reach of globalization. Of course, legal services are not alone in performing this role. Nonetheless, it is tempting to think that lawyers operating globally might be among the key carriers and even constitutors of new, worldly ideas and practices. In their study of commercial arbitration, Dezalay and Garth suggest that international business lawyers are now a major challenge to state sovereignty and in particular the power of the state to govern the economy, the law and the legal profession. Through their practices, these lawyers are producing new transnational law as well as applying the laws of the nation states.[1]

We might start with a supposition that trade in legal services is promoted by the globalization of the activities which lawyers service. These activities include the operation of financial markets, the coordination of manufacturing systems and the provision of consumer products. By so linking legal services to the developments occurring in their 'product markets' or the demands of their customers, we could trace how certain lawyers have followed their home country multinationals into foreign locations. They have facilitated sale of goods transactions, construction and natural resources extraction projects, manufacturing ventures and increasingly the placement of direct foreign investments. With the radical innovations being made in international financial and securities markets, together with the stepping up of merger and acquisition activity in the markets for companies, lawyers have gathered further work. They are putting together transactions, guarding against risks and dealing with regulatory requirements. Privatisation has given this work another major spurt. An ongoing source of work is regulatory arbitrage and the construction of offshore legal arrangements for the purpose of minimising various liabilities faced by wealthy individuals and corporate clients. Now foreign lawyers are eyeing the domestic markets of growing economies. They seek to capture the business of local corporations which are looking outward, even to tap into the domestically oriented custom of small/medium size business and household clients.

In this context, chapter two identified an emerging legality to be a new supra-national and possibly a-national type of business law, sometimes called the new *lex mercatoria*. Business operators not only express preferences between national jurisdictions, they promote types of law that are not dependent on assimilation into national schemes. The clearest examples are the large-scale but exclusive contracts which are fashioned to regulate special projects such as minerals exploitation or hotel and office construction. In addition to the actual terms devised for these contracts, the determinations made through commercial arbitration help to define norms and procedures which are suited to the requirements of transnational business.

Conventionally, the study would proceed on the basis that the lawyers who are successful in providing these services are responding in an instrumental fashion to the demands of their clients. Their strategies are determined by the fields of economic activity in which they operate. Yet the relationship between lawyers and capital is better seen now as a reciprocal one.[2] Recent work attributes a proactive, formative role to lawyers. They are given an important role in the social construction of world markets and not just in markets in law. International business lawyers are involved creatively in the production of symbolic forms.[3] Thus, lawyers are involved in the construction of market subjects (such as corporations), exchange commodities, forms of security, media of exchange, as well as the necessary bonds of social solidarity for economic activity, such as trust, legitimacy and morality, and the avenues for dispute resolution.[4] A good example is their role in the innovation of legally tradeable financial instruments such as securities and derivatives; another is the creation of special devices to effect management buy-outs and other forms of corporate takeover.

Entrepreneurial legal services

If this activist role is acknowledged, we can see that the provision of legal services involves competition between lawyers with differing styles and values. For instance, Dezalay and Garth identify a competition in which, to their mind, the aggressive, technocratic style of the big Anglo-American firm is prevailing over the more gentlemanly, almost aristocratic traditions of Europe. If this trend is true of international business law generally, then, thinking of lawyers in terms of institutional economics, these firms are taking advantage of their scale and scope economies. We know that already there are international firms with hundreds of

147

partners and offices in many locations. Less tangibly, these lawyers gain advantages by practising proactive deal making and conflict management skills. These skills build on their learning from home country experiences and their early movement into foreign work. Theirs is both a professional and organizational technology. This competition has consequences for the way that economic and other social relations are conducted. It seems to suggest more law and more litigation, generating more work for certain kinds of lawyers. For example, in corporate law, it seems to suggest that more innovative and adversarial methods will be used to determine mergers and acquisitions, rather than the informal resolutions of the 'old boy' networks.

The introductory chapters recognised the force of the contention that globalization would push national governments in the direction of generic types of business law. Localised legal differences would be reduced and law even stripped of its diverse political and cultural associations altogether. But that contention is counterbalanced by the sense that differences are still sustainable. In particular, it is recognised that a transnational field of business, if it were to be built on the strength of contractual accords, would not be able entirely to overcome the claims of national jurisdictions. Contract laws themselves, as well as what might more conventionally be called regulatory laws, express local resistances too. Even where localities are trying to attract foreign trade and investment with openings and assurances, the legalities they take on board are adapted to take account of local conditions.[5] With the different organizational forms of capitalism around the world, transnational legal links will be forged across other cultures too. Evidence for this is to be found in the case of Singapore lawyers who are operating now in locations like Hong Kong, Vietnam and China.

Nonetheless, the effect of this pluralism on the supply of legal services remains complex. The transnational lawyer may still prosper because of his or her unique capacity to compare, select and package these regulatory differences – to provide 'one stop shopping'. A trend in this direction is the demand for lawyers who can manage such differences, not across the board, but in specific areas of practice like securities markets. But, if this is the case, the expertise becomes of necessity an expertise in differences as well as an expertise (or enterprise) in convergence. The existence of differences suggests that local knowledge and local contacts can prove an advantage. Thus, in a study of the use of lawyers' knowledge in a field relevant to this book – computer law – Lewis finds that the lawyers' expertise is fundamentally one of translating the clients' needs into an acceptable legal language.[6] As well as borrowing models from elsewhere, this expertise builds on already existing local forms. Competition law displays these features too.

Relations with states, civil societies, communities
Even in their role in the making of markets, lawyers must be involved with
the state and its expectations. But lawyers are often involved in the construction of politics itself. Their skills can contribute to the strengthening
of state institutions. In this role, they have on occasions been linked with
authoritarian states. However, they display a particular affinity with Western political liberalism in their promotion of constitutionalism and the
separation of powers, in particular the idea of an independent judiciary
and a private legal profession. In acknowledging such a contribution, it is
worth noting that political liberalism is not always to be equated with economic liberalism. Indeed at times political or legal liberalism may place a
check on the excesses of economic liberalism, while lawyers active in promoting markets may severely undermine the legitimacy of the nation state
and even the liberal legal system itself.[7] This tension surfaces in the dualism which lawyers themselves exhibit. On the one hand, they are ready to
proclaim themselves unsentimentally and fiercely competitive in furtherance of the interests of their clients. On the other, they affirm the legitimacy of their calling through their devotion to national, and now to
international, public service of various kinds.

Lawyers also contribute to the creation and maintenance of civil society, which we appreciate is not just a function of autonomous market
institutions but depends on a range of voluntary associations, intermedi-
ate bodies and citizenship rights. Moreover, if their focus is often on core
civil and property rights, historically there have always been lawyers who
champion the cause of those who are experiencing economic and social
injustices. In some cases, foreign lawyers may be freer to intervene effectively between the local subject and the powerful state or at least be able
to give support to the local lawyers who are trying to do so. Of course, it
remains an open question how central the work of lawyers has been to
the advancement of these causes. Some of us are familiar with the 1960s
critique that lawyers divert these causes into unproductive channels and
even help to legitimise the systems which create the injustices. Today,
attention is again being paid to the role of lawyers in societies which are
undergoing transition.[8] Such questions are much too big to be
attempted in a study like this; they are noted strictly to help understand
why foreign lawyers may receive a mixed reception.

Finally, following in this vein, it can be recognised that lawyers take
part in building communities. These communities can be informal personal networks stretching across national borders, like those in the field
of international business law or ecclesiastical law. But they can also be
deeply and perhaps resiliently embedded in local communities, within
towns, inside associations or around courts. Lawyers can thus act as reser-
voirs of local legal cultures. Arguably, these types of law lend themselves

even less to the kind of abstraction and homogenisation which makes the foreign lawyer's entree easier.

Foreign or local lawyers

The arrival of foreign lawyers can provoke fiercely protective policies, but they are not excluded simply to preserve the markets of local lawyers. Political and cultural sensitivities continue to inspire policies which are designed to shield certain areas of law and legal practice from foreign influences in an inward looking way. If there is strength in the state's authority, the bureaucracy's autonomy or the organization of civil interests, liberal legality may be resisted. Such factors certainly influence the degree to which laws formally giving foreign lawyers access are actually respected.[9] They may also influence the position adopted on the foreigner's right to practise. Thus, governments may say that greater access for foreign lawyers is incompatible with political traditions of decision making or cultural practices of conflict resolution. It may be argued that foreigners lack empathy with local customs, introducing a style of legal practice (such as litigiousness) which will sour government, business or social relations. Or it may be stressed that lawyers are officers of the court and must show commitment to the local administration of justice, even, in some states, to national political institutions. On this basis, bans on family law, land law, testamentary or criminal law work show up regularly in restrictive policies, as well as prohibitions on representation and associated court work.

The argument that the practice of law is not just a business fuels resistance to what is cast (stereotypically perhaps) as an Anglo-American style of legal practice. As the Common Market developed, Whelan and McBarnet detected a tension developing between the claims of professionalism and commercialism.[10] Commercialism was being seen as a threat to the traditional professional ethics of collegiality, independence and public service. Conservative practitioners viewed with disfavour the prospect that more and more legal practice would be driven by private market forces, oriented to high paying corporate clients and commercial work. Baxi identifies a similar contrast being made, while appreciating that the critics are often idealising past practices.[11] So, for example, there may be suspicion of foreigners who do not seem to put something back into the development of the local profession or the provision of legal aid. To locals, such lawyers may seem detached from a traditional sense of 'noblesse oblige' or from a commitment to the welfare state. Consumer protection is often given as a more down to earth reason for distrust of foreign lawyers. On this view, it will be said that foreign lawyers lack the necessary understanding and competence to serve local needs properly, locals have no effective means of redress against the mobile foreigner, and the foreigner does not feel bound by the domestic standards of professional conduct.

Whatever the reasons given, it is clear that the impacts of lawyers on state, civil society and community are also borne in mind when the policies towards foreign lawyers are being formulated. In this way, independent lawyers can be seen as a threat to the power of the state and to the corporatist relationships it may have enjoyed with certain economic interests. These interests are often local elites, but they might include those foreign suppliers and investors who have obtained the inside running. Lawyers can also be seen as threats to the associations of civil society and community, a salutary example being the soul-searching in the United States over competitive lawyering, the assertion of rights and resort to litigation.

However, it would not do to exaggerate the degree of unity at the national level. We have made the general point that global pressures aggravate national disjunctures. We might make a rough contrast here between the large firms and the sole practitioners, between internationally oriented and locally dependent practices, between, as it were, the modernisers and the traditionalists. Transnational lawyering will have appeal to those lawyers who wish to cut loose from the constraints of their locality and tap into the opportunities of a global economy. It is likely that the main opposition to international competition will be found amongst the many smaller-scale members of the profession. Thus, the internal characteristics of the local legal culture, the structure of the profession and its links with the state all play a part in the competition. If, for instance, the local profession is not well organized and cohesive and its legal monopoly is not widespread and entrenched, it may be easier for foreign lawyers, or other professionals such as accountants for that matter, to gain access.

LOCATIONS FOR LEGAL WORK

Cross-border supply

To this point, the discussion has focussed on the complex relationship which competition between lawyers bears to the competition being experienced between certain types of law. The location of law making also affects the relative advantages enjoyed by global and local lawyers. Globalization of communications media, for instance, might render it unnecessary to be present in a particular locality in order to provide a legal service. Law's capacity to be conveyed abstractly and symbolically seems suited to these media; such ideas have no natural physical boundaries. Qualitatively speaking, some of the biggest legal influences have been transmitted through very small numbers of key individuals and transactions. Entrepreneurial and diplomatic lawyers have used their skills to engineer major changes in legislative regimes around the world. Today, once again, these kinds of consultants are abroad, rendering advice to the many countries which are undergoing transition to market economies, in some cases through the sponsorship of an exporting state, a multinational corporation, a philanthropic fund or an international organization. Such an influence can also be obtained by the students of law travelling to the site of the supplier. In certain countries, the best students tend to gravitate towards the metropolitan centres for an advanced legal education.

Could more conventional legal services be supplied in a similar way? A major service activity has been the competitive offering, in some small jurisdictions, of fora of convenience, especially for the construction of financial and accounting transactions. These services have ridden on the back of money flows, which governments have found difficult to control. We have already noted that the electronic media may make such services accessible to a wider range of people. Such an on-line mode of supply will be difficult to police. Does it matter then whether presence in the jurisdiction is regulated, if services can be sourced electronically?

So, for the state that wishes to maintain distinctive regulatory standards, the issue becomes the power of its location to pull these services flows down to earth. Do the suppliers and customers enjoy unfettered freedom to move from one place to another or to construct paper and electronic relationships across territorial spaces? Or are they rather still tied to a certain extent to a physical site or perhaps attracted to one which can offer a competitive service that is based on individuality, quality and security? In the realm of legal services, the question can be explored in several ways, each connected, I think, with whether effective supply depends on such advantages as proximity and familiarity.

The power of presence

At this point, we should entertain the possibility that the tradeability of legal services might be overestimated. To think again in terms of industrial economics, recent studies have detected clusterings of international industries on a regional basis. These clusterings represent networks of researchers, suppliers, manufacturers, distributors and customers. In these analyses, place still matters: these configurations build on their historically and geographically determined strengths. Thus Sassen, for example, locates the design, financing and management functions of the international economy in a few 'global cities' (such as New York, London, Frankfurt and Tokyo), together with associated producer services such as lawyering.[12] The hierarchy might extend down to some regional sub-centres. These centres become a focus for international lawyers, which is a reason why Tokyo's barriers are such a concern. It is quite correct to call such cities 'centres', yet they are still spatially based and they continue to exhibit local differences.

These cities are centres for a certain kind of legal service, partly of course because this is where the product market is concentrated. If this is true to some extent for financial markets, then we can expect it to hold for more traditional markets, for example in goods, and maybe even for new products such as information technology. But it is a two-way flow: producers gather here because of the agglomeration of services. What the producers are seeking is not so much a high degree of specialisation in legal areas as packages of services which spill over the conventional bounds of legal services. It is the ability to deliver these packages which makes accounting firms, for example, such genuine rivals to law firms. In this global competition to attract business, a locality can gain an advantage by the way it regulates these services. Regulation may be liberalised to make it easier for these kinds of services to operate, for example by removing restrictions on multidisciplinary partnerships and the incorporation of practices. But the sound regulation of professional conduct might also prove an advantage, for instance by reassuring clients that their interests will be protected.

Notwithstanding the importance for everyone of the kind of services which are being provided in these global cities, most lawyers continue to be associated with the conduct of business in domestic, home markets. These businesses need to be close to their customers and suppliers if their demands are to be met responsively. The desire for face-to-face relations remains a strong force. It is often said that legal services depend on personal contact with the client and a knowledge of local customs and conditions. In such ways, lawyers are immersed in their local spatial communities. The local advantage draws its strength from the richness of local legal knowledge and professional practice. Such operating imperatives most clearly apply in the case of appearances in court, together with the practical consideration of the availability of witnesses and other evidence. To acquire local knowledge, it is necessary to maintain a presence within the jurisdiction; it cannot really be achieved from afar. And the presence is not just a matter of being in the same space as the client or the legal institution. Time is an important dimension: the provider must have the time to observe local procedures and wait till they run their course.

These advantages are also bolstered by formal conflict-of-laws criteria, which tend to allocate jurisdiction to the place where cases can conveniently be tried and make the applicable law the law of the *lex fori*. Venues tend to diverge along procedural as well as substantive lines, such as their styles of argumentation. Another version of this constraint is the need to deal face to face with regulatory agencies that exercise discretion and develop unwritten law in government centres, whether regionally (say in Brussels) or more locally. Shapland contends that: 'A lawyer's corporate practice and usefulness to clients may depend much more upon the solidity of its alliance with the state than upon lawyers' creative ability to solve clients' problems.'[13] As chapter two suggested, even where the client is an international one, clearance for an activity or pursuit of an infringement may require localisation of the process.

In such circumstances, provision from another country or through temporary visits by travelling lawyers may not prove attractive; a real presence is advantageous and it may even be necessary to work through locals. This observation is especially apposite to domestic markets. But even externally oriented business clients can be hard to attract if they have a tradition of close informal links with the local profession, as for example in Germany or the City in London. A foreign lawyer complained of the Japanese market recently: 'Japanese businesses just don't know how to utilise foreign lawyers efficiently while spending a lot of money on those lawyers who have their continuing relationships.'[14] The organizational style of the local lawyers comes into play, even if they are outwardly oriented. Consider, for example, the tendency of European lawyers to connect through networks and clubs of independent practitioners rather than by merging into large-scale firms. To adapt, foreign lawyers have to practise more like locals.

At the same time, it is said that younger lawyers are prepared to travel anywhere and adapt to local conditions. Perhaps mobility and reflexivity are general attributes of that class of workers now styled as 'symbolic analysts', but the attractiveness of living conditions in different locations is still a subtle and influential consideration. Generally, we need to say that the mobility of labour in a global economy has been far less pronounced than that of capital. Besides, some markets simply do not justify the expense of establishing a local branch office. Yet, working through locals in a network of referrals or affiliations may not provide the capacity to control from the centre. While there are efforts to standardise and routinise legal work, so, we might say, it can be delegated, franchised and downloaded, some aspects remain highly skilled in a tacit, person-specific way. In some cases, the locals may lack the kind of expertise and organization necessary for international work.

Foreign and local lawyers

Nevertheless, the implications for the regulation of foreign lawyers are not predictable. As we have said, if the availability of services which are expert in certain global types of law is necessary to attract international business, the national government may be prepared to sacrifice the local profession. A government so inclined shows itself willing to break down the monopoly of a seemingly insular profession, creating a single market where sub-national or functional divisions existed, and letting in foreign providers. Increasingly, then, legal services are assimilated to a model of industry and competition rather than government and civics. For example, with an economic policy geared recently to internationalisation, Australia is starting to debate this strategy for the profession. The strategy has its critics: several eminent judges have expressed concern about commercialisation.

Yet the aim, even of an externally oriented government, may be to give an indigenous ('infant') legal industry time to develop the strength to compete in international law markets, especially for the custom of home-based clients. The result may be a green light to an increase in the number of local lawyers, the amalgamation of firms and the establishment of branch offices. Reforms may also be made to local legal education, including the development of research and teaching in the realms of comparative and international law. In these circumstances, multilateralisation becomes an uncertain strategy. Will the gains to domestically based firms outweigh the losses from increased foreign competition?

The desire to enhance the competitive capacity of local lawyers also influences the particular regulatory strategy adopted towards foreign lawyers. For example, foreigners may be allowed to work for local lawyers in the belief that they will impart skills or transfer technology to them. At the same time, they might not be permitted to employ local lawyers or form partnerships with them, out of a concern that they might control the locals' practices or siphon off their revenue. Likewise, the foreign lawyers may work for foreign but not local clients. However, in certain categories or locations of law, national authorities still make the judgement that the international services which the foreign lawyers can provide are not worth the risk to local legal culture. The authorities may continue to fear that, if they are afforded a presence, foreign lawyers will insinuate their way into home country work, despite the formal controls placed on the scope of their activities. The presence of foreign lawyers will encourage undesirable practices among local lawyers. Indeed, the reforms necessary to accommodate the foreigners will unsettle the whole profession. As a Japanese lawyer commented when entry was being relaxed in 1994, why make such big changes to the profession just for a few foreign lawyers?

NATIONAL REGULATION

Modes of supply

To move into the impersonal language of the GATS, this discussion indicates that international legal services assume various modes of supply. In turn, we shall see that each mode seems to attract the interest of national regulation. As we discuss the modes of supply and the national measures which regulate them, we should keep in mind what we have said in chapters three and four about the GATS norms of national treatment and market access. The modes which are subject to control range from dis-embodied provision across borders to supply by natural presence in the jurisdiction, either temporarily or on a continuing basis. They also include supply via a commercial presence. Commercial presence can be achieved through different means such as a local office, employment and partnership with locals or, conceivably, financial acquisition of existing local firms. A particular feature of the interaction between service supply and local regulation in this sector is the basis on which foreigners may gain admission to the profession and thereby access to the work which is reserved exclusively for the profession. Increasingly, as nationality con-trols are lifted, the nature of the required educational qualifications is the key to this admission. Failing admission, the issue becomes the scope of activities which are permitted outside this monopoly, for example work in the capacity of a licensed foreign consultant.

Despite the freeing up of financial and like transactions, we find that some limits may also be placed on consumers who wish to take advan-tage of legal services supplied across the border from abroad. Restric-tions may certainly be placed on the free movement of natural persons into the national territory, such as temporary visits made by travelling professionals. Countries have used entry regulation such as visas and work permits to screen foreign lawyers and to ration opportunities and limit stays, according to the perception of local needs, even in the case of limited consultancy activities. Bars to the acquisition of permanent residence or national citizenship are significant too, most directly where they remain prerequisites for practice as a member of the local profes-sion proper. But effective supply may depend in any case on the ability to consolidate a presence.

Likewise, obstacles may be placed in the way of establishing a com-mercial presence. Lawyers may seek to establish a presence by setting up a representative office, branch or subsidiary of their home firm. Regula-tion of establishment takes a variety of forms. Establishment may of course be barred or perhaps limited in some way, say to a representative office or to a single branch. Paradoxically, if some supply is allowed, establishment may be preferred over cross-border supply – there may be no right to non-establishment. Establishment may thus be demanded, though a variation is to insist on natural presence. For example, consul-tants may be limited to natural persons who must satisfy minimum resi-dency periods. The firm may not be recognised, or it may not be allowed to use its home country name despite the considerable cachet the name carries. Such obligations inhibit the foreigner's capacity to compete with locals, but they are said to be necessary to ensuring responsibility to local consumers, benefits to the domestic economy and the capacity of the host state to supervise. The form of establishment may also be regulated. We noted above that, unlike the policy in other service sectors, foreign lawyers may not be permitted to form joint ventures with locals or employ them. Similarly, the acquisition of local firms might be blocked.

Regulation commonly limits the scope of activities of foreign lawyers; in other words, it circumscribes the services sub-sectors in which they may operate. As noted above, certain areas, especially court work, may be completely off limits. Advisory work may be confined to advice on home country law and perhaps to international law, though even then it may be restricted to public rather than private international law. Here again, in the highly refined nuances of these regulatory nets, we see the national authorities trying to limit exposure to foreign influences to those situations in which their expertise is essential. Thus too, the foreign lawyers may be limited to working for foreign clients; they may be allowed to work for local clients offshore only; or they may be permitted to provide documentary and representational assistance in international fora so long as the fora are convened outside the host state.

At the same time, the regulation may seek to make the foreign lawyers accountable to local constituencies. In order to operate, foreign legal consultants may also have to meet certain requirements for registration, such as qualifications and length of experience in the home country or other law. Host country rules of professional conduct may be applied. We should remember that the local profession often has highly developed, if variable, ethical standards. Such rules can be a means to sheet home responsibilities, not simply to the lawyer's clients, but to the locality as it is constructed in various ways, such as the profession, public institutions, customs and traditions and maybe some concept of the 'law' itself. These kinds of rules may also impose financial responsibilities, including requirements to take out insurance locally or contribute to a guarantee fund.

Admission to the profession

These controls on activities may deal with foreign lawyers specifically, but they work in the shadow of the general controls on those who may provide legal services. National (or in some cases, sub-national) regulation is likely to give those admitted to the legal profession proper a monopoly over certain core types of work to the exclusion of the claims of various professional competitors. Within the OECD, a recent survey identified these controls as now representing the main barrier to trade in legal services.[15] Entry to the profession may be restricted, if not by official or unofficial quotas, then by the requirement for recognised education and training qualifications. Furthermore, the ways in which the profession organizes and operates may be closely regulated. Such regulation may include restrictions on business structure, restrictions on association with non-lawyers (such as multidisciplinary practices), restrictions on size, and restrictions on the number and location of offices which may be maintained throughout a jurisdiction.

As chapter four has indicated, the reasons for these restrictive practices go well beyond a concern with foreign competition. But they may well prove to present an extra burden for foreigners to meet, even though they are not openly or facially discriminatory in the way that nationality requirements tend to be. For example, if the foreigners' home country qualifications are not recognised, they must then face the hurdle of passing local professional examinations and possibly serving local apprenticeships too. If the mere failure to recognise the foreign qualifications does not constitute a denial of national treatment, then the way the local examination is styled might do so. For instance, conduct of an oral examination, especially in a different language, might frustrate the legitimate expectations of the foreign applicant. Furthermore, it may be argued that some controls, even if they do not treat foreigners less favourably, impede market access. Thus, quotas which were placed on admission would act as quantitative limitations, affecting access by foreigners as well as locals.

IMPACT OF THE GATS

In such a field, when global flows are met by an array of behind the border regulations, the assistance of a mediating device might prove attractive to some 'traders' in legal services. In chapter four, we acknowledged the significance of the GATS submission of services regulation to the norms of trade liberalisation. Trade in legal services was to be a prominent agenda item during the Uruguay Round. The GATS is notable for rejecting the argument that legal services are so closely tied to the exercise of government functions that they should be excluded from trade talk altogether, an argument that also failed at the time of the formation of the Treaty of Rome, though it was still to restrain the course of actual liberalisation (see below).[16] Once embraced, the GATS carried serious implications for legal services regulation because, as we know, it encompassed all modes important to effective supply, including commercial and natural presence in the territory of another country.

The GATS norms have major implications for legal services regulation too. We should first note the implications of the general obligation to provide MFN (article II). Another feature of the national regulation of foreign services has been an insistence on material reciprocity. Where access is made available to the nationals of other countries, it is on condition that the host country's nationals are granted access to the home country market in return. We shall see from the country studies below that such a condition has been common. The MFN obligation militates against these arrangements.

Of course, the national treatment norm puts pressure on regulations that discriminate in favour of local lawyers (article XVII). At this point, it is useful to reiterate that national treatment is not necessarily satisfied by according foreigners formally identical treatment; the test is said to be the effect on their opportunities to compete with locals. What national measures therefore will come to be seen as placing foreigner lawyers at a competitive disadvantage? National measures that single out foreigners, like controls on entry to the jurisdiction or nationality and citizenship requirements for admission to practice, are clearly within the purview of the norm. But, as we began to identify above, the interrogation soon extends to measures – such as a requirement of a local presence or a local educational qualification – that apply both to foreigners and locals. Measures which on their face do not discriminate may impose additional burdens on foreigners.

We have observed that the national treatment norm will not be breached if entry into a services market is restricted, or for that matter prohibited, for locals and foreigners alike. But we know that the GATS goes on to encourage members to negotiate over commitments to 'market access'. If market access is to be effective, countries may be pressed to lift non-discriminatory regulations and liberalise competition across the board. Support for this message was derived from the agreement's 'proscription' of certain measures (article XVI:2). It provides that, in the sectors where market access commitments are made, there are certain measures which a member shall not maintain, unless they are specified in the member's schedule.

The list covers limitations on the participation of foreign investment in a services sector. However it also includes measures that restrict (or require) specific types of legal entity or joint venture through which a service supplier may supply a service. In many countries, these types of measure are employed to regulate the structure of the local profession overall; good non-trade reasons are given for doing so. For example, members of the profession may be required to practise as individuals or in partnership. They may not practise in the guise of a corporation. This is said to promote personal accountability, both to fellow practitioners and to the clients of the service. Of course, the two kinds of control interact. Corporatisation makes it easier for non-practitioners, such as people abroad, to own and control legal services. Article XVI:2 further proscribes limitations on the number of service suppliers, transactions, operations, output or employees. Again, this proscription is applicable to legal services. We could ask here whether it extended not just to official quota systems but to local arrangements which limited the number of students in law courses or fixed a failure rate for examinations.

We should note that the agreement does provide exceptions for some non-conforming measures (article XIV). These exceptions allow for measures necessary, for example, to protect public morals or to maintain public order, to secure compliance with laws, to prevent fraudulent or deceptive practices, to protect privacy of individuals or to ensure collection of service taxes. Some of these exceptions could be invoked to justify specific regulatory measures within the legal services sector. The agreement does not however provide scope for a general cultural clause to be invoked in defence of local regulation.

The strongest antidote to speculation about the reach of the norms is the listings approach of the GATS. We know that the members were allowed to decide the extent to which they exposed their measures to the norms of the agreement. At the end of the Uruguay Round, the schedules of commitments to legal services liberalisation were restrained, reflecting the reservations about access to this sensitive sector which continue to be held in many countries. One strategy was to leave the sector out of their offer entirely; many of the newly industrialised and developing countries adopted this position. This is not to say that these countries necessarily exclude foreign lawyers entirely. But they were concerned that entry into the multilateral negotiations and the making of binding commitments under the GATS would limit their freedom to impose and adjust regulations. The decision not to inscribe the sector also withholds information about the nature of these countries' regulations. Another strategy was to limit the sub-sector in which commitments would be made, say, to advice on home country and public international law; a related strategy was to confine the commitments to a particular mode of supply. Where commitments were made and a sub-sector and/or mode of supply was exposed to the norms, a further strategy of course was to enter specific limitations explicitly on national treatment and market access.

In the Uruguay Round, some forty-five countries (including twelve from the European Communities) made commitments in legal services.[17] Nearly all these countries made commitments in the home country and international law sub-sectors, though half of them confined them to advisory services, excluding representational work. About half the countries which made commitments made them in relation to host country law, here including representational work as well as advisory work. In these cases, where sub-sectors were exposed, the most common limitation on national treatment was a residency requirement. The most common limitation on market access was a restriction on the style of legal entity which the legal service supplier could assume, the limitation requiring supply to be by a natural person or in some cases a partnership. Furthermore, six countries did not commit to cross-border supply, six did not commit to commercial presence, and the majority of the commitments to supply by a natural presence were 'unbound'.[18]

Over half the countries scheduled domestic regulatory measures. Most of these measures related to licensing and qualification requirements. However, as the WTO's background note points out, scheduling such domestic regulatory measures was not strictly necessary. 'Both home country law qualification requirements and home/third country law qualification requirements are domestic regulatory measures according to the GATS and therefore not subject to scheduling under articles XVI and XVII.'[19] They are nonetheless subject to the other disciplines of the GATS and notably to article XIV.

Significantly, the advanced industrial countries, and especially those in the Triad (Japan, the European Union and the United States), were prepared to submit legal services to the negotiations. They resolved not to enter MFN derogations which would insist on material reciprocity from individual countries. Nonetheless, the norms of national treatment and market access created quandaries for these countries as well as others. Because their general regulatory policies for entry of natural persons and direct foreign investment are implicated, such countries notified 'horizontal limitations' in their schedules, that is restrictions which apply across the board to those modes of supply. Where sub-sectors were exposed, specific limitations were also listed. We will now look at the positions which these major economic powers, the Triad countries, took, before returning to the general terms of the agreement.

COUNTRY PRACTICES

Japan

We commence with the situation of Japan which is an interesting one because the country combines a major role in international trade with strong local cultural traditions. Before a new statute was introduced in 1987, Japan effectively barred foreign lawyers from local practice. Such a characterisation is however subject to the kinds of qualifications we made above, for instance in Japan's case that non-lawyers were free to compete with lawyers for certain kinds of work. The lawyer's monopoly was not tight.

Still, the 1987 law was significant for institutionalising and perhaps liberalising the access of foreign lawyers to the Japanese market. The law allowed foreigners to apply for admission to the local profession, provided they met the same requirements as the local applicants. Failing admission to the profession, they could provide legal advice in certain restricted areas if they obtained registration as a foreign consultant.

If we speculate on the reasons for this change in attitude to foreigners, we might expect that economic factors played a part. Japanese corporations needed access to expertise on foreign law if they were to expand abroad. So too, foreign corporations trying to penetrate Japanese markets needed representatives with knowledge of often very subtle public and private regulatory practices. More directly, the United States made access a trade issue when its Trade Representative pressed Japan for concessions in the early 1980s. Lack of access for United States lawyers had been the subject of a United States Trade Act section 301 watch listing. By 1985, market access was on the Uruguay Round agenda and the Japanese Government seemed prepared to override the concerns of the Japanese Federation of Bar Associations (JFBA).[20]

However, the 1987 law did not relieve many of the barriers to practice for foreigners. Admission to the profession, with the right to practise as a *bengoshi*, was not a realistic proposition for most foreigners. While it was no longer necessary to be a Japanese citizen to be admitted, the need to pass the national examinations in Japanese law was an effective barrier. One might ask whether this requirement discriminated against foreigners. It has been extraordinarily difficult for Japanese students to pass the examination and the numbers entering the profession have been strictly controlled. Still the law provided no recognition for foreign degrees or special tests for foreigner applicants.

The most realistic option was registration as a consultant. But the activities of foreign consultants were limited to advice on home country and public international law; bans included advice on host or third country law and court or commercial arbitration work in Japan. The consultants were not to employ or partner *bengoshi*, though *bengoshi* could be engaged on a one-off transactional basis. To be eligible for registration, the consultants would need to show five years experience in home country law. In addition, they would have to maintain both a commercial presence and a natural presence, including residence for 180 days per year. They would have to operate primarily in their individual rather than their firm's name. The impact of some of these restrictions was obvious, while others were to be felt indirectly. For example, the measures limited flexibility to rotate staff. They added to operating costs by requiring a separate office to be maintained in locations like Tokyo. The policy also made access conditional on material reciprocity, which only some United States and Australian states, together with the United Kingdom, were regarded as providing.

One can speculate about the reasons for this policy. One possibility is economic protection for the domestic profession and especially for those practising in international law, at least until such time as they had developed the necessary expertise themselves. But cultural considerations are evident too, and the authorities have drawn a contrast between a Japanese style of consensus seeking and alternative dispute resolution and an American tendency to litigiousness and lawyer dependence.

Foreign lawyers found access difficult (registrations reached into the low hundreds) and, in addition to further bilateral approaches, Japan's legal services market was targeted in the Uruguay Round negotiations. The JFBA resisted relaxation of controls but the Government set up a study commission on the issue of foreign lawyers in preparation for making a commitment. Serious negotiations took place at a meeting in Evian and, despite scepticism in certain quarters, the United States Ambassador fashioned a deal at the last gasp of the Round.[21] In keeping with the multilateral process, the Japanese Government did not pursue a reciprocity requirement. But, within the negotiations, its willingness to commit was conditioned by the offers which the European Union and United States representatives could themselves make (see below). Here we see an illustration of the schizophrenic nature of the GATS.

Japan's schedule of commitments limited the sector to 'consultancy on law of the jurisdiction where the service supplier is a qualified lawyer'.[22] Its sectoral limitations on national treatment and market access listed requirements of supply by a natural person and commercial presence, while horizontal limitations confined a stay by natural persons to five years. Work preparing for juridical procedures in courts and other government agencies was still barred and other restrictions applied. Representation in commercial arbitration was permissible, provided that the applicable law was the law which the service supplier was qualified to practise in Japan. However, a further study commission was to put the issue of arbitration on hold. The practice of international law was permitted, again with a proviso that it was the law in force in the jurisdiction where the supplier was qualified. But only Japanese lawyers were to be free to advise on host country law or third country law. Providing some access to foreigners was making the national regulation more complex.

By way of implementation, a new law was introduced in 1994, which allowed a limited form of association between foreign and local lawyers – a joint enterprise in which fees could be shared. The joint firm would be permitted to act under Japanese law but only if the case involved other countries' laws as well and only if the case was not confined to Japanese nationals. But the Japanese lawyers would need to maintain independence and the enterprise would have to be a contractual venture rather than an integrated entity. The law conceded that two years of the foreign lawyer's necessary experience could now be in Japan.

In the wake of the liberalisation, a few more foreign law offices were opened and two joint enterprises were established. However, by February

1995, the *Japan Law Journal* was headlining: 'Exodus of foreign lawyers has begun, Japanese legal market not lucrative'. Instead, a government committee on regulatory liberalisation was reported to be considering allowing more local candidates to pass the bar examination; there were signs that some Japanese law firms were remodelling along the lines of large Anglo-American firms.

The European Union

The European Union provides another interesting test of the resilience of local diversity. It is of course a big market within the world economy and increasingly it responds to 'outsiders' as a single economic and political unit. Yet, as it is constituted itself by a trade agreement, it is internally the most developed source of jurisprudence on free trade, for instance in the supply of services.

The liberalisation of market access internally would in theory put the Union in a good position to negotiate for commitments from other parts of the world. But of course the degree of unity in internal policy should never be exaggerated. Furthermore, liberalisation within the Union might be coupled with a defensive attitude externally, for example in encouraging combinations of lawyers across Europe so that they could match the strength of competitors from the United States. However, this is not the place to attempt a history of the implementation of the treaty's principles in the legal services sector.[23] Briefly, it should be noted that a 1977 Directive addressed the issue of freedom of movement for those providing services on a temporary or travelling basis. In terms of commercial presence, it allowed the host state to regulate the scope of the foreigner's activities so as to reserve certain areas including advice on host country law; yet litigation work was to be allowed if performed in conjunction with a local practitioner.

A realistic right of establishment was seen to depend on admission to the local bar. Some basic discriminations such as citizenship or single-office requirements were soon disallowed, but the really significant step was the 1988 Directive on Mutual Recognition of Diplomas. The Directive required host countries to take account of home country qualifications. However, if the qualifications in the two countries substantially diverged in length or content, they were permitted to impose one of three requirements. The requirements were a period of professional experience in the home country, an adaptation period (supervised practice in the host country together with assessment) or a test of aptitude on host country law. In this way, the reference point continued to be the extent of local knowledge.

The experience with this Directive reveals the existence of reservations within Europe about free access to the local legal profession, even for the nationals of other member states. Notably, France enacted a new law in 1990 to comply with the 1988 Directive. It collapses the post-1972 category of *conseil juridique*, which had provided an opening for foreign lawyers, so that all must apply to be advocates. Lawyers from other member states were given the option of sitting a special examination to gain admission. However France was accused of manipulating this option by failing to draft a written examination. Also, the examination was conducted in French, which favoured applicants from countries such as Belgium and Luxembourg.[24]

At the same time, the law raised the hurdles for non-Union lawyers. They would now need to show a French or equivalent Union qualification as well as sitting the special examination, and this avenue was only open to nationals from countries which reciprocated materially. All non-French lawyers would have to adopt the French forms for professional association, meaning no branch offices, but association with French lawyers was permitted.

When negotiations in the Uruguay Round reached the stage of sectoral commitments, the European Union felt inhibited by these kinds of national reservations, despite its vigorous pursuit of Japan. It notified general horizontal limitations on commercial presence, particularly the establishment of branches, and, for some member states, on foreign investment in local enterprises. The presence of natural persons was 'unbound', countries retaining the freedom to introduce measures inconsistent with national treatment and market access, except for commitments to entry and temporary stay by certain limited categories of service suppliers. In its sector-specific commitments, the Union listed the sector as 'Legal advice, home country law and public international law (excluding EC law)'. In respect of cross-border supply, it notified national treatment limitations by France, Portugal and Denmark and market access limitations by France and Portugal; in respect of commercial presence, national treatment limitations by Denmark and market access limitations by Germany and France. The presence of natural persons was generally unbound, with Greece, Luxembourg, France and Denmark entering additional specific limitations.[25] Grondine suggests that the Union did not back the United States requests at Evian that Japan lift partnership and employment bans.[26] The smaller European bar associations, away perhaps from the centres of international business lawyering such as London, were themselves apprehensive about being swamped by more resourceful foreign firms.

We should note developments since the completion of the Uruguay Round. A further EC directive on establishment has long been in the process of negotiation, presenting the possibility that local qualifications requirements would be lifted altogether, along with restrictions on associations with local lawyers or the establishment of branch offices, so that truly multi-state firms would be a realistic proposition. A directive on lawyers' establishment has now been approved with implementation scheduled for the end of 1999.[27] Under this directive, lawyers will be able to practise host country law in another member state by showing that they are already registered to practise in one Union country. After three years practice in the host country, they will be able to register as members of the local profession. But the free trade imperatives which are operating within the Union produce no requirement for such benefits to be extended to non-Union lawyers. We should note too that the GATS accepts the existence of regional economic integration agreements which are designed to facilitate trade between their parties (article V). But to what extent should such agreements give preferential treatment to members or be generally non-discriminatory? As we saw in chapter four, the GATS states that such agreements shall not raise the overall level of barriers to outsiders compared to the level applicable prior to the agreement.

The United States

In the United States, regulation of legal services has been traditionally a sub-national, state-by-state concern. We noted that the GATS requires members to make reasonable efforts to address sub-national as well as national measures. Still, such a political division limits the capacity of the Federal Government to negotiate agreements with other countries, even if it favours liberalisation of markets. Among the American states, it was New York which took the initiative in 1974. Foreigners from 'common law' countries were permitted to sit the bar examination but no credit was given for home qualifications. Civil lawyers faced additional hurdles. However, provision was also made for foreign legal consultants. New York's groundbreaking rules excluded representation in court and certain other work, but allowed consultations on home country law, international law and third country law, and even on host country law after advice was taken from a licensed local attorney. Some other states (around eighteen, including California and Washington DC) have also established the consultant category, though not necessarily providing the same scope of activities. To obtain a licence, recent experience in home country law may be necessary; also residency and an in-state office. New York permits association or partnership with local lawyers but other states may not; on the other hand they may allow employment of local lawyers. To further integration, the American Bar Association has since proposed a set of model rules for licensing foreign consultants.[28] It is not hard to see why the states we have mentioned have liberalised. However, we would expect the many more parochial states to act cautiously.

According to Stewart, the United States Government was prepared to lay down legal services like a sacrificial lamb on the Uruguay Round negotiating table.[29] Access to legal services could serve as a trade-off for offers of access to other more important sectors abroad. Certainly, its own initial claims looked broad.[30] Its schedule was to make commitments, both in respect of practice as or through a qualified United States lawyer, and in respect of consultancy on law of the jurisdiction where the service supplier is qualified as a lawyer. But the nub of its commitments was an offer to bind the rules of the states which have made provision for foreign access. This position meant that, for many states, commitments to market access, through either commercial presence or presence of natural persons, were to be unbound.[31] Interestingly, the approach of the United States to other countries was restrained by its own domestic reservations.

Other countries

Many other countries were to be even more cautious in their commitments. The diversity of responses could only be done justice in a country-by-country survey, and it is really not possible for this study to work its way through all of the commitments. Nevertheless, it is worth noting that few of the ASEAN countries listed the sector. In keeping with the analysis above, the reasons for this position will vary, and, in some developing countries, market access may even give rise to fears of 'neo-colonisation'. Mexico's position of scepticism on the question of trade in legal services within NAFTA is also revealing here. To mention one additional case, the People's Republic of China, which is seeking entry to the WTO, provided its first authorisation of foreign firms in 1992, limiting them to home country, third country and international law.[32] Licensing of foreign firms was initially restricted. Approvals have been needed from city authorities as well as two national departments. The policy has allowed for branches, but this presence is limited to one location. Chinese lawyers cannot be employed. At the same time, China's own legal profession has been engaged in a major but unsure process of expansion and detachment from the state. Eligibility for admission has been extended to nationals of Hong Kong, Taiwan and Macau.

FURTHER DEVELOPMENTS

Modes of supply

What pattern is the liberalisation and regulation of international legal services likely to take in the future? The book is meant mainly to serve as an appraisal of the Uruguay Round agreements, but we should begin to look ahead to the next round, which is beginning to take shape. We shall do so in terms of the various modes of supply, commencing with cross-border supply.

The case of legal services represents the dilemma which national governments generally face when they are asked to guarantee both the freedom and the security of trans-border data flows. Freedom of access is coupled with an expectation that the confidentiality of the lawyer's communications with clients will be preserved. However, freedom of flows and data security are also seen as affecting government capacity to exercise regulatory oversight, for example in relation to tax avoidance practices and criminal activities such as money laundering. The two legalities may be difficult to reconcile. The Clinton Administration's proposal for the government to hold an encryption key in escrow highlights this quandary at the national level. These tensions are to be found within the GATS too. In chapter four, we have seen how the GATS allows for non-conforming measures which further certain regulatory objectives such as the prevention of fraud. Yet, in its provisions for basic telecommunications and financial services, it conveys expectations that transfers of information will be both free and secure.

In the legal sector, as in most others, freedom of movement of natural persons remains a delicate issue. Chapter four noted that the GATS gave this particular mode of supply attention across the board by providing a specific Annex on Movement of Natural Persons Supplying Services under the Agreement. Part of its intention was to hive off issues of entry and temporary stay from the broader and more sensitive issues of access to employment markets and citizenship, residence and employment on a permanent basis. The developed countries had a particular interest in assuring the passage of business visitors and intra-corporate transferees. We noted in chapter four that other countries were not so ready to accept this demarcation but, in any case, the case of professionals proved hard for a range of countries. The horizontal limitations on entry were joined by sector-specific limitations. There is opposition within the developed countries to granting more foreign professionals entry and the right to practise. A working party sought to extend the negotiations on the movement of natural persons beyond the Round. But they yielded few further commitments.

As we have noted, the GATS has become one of the main vehicles for liberalisation of investment regulation, particularly since it defined commercial presence in such an expansive way. Yet the outcome in the legal sectors, as much as in other service sectors, was that countries continued to place limitations on foreign investment. Most likely, liberalisation would lead to further mergers and acquisitions in the legal sector. Whelan and McBarnet found that the liberalisation of the European market was intensifying such activity.[33] Now we are seeing moves from the much more internationally organized accounting firms to take over legal firms.

In the legal sector, firms generally need to be owned and controlled by local professionals to be recognised as professional firms. As well as overt foreign investment controls, the restrictions on business structure present an obstacle to this kind of transnational legal practice. One commentator argues that 'the very strict rules intended to maintain the necessary independence of lawyers and ensure that the practice of law remained a liberal profession ... have also prevented the establishment of large multi-speciality law firms, especially in the field of corporate law, despite a clearly growing demand from businesses'.[34] Consequently, relaxation of the restrictions on choice of business structure, for example to allow multidisciplinary partnerships or incorporation and shareholding, would have significant implications.

Multidisciplinary partnerships would obviate the need for foreigners to qualify as lawyers if they wished to associate with locals. This would provide openings for other professionals such as accountants as well as professionals who were lawyers at home. Multidisciplinary practices would be geared much more to specific services markets than organized along professional lines, leading to a blurring of the boundaries between law and business. As well, the Chairperson of the GATS Working Party on Professional Services has observed that mutual recognition of firms would disconnect the practice of the professional activity from the ownership of the capital, allowing for a freer flow of capital among the professional community.[35] But it would also have the potential to let in investors from outside the sector, as it has done in the health services sector, for example.

As we shall learn from chapter eight, further liberalisation of investment is a spur to the formation of an international competition policy. Reichman supposed that small and medium-sized firms might realise a common interest cross-nationally in the right sort of competition policy disciplines.[36] However it has to be said that competition policy is likely to be viewed with ambivalence in sectors such as legal services. Its main impact might well be to prise open the controls which the local profession continues to apply for a variety of reasons to competitive practices. In any case, despite their implications for the nature of legal services, few mergers would be likely to achieve the high thresholds of market power which must be met before the scrutiny of conventional competition laws is attracted. It would depend in part on how markets were defined and whether the accumulation went the way of accountancy, where internationally there is now a small number of very big firms. If firms were able to achieve dominance in one market, or control essential services, competition law might be on the watch for attempts to leverage that power and force patronage of related services. It seems one argument against access for the accountancy firms is that they might tie their in-house legal services in with the supply of their accountancy services.[37]

Professional standards

If access is to reach to the full range of professional activities, then national standards regarding professional qualifications, training and experience are implicated. The initial thrust might be to seek the removal of such requirements for entry into the sector altogether. But there seems at present to be an acceptance that some sort of standards will remain. Mediation of national, sub-national and regional regulations would of course have the benefit of overcoming the cost of compliance with multiple and differential requirements. However there is a substantive issue here too, very much connected with the competition between models of legal practice. What standards of preparation and conduct should prevail? For example, the United States and the European Union have been proceeding informally to bring their requirements into line. They find much in common, but a contrast has been made between the Union's equal stress on the lawyer's obligations to the client, the courts, the legal profession, and the general public and the United States attitude, drawn from its common law tradition, which gives greater prominence to the lawyer's obligations to the client. The issue of standards for lawyers is also connected to the broader question of codes of conduct for their international clients, such as the multinational enterprises and financial markets.

A focal point might be the responsibilities which international lawyers owe to the governments and societies which are hosting their clients. Sensitivity might be enhanced by making some comparative study a requisite for mutual recognition of qualifications as well as the study of international law. But ultimately the process of standardisation may need to address the question of the appropriate standards for professional conduct. These standards would include the kind of conduct which was to be shown to members of the local host profession. However their concerns might also range wider. To offer one example from an Australian perspective, the International Commission of Jurists became interested in the role which one legal firm had played in Papua New Guinea. It was alleged that the firm had drafted legislation for transmission directly to the national parliament. The legislation aimed to outlaw the taking of legal action against the firm's client, an Australian multinational company, for pollution of farm and village lands.[38]

Perhaps then, codes of conduct will become bound up with the question of recognition of qualifications. Chapter four indicated that GATS article VI on domestic regulation pays special attention to measures relating to qualification requirements and procedures, technical standards and licensing requirements. It acknowledges these national measures, while at the same time subjecting them to certain disciplines. Article VII went on to enable members to recognise the education or experience obtained, requirements met, or licences or certifications granted in another country. Recognition could be based on agreements or arrangements with other countries, and third party countries were to have an opportunity to negotiate accession or to negotiate comparable ones. Where appropriate, recognition was to be based on multilateral criteria and members were to work in cooperation with relevant inter-governmental and non-governmental organizations on common international standards for the recognition *and* practice of relevant services, trades and professions (article VII:5).

At Marrakesh, the Decision on Professional Services set in train a Working Party which was assigned the accountancy sector as its first priority. In May 1997, the Council for Trade in Services produced Guidelines for Recognition of Qualifications in the Accountancy Sector.[39] Many of the Guidelines were preoccupied with the procedural standards (such as transparency) which should apply to the making of agreements between members to provide recognition. But, at the same time, they allowed for members to safeguard local integrity. For example, they conceded the place for additional requirements ('compensatory measures') such as knowledge of local law, practice, standards and regulations. Thus, the value of local specificity was given some support.

The Guidelines also acknowledged requirements, apart from qualifications, such as establishment or residency requirements, or compliance with the host country's ethics (for instance of independence and incompatibility). But the Guidelines did not seek to take on the question of the content of such standards at all, in the sense of formulating common standards at the international level. Elsewhere, the Chairperson of the GATS Working Party has sounded a note of caution: 'Such an approach would obviously bring in a very high level of liberalisation but could likewise present a risk to the protection of the public interest. In the absence of any proper harmonisation of laws and regulations in a number of areas, this approach will have to be used with the greatest prudence.'[40] In other words, without an attempt at harmonisation, mutual recognition might lead to a lowering of standards. The Chairperson added that this was no reason, however, to drop the idea at the outset.

In December 1998, the Council for Trade in Services produced a set of disciplines on domestic regulation in the accounting sector.[41] The disciplines are applicable to the measures of members who have scheduled specific commitments for accounting under the GATS. In addition, all members have agreed to take no new measures which would be inconsistent with the disciplines. At the same time, it should be noted that the disciplines do not apply to measures which are the subject of scheduling by virtue of articles XVI and XVII of the GATS. These measures are to be addressed through the negotiation of specific commitments.

The disciplines deal with licensing and qualification requirements and procedures. Their general thrust is to impel members to choose those measures which are no more trade restrictive than necessary to fulfil a legitimate regulatory objective. The disciplines recognise as legitimate objectives (inter alia) the protection of consumers, the quality of service, professional competence and the integrity of the profession. Of the more pointed of their demands, the first is for transparency. Licensing requirements are to be pre-established, publicly available and objective. More substantially, the member countries are urged to consider measures less restrictive than a residency requirement. Requirements relating to qualifications should take account of qualifications acquired in the home territory on the basis of equivalence in education, expertise and/or examination requirements. Procedures for qualification should be timely, with examinations held regularly. The disciplines make no mention however of language requirements. Generally speaking, they are very tentative. With their release, the Working Party was to move on to develop disciplines for professional services generally.

CONCLUSIONS

The case of cross-national legal services and the reception given to foreign lawyers provides a useful indication of the complexion of globalization. This chapter has acknowledged the spread of a certain contemporary kind of global lawyer. This is identified most strongly in the studies with a competitive Anglo-American style based on transactions and disputes. Globalization of this style proceeds somewhat under its own steam and it has not been my intention to play down its significance. In giving shape to a transnational field of private business justice, its impact may be profound. However a range of economic, political and cultural differences suggests why, at the same time, it encounters local resistance. Legal practice remains subject to restrictions and requirements. In part, they represent the evident desire of nation states to maintain their own different laws and the jurisdiction to apply them; in other words, not only lawyers make law. But the free flow of these global lawyers is also hampered by factors particular to the supply of legal services themselves. There are limits to the tradeability of legal services. For many kinds of legal services, local presence, proximity and familiarity still provide advantage. Lawyers must work closely, not only with business clients, but with state agencies, courts, civic organizations and local communities, including local professional legal groups. Global legal services must negotiate the national regulations which reinforce those advantages and indeed make it difficult to acquire them.

A brief examination of regulatory arrangements, even in the countries most generally disposed towards open trade and free markets, shows how sensitive this sector remains. Strong concerns are held about direct competition from legal businesses in the other northern countries, as well as the entry of individual lawyers from around the world into their domains of professional practice proper. The concerns extend beyond economic protection into a host of cultural and social reservations about the accessibility of foreign lawyers and legal services.

Where unilateral and bilateral arrangements for transmissibility have foundered, the GATS has become a crucial device to mediate the encounters of global services with local policies and practices. These local policies and practices will increasingly be shaped by their relationship to the global pressures for open trade and free markets. The GATS circumference is wide enough to promote all modes of supply of legal services and begin to scrutinise the full range of relevant government measures. Included here are regulations which do not directly discriminate against foreign services, but which make prescriptions regarding the structure, competence and conduct of the local profession for non-trade reasons also.

However, the GATS listings approach was to provide the opportunity for countries to hold the line, if they saw fit, against global supply. The evidence indicates that many did so. The concessions were minor. Nevertheless, we can expect that 'horizontal' economic connections will continue to promote the global flows of legal services, making changes, as it were, over the heads of the national regulators. It looks as if multidisciplinary practices will be a spearhead. Successive rounds of GATS negotiations, commencing with the 'Millennium Round', are likely also to advance these inroads. In these circumstances, the need to internationalise professional standards is likely to grow. The GATS contains some recognition of this need, but it remains to be seen whether it will provide an impetus for the kind of regulation which can fill the void created by the challenge to national regulation.

PART III

INTELLECTUAL PROPERTY

THE AGREEMENT ON TRADE-RELATED INTELLECTUAL PROPERTY RIGHTS

Like chapter four, chapter six has a modest aim of informing the reader. After recounting briefly how the Uruguay Round brought them into existence, it lays out the provisions of the TRIPs agreement for consideration within the context of the book. The chapter identifies how the re-regulatory requirements of intellectual property protection have become an essential component of the WTO's interface. Thus, the regulatory reform agenda is not confined to the deregulation of those national legalities which are identified as barriers to liberalisation. It can involve the enactment and enforcement of a set of proactive international standards.

Working through the agreement, we note how the principles of non-discrimination require members to give foreigners no less favourable treatment in their protection of intellectual property. In this respect, the agreement is not much of an advance on existing conventions. In making standards of protection multilateral rather than bilateral obligations, the MFN obligation has the most significance. However, the real potency of TRIPs lies in its requirement that members guarantee high levels of substantive protection to foreigners. Taking each of the agreement's categories of protection in turn, chapter six indicates the nature of the subject matter which they make amenable to protection as intellectual property. It identifies the uses which the property rights control. We take most interest in the categories of copyright and patents, as they are central to the case studies pursued in chapters seven and eight. Chapter six also acknowledges the detailed prescriptions which TRIPs makes in an attempt to overcome differing national administrative and judicial approaches to the enforcement of protections.

This analysis of the agreement's substantive provisions begins to reveal how far reaching is its impact on different legalities. The agreement specifies the nature of legal protection where products are shipped across national borders and they encounter unsympathetic legalities of copying and borrowing; it also lends support where foreigners seek to manage production processes inside the territories of member countries. But the agreement is not comprehensive. It draws on the rules and resources of the established intellectual property conventions which are administered by the World Intellectual Property Organization (WIPO). At the same time, it leaves spaces to be filled, first by various government and private legalities within the member countries, subsequently perhaps by other international agreements. Again, the generality of the norms leaves room for divergence. However the spaces also result from the agreement's hesitation in covering certain new types of subject matter and use rights. The agreement also makes concessions to alternative legalities by explicitly allowing in the text for members to take exceptions and to apply limitations.

The chapter identifies tendencies in TRIPs to promote the kind of regulation that counterbalances the market power which it has helped to bestow on global suppliers. The circumstances in which the agreement will permit non-voluntary licensing are considered. We identify the limited extent to which the agreement supports competition policy's approach to disciplining the abuses of intellectual property power. Again, one aim is to set the scene for the case studies which follow.

THE URUGUAY ROUND

The course of events

Like the GATS, the TRIPs agreement is an integral part of the Agreement establishing the WTO, comprising Annexe 1C to that Agreement. As one of the multilateral trade agreements, it is binding on all members and hence also a condition of membership for countries which have not yet joined the WTO. Such a condition is a significant one for countries seeking to join the WTO such as the People's Republic of China. Compliance with its provisions also figures as a substantial obligation for many of the initial members of the WTO. If it is faithfully applied by the members, the TRIPs agreement will make a major contribution to the international rules and resources available for the protection of intellectual property. The agreement will have broader symbolic significance as well. It is by far the most emphatic substantiation of the security dimension of the concept of secure access, exemplifying the fact that the WTO interface involves re-regulatory as well as deregulatory requirements. So far as it requires members to provide a high level of substantive protection for intellectual property, it is standardising regulation in this field right across the world.

For most of its life, the GATT's interest in intellectual property was marginal. It did recognise that local procedures for intellectual property protection could act in a discriminatory way. The GATT agreement afforded special permission for measures necessary to secure compliance with laws or regulations relating to the protection of patents, trademarks and copyrights. The United States has twice run into trouble with the GATT norms because it offered domestic holders of patents more accessible procedures for enforcement than foreign holders. In the first of these disputes, the procedures were saved by the exception.[1] In the second dispute, however, the procedure was held to be in violation.[2]

Lack of intellectual property protection on the other hand did not begin to surface as a trade issue until the round preceding the Uruguay Round, the Tokyo Round. During this Round, the United States flagged trade in trademarked counterfeit goods as an issue of concern. Here we see the origins of the idea that intellectual property protection was pro-trade, rather than a necessary evil which was to be tolerated in some circumstances because it promised its own benefits. Failure to provide adequate and effective protection for intellectual property was to be seen as a barrier to free trade or rather perhaps as a form of unfair trade. In other words, traders expressed their interest in obtaining security for their products and processes as much as freedom. Once they had obtained market access, they were not going to rely solely on economic advantages such as earlier innovation, superior quality or cheaper prices, when faced with competition from local secondary producers.

No agreement was reached in the Tokyo Round, but the United States continued to pursue the issue informally with the other members of the QUAD – the European Community, Japan and Canada. It also began to deploy in earnest the sanctions of its own trade legislation (such as sections 301 and 337) in order to obtain bilateral concessions towards greater intellectual property protection. This omnibus legislation sets out circumstances in which the Office of the United States Trade Representative was to take action to safeguard the intellectual property of United States producers. This action commenced with placing countries on a watch list for failure to provide adequate and effective protection. They could then be upgraded to the priority watch list. Countries that did not institute satisfactory protection faced trade sanctions. The main targets of the legislation were to be the newly industrialising countries such as Thailand, South Korea, Taiwan, India, Brazil, the Philippines and the People's Republic of China.[3] However, all sorts of countries were to be placed on notice, including countries with well developed intellectual property regimes such as the members of the European Union and Australia. The United States acted on any derogation from the rights which it felt were appropriate to intellectual property, and not just the situations in which basic protection was lacking.

To return to the Uruguay Round, it is worth recounting the main stages of the negotiations, for they cast light on the nature of the eventual agreement. Trade in counterfeit goods was included in the works program for the Round which was settled at the ministerial meeting in 1982.[4] However, at this stage, some of the developing countries, notably Brazil and India, questioned the competence of the GATT to regulate intellectual property protection. Consultations were ordered with the traditional international body, WIPO. But, at the same time, the United States intensified the pressure of its strategic bilateral initiatives. Its own multinational industries were lobbying hard for action, particularly on counterfeiting and the piracy of contemporary consumer goods such as fashions, sound and video recordings, films, and software. Protection for brand name pharmaceuticals and chemicals was to become another key objective. Counterfeiting and piracy were considered widespread practices in certain markets, with the losses in terms of sales of legitimate products calculated by United States industry to be running into many billions of dollars per year.[5]

Through 1985–87, again largely on the initiative of the United States, the intellectual property agenda broadened beyond trade in counterfeit goods to embrace the trade distortions resulting from the inadequate treatment and enforcement of intellectual property rights generally. The general economic and ideological origins of this convergence on an international intellectual property code have already been considered by others.[6] The references here are intended to serve the purpose of understanding the agreement itself. In terms of the specific events which led to its formation, we should note that the United States made representations to a special session of the contracting parties in 1985 and to the committee preparing the ground for the launching of the Uruguay Round of the negotiations. After initial disinterest, the European Community and Japan aligned with the United States on the basic issue, and some of the newly industrialising countries softened their opposition to the TRIPs agenda at this stage. As a result of the good offices of the Swiss and Colombian ambassadors to the GATT, a text on TRIPs was adopted for inclusion in the Punta del Este ministerial declaration of the terms of reference for the Uruguay Round.

The mandate given by the declaration to the negotiating group on trade-related aspects of intellectual property rights was expressed in composite terms. It recognised the interest in furthering protection, while conceding concerns about the restrictive uses of intellectual property:

> In order to reduce the distortions and impediments to international trade, and taking into account the need to promote effective and adequate

protection of intellectual property rights, and to ensure that measures and procedures to enforce intellectual property rights do not themselves become barriers to legitimate trade, the negotiations shall aim to clarify GATT provisions and elaborate as appropriate new rules and disciplines.[7]

Yet the agenda still seemed to be quite narrowly drawn: 'Negotiations shall aim to develop a multilateral framework of principles rules and disciplines dealing with international trade in counterfeit goods, taking into account work already undertaken in the GATT.' It also established a link with other international bodies: 'These negotiations shall be without prejudice to other complementary initiatives that may be taken in the World Intellectual Property Organization and elsewhere to deal with these matters.'

Little progress had been made on TRIPs by the time of the mid-term review of the Uruguay Round in 1988. Two opposing positions had emerged. One was supportive of a general agreement on intellectual property within the framework of GATT. The other, however, sought to confine any agreement strictly to the trade-related aspects of intellectual property, leaving the substance of intellectual property rights to be resolved in their traditional domain of the World Intellectual Property Organization. The mid-term review did nonetheless resolve to proceed with TRIPs and, over the period 1989–90, many countries made submissions on various aspects of the issue.[8] In 1990, the European Community was first to come forward with a draft of an agreement, with the United States, Japan, Switzerland, and then India on behalf of fourteen developing countries, following suit. A number of countries, including the Nordic countries, Canada and Mexico, are reported to have interceded at this stage to try to bridge the gaps between the positions. The chairman of the negotiating group produced a composite draft agreement, but several important matters remained outstanding.

Notably, there were differences among the developed countries in addition to the basic contrast with the position of the developing nations. These differences included patents for plant and animal varieties; the first-to-invent/first-to-file choice for patent recognition; the term of protection for patents; the scope of protection for computer software; the choice of copyright or related rights for performers, the producers of sound recordings and broadcasters; moral rights; the term of protection for sound recordings; the level of protection for industrial designs; the strength of rights over layout circuits; inclusion of coverage for undisclosed information; and the extent of provision for geographical indications.[9]

Other supra-national bodies were endeavouring to influence the intellectual climate during this period. The Science, Technology and Industry Directorate of the OECD had expressed a concern for the adequacy of intellectual property protection of the new technologies for some time.[10] Its Trade Directorate now also turned its attention to intellectual property and particularly the problem, as it saw it, of international piracy.[11] At the same time, two United Nations bodies, the United Nations Conference on Trade and Development (UNCTAD) and the United Nations Centre on Trans-National Corporations, continued to express reservations about further international protection.[12] Their concern appeared to lie with the restrictive business practices which might be built upon increased intellectual property power, particularly in terms of their impact upon the developing nations.

Of course, the international organization most directly affected by the Uruguay Round agenda was the World Intellectual Property Organization. As we noted in chapter three, WIPO is responsible for the administration of a number of long-standing intellectual property conventions, the main two being the Paris Convention for the Protection of Industrial Property and the Berne Convention for the Protection of Literary and Artistic Works. According to Australia's Attorney-General's Department, WIPO was rather taken by surprise by the TRIPs agenda.[13] It was presented with a novel situation in which some countries were seeking to shift the focus of initiatives in international protection to a trade body. Other countries responded by arguing that WIPO should remain the forum for determining any matters of substance regarding intellectual property protection. A potential for rivalry opened up. However, we know now, after the event, that a dynamic, almost dialectical relationship has developed between the WTO TRIPs agreement and WIPO's own conventions and treaties. At this stage, WIPO was to take up an offer of observer status within the Round.

Reaching agreement

Late 1990 saw the introduction of a comprehensive draft document by the negotiating group. Negotiations on the text took place in 1991. At this point, the developed nations seem to have buried their differences. Despite lingering reservations, many of the newly industrialising countries and the developing nations also withdrew their categorical opposition. Of course, it would require a thorough investigation to identify the reasons for the successful conclusion of the agreement. This task cannot be attempted here, but a few of the reasons which have been given are acknowledged.

As the consideration of the implications of the agreement will reveal, TRIPs hazards costs and benefits for various countries. The agreement had obvious attractions for producer nations such as the United States. In a globalizing economy, when other countries were undercutting its traditional commodities, and trade imbalances had developed with certain developing countries, high technology and popular culture were seen as a vital source of competitive advantage. Perhaps, as the catalogue of differences reveals, other developed nations saw the benefits of protection as far less clear-cut and uniform. However, for the larger northern nations, especially those in the Triad, extensive cross-investments and strategic alliances create pressures for convergence of legalities in intellectual property and related fields. In addition, some of the smaller countries, particularly those beginning to innovate and export in a commercial way themselves, saw virtue in a multilateral regime. Multilateral rules seemed preferable to the bilateral pressures which countries such as the United States had been applying so vigorously. If a country was already adopting high standards of protection, the agreement would be an effective way to obtain them from others. Such smaller countries could not expect to rely on diplomatic offices or trade sanctions to obtain reciprocal protections for their own nationals.

Yet many such countries still wished to be selective about the sectors in which they advanced protection, so we might need to look for other reasons why countries were prepared to accept such a comprehensive multilateral agreement. One reason refers to the calculation of their material interests. For the many countries which are net importers of intellectual property, TRIPs seems contrary to their overall interests. However, it is to be remembered that intellectual property protection was part of an overall Uruguay Round package of agreements. Countries were offered market access in other sectors of the international economy as the trade-off for swallowing TRIPs whole. General acceptance also signified the power of an idea. Affirmation of intellectual property protection was an indication that they were prepared to participate in a global economic system. The northern delegations used their powers of persuasion, expertise and authority to get this idea across.

We turn now to the provisions of the agreement. The implications of the agreement may be pursued under three broad heads. First, the agreement establishes the general principles which are to apply, such as the norms of national treatment and most favoured nation treatment. Second, the agreement raises the level and extends the scope of substantive protection for intellectual property. Third, the agreement introduces new methods of dispute settlement and redress for non-compliance into the international area.

GENERAL PROVISIONS AND BASIC PRINCIPLES

After its preamble, the agreement makes general provisions and establishes basic principles. The first concern the nature and scope of the obligations arising under the agreement. Article 1:3 requires members to accord the treatment provided for in the agreement to the nationals of other members. It goes on to say that those nationals are to be understood as those natural or legal persons who would meet the criteria for eligibility for protection provided under the Paris Convention, the Berne Convention, the Rome Convention or the Treaty on Integrated Circuits.[14] We should note here that the benefits of the protections are meant to be given to private persons. In other words, when implemented, the protections are meant to give rise to enforceable private property rights, but the individuals must be nationals of the members of the WTO. However, with so many countries becoming members of the WTO, the need to determine nationality will not be a big issue.

We have said that one of the most interesting features of the TRIPs agreement is the use it makes of the established intellectual property conventions. In this respect, TRIPs identifies the articles of the conventions it wishes to apply, but it does not actually set them out in its text. Reference must be made to the conventions themselves. This opening part of the agreement prescribes that members comply with articles 1 through 12 and article 19 of the Paris Convention (1969) (see article 2:1). Later, in the section specifically concerning copyright standards, it requires members to comply with articles 1 through 21 of the Berne Convention (1971), save for article 6bis. They should also comply with the appendix to the convention (see article 9:1). We shall return to these provisions in our examination of the different categories of protection.

National treatment

Article 3:1 of the agreement concerns national treatment. It requires members to accord to the nationals of other members treatment no less favourable than it accords to its own nationals with regard to the protection of intellectual property. We know that national treatment permits countries, provided they do not discriminate between foreigners and locals, to vary the level of protection they give to intellectual property according to what they see as their needs at any one time or in any one sector. Yet, to the country which does provide protection, it may seem like an onerous requirement if one's own nationals do not receive the corresponding level of substantive protection in the foreigner's home country.

The TRIPs agreement moderates this effect by standardising levels of protection between the members. Still, it is important to appreciate that the TRIPs requirement of national treatment extends beyond those 'matters affecting the use of intellectual property rights specifically addressed in the agreement'. It applies to the matters which a member country embraces generally 'affecting the availability, acquisition, scope, maintenance and enforcement of intellectual property rights' (footnote to article 3:2). There will be many ways in which a member's protections might run beyond the terms of the agreement. We should remember in particular that article 1:1 envisages members implementing more extensive protection than is required by the agreement, provided that such protection does not contravene the provisions of the agreement. Nevertheless, we should appreciate that this treatment need only relate to matters affecting these itemised aspects of intellectual property. For the purposes of the agreement, article 1:2 defines intellectual property to refer to the categories for which the agreement specifically provides standards (see below). There are categories in national law with which the agreement does not deal.

In addition, an explicit exception to this broader coverage for national treatment is made in respect of the rights for performers, producers of phonograms and broadcasters. Here, national treatment only applies in respect of the rights provided under the agreement. In contention here are the rights which some countries grant to receive a share of the revenue from payments of equitable compensation. These payments are made where there is non-voluntary licensing, for example of the reproduction, public performance or broadcasting of sound recordings.

Among the provisions of the Paris and Berne Conventions which TRIPs applies are their principles of national treatment. We should appreciate that they have their own complex idiosyncrasies which have been explored over time.[15] They do not entirely correlate with the way TRIPs itself prescribes national treatment. Article 2:2 states that nothing in the substantive parts of the agreement (compared to the dispute settlement provisions) shall derogate from the members' existing obligations under the four nominated conventions, so we must try to look at things in a cumulative way. In particular, we should understand that the conventions create 'points of attachment' for national treatment other than nationality. For example, the benefits of protection may be available if a work is published in a union country (that is, a country which is a member of the union associated with the convention), notwithstanding that the author is not a national of a union country.

In addition, article 3:1 makes the TRIPs requirement subject to the exceptions which are already provided in the four WIPO conventions the agreement has identified. However, article 3:2 limits the availability of the exceptions which have been accommodated in relation to judicial and administrative procedures. Relevant, for example, is the Paris Convention's reservation of national laws relating to judicial and administrative procedures, to jurisdiction and to requirements of representation (Paris article 2(3)). In language redolent of the GATT provisions, article 3:2 says that these exceptions can only be used where they are necessary to secure compliance with laws and regulations which are not inconsistent with the provisions of the agreement and where such practices are not applied in a manner which would constitute a disguised restriction on trade. Especially in relation to patents, foreigners have developed suspicions that the delays and complications they encounter within administrative and judicial procedures conceal discrimination. However, to what extent should members have to make allowances for the extra difficulties foreigners experience negotiating unfamiliar political, legal and possibly language systems? Furthermore, the imperatives of regulatory competence may demand that foreigners be treated differently. Evans provides the example of a requirement that foreigners deposit a certain sum as security or bail for the costs of litigation.[16]

Most favoured nation treatment

In article 4, the agreement embodies another principle or norm characteristic of the GATT. With regard to the protection of intellectual property, any advantage, favour, privilege or immunity granted by a member to the nationals of any other country shall be accorded immediately and unconditionally to the nationals of other members.

Again, this principle mediates against discrimination, in this case between nationals of different states. Thus this requirement aims to 'multilateralise' the benefits extended to the nationals of a particular country. They cannot be confined, for instance, to those whose governments have offered protections in return. Under article 4, this obligation to multilateralise extends to the benefits granted to any other country and not just members of the WTO, though the obligation itself is only owed to nationals of the members. Moreover, like national treatment, it applies to a member's protection of intellectual property generally and not just those matters affecting the use of intellectual property rights specifically addressed in the agreement.

Some exceptions are made in article 4. The most notable exceptions are benefits deriving from 'international agreements' relating to the protection of intellectual property which entered into force prior to the TRIPs agreement. An example might be the semi-conductor agreement which the United States has made with countries like Japan, though we would still expect members to have to comply with the substantive protections TRIPs demands in such categories. As well, TRIPs attaches a general proviso to the exception that the agreements do not constitute an arbitrary or unjustifiable discrimination against the nationals of other members.

A more specific exception recognises benefits granted under the provisions Berne or Rome make for material reciprocity. In addition, freedom to base extra protections upon reciprocity is permitted in respect of the rights of performers, producers of phonograms and broadcasters, so far as they are not provided under the agreement. Again, rights to share in equitable remuneration are a case in point. In particular, the European Union has only been prepared to give United States audiovisuals exporters a share if the United States has a scheme which reciprocates.

TRIPs SUBSTANTIVE STANDARDS

The heart of the agreement is the prescription of standards concerning the availability, scope and use of intellectual property rights. By standardising protection, the agreement seeks to manage the issue of conflict and competition between national laws directly. Thus, the issue of jurisdiction loses its edge. Countries have much less opportunity to decide whether it suits their situation to offer high or low levels of protection. In some cases, they must substantially rework their specific intellectual property laws or even their general legal traditions in order to comply.

Copyright and related rights

The standards start with copyright and related rights. This category bears most relation to the cultural content which is carried around the globe through various media as well now as having application to what we might call carrier technologies such as computer software. It will form a major part of the case study in chapter eight of the on-line media. Here, we shall analyse the basic TRIPs provisions, first looking at the connection it makes to the Berne Convention and then identifying the protections it introduces directly.

Protection for works

TRIPs is making use of the resources of a well established international convention. The Berne Convention was formed back in 1885. It has experienced several revisions since that time and TRIPs is applying the convention as it was last revised, in 1971. As of 31 January 1998 there were 130 states party to the Convention, a number similar to the membership of the WTO, though the fact remains that not all of those states have subscribed to the most recent revisions to the Convention. As well, its provisions have not been entirely attractive to some countries and we should note that the United Nations, through UNESCO, formulated another convention, the Universal Copyright Convention, where the protections required were milder.

What is the substance of the Berne provisions which TRIPs applies? TRIPs largely leaves out the Berne provisions relating to the machinery – the internal workings – of the Convention and the union it establishes. The most substantive provision which TRIPs omits is the provision (article 6bis) for authors of works to claim moral rights rather than economic rights. Otherwise, it applies the substantial copyright protections which Berne provides. It is not possible to give a fulsome and precise account of those Berne provisions here. The reader is advised to consult the scholarly literature.[17] Briefly, it should be said that the Convention requires protection primarily for literary and artistic works (Berne article 2). These works are to include every production in the literary, scientific and artistic domain, whatever may be the mode or form of expression. The Convention goes on to offer an illustrative list of such works which does not run to some of the more modern media, though cinematographic works are embraced by the Convention. For explicit protection of the modern media of sound recordings and broadcasts, we need to look elsewhere, such as to the Rome Convention (see below).

We should understand, nonetheless, that these modern media put original works, such as musical scores, the plots and dialogues of books and the images of paintings, to new uses. The issue here for Berne becomes the nature of the rights which are to be exercised over the 'underlying' works. For literary and artistic works, Berne now recognises explicitly the right to authorise reproduction of the work in any manner or form (Berne article 9(1)). Other rights have longer standing. Rights of translation and adaptation recognise that the works will not necessarily appear in their original guise. Rights concerned with immaterial disseminations of works have included the right to authorise the broadcasting of works, the communication of the work to the public by any other means of wireless diffusion, or the communication of the work to the public by wire (Berne article 11bis(1)). We can see that these rights are tied to specific media. The right to control public performance is not so tied, but it seems it only applies to dramatic and musical works.

If the copyright provisions of the TRIPs agreement were confined to these articles of Berne, it would carry over the uncertainties which surround the Convention's potential to cover the new kinds of subject matter and new kinds of exploitation which are bound up in the current wave of technological and organizational innovations. The TRIPs agreement proceeds explicitly to require that computer programs, whether in source or object codes, be protected as literary works under the Berne Convention (article 10:1). Nonetheless, in this area, as in others, such a general requirement leaves open all sorts of issues concerning the precise extent of protection which national copyright affords to software. Article 9:2 does attach the basic proviso that copyright protection is to extend to expressions and not to ideas, procedures, methods of operation or mathematical concepts as such. But how to make the problematic idea/expression distinction work in the case of computer programs remains a matter for national jurisprudence.[18] Perhaps the WTO dispute settlement bodies will be asked to have a say at some stage.

Under the agreement, protection is also to be afforded to compilations of data or other material, whether in machine-readable or other form, which by reason of the selection or arrangement of their contents constitute intellectual creations (article 10:2). Such protection is to be without prejudice to any copyright subsisting in the data or material itself. This provision appears to pick up on the provision in Berne article 2(5). As we shall see in chapter eight, certain functional or utilitarian databases are not likely to meet these criteria and would need to be given their own category of protection internationally.

Under Berne, the beneficiaries of the rights which its protection confers are the authors of the works. By relying largely on Berne, the TRIPs agreement has also made the author the starting point for the holding of rights. So much is done today under conditions of employment or commission from industrial corporations that it was thought this concept might have been bypassed. Of course, the work often leaves the author and enters an elaborate network through which it is reproduced, recombined and diffused. Commercially, it becomes important that the author assign or license the rights to others by way of marketplace contractual transactions. In speaking throughout of 'successors in title' and 'other right holders', it would seem that the agreement envisages 'free' transferability of rights in the marketplace. It also envisages that those holders may be legal as well as natural persons. Moral rights, on the other hand, would have placed some limitations on the author's alienation of the works in the marketplace.

Use rights

Which rights does the holder enjoy in controlling access to the works by potential competitors and consumers? We have noted the rights on which the agreement insists by applying the Berne Convention. But innovations are of course presenting ever more opportunities to exploit works apart from making and selling hard copies. We are thinking here in particular of the other ways in which works may be distributed. As chapter eight will show, these rights also have particular relevance to control of the new digital on-line media. In this respect, the TRIPs agreement has already been characterised as 'backward looking'.[19] Its caution has given a spur to the formulation, under the aegis of a Diplomatic Conference, of two new WIPO treaties, the Copyright Treaty and the Performances and Phonograms Treaty. We shall discuss these treaties in chapter eight.

Still, the TRIPs agreement broaches this field by providing for rental rights. The agreement states that, 'at least in respect of computer programs and cinematographic works, the parties shall provide authors and their successors in title with the right to authorise or prohibit the commercial rental to the public of originals or copies of their copyright works' (article 11). What constitutes a rental is not indicated. In the case of cinematographic works, this provision was to be an advance on the rights conferred by article 14(1) of Berne. We shall deal with the limitations and exceptions which TRIPs allows to these and other rights later in this chapter.

Applying Berne, the term of the copyright protection is the life of the author plus fifty years. Article 12 goes on to say that, wherever the term is calculated on a basis other than the life of a natural person, it will be fifty years from the date of publication or, failing publication, from the date of making of a work.

Related rights

In article 14, the agreement explicitly requires protections to be given to performers, producers of sound recordings and broadcasting organizations. Some countries have chosen unilaterally to offer them copyright protection. In the TRIPs agreement, their rights are cast instead as rights which are related to copyright. This approach is consistent with the Rome Convention, but the provisions of the Rome Convention are not applied directly like the Berne provisions. It is worth noting that the Rome Convention has not attracted as many signatories as Berne.

The protection offered to performances is the mildest. The agreement states that performers are to have the possibility of preventing (when undertaken without their authorisation) the fixation of their unfixed performance and the reproduction of such a fixation (article 14:1). Here, the agreement has in mind the practice of bootlegging, which is the unauthorised taping of live performances and the subsequent sale of copies. TRIPs extends its protection to control over the broadcasting by wireless means and the communication to the public of live performances. However, in speaking of the possibility of preventing, the protection seems weaker than the clear property rights given to the authors of works. Furthermore, it does not afford performers control over reproduction of their performances, once they have authorised the first fixation of the performance. Here, the interests of performers as authors of a performance may run up against the interests that the producers and distributors of audiovisuals have in easy access to such content resources. Performances are embodied in such media as sound recordings, films, broadcasts and CD-ROMs, which are then exploited in a number of ways. In chapter eight, we shall see that these practices became an issue at the WIPO Diplomatic Conference.

The agreement requires that producers of sound recordings shall enjoy the right to authorise or prohibit the direct or indirect reproduction of their sound recordings (article 14:2). But it does not adopt the other rights enumerated by Rome such as the right to control the broadcasting of recordings. Commercial rental rights are extended explicitly to the producers of sound recordings and other right holders in sound recordings, though with provision at the same time for non-voluntary licensing (again, see below).

Broadcasting organizations shall have the right to prohibit (when undertaken without their authorisation) the fixation, the reproduction of fixations, and re-broadcasting by wireless means of broadcasts, as well as the communication to the public of television broadcasts of the same (article 14:3). The agreement states that, where parties do not grant these Rome-type rights to broadcasting organizations (making the provisions permissive?), they shall provide the owners of the copyright in the subject matter of the broadcasts with the possibility of preventing such acts, subject to the provisions of Berne.

The term of protection available to performers and producers of sound recordings is to be at least fifty years; the term for broadcasting organizations at least twenty years.

Patents

Patents represent the second category of intellectual property which we shall treat as important to the global carriers. They form a major part of the case study in chapter seven. Patents started with industrial technologies but now extend into agriculture and service sectors such as health care. In doing so, they are offering a point of control over the processes of reproduction of life and specifically the genetic codes of plants, animals and humans. Again, the object here is to analyse the essential TRIPs provisions.

The provisions for patents commence with the application of the Paris Convention in article 2:1. The Paris Convention dates from 1883 and it has undergone several revisions. Today, around one hundred states are party to its union. As we shall see, the Convention deals with other categories of intellectual property too, namely utility models, industrial designs, trademarks and trade names, geographical appellations and unfair competition. In regard to patents, we should appreciate that the Convention does not require countries to provide substantive protection. Instead, through national treatment and independence of protection, it obliges them to offer whatever level of protection their laws demand to foreigners as well as to locals. The Convention also establishes a very valuable procedural facility. If an application for a patent or utility model is filed in one state of the union, it is to enjoy priority in the other states of the union too for twelve months.[20] For industrial designs and trademarks, we should note that the corresponding period is six months.

Patentable subject matter

In contrast to the Paris Convention, the key article of the TRIPs agreement, article 27:1, requires members to make patents available for any inventions, whether products or processes, in all fields of technology.

So, apart from the categories which the agreement itself excepts, members must not distinguish sectors where patents will be granted. To attach such a broad scope to patentable subject matter signifies a major extension in international protection, especially in the sectors where many countries have maintained gaps. These sectors include pharmaceuticals, foodstuffs and chemicals.[21]

The agreement uses the concept of the invention to identify patentable subject matter. Furthermore, it attaches the proviso that the inventions be new, involve an inventive step and are capable of industrial application. To take account of the variations in the way these criteria are cast by countries with patent systems, a member is permitted to deem the term 'non-obvious' synonymous with 'inventive step', and 'useful' synonymous with 'capable of industrial application'. Of course, these eligibility criteria are stated at a very high level of generality and it will remain necessary to fill them out through local jurisprudence and practice. However, it is important to note that the Paris Convention did not contain such criteria and that they import into the international field the kind of criteria which reward the science and technology in inventions. We shall find that this orientation is relevant to the competing claims for control of genetic codes (chapter seven).

TRIPs permits members to exclude inventions from patentability on broad grounds of public order or morality (article 27:2). There follows a familiar but significant exclusion for diagnostic, therapeutic and surgical methods for the treatment of humans or animals. For the purposes of our case study, we should highlight the final exclusion. Article 27:1(b) permits members to exclude: 'plants and animals other than micro-organisms, and essentially biological processes for the production of plants or animals other than non-biological and micro-biological processes'. However, this article adds that members must provide protection for plant varieties either by patents or by an effective sui generis system or by any combination thereof. Then, the whole provision is earmarked for review four years after the date of entry into force of the WTO Agreement. These allowances were hard fought and their significance is explored in depth in the chapter on genetic codes.

Use rights

The agreement specifies the rights which patent owners are to enjoy exclusively. To employ the language of the agreement again, they are said to be: a) where the subject matter is a product, to prevent third parties from making, using, offering for sale, selling or importing for these purposes, the product, and b) where the subject matter of the patent is a process, to prevent third parties from using the process or from using, offering for sale, selling or importing for these purposes, at least the product obtained directly by that process. This last clause is interesting. As we shall see, effective protection of a process may require control over products, especially if they are imported from a country that does not prevent infringements of the process. But what is the direct product, for instance, of a genetically engineered wheat plant – just the flour, or also the bread? Still, overall, these rights are substantial and we should note now that the right to prevent others importing, as well as making or using locally, has implications for the economic relationship between developed and developing nations.

The agreement is markedly silent on the issue which has divided the United States and other industrial countries as to whether to recognise the first to invent or the first to file. It seems that the United States backed away from insistence on its approach, which has been first to invent.[22] This difference complicates efforts to coordinate the processing of applications, just at a time when more inventors are identifying a need to secure their markets across a range of countries.

As we know, patents rely on a grant being made in the individual case after an application is made to the authorities. In contrast, in most countries, copyright does not depend on registration for its validity. Article 5(2) of Berne says that the enjoyment and exercise of its rights shall not be subject to any formality. However, article 2(1) of the Paris Convention specifies that the foreigner must comply with the conditions and formalities which are imposed on locals. TRIPs includes a general provision that is designed to discipline the procedures and formalities which members may require as a condition of the acquisition or maintenance of intellectual property rights (article 62). Procedures for grant or registration are among those disciplined. Broadly, the procedures must be timely and final administrative decisions must be subject to review. They are also governed by the general obligations of article 41 (see below). As well, we should note that TRIPs insists that members make available judicial review of any decision to revoke or forfeit a patent (article 32). Another provision which is favourable to the holder is article 34. It places the burden of proof in infringement proceedings regarding process patents on the defendant.

TRIPs makes the term of protection of a patent a minimum of twenty years (article 33). This period has to be seen as an increase for many systems, including those in the developed countries. At the same time, it makes no provision for utility models. Utility models and their variants offer an alternative to inventors where it does not seem feasible to make the investment involved in securing the full patent. The requirements are generally less demanding, but the protection is also less fulsome. The term of protection is short. They may appeal for instance to the small, local inventor. In a number of national jurisdictions, utility models are made available alongside patents, and the European Union has recently published a proposal for a directive on the protection of inventions by utility model.[23]

OTHER CATEGORIES

Trademarks

We turn now to the agreement's other categories of protection. These categories are complex and significant but we shall not be able to give them the same attention, either here or later, as we do copyright and patents. We begin with trademarks. We should appreciate that trademarks become desirable objects for protection as the global economy is increasingly built upon trafficking in signs, styles, images and associations.

TRIPs applies the provisions of the Paris Convention regarding trademarks. These provisions demand more substantive protection than they do for patents. In particular, they expect protection to be afforded to certain types of mark, namely well known marks, service marks and collective marks (see Paris articles 6bis, 6sexies and 7bis). They require countries of the union to protect marks which are registered in other union countries (Paris article 6quinquies). The protection is to include the seizure of imports which infringe (Paris article 9).

TRIPs elaborates on the Paris Convention substantially. In particular, it provides a definition of the term 'trademark'. The definition is broad: any sign capable of distinguishing the goods and services of one undertaking from those of other undertakings shall be capable of constituting a trademark and shall be eligible for registration (article 15(1)). It goes on to say that such signs, in particular words including personal names, letters, numerals, figurative elements and combinations of colours as well as any combination of signs, shall be eligible for registration as trademarks. It also says that, where signs are not inherently capable of distinguishing the relevant goods or services, parties may make registrability depend upon distinctiveness acquired through use. However, article 15(2) states that all this is not to be understood to prevent a party from denying registration of trademarks on other grounds, provided they do not derogate from the provisions of the Paris Convention. Provision must also be made for opportunities to oppose registrations and to petition to cancel registrations.

The agreement substantiates the trademark owner's position in regard to use of the trademark. The parties may make registrability dependent upon use but actual use shall not be a condition for filing an application, and an application shall not be refused solely on the ground that that intended use has not taken place for less than three years from a date of application (article 15(3)). Furthermore, if use is required to maintain registration, registrations may be cancelled only after an uninterrupted period of at least three years and only if valid reasons based on obstacles to that use do not exist (article 19). The Paris Convention has said that, where use is a condition of registration, it may be cancelled only after a reasonable period (article 5C(1)).

The registration of trademarks is to be renewable indefinitely, for periods of no less than seven years at a time (article 18). The use of a trademark in commerce is not to be unjustifiably encumbered by special requirements (article 20). Certain conditions may be placed on the licensing and assignment of trademarks, but TRIPs says that the compulsory licensing of trademarks shall not be permitted (article 21).

Trademark owners are to have the exclusive right to prevent all third parties from using in the course of trade identical or similar signs, for goods or services which are identical or similar to those in respect of which the trademark is registered, where such use would result in the likelihood of confusion (article 16). This provision is similar to the Paris Convention. Article 6bis of the Paris Convention is extended (in certain circumstances) to services; also, subject to certain provisos, to goods and services which are not similar to those in respect of which a trademark is registered.

At this point, we should note that the agreement also applies the Paris Convention's prescription concerning unfair competition. Countries of the union are bound to assure effective protection against unfair competition. Paris article 10bis identifies any act of competition contrary to honest practices in industrial or commercial matters to constitute an act of unfair competition. Such a standard is very open ended. Article 10bis goes on to require three specific kinds of act to be prohibited. They include the sort of conduct which 'passes off' goods as being those of another. Enjoining such conduct is a way of protecting the investment made in a sound reputation as a manufacturer.

In the contemporary, media-inspired economy, some national laws have given much wider support to the commercial value of reputation. They extend their protection to those who exploit their status or celebrity to endorse the products and services of others. In these cases, deception and confusion may not be essential elements of an offence. It may be considered unfair to trade on the broad recognition and positive associations which certain real-life or even fictional characters enjoy among consumers, at least without paying licence or royalty fees. However, the trend in protections gives rise to concerns that commercial interests might be able to commandeer symbols which form part of the common language or popular culture. At the same time, where commerce is prepared to draw on every available resource, religious and ethnic groups may object to the use of their traditional symbols in unsanctioned ways.

Geographical indications

The TRIPs agreement makes clear provision in favour of protection of geographical indications. Much of this is in line with the Lisbon Agreement for the Protection of Appellations of Origin and their International Registration,[24] but all of it is stated in express terms. Such protection was strongly sought by the European countries, particularly in its application to trade in wines, spirits and foodstuffs. An example which comes to mind is the French names for certain wines and cheeses.

The agreement says geographical indications are indications which identify a good as originating in the territory of a member or a region or locality in that territory, where a given quality, reputation or other characteristic of the good is essentially attributable to its geographical origin (article 22). Protection is to provide interested parties with the legal means to prevent either any use that misleadingly indicates or suggests that goods originate in a geographical area other than their true place of origin, or any use that constitutes the act of unfair competition with the meaning of article 10bis of the Paris Convention. Provision is also to be made for refusal to register a trademark if the use of the indication in the trademark for goods would mislead the public as to the true place of their origin. We can see here a particular application of the concern with passing off.

Additional protection is to be provided for geographical indications identifying wines and spirits (article 23). A legal means to prevent use of a geographical indication is to be provided, even if the true origin of the goods is indicated or the use is accompanied by expressions such as kind, type, style, imitation or the like. In other words, these indications are to have protection even if there is no deception or confusion among consumers. We all know the power of recognition and association bound up with the use of the magic word 'champagne'. On this basis, reliance on passing-off laws may not be sufficient compliance.

Furthermore, under article 24, the members have agreed to enter into negotiations aimed at increasing protection of individual geographical indications. It has been suggested that the agreement's provisions only represent a holding position and that the European countries will push for stronger protection; the ex-colonial countries, including the United States, continue to hold reservations. The Council for Trade-Related Aspects of Intellectual Property Rights began preparation for these negotiations in 1997.[25] Article 24 recognises several of the concerns we noted in relation to trademarks. Members are not to be required to proscribe indications which have been in continuous local use for a certain period of time or which are customary in common language as the common name for the goods or services.

Industrial designs

In a bald statement, the Paris Convention requires union countries to protect industrial designs (Paris article 5quinquies). In contrast to the large amount of discretion this allows such countries, the protection required by the TRIPs agreement is substantive. Generally, the parties are to provide protection for independently created industrial designs that are new or original (article 25:1). A patent-like requirement of inventiveness or non-obviousness is not required. Parties may provide that designs are not new or original if they do not significantly differ from known designs or combinations of known design features. An issue troubling some jurisdictions has been the extent to which design law should provide protection for functional features.[26] The agreement permits the parties to provide that protection shall not extend to designs dictated essentially by technical or functional considerations.

The owner of a protected industrial design is to have the right to prevent third parties from making, selling or importing articles bearing or embodying a design which is a copy, or substantially a copy, of the protected design, when such acts are undertaken for commercial purposes (article 26:1). Breaching another gap in the Paris Convention, the agreement specifies that the protection available shall amount to at least ten years (article 26:3).

Despite these prescriptions, the agreement largely avoids tying down the key concepts, which remain subject to differing interpretations in the various countries. It makes no mention of a system of registration. Nor does it address the relationship which is to be struck between copyright protection for designs and the sui generis industrial design law, except in relation to textile designs.

Layout designs (topographies) of integrated circuits

Though a treaty was reached on protection for integrated circuit designs (the Washington Treaty on Intellectual Property in respect of Integrated Circuits), the leading producer countries and especially the United States have preferred to adopt a strategy of obtaining reciprocal protection through bilateral agreements. The TRIPs agreement requires members to provide protection in accordance with articles 2 to 7, except for article 6(3), together with articles 12 and 16.3 of the Treaty. The agreement adds that the members must consider unlawful (if they are performed without the authorisation of the right holder) the acts of importing, selling or otherwise distributing for commercial purposes a protected layout design (article 37). The protection extends to the circuits which incorporate them and the articles which incorporate those circuits, in so far as they continue to contain an unlawfully reproduced layout design. Exceptions are to be made, however, for certain innocent commissions of those acts. The term of protection is to be no less that ten years, but protection may lapse after fifteen years (article 38).

One reason which has been given for the decision of certain countries to bypass the Washington Treaty was its provision for compulsory licensing powers. TRIPs does not apply the relevant provision of the Treaty (article 6(3)). However, in its own article 37:2, TRIPs both concedes that non-voluntary licensing will occur and applies the disciplines which it has formulated to control the compulsory licensing of patents (see below).

Undisclosed information

The inclusion of protection for 'undisclosed information' signifies a major development in international intellectual property. It introduces the potential to blow out the specific categories which presently delineate intellectual property. It seems that even some of the developed countries, such as Japan and Australia, held doubts about the need for its inclusion. But it was to be a key objective of the United States.

Despite its significance, we shall confine ourselves to noting the provisions of the agreement. The agreement says that members shall protect undisclosed information in the course of ensuring effective protection against unfair competition under article 10bis of the Paris Convention (article 39:1). In keeping, article 38:2 states that natural and legal persons are to have the possibility of preventing information within their control from being disclosed to, acquired by, or used by others without their consent, provided it is done in a manner contrary to honest commercial practices.

To attract such protection, the information is to be secret, is to have commercial value because it is secret, and is to have been subject to reasonable steps under the circumstances to keep it secret (article 39:2). These provisions appear to be modelled on the United States uniform trade secrets legislation. Secrecy is a constituent, but we should appreciate that it may not be enough on its own to justify protection. By employing the concept of a manner contrary to honest commercial practices, the agreement seems concerned at the same time with the way the information is treated by others, that is with the propriety of the conduct of the defendants.

A footnote indicates that 'a manner contrary to honest commercial practices' is to be taken to mean at least practices such as breach of contract, breach of confidence and inducement of breach, and to include the acquisition of undisclosed information by third parties who knew, or were grossly negligent in failing to know, that such practices were involved in the acquisition. Thus, the protection can be established by the obligations which parties have been able to secure through such relational dealings as contract. It tends to make the benefits very much a function of the power which parties can exercise in the marketplace. But the scope of the protection remains unsettled. We should recognise, for instance, that some jurisdictions have tried to draw a line around the concept of information itself. For example, they ask whether information can be separated out from the general knowledge and make-up of an individual or perhaps a group, so that it can be said to be appropriable by another.[27]

Article 39:3 requires members to protect certain data submitted to government agencies. This provision was potentially wide, but it was confined to data submitted as a condition of approving the marketing of pharmaceutical or agricultural products which utilise new chemical entities. The data should be undisclosed test or other data, the origination of which involves a considerable effort. Article 39:3 require this information to be protected primarily against unfair commercial use. It is also to be protected against disclosure unless disclosure is necessary to protect the public or unless steps are taken to protect against unfair commercial use. This kind of information is vital to decisions about the release of potentially hazardous substances and governments are often not in a position to generate such information themselves. They rely on the firms but the information is costly and sensitive. Governments will have to take care to safeguard the information against the commercial rivals of the firm submitting. In some situations, agencies of the same government can themselves become commercial rivals.

ENFORCEMENT PROVISIONS

Part III of the TRIPs agreement is a major addition to the international provisions for intellectual property protection. Berne and Paris do say that those persons entitled to their protections should have legal remedies. But, with a few exceptions, they do not specify those remedies. In contrast, the elaboration within TRIPs is striking. All members will need to make adjustments. In terms of general procedural legalities, the obligations will not be regarded as so onerous for countries with liberal legal systems such as Australia, but their impact on the administrative and judicial infrastructures of the developing nations may be profound. It is interesting then that the agreement attaches some qualifications. It makes it clear that the members do not have to put into place a judicial system for the enforcement of intellectual property rights, distinct from the system for enforcement of law in general (article 41:5). Nor is any obligation created with respect to the distribution of resources between enforcement of these rights and the law in general.

The agreement starts by imposing a general obligation on the members to make enforcement procedures available under their national laws so as to permit effective action against infringements (article 41:1). They are to include expeditious remedies to prevent infringements, together with remedies which constitute a deterrent to further infringements. At the same time, these procedures are to be applied in a manner as to avoid themselves the creation of barriers to legitimate trade and to provide for safeguards against their abuse. Such procedures are to be fair and equitable and are not to be unnecessarily complicated or costly or entail unreasonable time limits or unwarranted delays (article 41:2). On the other hand, they must meet certain natural justice or due process standards, including the opportunity for judicial review (article 41:4). We should note that these standards are to be for the benefit of all parties to the proceedings. Some jurisdictions can become rather zealous in their endeavours to prosecute infringements.

More specifically, the members are to make available to right holders civil judicial procedures concerning the enforcement of any intellectual property right covered by the agreement (article 42). But, at the same time, prescriptions are made regarding the access of all parties to a hearing and to legal representation. The agreement then proceeds to put some compunction into the procedures. Article 43 concerns the compellability of evidence. The following articles specify the remedies which the judicial authorities should be empowered to order. They authorise injunctions against the infringing party or imported goods (article 44), compensatory damages where the infringer knew or had reasonable grounds to know he was engaged in infringing activity (article 45) and disposal of infringing goods non-commercially (article 46). The authorisation is to extend to provisional measures so as to prevent infringements or to preserve relevant evidence (article 50). Procedural powers and corresponding safeguards are specified in some detail. It is clear from these articles that the drafters have gone to some trouble to ensure that the protections are backed up. However, we should note that the agreement does not actually require a member country's judicial authorities to provide an individual right holder with these remedies against infringement. The authorities retain discretion; the remedies are not as of right.

Even so, the agreement is not finished with enforcement. Special requirements are laid down relating to border measures (articles 51–60). For instance, right holders who have valid grounds for suspecting the importation of counterfeit trademark or pirated copyright goods are to be enabled to apply for suspension by customs authorities of the release into free circulation of such goods. This avenue of redress extends to goods which involve other infringements of intellectual property rights. Right holders are to be required to produce evidence and the authorities are also to have the power to require a security. The duration of any suspension of import or export channels is regulated; so too is ex officio action by the authorities.

In a notable development, the agreement provides that criminal procedures and penalties shall be applied, at least in cases of 'wilful' trademark counterfeiting or copyright piracy on a commercial scale (article 61). Parties are indeed permitted to provide for criminal procedures and penalties to be applied in other cases of infringement of intellectual property rights.

SPECIAL AND DIFFERENTIAL TREATMENT

Another principle which is familiar to the GATT is the principle of special and differential treatment. Such treatment has largely been included as a means of accommodating the needs of developing countries. The TRIPs agreement has highlighted the difficulties which the developing, and indeed the smaller industrialised nations experience when they reform their approach to intellectual property. On the one hand, the evidence suggests that protection for intellectual property is necessary to encourage leading foreign producers to provide sophisticated goods, make investments in local industry, and engage in technology transfer. Intellectual property protection may also become a condition of access to rich northern markets at a time when an export strategy holds out more economic promise than imitation at home. However, we should appreciate that the expert literature debates the importance of intellectual property protection to investment decisions. We should also acknowledge the caution that high technology is not always a boon to the people of the developing world.[28]

Moreover, in the short term at least, protection carries costs as well as benefits for importing countries. Instead of releasing foreign technology and encouraging local working, with all the important spin-offs for domestic capability, local protection might be deployed to cover imports and keep technology in-house. Certainly, it remains the case that much foreign intellectual property is not worked locally. Where intellectual property is worked locally, conditions may be applied which restrict research, production and sales by local subsidiaries or external licensees. Through market partitioning, it might be used to keep locally based firms out of export markets. It can also work directly to delay access or add to the price of certain products on the local market. India, Brazil and Peru were among the countries which expressed concerns about protection of this nature during the Uruguay Round.

We noted earlier that the WIPO conventions have in many respects been sufficiently non-prescriptive to allow developing nations leeway in how they cast their domestic arrangements for protection. To a certain extent, the arrangements could fit with their perception of their economic needs and cultural values. Poignantly, Dhanjee and de Chazournes note that the Western nations, including the United States, maintained gaps in their own intellectual property protection which were commensurate with their stage of local economic and cultural development:

> Thus this freedom has been used by states to promote their national technological and industrial development. In order to do so they have attempted to find a proper balance between the encouragement of creativity, and the maximization of social welfare arising from the diffusion of the fruits of that creativity, and from free competition and trade. Such a balance underlies all national legislation on IPR's.[29]

In its established rules for freer trade in goods, the GATT itself has provided for special and differential treatment for developing countries. The TRIPs agreement is significant for providing an allowance in terms of time to comply rather than the level of compliance. Under article 66, 'least developed' countries are relieved of the requirement of applying the substantive norms of the agreement (but not the national treatment and MFN principles) for effectively eleven years. A category of 'developing countries' is entitled to delay the same implementation up to five years from the date of the application of the agreement (article 65:2), with an extra five years grace conceded for product patent protection in those areas of technology which had not previously been protected (article 65:4).[30] This period of grace is extended to members which are in a process of transformation from a centrally planned into a market, free-enterprise economy and which are undertaking structural reform of their intellectual property system and facing special problems in the preparation and implementation of their laws and regulations (article 65:3). The agreement goes on to charge developed countries to provide these categories of country with technical cooperation (article 67).

One of the sticking points is likely to be the definition of least developed and developing countries. In the past, the GATT has essentially allowed countries to categorise themselves. It has been suggested that the main object of the TRIPs initiative is the newly industrialising countries which have moved to a stage of development where they are both exporting successfully and offering attractive markets for imports. Other countries may be implicated because they represent a base for the copying and transmission which the new technologies make so much easier. But protection provides a means to control access to intellectual resources. By confining differential treatment to transitional time limits, the agreement is really casting into relief the stringency of its substantive standards. It will be necessary in the discussion below to see whether the agreement places any counterbalancing obligations upon right holders. This inquiry is doubly apt, given we are suggesting that the issue relates not just to the contrast between developed and developing nations – a spatial dimension – but to the general balance between right holders and other scientific researchers, industrial competitors, supplier intermediaries and end-user groups. Just as there are constituencies in the developing nations which identify with protection, counter-constituencies can be found in the developed countries. The case studies should bear this assertion out.

DISPUTE RESOLUTION

One of the major attractions for supporters of the TRIPs agreement was the weight it would lend to the implementation of protection. But, at the same time, the use of trade norms to identify and sanction breaches will add a new dimension to the international law of intellectual property. As part of a Uruguay Round package, intellectual property protection comes into play with the regulation of trade in goods and services.

Transparency

The agreement begins to assure compliance by requiring transparency. Again, this obligation has the potential to require members to conform to a rule-based system of intellectual property. The agreement requires the publication of all laws, regulations, final judicial decisions, and administrative rulings of general application (article 63:1). If publication is not practicable, they must be made publicly available. To further the monitoring of member compliance, all such laws and regulations are to be notified to the Council for TRIPs. The Council was to consult with WIPO on the establishment of a common register and this item is now a subject of the cooperation agreement between the two organizations.

Determining non-compliance

To return to article 1, we can see that the agreement places the burden on member countries to give effect to the provisions of the agreement. Thus, it is these members' actions which will be the measure of compliance. Strictly, the question is whether they implement the provisions of the agreement. The substantive provisions generally do not specify the method, with the agreement containing a general provision which says that 'members shall be free to determine the appropriate method of implementing the provisions of this agreement within their own legal system and practice' (article 1:1). Upfront this seems like an important concession to the forms which different legalities favour. Implementation might generally be expected to take the form of legislation.

Certainly, this method would be the most direct and transparent. But the members have various legal traditions and cultures; even in the North, the contrast between the civil and common law styles is significant. For example, common law countries might contend that their courts already provide the protection which TRIPs seeks. However, the choice of implementation strategy may not be wide open. The rulings in the dispute between the United States and India over patent protection indicate that the chosen form should lend legal certainty and predictability to the protections (see chapter three).

Likewise, because the agreement is addressed to governments, we might argue that its provisions are not cast so much in terms of the kind of individual rights and obligations which can be directly activated in the courts. Furthermore, while its substantive provisions are cast to a large degree in imperative terms, they are still often expressed in generalities rather than specifics. Perhaps inevitably, they leave scope for the members to decide how to fill out the details of the criteria for protection. Therefore, we can expect legitimate differences to arise as to whether local protection is sufficient to amount to implementation of the agreement. Accordingly, it will not be a simple matter of comparing local law directly with the provisions of the agreement in order to determine whether members have made compliance. Nonetheless, we should not forget that the ultimate objective of the agreement is to promote private property rights. The primary obligation imposed on members is to accord the requisite treatment to the nationals of other members (article 1:3). Many provisions speak expressly of making rights available to individuals.

There is a further complication emanating from the GATT's traditional focus on the reduction of barriers to trade in goods. Where it was established, would a textual disparity between the requirements of the agreement and a member's national laws be sufficient to found a 'nullification or impairment' of the benefits of the TRIPs agreement? Or would an adverse effect upon trade need to be established in actual fact? Any need to demonstrate an adverse effect upon trade or injury to industry provides further room for argument about compliance. In an economic analysis, the impact attributable to the lack of intellectual property protection may prove controversial. For example, when will it be possible to say that the consumers would have bought the legitimate item if counterfeit or pirated versions had not been available? So too, given that other assets such as speed of innovation or manufacturing and marketing capability may provide a competitive advantage, when will it be possible to say that lax conditions of appropriability were the telling factor in a producer's lack of success?

Article 64:1 of the TRIPs agreement applies the provisions of articles XXII and XXIII of the GATT agreement 1994, as elaborated and applied by the new Dispute Settlement Understanding, to consultations and the settlement of disputes under the agreement. In chapter three, we saw that the GATT process first entertains 'violation complaints'. Where there is an infringement of the obligations assumed under a covered agreement, the action is considered prima facie to be a case of nullification or impairment of the benefits of the agreement (Understanding article 3:8). In the case of TRIPs, the violation would be the failure to institute the necessary re-regulatory legal protections. We should also note here that the protections are protections against infringements of intellectual property rights such as unauthorised copying. TRIPs is not directly concerned with the opportunity to sell products competitively, though one imagines this concern was one of the rationales behind its provisions. The really testing cases for TRIPs would come from non-violation and situation complaints. However the agreement chose to place a five year moratorium on these complaints (article 64:1). It charged the TRIPs Council to make recommendations to the Ministerial Conference about the scope and modalities for complaints of these types (article 64:3).

Chapter three outlined the WTO's general dispute settlement pathways in some detail. While the efficacy of this process remains to be established, member countries can see there is a means of direct recourse against other countries for failure to implement the requisite intellectual property protections. Arguably, this facility contrasts with the WIPO conventions which have provided a more remote and formal International Court of Justice avenue for members. Under Berne, for example, countries can declare that they will not be bound by the Court's jurisdiction (Berne article 33(2)). Recently, however, WIPO has established a conciliation and arbitration service. So too it has been working on a treaty to establish dispute settlement procedures, a Treaty on the Settlement of Disputes between States in the Field of Intellectual Property. But this prospect has raised an interesting issue. Where the TRIPs agreement overlaps with the WIPO conventions substantively, alternative procedures might produce conflicting interpretations of the parallel provisions. There are already understandings concerning the WIPO conventions. It has been suggested that one of the hesitations over the new WIPO Treaty concerns its relationship with the WTO dispute settlement process.[31]

Trade sanctions

Once intellectual property protection is fed into the general dispute settlement processes of the WTO, it is liable to be associated with trade sanctions. There are two sides to this association. Trade sanctions might be used to ensure protection of intellectual property. We would anticipate that most disputes will be settled by compliance. However, it can lead to the complaining party being authorised to suspend its own obligations or commitments. The main issue here is whether a retaliation for failure to implement the agreement is to be confined to the corresponding intellectual property protection. The Understanding says that retaliation starts there but can move on to other categories of intellectual property rights covered within the TRIPs agreement. It cannot move across, however, to other agreements (see article 22:3(g)(iii)). The other side of this coin is the possibility that members might seek to suspend their intellectual property protections as a ultimate sanction against non-compliance by another member in some other area of trade such as trade in goods.

It remains to be seen how TRIPs will fit with the other dimensions of the WTO. Yet, despite its problematics, it may prove to be a valuable testing ground. We have acknowledged that intellectual property protection involves positive re-regulation. It provides a foretaste of the kinds of issues that will be common if the WTO were persuaded to take on responsibility for regulatory standards generally.

COUNTERBALANCING REGULATION?

While said to be an important incentive for investment in the production and release of intellectual resources, paradoxically, intellectual property rights have the propensity to work at times against free trade. The GATT recognises this dual quality. Intellectual property rights can contribute to market power, enabling anti-competitive practices to be effected. Why, one critic asked, should government protection for intellectual property be treated as an essential part of the framework for international trade, unless the same is to be done for the regulation of restrictive business practices?[32] We have suggested that the TRIPs agreement is concerned as much with 'fair' trade as with free trade. If it is fair to provide protection from excessive or unfair competition, such as the competition of unauthorised copying or derivation, fairness might also demand that property rights be 'balanced' against competing claims for readier access. We find that such an outlook is indeed reflected within the body of the different national intellectual property laws. It also finds expression in their external regulatory regimes such as foreign investment review, industry-specific regulation and competition law.[33]

Within the body of intellectual property laws, this concern to find a balance is pursued in several ways. We should appreciate that the boundaries drawn round the subject matter which is to be appropriable represent a concern to leave certain intellectual resources in the public domain. Limiting the term of protection is another such way to do so. Furthermore, explicit exceptions may be made. So, in relation to the coverage of copyright, article 9:2 of the agreement is directive in stating that protection shall not extend to ideas, procedures, methods of operation or mathematical concepts as such. The exceptions to patentability are on the other hand permissive. Members may exclude plants and animals for instance from patentability (article 27:3). A second approach is to demand a concession in return for the property right. So the agreement charges members to require patentable inventions to be disclosed to the public (article 29:1). However, we shall see that publication is not made a condition of copyright.

In each category of protection, there is a general allowance for members to provide limited exceptions to the rights which are conferred. But the allowances share a proviso that the exceptions do not unreasonably conflict with the normal exploitation of the subject matter and do not unreasonably prejudice the legitimate interests of the right holder. The application which this discipline is given will be crucial in determining the extent to which the exclusive rights are counterbalanced. The wording is borrowed from a provision of the Berne Convention, article 9(2), but TRIPs is generalising the discipline at the same time as it is requiring it to be translated into the specifics of the use of each category of intellectual property.

For each category, a set of inquiries will be demanded. It will be necessary to determine what constitutes a normal exploitation of the subject matter and which practices might then conflict unreasonably with it. For instance, the normal exploitation may be to promote high volume sales of the products in which the subject matter is embodied. Wholesale copying of those products provides the obvious conflict. Then it will be necessary to identify the legitimate interests of the right holder and which practices unreasonably prejudice them. For instance, the legitimate interest may be a financial return on the sales. Failure to pay a licence fee or a royalty to the right holder prejudices that interest. In these circumstances, it might be possible to argue that isolated, non-commercial uses do not infringe the proviso. But what if the exploitation lies in making sales to researchers? What, moreover, if the interest is in exclusivity and not just financial returns? The use of general criteria like these leaves scope for interpretation.

Copyright and related rights

Let us start with the copyright category. We should note first that the TRIPs agreement applies several provisions of the Berne Convention for specific exceptions. Berne article 11bis(2) permits countries to determine the conditions under which authors of literary and artistic works shall enjoy control of the broadcasting or communication to the public of their works. So they may authorise non-voluntary licensing, subject to the proviso that equitable remuneration be payable for such uses of the work. Berne article 13(1) envisages reservations and conditions being placed on the right of the author to authorise sound recording of a literary or artistic work.

The most general provision makes it a matter for national legislation whether to permit reproduction of the works. But Berne article 9(2) confines the permission to 'certain special cases'. It goes on to attach the proviso we identified above. Article 13 of TRIPs adopts the language of the Berne, while at the same time extending this allowance for exceptions to each of the rights which it affords and not just the right of reproduction.

What sort of practices might this allowance accommodate? Foremost, we can say, right holders want to eliminate copyright piracy. The literal and wholesale copying of successful products, such as books, programs, sound recordings and films, may drastically undermine sales. The copying may be done by secondary producers for commercial trade. It may be done by consumers for home use. The copying by home users has proved difficult to eliminate and producers have sought to attach liability to intermediaries and the providers of copying technologies. So, in some situations, the non-voluntary licensing schemes benefit producers by raising revenue from home users they could not otherwise collect. We should also appreciate that, in some situations, the users would not purchase the authorised copy, even if no other copy was available for free or at a cheaper price. So it may be arguable that non-voluntary licensing, especially if it is coupled with a financial levy, will not undermine sales.

Beyond piracy, copies are made for more legitimate purposes. Here, the balance becomes less obvious. Copies may need to be made, for example, for the purposes of research and study. The student may be seeking to become familiar with the state of the art generally. However the copy may be made, more purposefully, with the intention of producing a better version of a particular product. In certain sectors, decompilation and the reproduction of interfaces may be necessary to ensure that related products are inter-connectable and inter-operable with a core technology. We shall consider these situations of competitive derivation in our case studies below. We can say that access is important to further innovation, especially if the right holder is refusing to license the property altogether. But what if the right holder is simply seeking to charge a fee for use of the material? We pursue these questions in chapter eight.

A further issue in this complex area concerns the freedom with which media developers and distributors can exploit a whole range of original materials which are found in music, text, images and performances. Exploitation takes on an extra dimension when the materials can be transmitted on-line. For instance, the commercialisation of these materials may include taking bits of them, recombining them in new media, and distributing them further afield. If such acts do not involve reproduction of the works, they may cut across other rights that are being extended under the banner of copyright. But it may prove costly for the distributors to obtain clearance every time they wish to use original material, however transient the use may be. We can see that Berne articles 11bis(2) and 13(2) relate to these practices. TRIPs allows exceptions to its rental right for cinematographic works 'unless such rental has led to widespread copying of such works which is materially impairing the exclusive right of reproduction' (article 11).

The related rights given to performers, record producers and broadcasters are also affected by these practices. TRIPs allows members to provide conditions, limitations, exceptions and reservations to the extent permitted by the Rome Convention (article 14:6). Rome allows non-voluntary licensing of the use of recordings in broadcasting or communications to the public, provided equitable remuneration is made payable (Rome article 12). As well, exceptions to infringement may be made for private use, the use of short excerpts in connection with the reporting of current events, ephemeral fixation as part of a broadcast, and use solely for purposes of teaching or scientific research (article 15). We can identify in this allowance a mixture of motives for allowing exceptions to infringements.

Patents and other industrial property

The TRIPs allowance made for exceptions to the protection of industrial designs is in very similar terms to copyright (article 26:2). However, it introduces into consideration the legitimate interests of third parties. Limited exceptions are allowed to infringement of trademarks, provided they take account of the legitimate interests of the owner and of third parties (article 17). But we noted that compulsory licensing of trademarks is not permitted (article 21).

Again, in respect of patents, limited exceptions have been permitted (article 30). But, because the subject matter of patents is inventions, we might expect the discipline to operate in a different way. Sales will not necessarily be the normal exploitation of an invention, nor revenue the main interest of the holder, though the situation becomes complicated when the invention and its product merge. The holder may wish to prevent others from using the invention altogether for one reason or another. The beneficiary then of a compulsory licence may be a local manufacturer, or another kind of producer/user such as the farmer who resows the seeds from a genetically engineered plant. The Paris Convention has allowed countries to license compulsorily, in order to prevent abuses of rights, such as failure to work the patent (Paris article 5(2)). TRIPs imposes stricter and more detailed disciplines on any national law that allows for use without the authorisation of the right holder (article

31). For example, an attempt must first be made to obtain a licence from the patent holder on reasonable commercial terms.

Partial relief from these conditions is given if the licensing is ordered in judicial proceedings to remedy anti-competitive practices. But we should accept Reichman's argument that the licensing in contemplation is not confined to this objective. He adduces article 8:2 in support.[34] Here, the agreement recognises that appropriate measures, provided that they are consistent with the provisions of the agreement, may be needed to prevent the 'abuse' of intellectual property rights by right holders or the resort to practices 'which unreasonably restrain trade or adversely affect the international transfer of technology'. We return to this issue in chapter seven.

Restrictive trade practices regulation

At the same time, the patent provisions would suggest that one interest of TRIPs is the relationship between intellectual property practices and competition policy. In national systems, this interface has not proved an easy one. We can make the general observation that the present regulatory systems display difficulty in reconciling the thrust of the two policies. Their relationship fluctuates, in part with the economic theories and legal currents which prevail at the time. Explicit exception from the proscriptions of the competition law is often made for the intellectual property rights as such. Of course, on this approach, opinion may vary as to what is to be regarded as within the legitimate scope of the right and what is to constitute an illegitimate extension of its power. Increasingly, this kind of categorisation is giving way to a judgement in the individual case. Authorities then face decisions about which uses of the right are to be treated (as they may) as pro-competitive rather than anti-competitive and which anti-competitive uses are to be regarded as providing benefits that outweigh their costs. Such ambiguity and ambivalence lead to disparities in national practices. This phenomenon will be explored in some depth during the case study of on-line communications media (chapter eight).

One genuine concern about the prospect of a TRIPs agreement was that it would alter the balance between the two policies (or legalities, to use our preferred terminology). The agreement insists on backing for property rights without prescribing competition standards at the same level. However, the agreement contains a section of relevance which is headed 'control of anti-competitive practices in contractual licences'. Here, in article 40:1, it states that: 'Members agree that some licensing practices or conditions pertaining to intellectual property rights which restrain competition may have adverse effects on trade and may impede the transfer and dissemination of technology.' Interestingly, this statement links competition back to trade and technology transfer.

The agreement next focusses on competition by providing that: 'Nothing in the agreement is to prevent members from specifying in their national legislation licensing practices or conditions that may in particular cases constitute an abuse of intellectual property rights having an adverse effect on competition in the relevant market.' Article 40:2 goes on to permit the parties to adopt appropriate measures to prevent or control such practices. The measures must remain consistent with the other provisions of the agreement, which leads back to the issue of identifying what constitutes an abuse of the rights as compared with a mere use. It is salient that the members were only able to agree on a short list of examples of such practices. Article 40:2 says they: 'may include for example exclusive grantback conditions, conditions preventing challenges to validity, and coercive package licensing'. National competition laws have recognised many more examples of restrictions. In particular, the cases extend beyond conditions which are included in licences to contemplate refusals to licence at all or decisions to license on an exclusive basis. But the guidelines which national authorities issue are an indication that their policies towards licensing practices rarely take a categorical stance. Attitudes depend on the situation-specifics and in particular whether the right holder is in a position of market power.

In any case, the TRIPs provision is a permissive rather than a directory one. It can do little to deter regulatory competition between countries. As we suggested in chapter three, some countries may wish for stronger pressures to be placed upon all members to cooperate in mutually reinforcing regulatory regimes. The TRIPs agreement merely obliges the parties to give full and sympathetic consideration to requests from other parties for assistance to deal with the anti-competitive practices of their nationals (article 40:3). Its language is very respectful of the autonomy of each member's jurisdiction. Intriguingly, it is the intellectual property rights of the TRIPs agreement which offer us the strongest example of international regulatory coordination. In the case studies of chapters seven and eight, we ask after the capacities of international competition law to provide some counterbalance to this global intellectual property power. As the book has been urging, this question is all the more pressing because the trade agreements, especially agreements on services and investments, are at the same time chipping away at the alternatives to generalist competition law, such as industry-specific regulation and foreign investment review.

CONCLUSIONS

This chapter has proffered an analysis of the provisions of an emphatic multilateral trade agreement. The formation of the TRIPs was fiercely contested but, despite the appreciable reservations held in many quarters, it has become a feature of the new public international law. An examination of its provisions indicates how it embraces the full range of Western intellectual property categories. Yet, TRIPs is not the first multilateral convention on intellectual property. It draws substantially on existing conventions and notably on the Berne Copyright Convention. So it provides an example of the kind of cross-referencing we identified in the introductory chapters. This reliance on the existing conventions helps the WTO to mediate the cognitive and normative demands being placed upon it by inter-legality.

Nonetheless, TRIPs has firmed up the protection being made available for high technologies and commercial products. In areas such as patents and trademarks, the coverage has been strengthened. In addition, the agreement has confirmed protection for such key resources as computer software and secret information, which could previously only be assimilated under very general provisions for international protection. Moreover, TRIPs is resolute in requiring members to provide effective means of enforcing the rights which it has nominated. Furthermore, in order to ensure that members respect their obligations, it is backed by the WTO's government-to-government system for dispute settlement. Questions of interpretation and redress for non-compliance are accordingly to be considered from within the trade perspective of the WTO. As the early disputes are suggesting, such back-up may prove particularly significant for those countries which are finding implementation onerous and are encountering domestic opposition.

It is fair to say that the TRIPs model of intellectual property is very much one of individual property rights freely assignable in the marketplace. Moral rights were not stressed. On this view, it would seem that TRIPs had little to offer secondary producers and end users, even independent local inventors, developers, artists and performers, who are not necessarily antagonistic to the notion of property rights. Nonetheless, a close analysis reveals that the TRIPs leaves spaces to cater for national sensitivities regarding, for example, the ownership of plants and animals or rights to control on-line communications. It leaves openings for other international fora, such as WIPO, UPOV and the Biodiversity Convention, to re-enter the field. So too, TRIPs makes concessions to counterbalancing regulation. It allows national legislatures to attach limitations and exceptions to the rights. In the past, these kinds of allowance have been utilised to afford access for such purposes as research, criticism and education. The availability of these allowances mediates the clash between differing attitudes to the use of intellectual resources.

For importing and developing countries, one crucial objective has been technology transfer and the local working of the intellectual property. TRIPs became an opportunity to discipline the national use of compulsory licensing. In any case, a mere allowance for compulsory licensing is of little help to the nation state today. Unilateral regulation is a risky proposition when trying, at the same time, to attract foreign investment and link locals into international production and distribution networks. Having bolstered market power, TRIPs proves very weak on international regulation of the restrictive practices of the transnational corporations. It is true to say that the costs and benefits of intellectual property are not so neatly distributed today. All the same, if the WTO is asking all countries to provide protection, it may still have to give something more in return.

CHAPTER 7

THE CASE OF GENETIC CODES

Chapter seven selects as its global carrier the essential life force of the genetic code. It considers how control of the code may exercise a powerful influence over the plants which are produced across the world. Just as importantly, it may shape the pattern of the benefits which stem from their production, such as farming livelihoods, food sustenance and health care. Links are made to the manipulation of genetic codes in animals and humans, partly because the technology now crosses over directly, partly because the legal issues have increasingly become the same.

In keeping with the general approach of the book, the chapter offers reasons why the technology is not all powerful and legal control matters. The dynamics of the technology do not allow entirely for production to cut loose from the ties of the locality, and protection still relies on a legal foundation rooted in the national legalities of intellectual property. In this field, the main means for legal control has been the patent. Legal pluralism stems from the differences in the criteria for recognition of genetic codes worthy of protection. By way of illustration, we take up the example of differences to be found in the application of the distinction between discovery and invention. A contrast is drawn here between recent European and United States jurisprudence.

Some of the industrialised countries of the North continue to make explicit exceptions from patentability on public policy grounds. Such exceptions have provided a space for environmental and moral interest groups to intervene and express opposition to the technology. The chapter recounts the debate over the retention of the limited European Union exception for plant and animal varieties. Yet, when high technology producers seek to protect their contributions to genetic codes across the world, they encounter even more diverse legalities. An inter-legality is created by the lack of patentability in some countries of the South. Provisions for compulsory licensing and the 'farmer's privilege' must also be taken into account.

Previously, legalities in the South sought to maintain a space outside the field of appropriation for a common natural heritage. Chapter seven recognises how globalization is stimulating a positive assertion of national interests and, in some instances, the interests of those local communities and indigenous peoples who have conserved and managed the essential resources for the genetic codes. Those interests are seeking new legal means to obtain material rewards for their contributions to the resources, perhaps the right to prevent incompatible uses. If patents are not fitted to providing recognition to these contributions, then support is sought in other forms of property. We examine the experience with a form specific to plants, the plant breeder's right. The right has achieved international status through the UPOV Convention (International Convention for the Protection of New Varieties of Plants).

The chapter brings the study around to the impact of the TRIPs agreement. The agreement strengthens patent protection, but the need to mediate has seen the insertion of a very relevant exception to patentability. This exception is discussed. At the same time, take-up of the exception is conditional on institution of an alternative system of protection, and in this regard the relationship between TRIPs and UPOV (which itself has been undergoing revisions) remains indeterminate. Furthermore, the chapter appreciates that globalization is provoking searches further afield in order to broaden the positive re-regulatory potential of intellectual property. We assess the progress which the Convention on Biodiversity has made with alternative forms which might give better recognition to the knowledges, practices and innovations of local communities and indigenous peoples.

Global carriers?

We might begin the case study with some remarks on the capacity of the technology to put these codes to use. We know that, from the time cultivation began, people have been selecting, swapping and nurturing seeds and cuttings. The application of scientific and industrial techniques, however, has far greater potential to alter the balance between labour and capital, between the local and the global, even between nature and humankind. At the beginning of the twentieth century, the techniques extended to systematic cross-breeding, combining favoured characteristics of sexually compatible plants within the same variety or species. In the second half of the century, with the innovation of genetic engineering, they moved to the laboratory. Here, they began to work at the level of the micro-organism, the cell and the gene sequence. Through the application of techniques such as tissue culture, somatic cell fusion and gene splicing, genes can be introduced into sequences or removed much more directly. The process bridges the gap between varieties or species, overcoming the obstacle of sexual incompatibility. Flounder genes have been inserted into tomatoes to make them more resistant to frost; human genes have been placed in mice to make them more susceptible to cancer.

Such genetic engineering has clearly enhanced the techniques available for use in food production. We can acknowledge that the techniques will be used for a whole host of utilitarian purposes. To list a few, they can increase crop yields through greater growth; strengthen resistance to insects, weeds, adverse weather or disease; build up tolerance to chemicals used for example as fertilisers, herbicides or insecticides; make crops more amenable to mechanised harvesting; enhance food quality and taste; manipulate colour and other appearance; or improve storage capability.

Nonetheless, we should appreciate throughout this chapter that the genetic codes of plants are being explored and altered for other purposes too. In particular, there is renewed interest being shown in the medicinal qualities of plants. This interest crosses over into the genetic engineering of animals and humans. We shall see that the legal issues overlap too. Genetic engineering is able to make this instrumental approach much more applicable to the higher levels of life. Indeed, in a direct link, human genes have been introduced into animals. Now, a comprehensive mapping of the human gene is pointing to the location of genes that influence, not only health, but a range of other attributes including performance and appearance. Already, we hear of athletes taking growth hormones. Thus, the genetic codes embody ideas and practices which carry profound implications for society worldwide.

Could the technology contribute to the globalization of food and medicine production? We can note that the potentialities of biotechnology have inspired reorganization of research and development increasingly on a global scale. Scientists have taken part in large-scale, cross-national research programs. Multinational companies have established a presence, sponsoring and licensing work in the public sector and buying into small private companies.[1] Now, more research is being brought in-house, as well as being centralised in the Triad countries. Research is further geared to commercial success in areas such as elite cultivars and boutique foods, with these companies tempted to do little work elsewhere except to tailor the products to local markets.

The technology makes an impact on the organization of food production. An OECD report identifies the high rate of structural change occurring in agriculture.[2] This change is proceeding along the lines of greater integration among sub-sectors down the food chain as well as the formation of further inter-sectoral linkages. In the process, the farmer is linked more closely to the suppliers of industrial inputs, such as machinery, chemicals, know-how and capital. So too, largely through the medium of production contracts, the farmer is joined to food processors and retailers.[3] The technology plays a role in creating that relationship by supporting two basic strategies, appropriation and substitution.[4] Within appropriation, the technology tends to favour those plants which are most compatible with the industrial inputs. Here, the seed becomes the 'delivery system' for a mode of production which favours farms that are technically sophisticated and capital intensive. While achieving certain efficiencies, farming becomes further detached from its traditional state of autonomous reproduction.

This industrialisation of agriculture may produce uneven distributional effects. As well as favouring high technology farms, it produces a broad split between developed and developing countries. Developed countries tend to specialise in the production of low-value, high-volume basic grains and cereals with the use of capital-intensive methods. On the other hand, developing countries farm more labour-intensive produce for local and foreign middle-class markets, such as fruit, flowers, eggs, vegetables, milk, pork, fish and poultry, both as fresh produce and as constituents within processed foods. Thus, this organizational structure – of centralised large-scale production of generic foodstuffs and flexible consumer-segmented production of high-value items – also assumes a distinctive geographical pattern. Such developments also promote a wider range of differences within each sector and locality as well as across the world. Successful farmers connect up to agro-food networks, while others, and especially the family farm, move to the margins. But Lawrence's second strategy, substitution, attenuates this process.[5] Traditional natural foods are replaced by the synthetics made in the factory and the laboratory, allowing production to be clustered in the advanced industrial regions. The replacement of natural sugars with artificial sweeteners provides an example.

The social and environmental consequences can be mixed. We should acknowledge that yields may be increased, making more food available to the poorer consumers. At the same time, however, a central source of work for many people, and even a vital space outside a capitalist economy, is lost. While by no means providing the only reason, this development contributes to the huge population movements into the cities which the world is currently trying to accommodate. Furthermore, if yields are increased, the technology increases the risks of crop failure. It has been suggested that monoculture may make food sources more vulnerable to the devastation of disease, pests or weather.[6] While more efficient, the individual plants tend to lack versatility. In addition, product specialisation and large-scale farming dedicate whole areas to the one crop. Overfarming and the use of chemicals exacerbate environmental problems such as soil erosion and hazards to human health and wildlife. Of course, the engineering of animal and human life is seen to raise even more fundamental questions about the extent to which we should try to alter nature.

Strength of local resources

However, it would be premature for us to conclude that food production has become detached from the ties of the locality. We should understand that the development of the technology often involves high-risk and large-scale investments with long lead times for commercialisation. Gene transplanting is in its early stages and it appears that not all crops are taking to new genes from alien sources or responding to cloning in tissue cultures. Limits to the technology also impede progress towards appropriation. For example, some plant varieties have been resistant to hybridisation, particularly where the aim is the production of sterile plants, that is plants which do not generate seeds. Recently, this strategy has attracted social protests too. Monsanto's use of a patented 'terminator gene' has borne the brunt of the protests and the company has agreed not to proceed with this strategy for the time being. In these circumstances suppliers must try to control the use of seeds (or other progeny) down the line, if they are to obtain the desired return on their investments. Such a strategy is likely to be problematic in a sector where the technology is so easily replicated. In addition, the potential users may be too dispersed or divergent in their practices to be contained through the use of licence contracts or infringement suits.

We should note that consumer demand creates a variable too. While there is much interest now in the production of cheaply priced staples, longer term, it is suggested, both local and international consumer tastes may become more discerning. Paradoxically, segments of more affluent middle-class markets already seek out natural foodstuffs and medicines, such as free range, organic, fresh and environmentally sound produce. As we saw in chapter three, a major issue now is the extent to which the presence of genetically modified organisms should be identified by product labelling. Release of the organisms into the environment also faces regulatory controls. Here too social protests have been encountered, environmentalists taking direct action to destroy genetically modified plants.

Substitutions are also limited because certain crops can still only be produced in specific climes and habitats. Accordingly, local knowledge and cooperation remain important ingredients in successful farming. This reliance hints at a far broader mutual dependence between North and South. Much of the high technology draws on the genetic pool of wild and indigenous plants which has been sustained on the ground by local farming and indigenous communities. The gene-rich regions of Latin America and west central Asia have been major contributors to this pool. Today, scientists are even more systematically prospecting for genes throughout such natural plant habitats. Their 'finds' extend to animals such as periwinkles and frogs and indeed to native peoples whose gene lines seem to carry resistance to the diseases which afflict us in the urban industrial North. Now the government of Iceland proposes licensing access to the exclusive genetic lineage of its people. The prospect of finding a cure to the terrible diseases of the nervous system, cancer or AIDS, gives a powerful stimulus to this work.

INTELLECTUAL PROPERTY REGULATION

We need to consider what role intellectual property has to play in these uses of the genetic code. The evidence suggests that technical and economic strategies will not always be adequate to capture the benefits of this trade in technology. Consequently, the suppliers are likely to seek positive legal recognition for their genetic codes. In the field of biotechnology, the most relevant category of intellectual property is the patent, though it is necessary for us to think in terms of other categories such as the plant breeder's right as well. Across industries, the importance of intellectual property is often debatable but, in the biotechnology field, the commercial interest is demonstrable. Intellectual property offers a form of security against those who would reproduce the technology directly or use it to develop derivative products. By discouraging unfair competition, it permits a return to be obtained on the investment made in the innovation. Thus, intellectual property enables the right holder to charge a price for purchase of the technology, even to control its uses by others where they might compete with its own uses. In this way, it provides an economic incentive to research, release and commercialise inventions.

Role of property rights

Within the biotechnological field, it is again useful to appreciate that intellectual property serves not merely as a protective, exclusionary device; it is often employed as a negotiating and organizing tool.[7] For example, intellectual property agreements can be a medium to communicate preferred lines of research between industrial sponsors and research institutes. Furthermore, cross-licensing agreements may be structured to combine specialised assets and coordinate operations amongst industrialists. Likewise, external licensing allows quality and quantity controls (as well as other specifications) to be applied downstream to assemblers, distributors and users, such as farmers.

These controls have various purposes, some more positive and benign than others. After all, we should expect some control rights to come with the grant of property. However, it would remain of concern if the intellectual property rights were to be used, say for the purpose of suppressing genuine competition. Certainly, licensing practices have been deployed in attempts to inhibit the progress of research and development by potential rivals or to make end users dependent on the one source of technology. In the realm of plant production, the control issue takes on a special complexion because the working of the 'invention' is one of the uses which farmers wish to make of it. In other words, the technology is bound up with its products in a special way. Replication may also be necessary to the conduct of research and development on further strains and varieties.

As Pavitt observes, these arguments about the proper reach of intellectual property power were previously conducted within the confines of the nation state and the discipline of industrial economics.[8] But now they carry with them a whole range of international, cultural, social and environmental dimensions. Furthermore, they need to be appraised within the context of the other pressures to open localities to global trade and investment flows. That is, the localities are relinquishing many of the traditional regulatory controls which they were able to apply. For example, some countries are being encouraged to introduce private land titling and facilitate the alienation of resources which were once held as part of their rural and wilderness commons. Liberalisation pushes back the barriers which many countries have placed before foreign investment in their farm supply and services sectors, food processing and retailing sectors. Even the core farm ownership and operation sectors are being opened up to foreign investment in some countries. Moreover, we realise that the Uruguay Round itself brought the many controls which countries apply to trade in agricultural products within the purview of the WTO. McMichael suggests that bringing agriculture into the WTO was a crucial way of promoting world market integration, precisely because of farming's identification with place and nation.[9]

Support for property rights

If we are to think in terms of the costs and benefits of property rights, then our reference point ultimately is the innovations they help to promote. Within this study, it is the impact of the production of new foods and medicines. In much more direct and immediate terms, property rights confer benefits on those who hold them. With this interest in mind, studies of patent holdings suggest that in the past the major sources have been in the northern countries like the United States, United Kingdom, Germany and Japan.[10] Such a pattern reflects the focus of the patent on the contribution of science and industry to technologies such as biotechnology. Research and development has been concentrated in these countries.[11] Again, the main destination for patent registrations has been the Triad countries (Japan, the European Union and the United States), as these countries are where the competition commonly takes place. However, where biotechnology is concerned, patent protection becomes important to the prospects for commercialisation in other parts of the world too. The developing countries are already significant locations for production, potentially they are also large markets for new foods and medicines. We can think in terms of the technology being imported into such countries. But it is technology which is often easily replicated through such activities as the resowing of seeds or the manufacture of generic drugs. Thus recognition for patents in these places is important to protection too.

In the northern countries, we can identify a variety of contributions to the technology, ranging from public research centres to private start-up firms. Yet a characteristic of the patent is the right to assign or license it in the marketplace. The patent can end in private hands, not just because private firms are active in research, but because well endowed companies can sponsor public sector research in exchange for property rights, acquire patents on the open market, or take over the institutes and small firms when they go searching for the large-scale capital needed for commercialisation. Thus, a growing trend has been for the independent seed centres and companies to be acquired by agricultural chemical and fertiliser conglomerates such as Monsanto.[12] A uniform system of patents helps such corporations spread their acquisitions around the world.

However, we should not be too quick to set up a dichotomy. It is also true that certain local interests within the importing countries identify with the virtues of intellectual property protection. Especially in middle-income countries, such as the newly industrialising countries, we would expect a direct identification to be made by those whose role it is to act as local distributors, compilers and servicers of technology imports. Protection also offers those local inventors, public and private, something with which to bargain. More countries appear to be submitting to the weight of the argument that it is necessary to offer intellectual property protection if direct foreign investment and technology transfer are to be encouraged. Long-time sceptics such as the United Nations organization, UNCTAD, have begun to advocate a more moderate line, a balanced approach to intellectual property. A move to high technology farming provides opportunities for local capitalists who, to quote the Indian Minister for Agriculture, are product, surplus and export oriented.[13] In countries such as India, Chile, Argentina and Mexico, local leaders often give support to such strategies of economic liberalisation and privatisation.

Furthermore, whatever the net material gain to a particular country might be, intellectual property protection is increasingly viewed as the symbolic price to pay for participation in a global economy. A commitment to its protection acts as an indication of a country's goodwill to abide by the rules.[14] On this basis, World Bank and IMF funds have been made available to developing countries on condition that their programs of structural adjustment include the institution of intellectual property and other liberal legal provisions. In earlier chapters, we noted how the newly industrialising countries, notably those in South-East Asia, have also been met with the threat of trade sanctions if they do not provide intellectual property protection for high technology. Patent protection, for instance for agricultural chemicals and pharmaceuticals, has been a major target of those bilateral pressures.[15] Of course, the Uruguay Round itself was to be a multilateral process for linking agreement to intellectual property protection with greater market access for agricultural and manufactured goods.

Yet some observers continue to doubt whether market forces alone have the capacity to produce genuine technology transfer, or to promote applications which translate the technology into farming methods and ecological practices suitable for local conditions. With the public sector resiling from its involvement in farm extension work, the OECD recognised that these market forces were all the more central. It counselled that new institutional procedures were needed to ensure that technology transfer occurred through the private sector. Otherwise, there was a risk that the differences in agricultural wealth between the developed and the developing countries would widen.[16] The OECD also noted that commercialised biotechnology is less likely to find application in the more marginal, smaller-scale spheres of activity where, for example, the farmer saves seeds for the following season or otherwise the market is not seen as especially valuable to industry.

Indigenous property rights

We should appreciate that the opposition to patent protection is not confined to the developing countries. The possibility that the traditional farmer might be priced out also creates a lobby in the developed countries. This lobby is often focussed and vocal. Yet, at the very same time, it is now being asked whether intellectual property might carry an additional potential for countries which are usually receivers of high technology. Not only will they receive valuable products from the North, but they too might capitalise on the contributions they have made to the development of the technology. Increasingly, their laboratories will work on high technology innovation. But, already, they make a more fundamental contribution which is deserving of recognition. We should remember that the tradition has been to regard the pool of genetic resources as part of a common heritage, a free gift of nature, which can be drawn on by all. Now, it is recognised more widely that much insight, care and effort have been devoted to the identification and preservation of wild plants and the shaping and strengthening of primitive cultivars and localised varieties. On this view, it would be unfair for that value to be appropriated without any acknowledgement or recompense.

In pursuit of this objective, there may be reference to the internal criteria of patents law, or other forms of intellectual property with Western origins such as plant breeder's rights, to see whether they can recognise and reward these particular contributions to genetic resources. Another strategy is for the state in these localities to assert dominion over flora and fauna resources. Yet this strategy leaves in question the role of non-state entities, such as local farming communities and indigenous peoples who have sustained the genetic materials. In such cases, the materials may well carry a spiritual significance that is bound up with the meanings, traditions and customs of the group as a whole. Just like their scientist counterparts in the North, the locals may be as much interested in moral as in economic rights, collective as in individual rights.

Some members of these groups, along with ecological and ethical movements in the North, remain opposed to the application of any kind of economic property rights to natural genetic materials and higher life forms. Supporters of patents suggest their concerns lie really with the nature of scientific research and the uses to which the results of this research are put by industry and the service sectors. The ownership question is not strictly germane.[17] Nonetheless, it seems that, at the very least, public concerns have found a convenient forum in the property issue. In Europe and the United States, also India, for instance, the issue of patentability has provided a point of entry to the debate for these environmental and other non-government groups. As we shall see now, there have been third party interventions in patent proceedings and lobbying in the legislatures.

We seek now to gauge the extent of legal pluralism in this field. While many countries now have patent laws on their books, the laws reveal significant differences in their coverage and strength. The space for mediation can be opened up in several ways. As we shall see, the defensive response is to employ strict criteria for the recognition of patentable subject matter, oppose grants in individual cases, maintain categories of exception to patenting as a matter of public policy, and provide for compulsory or non-voluntary licensing in certain situations. Variations are to be found in the texts of the national legislation but, less transparently, they are shaped by the practices of the administrative offices and the decisions of the ordinary courts. Sell finds that, even where countries have responded to pressures to institute protection, implementation and enforcement of rights have lagged behind.[18] Of course, we should appreciate that such policies do not always signify opposition to intellectual property. Sometimes, they are evidence of a lack of technical resources or a preference for other strategies such as informal arrangements with potential transgressors.[19] Once again, it would be too ambitious to try to capture the full extent of this legal diversity here,[20] and we shall focus on a couple of aspects which will serve as illustrations. The first involves the distinction made in patent law between a discovery and an invention.

THE CONCEPT OF INVENTION

Patent law practice

If patents are to operate in an instrumental fashion, to serve the purpose of stimulating innovation, the law is meant to apply the kind of criteria which determine whether individual applications do in fact constitute inventions. For a long time, the threshold requirement that claims constitute an 'invention' was read to restrict patents to the products and processes of secondary manufacturing. But in acknowledging developments in science and economy, the concept has been relaxed in many northern jurisdictions to embrace the commercially valuable technologies which are employed in the agricultural and service sectors. Did such liberalisation empty the concept of all its content? Biotechnology is notable for employing processes and products which are alive. Patent law has allowed that inventions can be living things. However at the same time a distinction between naturally and non-naturally occurring products or processes came to the fore. Yet selective plant breeding and genetic engineering cannot help but involve the interaction of natural and non-natural elements. The law is then called to decide whether the role of human agency is enough to transform a living thing from a discovery into an invention, to distinguish something found in nature from something made by man. Understandably, such a distinction can be hard to make. How ready the courts and patent offices are to do so is an important indicator of national divergence.

In certain jurisdictions, patent law is highly developed. We should note several features here, while conceding that anything we say will only be a crude summary. First, it is worth appreciating that, in seeking to identify real innovations, the office or court may break the claim for a patent into constituent steps or parts. Thus a patent may cover a process, product, use or application. In biotechnology, a process may be invented to constitute a product (from composite materials) which in turn is incorporated in another product or employed in another process, all with uses and applications in mind. Disaggregation along these lines allows the patentable to be divided from the non-patentable, though the decision makers naturally may resist too much discernment of this kind. One example is the product by process patent. In this category, the product is deemed patentable because the process by which it is made satisfies the criteria.

On the other hand, patent law may extend the reach of rights if it is to ensure that its protection is effective. Because the rights of the patent holder are meant to encompass the making, use, selling and maybe even the importing of an invention, the rights may reach to control over the kinds of materials which embody the invention. In the case of plant technology, control issues run to the seeds, fruits, flowers, leaves, meal, foodstuffs and medicines which contain the product or process and which in some cases enable the re-making of it.

Given these possibilities, it might not matter to science and industry whether the basic genetic material is patentable. The focus will be on the 'value-added', the processes employed in extracting and recombining these materials, together with the end products which are so constituted, and the uses or applications to which they are put. But it seems unlikely that patenting would be so selective unless the law insisted, and the evidence is that the claims extend to the genes and gene sequences themselves. One immediate reason for the interest in the patentability of the genes is that the attendant processes and products are, in becoming more routine and predictable, unable to satisfy the criteria and anchor the claims in their own right.

In this respect, we should consider the criteria which the patent systems of the North have developed for identifying patentable subject matter. We might characterise these criteria as internal and technical criteria. They are internal in the sense that they do not set the boundaries to the subject matter. Rather, they tend to judge the eligibility of the individual claim. They are technical in the sense that they are interested in the quality of the scientific input into the claim and its relation to the prior art. These criteria are said to reflect the system's concern with encouraging or rewarding only true innovation. The criteria are novelty, inventiveness (or, in some systems, non-obviousness) and utility (or industrial application). Generally put, novelty requires that the invention not be already known to the public, in the sense that someone skilled in the science would be in a position to replicate the invention. An invention involves an inventive step if it amounts to something more than the skilled practitioner could have worked out how to do. In turn, utility requires the invention to be developed to the point that it demonstrates a practical application of economic value.

We might see how these science and industry-oriented criteria would not recognise indigenous knowledge. Yet they could also serve to put a brake on their appropriation by biotechnology from the North. For example, it may be hard to say that something which has existed in nature and has been put to use by local people remains novel. The pro-technology response is to look for the intervention which transforms a discovery into an invention and to say that the characteristic way in which biotechnology intervenes fits the bill. Specifically, the response is to say that the ingredients of novelty, inventiveness and utility, which are involved in the isolation and purification of a gene sequence, render it an invention.

Evidence of this approach is to be seen in previous patents office guidelines for applications. The guidelines seek to carve out a category for the science which is working so ingeniously with these natural materials. For example, European patent office guidelines once advised that it would be considered a mere discovery to find something freely occurring in nature; Japanese guidelines indicated that the question was whether the materials were still as they would be in nature without interposition of artificial means; the United States system granted patents for the pure cultures of organisms if they subsist in nature only in an impure form.[21] Accordingly, claims have tended to recite a formula of a substantially isolated and purified form, rather than simply 'read on' the genetic sequences. Thus, the current Australian industrial property organization notes for applicants allow: 'the DNA coding sequence for a gene; this is claimed either in purified or recombinant state (otherwise it is claiming something which occurs in nature)'.[22] The result is that a number of patents have been granted for genes. The patented matter includes genes carrying codes for the expression of such proteins as adreline, interferon, vitamin B-12, L-arterol, relaxin and erythropoietin.

Recent cases

As we know, patent office practice faces review by the courts when proceedings are taken to restrain infringements of the patent. In this area, an issue for the courts is whether to treat the concept of an invention as having any real content beyond the requirements of what we have called, for convenience sake, the internal, technical criteria. Where the legislation simply posits a general concept like 'invention', we might expect the effective standard to depend on the course of judicial decision making. The study will now make reference to several recent cases in order to indicate how movement to this level can sustain pluralistic national jurisprudence. Yet, when the parties are major industrial corporations and social movements, interested in patenting worldwide, such divergence between jurisdictions becomes an international inter-legality. The cases we shall mention now reveal a divergence between United States and European jurisprudences. All of these cases concern human genetic codes, but it is suggested we can accept their application to the technology overall.

Where the process of arriving at the genetic code was not itself inventive, the United Kingdom courts have acknowledged the possibility that they would be patenting a discovery. A key case concerned Genetech's attempt to enforce a patent to a DNA sequence coding for an enzyme that dissolved blood clots.[23] Here, the Court of Appeal found that the method of arriving at the sequence had become routine; it also said that the product was to be regarded as known and obvious. There being nothing new in the claims, apart from the use of the sequence, at least one of the judges took the view that the claims were founded on the ascertainment of an existing fact of nature, in other words a discovery. In contrast, the Court of Appeal was able to rule in favour of Chiron's patent over a sequence that encoded a polypeptide providing antigens to Hepatitis C.[24] It characterised the invention as finding and sequencing the initial clone of the virus. If the Court thought that the clone was derived from a discovery, it would not entertain the idea that the patent would be claiming the discovery as such.

This favourable decision was followed, however, by a ruling against Biogen's claim to a sequence coding for proteins displaying antigen specificity to Hepatitis B.[25] The Court of Appeal said that, as the process of arriving at the sequence had not been inventive, but had just searched at random for DNA segments, the cloned molecule did not constitute an invention. The process could not make the product patentable. However, it is significant that, in parallel proceedings, the European Patent Office's Technical Board of Appeal was satisfied that the same method was inventive and that there was an invention.[26] Yet, subsequently, the House of Lords was to uphold the Court of Appeal decision against Biogen on the ground that its application involved no inventive step.[27] In passing judgement, Lord Hoffman was of the opinion that it was unlikely that anything which satisfied the internal criteria would not also be an invention. While in theory there might be such cases, the present case was not one.

The United States courts have overcome the uncertainty which the British courts have experienced by emphasising the distinction between the natural and cloned genes. A good example comes from the Federal Circuit ruling on Amgen's claim to a sequence encoding a protein which stimulates the growth of red blood cells.[28] The court pointed out that the claimants did not invent the gene as such – their claim was to the novel isolated and purified sequence. This sequence could be regarded as novel because 'you had to clone it first to get the gene sequence'. This decision was followed by, among others, the decision in re Deuel supporting a patent for a sequence encoding the production of human and bovine heparin-binding growth factors.[29] Here, the court felt that the method of isolation was not inventive. However, the sequence itself was novel because prior knowledge of the protein was at too general a level to identify the sequence before it was extracted. Analogs could not be used because ultimately each sequence is to be regarded as structurally different.

The viability of the distinction

This focus at the level of court decisions shows how differences remain possible. The choice of jurisprudence is a critical one from a policy point of view too. We can readily concede that the isolation of the genes involves more than mere recognition of a natural resource. But can we say that the technical human intervention really alters them? In a critical piece, Looney argues that the Amgen approach confuses the threshold and technical criteria of patentability or, more precisely, it squeezes out entirely the policy layer represented by the threshold criterion of an invention. She comments: 'The interpretations draw a distinction where none may exist – an object of nature (a gene), unaltered by human innovation, does not necessarily lose its status as such simply because it is outside the body and has an identified function.'[30] Equally critically, Ducor argues that the re Deuel approach turns non-obviousness into nothing more than novelty. In any case, even if the precise structure of the DNA molecules is never fully known until they are isolated, that is, assuming they do not have structural analogs, they may well express the same informational content and operative function. While the isolated DNA is always different from the natural DNA, because it drops off redundant material, such differences might also be viewed as insubstantial or incidental.[31]

On the other side of this important debate is the understandable desire to provide reward, and so to give encouragement to the considerable degree of research activity and expenditure which goes into discoveries. For example, Karet criticises the decision in Biogen as

> difficult for the biotechnology industry because the production of known targets having new levels of purity has often represented an immense research effort ... The work that has gone into making these previously identified but scarce products will not, under this decision, be patentable unless a patentee can show surprising research results or the development of a new and non-obvious method.[32]

In the past, some of the greatest contributions to medicine have come from the insights and forays of the natural scientist. But Ducor argues that the explicit purpose of the patent system is to single out the exceptional

activity of invention. He argues that a sui generis form should be insti-
tuted if useful scientific or industrial work is to be recognised. [33]

A related debate concerns the breadth of individual patent grants. An
applicant may have invented a process that is capable of many applications in the future; likewise, a product may suggest a number of analogs,
complementary sequences, allelic variations, or similar species. It is not
hard to see how a patent over the basic genetic starting material could be
used to block researchers down the line. The United States office in particular has been criticised for granting very wide and sometimes overlapping claims. Crespi comments: 'In a high proportion of biotechnology
patents the broad product claims are in effect directed to the objectives
of the research or the results of research and do not pinpoint the actual
inventive solution of the problem.'[34]

The NIH claims

The difficulty of this issue was highlighted when the National Institutes
for Health (NIH), together with their employee, Craig Venter, applied to
patent sequence tags which were used to mark the location of gene
sequences coding for basic human brain functions. The tagging of these
sequences was the result of participation in the human genome project,
a multi-million dollar, cross-country effort to map the human genome.
Rejection of the NIH's sequences, on the ground that they were products
of nature, would bring down other patents issued to the biotechnology
industry. But the scientific community was concerned that such patents
would obstruct applied research work down the line. Collaborators in the
public project from other countries, including Britain, France and Italy,
regarded the applications as a breaking of ranks.[35]

The United States Patent Office rejected the applications on the basis
that they failed to meet the internal technical criteria. The requirement
of novelty presented one problem for the Office because, at the level disclosed, some of the sequences were already recorded in existing databases. The Office also took the position that the applications used a
method obvious to others, did not identify any non-obvious properties of
the sequences, and did not solve a problem in a way not previously
recognised. The main objection mounted to the applications was lack of
utility or industrial application. The applicants were said to be seeking
patents when the uses of the genes were still unknown. On this objection,
patent systems should only be used to reward those who have invented a
use for the material; the grant can then be limited to that use and others
afforded scope to devise further uses. The Office did not accept the
applicants' argument that the tags were already being used in research
work as genetic markers or tissue probes.[36]

Ultimately, the rulings were not to be tested in the courts, for the applicants withdrew the claims. Craig Venter was permitted to move out of the NIH and to contract with the pharmaceutical company, WR Grace, for the development of the technology. Here, we see the dilemmas for science highlighted. Paradoxically, it is possible that the grant of a patent to the NIH would have provided the public sector with an opportunity to obtain a return on its huge investment of taxpayers' monies. As Cohen and Boyer (and their universities) were prepared to do in the case of the basic gene splicing technology, the NIH might have been prepared to license all comers at a modest fee.

EXPRESS EXCEPTIONS

Plants, animals, people

Given the complexity of the internal, technical criteria, we might not be surprised to see that the focus of opposition often turns instead to the availability of any public policy grounds for denying patents. However, in recent years the offices and courts have shown an understandable reluctance to take on the large economic and moral arguments involved in these kinds of objections to patenting. In the landmark Chakrabarty case, for instance, the United States Supreme Court was most emphatic in its deference to the legislature as the arbiter of public policy in such matters.[37]

The appeal bodies in Europe also tried not to take sides in these debates. But latterly the activism of environment groups has obliged them to rule on objections expressed in terms of morality and *ordre public*.[38] For example, in opposing the Plant Genetic Systems application (see below), Greenpeace raised arguments based on common heritage, free access to genetic material for plant breeding, and biological diversity. So too, the Green Party questioned the morality of the use of women's bodies for a technical process when it opposed a patent for human relaxin gene. Proceedings in relation to the patent for Harvard University's onco-mouse had to be extended due to opposition from some seventeen ecological and animal welfare organizations, together with over one thousand individuals. A large hall had to be hired to hear all the objections.

At the same time, the environmental groups, as well as local industrial interests, have pressured the legislatures to maintain or to extend the explicit statutory exceptions. It should be noted that many countries have maintained exceptions for processes or products in which these natural resources are being incorporated or employed. These exceptions include pharmaceuticals and methods of human treatment. What of the genetic materials themselves? Perhaps because the technology was not anticipated, few statutes make explicit exception for human genes and life forms, though this issue is now on the agenda of certain legislatures.

When it arose in Australia, for instance, the national parliament chose not to adopt an exclusion for genes but instead excepted 'human beings and the biological processes for their generation'.[39]

The most directly relevant exception has been made for categories of plants and animals and for processes for their production. In his survey, Lesser found that fifty-two countries (out of 115), ranging from very low to high income countries, excluded plant and animal varieties; forty-two excluded essentially biological processes.[40] Of the main locations for systematic cross-breeding and genetic engineering, the United States and Japan are notable in not maintaining such exceptions. As a location for high technology innovation, the European Union carries perhaps the most well known exception. But other countries are also reported to have excluded plant and animal varieties from patentability, including Argentina, Brazil, Canada, Israel, Mexico, Switzerland, Taiwan, and China, at least prior to the recent bilateral and regional initiatives to extend patent protection (see below).

Experience with the European exception

The exception contained in the European Patent Convention has been the focus of much contention. Again, the object in this study will be to use it as an illustration of the scope for divergence. The exception provides that patents shall not be granted in respect of plant or animal varieties or essentially biological processes for the production of plants or animals. However, this provision is then said not to apply to microbiological processes or the products thereof. Arguments have been made that it should be read down restrictively by the courts. For instance, it has been argued that it does not apply to individual plants and animals where they do not in themselves constitute a variety. Neither is it meant to encompass the basic genetic constituents, at least so long as they do not provide by themselves the means to reproduce the variety. Furthermore, it has been suggested that little human intervention is needed to render a process non-biological and, in any case, biotechnology really produces plant and animal varieties by microbiological processes.

Despite the momentum in these contentions, which saw a European patent granted for the Harvard onco-mouse, a recent decision by the European Patent Office's Technical Board of Appeal gave the exception new vitality.[41] Greenpeace opposed a claim by Plant Genetic Systems to a gene that coded for a protein which nullified the effect of a herbicide on a range of broad leaf plants which included potatoes, sugar beet and tomatoes. The Belgian company also claimed the process for transferring the gene and the 'resulting' cells, plants and seeds.

The Board ruled that plant cells cannot be considered to fall under the definition of a plant variety. But the claim to the plants and seeds was a claim that encompassed or embraced a variety and could only be allowed if they were the product of a microbiological process. It conceded that the initial microbiological process step, the transformation of the plant cell, had a decisive impact on the final result. It was by virtue of this step that the plant acquired its characterising feature that is transmitted through generations. However, the Board considered that the subsequent steps of regenerating and reproducing the plants also had an important value and contributed to the final result. Hence, the multi-step process could not be regarded merely as a microbiological process. The case went to an enlarged Board of Appeal that took the view that the claim was directly to a variety – the genetic modification which made the plant distinctive and stable through generations made it a variety.[42]

Greenpeace regarded the decision as a success. But, interestingly, Plant Genetic Systems, which held the patents with Biogen of Cambridge, Massachusetts, said that it was also happy with the ruling. Anyone who wanted to sell plants that were resistant to the herbicide would still have to use the company's gene and its technology for inserting the gene. Selling seeds from one year's crop to be sown the next year was not a realistic option because the plants from the second generation seeds were vastly inferior to those sold by the company.[43]

At this time, the pro-patent groups were entitled to expect the exception to be removed from the European Patent Convention. Indeed, since the 1980s, the European Commission had sought to introduce a Directive that would clarify and strengthen patent protection for biotechnology. In doing so, the European Union's executive bodies were responding to arguments that European industry would be placed at a competitive disadvantage if adequate protection was not available. For example, companies would be inclined to fund research and transfer operations to jurisdictions such as the United States where such exceptions were missing. These bodies have also been lobbied by foreign producers. In these ways, we can see how the position on exceptions produces another inter-legality.

Yet, in early March 1995, the European Parliament voted to abandon the Directive. Aspects of the Directive had been opposed by local economic interests, such as the farming lobby in some member states. It had also been opposed by Greenpeace, the Genetics Forum and Genetic Resources Action. In its tortuous path, amendments were introduced in the Parliament to exclude from patenting parts of the human body as well as to retain the current exception for plant and animal varieties. The Parliament was unable to reach agreement on changes. Environmental groups described the result as a victory for 'conscience over capital'.[44] But the Bioindustry Association also expressed relief. It had been concerned about the ambiguity of the compromises in the Directive. The woolliest it said had been the attempt to draw a distinction between human genes and cells removed from the body – which were deemed unpatentable – and synthetic versions of those genes produced in the laboratory – which the draft Directive suggested could be patented.

However, the story of the Directive was not to end there. In December 1995, the Commission issued a fresh proposal. After several further revisions, it was given a preliminary approval by the Parliament in July 1997. The draft Directive declared that plants and animals may be patented if the practicality of the invention is not technically confined to a particular plant or animal variety. It also provided that the human body, at the various stages of its formation and development, and the simple discovery of one of its elements, including the sequence or partial sequence of a gene, cannot constitute patentable inventions. But an element isolated from the human body or otherwise produced by means of a technical process may constitute a patentable invention, even if the structure of that element is identical to that of a natural element. The Directive has since been confirmed.[45]

COMPULSORY LICENSING

A further source of the pluralism has been the provision for exceptions from infringement and for non-voluntary licensing, usually called compulsory licensing in the case of patents. In this field, borrowing from the approach taken within plant breeder's rights regimes (see below), amendments to the European directive had sought to instigate a 'farmer's privilege'. Farmers would be entitled to use the seeds from a genetically engineered plant to sow another crop. Now the new proposal for a directive extends the idea of a privilege to animals, proposing a right to use patented livestock for breeding purposes on one's own farm. In recognition of the same small farmers' lobby, proposals for a farmer's privilege have been put before the United States Congress.

We have noted that replication is also liable to be regarded as infringement when experiments are conducted by researchers who are seeking to make advances on the technology. Most of the Western European countries already make explicit statutory exception for experimental use. In the United States, the courts have entertained the idea of reading such an exception into the legislation, so long as such use is not regarded as depriving the patent holder of the commercial benefits of the invention. Because the research sector may itself be regarded as a commercial market for biotechnology inventions, this approach has proved problematic and an express exception would seem to be needed. We have seen that the NIH claimed the sequence tags could be used as genetic markers or tissue probes.

Compulsory licensing powers have also been invoked by some importing countries as a means of requiring that individual patents are worked
locally. Local working is thought to generate business for local industry,
as well as increasing competition in the product market. It may lead to
more lasting benefits, such as the transfer of technology to indigenous
firms and workers becoming skilled in the development of technology
centred on local needs. Requirements of external licensing and joint
ventures have also been applied to try to spread the benefits. Such policies respond to a concern that the foreign producers will keep the technology in-house.

Correa notes that some ninety-six countries or seventy-one per cent of
all countries enable one form of compulsory licensing of patents or
another.[46] Compulsory licensing powers may be incorporated in the
operation of the patents scheme itself. Also by operating on a case by case
basis, local working and technology transfer have been made conditions
of foreign investment approvals in some countries. They may at least
theoretically be the subject of a remedy in competition law, where
refusals to license local firms at all or the grant of licences exclusively to
affiliates are treated as being anti-competitive. Licences to 'outsiders' can
also be hedged in with all sorts of restrictive anti-competitive conditions,
such as requirements to license back any improvements made to the
technology, or promises not to challenge the validity of the patent itself.
As, from one direction, trade liberalisation attacks these national instruments of policy, say through investment liberalisation initiatives, it
becomes increasingly important that the international agreements provide a coordinated counterbalance to such uses of property power.

THE UPOV CONVENTION

We turn now to another form of property in plant technology, the
plant breeder's right (PBR). We shall acknowledge how national differences in the definition of this right have created an inter-legality,
but so too the divergence between its content and that of the patent.
Several of the national PBR schemes, predominantly those in Europe,
preceded the formation of an international convention in 1961. But
that convention, the International Convention for the Protection of
New Varieties of Plants (UPOV), has given a fillip to the spread of such
schemes worldwide.

While conferring some of the familiar bundle of rights on breeders,
this UPOV scheme may have been attractive to a wider range of countries
than the patent system. We shall see that it has attempted to balance the
owners' rights against the need of other groups to have access to the
varieties. It has also seemed to offer something positive to those breeders

whose contribution went largely unrecognised by the high technology focus of the patent. Nonetheless, it is important to appreciate that the several revisions to the Convention, notably 1978 and 1991, have moved it further in the direction of a fully blown property right. Furthermore, its articulation with the patent has altered.

Plant breeding

We should take some time now to compare and connect the PBR. We begin by saying that the subject matter of the PBR is much more specific than the patent. It is settled on new plant varieties. It is thus available only for a product and not for the processes of arriving at it. Moreover, it subsumes into ownership only the whole plant, and not its constituent parts, such as its genetic make-up. The 1961 Convention also allowed countries to exclude certain types of plant from the coverage of their national scheme. But the 1978 act set minimum numbers and the 1991 revision requires protection to be given to all genera or species within five years, for new members within ten years. In part, the aim of this stipulation is to move more member states to protect varieties that are not grown locally but are imported from states which do not confer PBR protection. In this regard it is possible to see the terminology 'bio-piracy' gaining in currency. Barry Greengrass (fittingly perhaps the Vice-Secretary General of the UPOV Convention) offers an example: 'thus far, the UK, as an importing country, has probably been uninterested in the protection of bananas. This will now change.'[47]

In order to say that a plant variety has been established, it must prove to be distinct, homogeneous and stable. These requirements call on characteristics that mark off the variety from existing plants and these characteristics must be sustainable across generations. These criteria are struck at such a level of generality that they allow room for differential recognition and practice. For example, Lesser asserts that the Europeans are more rigorous than the Americans in running field trials, the American PBR Office accepting whatever distinctions are claimed by the applicant. But how should a variety with such characteristics be achieved? The crucial question is whether it demands inputs akin to those required by patent law for an invention. It is evident that the variety must display novelty. However, the 1978 Convention was to equate that quality simply with lack of commercialisation. On this basis, the variety was to be regarded as novel if it had not been offered for sale (with the breeder's agreement) prior to the application for the right. The 1991 act altered this criterion slightly to specify that the propagating or harvested material should not have been sold or otherwise disposed of with the breeder's consent. But it also said that the variety had to be distinct from varieties whose existence was already a matter of 'common knowledge'.

We should remember that the right is styled as a right of the plant breeder and the 1978 act did require that a variety originate with the applicant. However, it is relevant to our discussion to note that it is quite possible for a variety to be discovered in nature and meet the general criteria of novelty, distinctiveness, homogeneity and stability. The indeterminacy of the Convention left the question to national legislation. For example, Jarvis thought that the criterion of origination in the Australian legislation – where a person carries out activities in relation to plants in the hope that a variety would originate by natural process – was not enough to catch plants found in nature.[48] Correa cites Argentina, Chile and Peru as countries where PBR legislation explicitly provides that discovered varieties have been protectable.[49] The 1991 act defined the breeder as a person who bred, discovered and developed a variety. The attachment of the word 'developed' complicates the picture; evidently the original proposal to the conference did not include it.[50]

Breeder's rights

In the 1978 version of the Convention, the plant breeder obtains the right to control production – for purposes of commercial marketing – of the plants of the variety and the reproductive or vegetative propagating material (such as seeds and cuttings). Such protection seemed to be aimed against those who deal competitively with the breeder in selling the variety as a commodity to users. But what of the farmer who generates reproductive material from the use of the variety? Significantly, the model left a gap in the rights. It permitted national legislators to afford farmers the privilege of using reproductive material to grow another crop, so long as the crop would be sold for food, fuel, fibre or some other secondary product, rather than sold as a plant for others to grow. Giving seeds to another farmer would seem also to have been permissible.

In addition, the 1978 model made provision for a breeder's privilege. A protected variety and its reproductive material were to be usable as an initial source of variation where the purpose was to originate other varieties. But of course ultimately the variation would have to be distinguishable from the original variety, otherwise its production would involve the reproduction of the original variety. The 1978 act also allowed for compulsory licensing.

Our study should appreciate that the Convention has been in transition. The 1991 act strengthens the breeder's rights over access to the resource. In a significant change to the onus of protection, it adopts the general position that any production, reproduction (multiplication), marketing, exporting or importing shall require the breeder's authorisation, whatever the purpose. Yet Greengrass points out:

the very widely differing natures of the agricultural industries of UPOV member states and the varying political situations in these states made it essential nonetheless to provide states with the option of excepting the planting of farm saved seed. Accordingly, member states may restrict the right in relation to any variety so as to permit farmers to use for propagating purposes, on their own holdings, the product of the harvest obtained by growing on their own holdings.[51]

At the same time, the Convention provides that the member states may only grant this privilege within reasonable limits, and subject to safeguarding the legitimate interests of the breeder. From chapter six, we see how this proviso mirrors a form of words increasingly prevalent in international parlance. Furthermore, the Convention counsels the parties to consider the merits of doing so on a variety-by-variety basis. The conference which negotiated the 1991 act recorded formally the understanding that the provision not be read to extend the practice to sectors in which such a privilege has not been a common practice. In this way, the allowance for a farmer's privilege is formalised, but it is at the same time heavily circumscribed.

The 1991 act also affords the owners' protection greater bite by extending control to the harvested material and the products made directly from this material. Both importing and exporting can now be proscribed, allowing members to attach material or product that is going to or coming from countries that do not confer protection.

Acts done for experimental purposes and acts done for the purpose of breeding other varieties are permitted by the 1991 version. But the 1991 model prohibits exploitation of an 'essentially derived variety' unless authorisation from the breeder of the original variety is obtained. This breeder cannot be compelled to do so, and generally the Convention only allows compulsory licensing where the public interest justifies it and, in that case, the member state must ensure that the breeder receives equitable remuneration.

In terms of mediating inter-legalities, UPOV is also extremely interesting because it has prohibited members from extending both PBR and patent protection to a plant variety. As we noted, the United States and Japan have not provided exceptions for plant varieties in their patent law and the prohibition was not applied to them when they joined the Convention. In any case, the 1991 act lifts that ban on double protection, providing opportunities, in those countries that now choose to allow both, to circumvent the limitations of the PBR.

Finally, in relating the experience with the Convention, we should indicate that the number of signatories to the 1978 Convention has been low, some eighteen to 1991. All of them were industrialised countries from the North.[52] Around fifty states participated in the 1991 conference, along with a range of inter-governmental and non-governmental organizations. Spurred as we shall see by the TRIPs agreement, more countries are now instituting their own PBR schemes, including several Eastern European and Latin American countries. But the absence of such schemes is still noticeable in parts of Asia. And, significantly, as we shall now see, many of the countries coming on board seem to prefer to adopt the 1978 version over the 1991 version.[53]

THE TRIPs AGREEMENT

The TRIPs agreement sought to place some order on this national divergence and strengthen the international security of intellectual property. We examined its general features in chapter six. Here, we shall focus upon the implications of its multilateral standard setting for biotechnology. As we noted in chapter six, to enter the GATT frame of reference, it was necessary to characterise national intellectual property protection as trade related. Some countries had difficulty seeing how local agricultural practices like the resowing of seeds could be placed in this category. Countries such as India and Brazil argued that protection would attach rights and obligations to the activities of individuals which took place behind the border, rather than addressing the cross-border movement of goods in the traditional GATT way. Another reason for leaving intellectual property matters out of the GATT was the considerable discretion which the Paris Convention had afforded national governments to tailor their policies to suit their stage of economic development and their other public needs. As we know, TRIPs lent the force of a trade agreement to many of the provisions of these conventions. But it went further in specifying and strengthening standards. Given that the Paris Convention lacked substantive prescriptions in relation to patentability, the standards of the TRIPs agreement are to be regarded as a major step in the direction of convergence.

Patentable subject matter

Our discussion in chapter six indicated that article 27:1 of the TRIPs agreement requires members to make patents available for any inventions, whether products or processes, in any field of technology. This requirement is supported by a prescription that patents shall be available and patent rights enjoyable without discrimination as to the place of invention, the field of technology and whether the products are imported or locally produced. Such a comprehensive standard was seen as a major gain for the exporting nations. When their initial positions are considered, it was to be a major concession by many of the developing countries. Yet, even as it standardises protection across the world, the agreement can be seen as placing a kind of control over the advances of the patent system.

TRIPs exceptions

The TRIPs agreement identifies the common internal criteria for assessing claims to patents. Patents shall be available for 'inventions', provided they are new, involve an inventive step and are capable of industrial application. To this extent, it institutionalises what we have termed the internal, technical criteria of the northern patent systems. Previously, the Paris Convention had not done so. But the agreement does not and, realistically speaking, could not at such a level of generality operationalise such criteria. Such a shortfall must inevitably leave space for the kinds of differences in the case law we have already identified.

Furthermore, the agreement has embodied and thus, it can be argued, provided support for certain national exclusions from the field of patentability. For the purposes of this discussion, the key allowances are to be found in article 27:3(b). Scalise and Nugent even suggest these allowances were such a major defeat for the biotechnology industry that some elements would have been happier if the agreement had not come to pass at all. Bilateral initiatives would have been able to obtain more protection.[54] The United States, Japan, the Nordic countries and Switzerland all submitted by way of their draft texts that there be no exclusions for plants or other living organisms.[55] But the European Union's text sought space within the agreement to maintain its own particular exception. Exceptions were also sought in a communication from a group of developing countries that included Argentina, Brazil, Chile, China, Colombia, Cuba, Egypt, Nigeria, Peru, Tanzania and Uruguay. On the issue of an exception, the final text was to be in issue right up until the close of negotiations.

The exception was to represent a curious compromise. It is perhaps significant that the exception is not worded exactly as the European Patent Convention. It provides that: 'Members may also exclude from patentability: ... (b) plants and animals other than micro-organisms, and essentially biological processes for the production of plants and animals other than non-biological and microbiological processes'. The exception is wider than the European Convention in that it is for plants and animals as such, rather than for varieties – a category which we have noted has been read restrictively in Europe. In making micro-organisms an exception to the exception, it is clearer than the Convention category of the products of microbiological processes, but arguably narrower. Like the European version, essentially biological processes for the production of plants and animals are also excluded, but in the TRIPs text, this exclusion is limited by the qualification 'other than non-biological as well as microbiological processes'. The effect of this qualifier remains to be seen.

Sui generis systems

The other side of the compromise over the final text is the requirement that 'members shall provide for the protection of plant varieties either by patents or by an effective sui generis system or by any combination thereof'. This requirement seems designed to spread the PBR, at least where countries continue to choose not to make patents available for plant varieties. The evidence for this is the use of the term 'plant varieties' when the exception speaks of 'plants'. Also, no similar protection is required for animals or animal varieties. But, at the same time, the text made no mention of the UPOV Convention explicitly. Certainly, it did not lend its powerful backing to the UPOV Convention in the explicit way it did elsewhere, for instance to the Berne Convention on copyright.

The absence of any final insistence on the patenting of varieties reflects the fact that a consensus was lacking among the developed countries. But the lack of prescription of the UPOV Convention as an alternative is more mysterious. Above, we noted that few developing countries had granted breeder's rights or were members of UPOV. Reportedly, a major source of concern in the drafting stages of the agreement was whether writing in a requirement of UPOV (as an alternative to patents) would apply the 1978 or 1991 versions of the convention.[56] The result is to leave considerable room for countries to develop their own 'effective sui generis systems'. In this way, paradoxically, it may have a de-standardising effect. It also raised the possibility that the WTO disputes settlement system would be brought into play in order to determine what is an effective system of protection. Here, it might be argued that any system must have the flavour of the protections which the agreement has conferred throughout. In particular, it ought to afford protection on the basis of private property rights.

At the same time, the clause in question is notable for scheduling a review of this provision to begin by the end of 1999. The review envisages a shorter time frame than the general allowances which are made for the least developed and developing categories to delay application of the requirements of the agreement in general. The review raises the question whether members who are opposed to patentability should be working to persuade the WTO to prescribe its own sui generis system. Below, we shall ask whether a link to the Convention on Biodiversity is possible here.

In all this, we should appreciate that the TRIPS provision does not actually require member countries to make this exception to patentability. It just allows them to do so if they see fit. They can if they wish provide both patent protection and sui generis protection for plant varieties.

The first evidence of the national response to this provision is to be found in Latin America.[57] The Andean Group – Bolivia, Colombia, Ecuador and Peru – together with Chile, Brazil and Argentina, have been strengthening their patent protection. Bilateral pressures from the United States and the prospect of membership in an expanded NAFTA have also played a part. In Mexico, which is already a NAFTA party, the 1991 law already admitted the possibility of patenting plant varieties. Its new laws are set to encompass biotechnological inventions. But Argentina and Chile have made exclusions for plant varieties and essentially biological processes for obtaining them. Brazil has made an exclusion for substances which already exist in nature, while, interestingly, the Andean Group's exclusion extends to those substances which replicate them. Argentina's law has excluded both pure biological and genetic material as it exists in nature and their 'replica', as well as the biological reproduction process.

Implementation has so far been less demonstrable in Asian countries. South Korea is enacting strong protection, covering inventions (other than humans) and the discovery of new genes. India, on the other hand, seems likely to rely on the exception. The People's Republic of China is currently seeking approval to join the WTO and its intellectual property protection is a major consideration in this process; it seems that animal and plant varieties are not patentable under Chinese law.

Counterbalancing regulation

Overall, the conclusion of the TRIPs agreement indicates that more countries are prepared to take on board the idea of intellectual property protection. But we should not be surprised if they remain sensitive to the need to ensure that the benefits of such protection flow through to their localities. They may not be confident that the globally secured market will assure this outcome simply by the workings of its own autonomous processes. Therefore, they may wish to qualify the patent holder's rights by deeming certain practices not to be infringements or by making provision to assume those rights. In this respect, we should recall that article 30 permits members to provide limited exceptions to the patentee's rights. It attaches a proviso that such exceptions must not unreasonably conflict with a normal exploitation of the patent and do not unreasonably prejudice the legitimate interests of the patent owner, while taking into account the legitimate interests of third parties. Would this proviso accommodate the kind of farmer's privilege which allowed resowing on the farmer's own land?

In addition, the agreement deals directly with compulsory licensing powers (article 31). We know that compulsory licensing was an aspect for which the Paris Convention made substantive provision. For the exporting nations, the TRIPs agreement became a means to apply new disciplines to the uses of such national powers. It lays down a number of safeguards designed to ensure that compulsory licences are confined to the purposes for which they are granted and that the title holders receive adequate remuneration. The agreement is prepared, however, to allow national legislatures to determine the grounds for granting such licences – for allowing other use without the authorisation of the right holder. Article 31 refers to such grounds as national emergencies, public non-commercial use, anti-competitive practices, and dependent patents. But others might be envisaged, such as public health and nutrition or environment protection.

The legitimacy for invoking such grounds might also be found in the aspirational or exhortative statements throughout the agreement. So, for example, if local working were the desired objective, member states might enlist the aid of the statement of objective in article 7. It recognises the value of the promotion of innovation and the transfer and dissemination of technology. Furthermore, the expression of principle in article 8 recognises the right to adopt measures necessary to protect the public interest in sectors of vital importance to socio-economic and technological development (provided they are consistent with the objectives of the agreement). Moreover, article 40 recognises the right to adopt measures (again if consistent) to prevent abuse of intellectual property or resorts to practices that unreasonably restrain trade or adversely affect the international transfer of technology.

Yet such good intentions have to interpreted in the light of the concrete protections of the agreement. Most significantly, the rights of the patent holder are slated to include the right to import a product which is the subject of a patent or the product of a patented process (article 28:1). Generally, patent rights are to be enjoyable without discrimination as to whether products are imported or locally produced (article 27:1). Correa suggests two interpretations of these provisions. One is that a country cannot require local working if the invention is being imported, while the other allows the national law to target lack of local working if it would equally target lack of importation.[58] Of course, lack of importation may also be an issue, if transfer is delayed altogether according to a worldwide strategy for production and distribution.

RECOGNITION FOR INDIGENOUS PROPERTY RIGHTS?

Intellectual property conventions

Now we return to one of our basic inquiries. Who ends up with access to rules and resources in this fluid and multi-faceted pattern of law making?

In the developed countries, it is fair to say that intellectual property is moving to embrace the powers of nature directly. In the key biotechnology producing nations, the conceptual inhibitions are being relaxed. However the powers of nature are said to be appropriable only so far as they are transformed through technical intervention into artificial processes and products. Thus, the internal criteria of the patent systems apply their own limitations to the capture of natural genetic resources. This means the patent and even the PBR are not available to the discoverers, keepers and transmitters of the natural materials. It is consistent with this approach to select out the contribution of science and industry. But if the appropriable element is that layer added by technical intervention, others continue to enjoy access to the starting materials for other purposes. We might sense that this balance begins to tilt, if the isolation and purification of the genetic material, its separation into transferable bits, becomes enough to attract a patent. In such a way, the patent rewards those who are ingenious enough to abstract and standardise the material.

From the evidence above, it is clear that one response to this firming of intellectual property protection is a defence of local spaces. The clearest example is the reservation for national law of the authority to maintain exceptions to patentability. So far the international conventions have continued to provide such national freedom. However, we now appreciate how this defensive response does not necessarily realise the value of local and indigenous resource conservation. As we have acknowledged above, a movement is growing to give such knowledges and practices recognition through some kind of property law regime. But, without a doubt, this movement has opened up a hugely complex and sensitive issue. It is not easy to see how a property right can cope with all these aspirations, especially if its tendency is to render the knowledges into a saleable form which is amenable to the individualised exchanges transacted in the marketplace. A sui generis form of protection may be more suited to the task of assimilating the knowledges bound up with the situation-specifics of local communities and natural environments.

Even if it were achievable, such a form would still present issues about control, both within the communities and in their relations with outsiders such as the nation states and the customer corporation. These issues are in starkest relief when the state assumes property in the resources and licenses prospectors and extractive industries. Within such contractual arrangements, conditions may be imposed in order to obtain royalties or the promise of assistance in kind such as technology transfer and opportunities for local research. Conditions may also be imposed for the safeguarding of natural habitats and environmental integrity. Already, this approach has been explored; the Costa Rican Government most notably fashioning an agreement with the drug company Merck.

In return for prospecting and extraction rights, the agreement provides money for conservation, equipment and local training, together with a share in any profits from intellectual property and the grant of licences to work the intellectual property locally.

We can readily appreciate that, if they are to be successful, such agreements depend on the bargaining power of the state. They also rely on the strength of its resolve to safeguard the interests of local communities, indigenous peoples and the natural environment. However, even if local people are involved in the construction of these agreements, control issues are likely to remain. For example, such property systems may give rise to disputes as to whom among such people have the right to represent or make commitments. Perhaps the NGOs and the international organizations themselves may need to provide support services to assist in the making of the agreements.[59] The simplest agreement will provide monetary compensation for the sale of the genetic material. It will be far more challenging, and ultimately more beneficial perhaps, if agreements can be constructed that contribute to the long-term capacity of the locals to participate in these global agricultural networks. This is especially so if it can be done in ways that are compatible with cultural and environmental traditions. We can suggest that the scale and structure of ventures are important considerations here.

Combining concerns for the preservation of natural genetic materials with access to the benefits of high technology is a good test of the potential of the global frame of reference. TRIPs makes only light provision for mechanisms to mobilise the developed countries and the multinational corporations to respect the needs of developing countries. As we have noted, the objectives and principles recognise the need for intellectual property rights to contribute to technological innovation and the international transfer of technology. But the follow-through is negligible. In any case, the developing nations are precisely those countries which lack the unilateral capacity to discipline the multinational corporations in such ways. Something more positive must be done internationally if duties are to be settled on them. In this regard, the most which the TRIPs agreement asks is for the developed countries to provide incentives to enterprises and institutions within their territories 'for the purpose of promoting and encouraging technology transfer to least developed country members, in order to enable them to create a sound and viable technological base' (see article 66:2). At the same time, it is fair to say that TRIPs makes no reference to environmental concerns.

Despite this growing attention to the conditions of exchange, there will be occasions when local peoples wish to place a veto on certain objectionable uses of the material. For, as we have noted, the material may carry spiritual and moral connotations as well as economic values. How can this attachment be represented when the private or state property holder wishes to license the rights to an economic developer? There is potential for a clash here which will be very difficult to mediate. Responding to the human genome diversity project, which is building a gene bank of endangered peoples, one representative of indigenous peoples exclaimed: 'After being subjected to ethnocide for 500 years, which is why we are endangered, the alternative now is for our DNA to be collected ... why don't they address the causes of our being endangered instead of spending millions to store us? How soon before they apply for intellectual property rights and sell us?'

Convention on Biodiversity

In keeping with the idea of the interface we have been pursuing, other international agreements might be linked with TRIPs in an attempt to broaden out the vision and to find a means to integrate values. In recent years, several international declarations have raised the question of indigenous property rights. But most have remained instances of soft law. With signatories from some 157 nations and already over seventy parties, the United Nations Convention on Biodiversity carries perhaps the most weight.[60] However, an examination of the experience with the implementation of the Convention suggests that a reconciliation is proving difficult to achieve. The Convention's convoluted language is symptomatic of this problem. It makes a tortuous attempt to accommodate the conflicting legalities.

One attempt the Convention makes is to reconcile intellectual property rights with access to technology. It states that the developing countries are to be provided with access to and transfer of technology under fair and most favourable terms – where mutually agreed. Recalling the language of TRIPs, the Convention insists that this access and transfer should be on terms that recognise and are consistent with the adequate and effective protection of intellectual property rights. For their part, the developed countries are obliged to take legislative, administrative or policy measures to ensure access and transfer of technology (which is protected by patents and other intellectual property rights) take place on mutually agreed terms. In particular, they are to do so for those developing countries which provide genetic materials. Furthermore, the parties to the Convention are obliged to cooperate in the fields of patents and other intellectual property rights which are subject to national and international law, in order to ensure that such rights are supportive of the Convention's objectives such as conservation, sustainable use and biological diversity.

At the same time, the Convention signifies a shift away from the ethos of common heritage. It recognises the sovereign right of states to exercise control over the biological resources within their territories.

The Convention requires these states to grant access to the resources within their control on reasonable terms, but access is to require prior informed consent on mutually agreed terms. Furthermore, the country providing the resources is entitled to benefit from the commercial use of its resources. Access is also subject to appropriate utilisation of the resources and to a fair and equitable sharing in the benefits which derive from them. In a further clause, the Convention then seeks to acknowledge the interest of local non-state groups. Article 8(j) places requirements on the states themselves to respect, preserve and maintain the knowledges, innovations and practices of indigenous communities.

In her critical evaluation of the Convention, Shiva questions whether third world countries really received enough from it to match its recognition of the intellectual property rights of the developed world.[61] Also in her view, not enough was done to assert the intellectual and ecological rights of indigenous peoples and local communities to conserve and make use of biodiversity. As the implementation conferences would later recognise, the means of recognition remained very hazy. Moreover, the Convention did not take on the issue of appropriate compensation for the substantial genetic resources which were already stored in gene banks. These banks are under the control of the developed countries, rather than the appropriate United Nations agency, the Food and Agricultural Organization. Shiva is also critical of the Convention for failing to give guarantees to third world farmers or public breeding institutes about access to the materials covered by intellectual property rights. Nor was any mention made of international safety or environmental regulation, when, as we have seen, national legislation faces the disciplines of the Uruguay Round agreements, such as the agreements on sanitary and phytosanitary measures and technical barriers to trade (see chapter three).

How substantial were these criticisms? Subsequent developments have probably not inspired much confidence in the Convention's ability to make its objectives work. Under a Republican administration, the United States Government refused to sign the Convention on the ground that intellectual property rights could not be compromised and that technology transfer should be effected according to terms agreed solely through the free market process. It also pointed out that the Convention's language seemed hollow, for many developing countries had no intellectual property protection for biotechnology whatsoever. The Clinton Administration subsequently did sign. However it circulated a letter of interpretation urging the parties to establish adequate and effective legal protection of intellectual property in inventions based on genetic resources and to secure voluntary acceptance of conditions for the distribution of advantages as well as for the transfer of technologies. The

United States did not become a party and it attends the implementation conferences as an observer.

The second conference in 1995 postponed implementation of rules regarding suitable conditions of access to biological resources. The third conference, in late 1996, took up the question of implementing article 8(j). A delegation from the association of indigenous peoples pressed for the development of an alternative sui generis system of intellectual property. A coalition of countries, South Africa, Ghana, the Philippines and Norway, saw the chance of a constructive linkage to TRIPs which, as we have noted, is due to review its provisions on plants and animals in 1999. They stressed the need for the WTO to take the objectives of the Convention into account, particularly when reviewing article 27:3(b) of TRIPs.[62] The conference declaration embodied a decision to work with the WTO.[63] But the main action was to commission a set of case studies into the relationship between current intellectual property rights systems, access to genetic resources, technology transfer and the knowledges, practices and innovations of indigenous and local communities. Sceptics fear that the case studies will simply be shelved when, eventually, they are completed.

In 1992, the OECD warned that the coupling of privatisation with globalization has created a demand for creative new institutional procedures. Of course, we have already heard arguments that intellectual property may not necessarily be the most suitable system of protection. We have also questioned whether competition law is really designed to bring into account the kinds of social and environmental concerns we have identified here. The Biodiversity Convention's secretariat has listed for consideration a whole range of alternative systems, including contracts, traditional resource rights such as land tenure rights, incentive measures, and the recognition of customary laws.[64] But these systems do not have the force of international law. Some inspiration might be sought in the codes of conduct which were formulated at the United Nations in the past. However, we have seen that they remain very good examples of international soft law, seemingly lacking the precision or the machinery necessary to be enforceable when parties do not wish to cooperate. Furthermore, they were formulated before these concerns with indigenous peoples and biodiversity came to the fore. Perhaps the Biodiversity Convention itself will eventually reach the point of translating its general principles into a workable code. It may derive assistance from the FAO commission on plant genetic resources which has been doing work on elements of a code of conduct for biotechnology. So too we should note that UNCTAD has been seeking to influence the terms of the exchange between North and South with its new moderating line on intellectual property. Other agencies such as UNIDO and UNESCO have been endeavouring to foster individual examples of positive joint ventures, but these examples represent very tentative initiatives. Furthermore, they may not be able to deal with the moral and spiritual aspects of the issue. At times, we must say, these aspects stand in opposition to the economic exploitation of the materials, whoever might happen to be the beneficiaries of that exploitation.

CONCLUSIONS

This study has provided one of the most substantial chapters of the book. As they are embodied – for example in the plant – genetic codes carry messages about the organization of fundamental social activities on a global scale. The new technologies provide opportunities for science and industry to appropriate, even in some instances to replace, the materials which have been used in the settings of diverse natural and communal environments. However global interdependence means that such strategies could not be wholly effective. Even if it were the aim, it would prove difficult to control access, and indeed the industries of the North must also rely on input from the knowledges, innovations and practices of the peoples residing in the gene-rich South.

In the North, patent laws are tending to give recognition to that layer of technical intervention which isolates and 'purifies' the genetic materials. However, to varying degrees, the relevant judicial decisions and legislative provisions still hesitate to make the criteria for patentability wholly technical. We can see evidence of reservations being expressed through the distinction between discoveries and inventions, as well as the categorical exclusions, for example in relation to plants and animals. Various research, environment and moral interest groups maintain opposition to patentability. In the South, the doubts have often been more fundamental. In this sphere, patent laws have been non-existent or heavily circumscribed.

The TRIPs agreement became a means to promote a strong and comprehensive standard of patent protection for the increasingly valuable contribution made by science and industry. But, at the same time, it conceded a space to members in which they could prefer sui generis systems for the protection of plants and animals. That space was left largely undefined. It seems that the concurrent strengthening of property rights within a related convention, the UPOV Convention, discouraged cross-referencing. A genuine consideration of alternative systems of protection may be possible when the provisions come up for review late 1999 and early 2000.[65]

Encounters with northern intellectual property law appear to have stimulated initiatives for international recognition of indigenous property rights. In part, the shift away from the ethic of common heritage is motivated by a desire to obtain some material recompense for the contribution made by local farming communities and indigenous peoples. However it might also be seen as a means to assert controls over the uses to which materials may be put. The materials may also bear social, ecological and spiritual significances. Such a desire will be more difficult to mediate. It is fair to say that TRIPs has done little so far to help with this inter-legality. Presently, the Convention on Biodiversity is giving the most emphatic international recognition, yet its progress has highlighted all the difficulties of reconciling the two perspectives. Compromised by a fuzzy text, it has failed to provide any effective link between national or indigenous rights over biological resources and the more dominant private intellectual property rights. It looks very much as if it needs the aid of the WTO. Thus the review can also be regarded as an important test of the WTO's capacity to mediate.

PART IV

CONVERGENCE

CHAPTER 8

THE CASE OF COMMUNICATIONS MEDIA

Chapter eight's case study is the new on-line communications media. The chapter detects a broad trend towards global integration of the media. However, the openness of the technology itself, the conflicting economic interests which the participants bring to bear (including contradictions within their own positions), and the varying cultural mores of production and distribution all suggest that pluralism is unlikely to be eliminated.

The chapter attempts to relate three legalities which shape most directly the pattern of the flows through this media. It identifies complex and shifting relationships between industry-specific regulation, intellectual property and competition law. We suggest how each of these legalities has been employed, both to stimulate the flows and to capture their value. Two connected issues are pursued to illustrate the significance of the different legalities. The first issue is the freedom with which to transmit various kinds of content on-line; the second is the conditions of access to the technological facilities needed for its transmission. The nature of the field provides an opportunity to consider the influence of the two WTO agreements in conjunction. So this chapter brings each of the strands of the book together.

Globalization is undermining the competence of the kind of industry-specific regulation which national governments have favoured in the past, such as public monopolies, licensing schemes and local content quota. Chapter eight examines the role which the GATS has played in obtaining commitments to roll back this regulation where it would deny foreign service suppliers national treatment and market access. It is clear that the communications sectors were regarded as sensitive by all sorts of countries. We note the reluctance to make commitments in the audiovisuals sector, and relate how the negotiations over basic telecommunications were extended beyond the Uruguay Round in an endeavour to obtain more concessions.

As industry-specific regulation is gradually undermined by globalization, a market-oriented legality like intellectual property regulation is allowed more play. Pursuing the two issues nominated above, chapter eight discusses the convergences and divergences between the various national intellectual property legalities. The focus here is on their provisions for copyright protection. The chapter then refers to the provisions which TRIPs made for copyright in this field, but the study is alert to the hesitations and ambivalences which are evident in the WTO's approach. We draw into the discussion the more recent initiatives of WIPO in relation to content on-line; the WIPO Copyright Treaty and Performances and Phonograms Treaty are discussed here. The field is able to provide a very good example of the interaction between two sources of international norms.

Yet, in turn, intellectual property gives way to the legalities of a market-based organization of the media. The big 'players' in the market employ organization forms, such as strategic alliances and functional integration, to assert control. We consider the national approaches of competition policy to the use of these organizational forms, and concentrate on the requirements they make to enable access to 'essential facilities' which are so controlled. The essential facilities under consideration are computer platforms and telecommunication networks.

The chapter asks whether the WTO agreements are providing independent and alternative producers, here of content and services, with the necessary rules and resources to benefit from the global on-line media. It finds a little support in the intellectual property provisions. The final inquiry of this kind concerns the potential which lies in their support for competition policy. Here we find that the support is extremely tentative and diffident. The provision with the most substance has been made through the telecommunications access obligations. They were prescribed in the GATS Annex on Telecommunications and in the subsequent negotiations over basic telecommunications. Once again, it is necessary to ask whether competition law can be expected to offer much potential in this regard or whether the WTO should now develop more sympathetic legalities, such as positive codes of conduct, for transnational operators. The chapter closes by gauging the tenor of the most recent debate over the WTO's new competition policy agenda. As members vacillate over the direction of this agenda, the WTO is at risk of wasting an opportunity to create a prototype for the kind of re-regulation needed to counterbalance global economic power.

Globalizing effects

There is clearly common ground among a variety of theoretical perspectives in assigning a central role to communications media in the process of globalization. The global role of such media is most evident in the capacities they provide traders, financiers, industrialists and suppliers to overcome the spatial and temporal limitations of the locality and operate in a coordinated and reflexive fashion across the world. Such capacity proves valuable in the communications sectors or industries themselves. Today, it is really possible to project communications into almost every corner of the globe, whether it be by medium of an extra-terrestrial satellite or a pocket cassette player.

The new on-line electronic media are expected to step up this process of deterritorialising and dematerialising the communications between us. In so doing, they present a challenge to the economic independence, political sovereignty and cultural integrity with which the locality seeks to regulate the communications media themselves. The media provide their own means for resourceful suppliers and users to circumvent the boundaries which have been drawn around the various sub-sectors of communications with a view to protecting local industries. Indeed, many localities may have to decide whether they can maintain communications industries of their own – such as equipment, content, infrastructure and services industries – at all. They are tempted to relinquish their protections and open up to the international networks. It is argued that their businesses and consumers will receive the benefits of the economies of scale and scope, investment and expertise, and other assets which these networks command. Such assets are needed, it is claimed, to keep traditional industries viable and to participate in the new sectors of electronic discourse and commerce.

In a rapidly destabilising environment, these decisions about economic strategy are hard to make. The challenge is capturing a share of the benefits which are to be generated through transport charges, intellectual property royalties, sales commissions, subscriber fees and taxation revenue, while giving up many traditional instruments of national policy such as public instrumentalities and other ownership controls. However control over communications and information structures is increasingly central to the fate of societies generally. Communications media carry cultural and social messages to the locality. These messages challenge the traditional certainties of ideology, allegiance and identity.

A more material message is their challenge to regulatory competence. The media provide opportunities for more producers and users to shop for sympathetic national regulation, manipulating the concepts traditionally used to attach conduct and entities to particular locations. The regulation in question can range right through product standards, gambling controls, fair trading practices and financial supervision to taxation measures and forms of industry assistance. Internet banking provides a good current illustration, while a more sordid example of the practices which are emerging comes from the international market for phone sex. For instance, it is reported that a company incorporated in Delaware, directors and investors unidentified and headquartered in the Virgin Islands, takes calls from American consumers through the Guyanese national telecom which the company has recently bought out.[1]

As we first heard in chapter two, in some scenarios this electronic trade breaks free of any connection to national jurisdictions. The communications media enhance the capacity of trade to float freely above the nation state, in self-regulating fields of commerce connected horizontally as spaces of flows. Current discussions about jurisdiction in cyberspace posit a world in which communications cannot be sensibly localised, whatever point of attachment is pursued, whether it be country of origin, country of emission, country of reception or country of infringement. Such communications can never be satisfactorily fixed to a particular point in time or a place on the ground.

Global communications do not simply create conditions for competition between countries; they expose disjunctures within nations too. Communications enhance direct linkages across national boundaries, not just within transnational corporate groups, but between global cities where design, financing, management and associated services (such as legal services) are concentrated. For example, voice and data transmission circulate through intra-corporate telecommunications circuits which are connected into the public and international networks. One proliferating private linkage takes the form of the intranets being constructed on the platform of the Internet, the network of networks.

Thus globalization both connects and fragments. Paradoxically, communications infrastructures reveal a spatial configuration, but the configuration which emerges is an uneven one, both cross-nationally and sub-nationally. Infrastructure is thickest in the metropolitan centres of the North. Yet, at the same time, in many countries, most people still do not enjoy access to a simple telephone line. Even in the relatively affluent North, only a minority of homes would presently be connected to the Internet.[2] Thus, we are also presented with the possibility that certain locations will be bypassed by the global flows or relegated to a marginal position. The configuration raises prospects of a new kind of inequity based on uneven access to information and technological resources.

Access to the media

Those who are optimistic about the new media suggest that they provide their own solution to this problem.[3] The media of the previous eras have allowed distributors to capture and exploit economies of scale and scope. At times, the state has assisted them with this project, but the new converging and interactive media are set to lower barriers to entry dramatically. The huge expansion in carrying and processing capacity will enable anybody to be a user or indeed a producer. With the prospect of interchangeable alternative routes, satellite for wire, cable for television, network for computer, there will be no incentive for distributors to bottleneck traffic and exclude non-affiliated content providers or small-time users. So, for example, intellectual property, which has been one way for distributors to control channels, again with state support, will assume a different complexion. While perhaps in the transition to the new media, some core content such as major sporting events, popular movies and iconic images will be rationed, the emphasis will ultimately shift to releasing, translating and reconstituting content as widely as possible – especially where it is possible to obtain payments for small uses of a work.

Thus, the new media offer ways to break loose from the political controls or cultural insularities of certain localities. But, furthermore, they provide means to surmount the economic limitations of the one-to-many communication channels, in which intelligence is controlled from the centre and a lowest common denominator product distributed to 'dumb terminals'. On this scenario, the new media finally provide the means to cut out the middleman. Independent content producers and service providers will be able to connect up directly with empowered, interactive users, all around the world.

The Internet is the medium carrying perhaps the most hopes for providing alternative channels for information flows, the sending of messages and exchanges of dialogue. For instance, the Institute for Global Concerns contends:

> The development of communications technologies has vastly transformed the capacity of global civil society to build coalitions and networks. In times past, communication transaction clusters formed around nation-states, colonial empires, regional economies and alliances … today new and equally powerful forces have emerged on the world's stage – the rainforest protection movement, the human rights movement, a campaign against the arms trade, and planetary computer networks.[4]

Control of the media

However, this early optimism has given way to scepticism in some quarters. One source of scepticism about this emancipatory potential is the nature of the media themselves. Far from putting people in touch with solid information sources again, or with like-minded communities, the electronic media are substituting a hyper-reality, which has the perverse effect of disguising the very absence of reality.[5] On a more practical plane, it is doubtful whether the electronic media can provide a complete substitute for face-to-face personalised and localised relations. Tacit knowledge, trust and understanding remain critical to the conduct of social discourse, even to the success of trade and commerce.

We must question whether the horizontal, private configuration of the communications sector can ever entirely detach itself from the ties of the locality. For the time being, local cooperation is needed to overcome the physical obstacles which the local terrain presents to the building, operation and maintenance of the infrastructure. Local terrestrial lines or large satellite receiver dishes provide a point at which controls can apply restrictions to transmissions. More subtly, a presence may be essential, involving collaboration with locals, if communications are to be adapted, not just to the many resilient traditional cultures and moral majorities, but also to fashion appeal to postmodern audiences which split into many specialist, expressive styles. 'International broadcasting satellites, not anchored in a national broadcasting culture and targeted at no audience in particular, have been a commercial graveyard.'[6]

Yet the biggest threat to access may lie in the way society chooses to configure the media. Might another – as yet indistinct – means emerge to capture this transactional space?[7] If, for instance, as Esther Dyson has argued,[8] property in content will no longer be central to supply, might value be captured by those who can lock-in users and exclude non-affiliates by integrating service systems in a functionally effective fashion? In particular, could those who control the fibre optic wire or the computer software platform exploit their position, using intellectual property power, as well as other strategies such as acquisitions and alliances, to control access to essential facilities? They might build on this strategic position to become the systems integrators and offer not just equipment but a range of services to those many producers and users who do not have the time or expertise to construct and operate their own networks. Such services may be targeted at the users, but they might also be designed to attract the support of content producers and service providers who are seeking to identify and reach a constituency. Of necessity, many participants will continue to turn to others to provide a speedy, facile, reliable and secure flow. For instance, they will want someone to filter, authenticate, check and customise messages for them. At the risk of ingratiating myself with my publisher, I note that the author and the reader will still need the services of an editor.

Convergence might present opportunities to assume this position. Convergence has been characterised as technical, functional and organizational.[9] If even the largest firms today do not attempt to adopt a 'stand-alone' position and provide the whole system, they seek to design exclusive arrangements with allies and affiliates. A feature of the current field is the exploratory alliances formed horizontally across previously separate markets – telecommunications and entertainment, computing and telecommunications, computing and information services. Another strong feature is the acquisitions of smaller firms with specialised assets which are needed by the large companies to incorporate in these systems. If economies of scale and scope can still be exploited, the systems integrators might be tempted not to act merely as neutral 'air traffic controllers' but to use their position to favour their own services and those of their affiliates, at the expense of independents.[10]

INDUSTRY-SPECIFIC REGULATION

It is clear that the prospect of this power puts many localities on the defensive. It is undermining confidence in the traditional means by which many countries provide access to local and less powerful voices, such as public carrier monopolies, media ownership controls, local content requirements and universal service obligations. In the recent past, the approach of the nation state has been to regulate competition on a categorical basis. Thus, local industry was protected from foreign competition, for instance through limits placed on the level of direct foreign acquisition or establishment in sectors regarded as sensitive. Restrictions have also been placed upon cross-border supply, by way of private telecommunications circuits or satellite services departing from nationally organized and often publicly owned grids.

Of course, communications have long involved a cross-national dimension but it has largely taken the form of the division of the market between national monopolies. In relation to supply both through telecommunications and satellites, such partitions have lately come under stress. Thus, Canadian and Mexican controls of this kind were a target in the NAFTA negotiations.[11] Another form of local protection consisted of the limits placed upon imports of personnel, programs and signals. The European Union's local content quotas for television have attracted the displeasure of the major importers, mainly from the United States which is strong, as my children know, in the production of popular entertainment. France has so far been unable to obtain its partners' agreement to extend the quotas to the new interactive audiovisual media.[12]

Not all controls have targeted foreign competitors directly; incumbents were further shielded by general cross-media ownership controls and lines of business restrictions. Moreover, in some sectors, whether by region or otherwise, licensing restricted the number of competitors overall. Governments also of course have supported public ownership, in some sectors in a monopoly position. But latterly, in both television and telecommunications sectors, for instance, these governments have allowed in more participants and privatised state-owned incumbents.

From a free market perspective, such industry-specific national regulations have been characterised as protections from 'competition'. The protections were justified on the basis that investments were high and resources were scarce (such as frequency spectrum or advertising revenue). But it should be remembered that, as well as guaranteeing the viability of the operators, the state had an interest in favouring a limited number of local operators. Licensing created a point at which to extract concessions towards local equipment or content purchase, the carriage of certain public good contents or services, and the cross-subsidisation of indigent users. Not all sectors benefited from this kind of direct protection. However we can argue that intellectual property provides an analogous, probably milder, sort of state security against competition for others such as those in book, record and software publishing sectors. Again, in return, the state considers whether to extract certain concessions from the property holders.

Of course, another rationale for the immunities was that the absence of such regulation would lead to more concentration rather than less. Public power would be replaced by private power. Given the role of the communications media, this power could even comprise a threat to democratic forms of local decision making and outlets for expression of cultural diversities. Thus governments are understandably reluctant to jettison these traditional instruments of public policy. Feeling sympathy, the World Bank has suggested that for the time being developing countries should refrain from privatising their national telecommunications instrumentalities.[13]

IMPACT OF THE GATS

If unilateral liberalisation can be hesitant and partial, the expansion of world trade and investment is adding another dimension to the framework for policy formation. As we have noted, bilateral and regional agreements commence this process. But the multilateral WTO agreements and specifically here the GATS are influential in shaping the framework too.

Audiovisuals sector

In the communications service sectors, the GATS places the onus on national governments to defend or relinquish their industry-specific regulatory measures. The general message is that this regulatory legality should give way to whatever legality of association and distribution the international operators find most rational. Let the market find its own form of ordering. As the analysis in chapter four established, submission to the norms and procedures of the agreement opens up to scrutiny a range of local arrangements. In the audiovisuals services sector, limits on foreign ownership, refusal of work permits to foreign artists and technicians, local content requirements for programming, and production subsidies for local ventures may be regarded as discriminating against foreign suppliers. Or the regulatory arrangements may simply have the effect of restricting market access for foreigners. Controls on concentration of media ownership, licensing restrictions on market entry, and bans on certain kinds of programs or advertisements may be viewed this way.

However, the negotiations revealed that many countries regarded this sector as extremely sensitive. As the agreement allowed, their commitments to national treatment and market access were markedly conservative. An inspection of the schedules reveals that a significant number of countries chose not to inscribe their audiovisuals sector in their schedules at all. These countries included developed countries, such as Australia, Canada and members of the European Union, particularly France, which felt exposed to the economies of scale and cultural imprecations of the American entertainment industries. Partly, this choice of response was a strategic one. Even a stand-still agreement would have limited a member's measures to its existing modes and levels of regulation. It would have restricted its choice of regulatory strategy in the rapidly developing new media sectors. Nonetheless, the resistance ran deeper. In France, a member of the right-wing parliamentary parties was to assert that cultural goods, which carry cultural identity, and the agricultural goods, which carry territorial identity, were not goods like others. It was not surprising that this resistance greatly exercised the United States industry lobby, but it was not helpful to look upon the reaction as simply a case of disguised industry protectionism; the dispute exposed cross-cultural static.

Telecommunications sector

Telecommunications was to be another sensitive sector. By the end of the Uruguay Round, forty-eight countries had scheduled commitments on telecommunications. Most were given over largely to the valued-added sub-sectors, though twenty-two countries inscribed basic telecommunications and made limited commitments, for instance in relation to mobile and cellular telephony.[14] Yet, like audiovisuals, many countries chose not to inscribe telecommunications sectors in their schedules at all. After all, we know that inscription opens up to scrutiny the restrictions which many countries still place on foreign ownership and operation of services and the controls they apply to the circumvention of public switched networks.

Nevertheless, a Decision was taken at Marrakesh to continue negotiations on basic telecommunications on a voluntary basis. Negotiations were to be comprehensive, with no basic telecommunications to be excluded categorically. A closing date of April 1996 was set for these negotiations. Negotiations were reported to be addressing all modes of supply, including cross-border supply and supply by resale, and the establishment of a commercial presence through foreign direct investment and the ownership and operation of networks.

Yet the United States continued to express concern about the value of the market access offers being made by the other participants, including such Asian countries as Malaysia, India, Indonesia and Thailand. Their restrictions on foreign ownership were being targeted. We identified in chapters three and four the effects of permitting countries to take exemptions from the general obligation to accord MFN treatment. The basic telecommunications sub-sector was one in which the United States had threatened to apply an MFN exemption across the board. Now the European Union was worried that it would exclude international services from the agreement. The United States was said to be concerned that other countries would seek to free ride on the cheap international connections which competitive markets such as its own and those in Europe had made available. Yet the WTO Director-General stressed the futility of maintaining a bilateral approach. He argued that national boundaries were being abolished and national monopolies rendered obsolete.[15]

Just before the deadline, the negotiations froze. The Director-General of the WTO successfully proposed that the participating countries preserve the offers they had made and re-examine them during a thirty-day period that was to begin on 15 January 1997.[16] This further 'window of opportunity' produced offers of further liberalisation, representing fifty-five schedules of commitment and sixty-nine countries.[17] It finalised a Fourth Protocol to the GATS which came into force at the beginning of 1998.[18] It is reported to have led more countries to relent on foreign ownership and control of basic services, amongst them the United States itself. However, it is clear that the issue remains a sensitive one for many countries, especially in regard to local services. The Protocol also includes a list of nine MFN exemptions which members had taken.

These post-Uruguay Round negotiations also stimulated work on conceptual, technical and regulatory issues. The regulations under consideration included those which might constitute barriers to trade. Interestingly, in the light of what we have said about market access, non-discriminatory limitations on the number of providers were mentioned here. But the work was also to do with the character of the national regulations which were seen as necessary to safeguard liberalisation. The topics included licensing, frequency and numbering, standards and type approval, tariffs and accounting rates, termination services, rights of way, and universal services. Given the continuing role of regulation in this sector, transparency and impartiality were regarded as key issues. High on the agenda were the terms and conditions for interconnection between telecommunications and other service suppliers, together with the nature of the safeguards required to prevent abuse of power by dominant network operators. The case study returns to this aspect of the GATS work in its discussion of competition law below.

For the time being, we should underline the point that the work on legalities is not simply deregulatory. We can concede that national governments are increasingly reluctant to invest funds directly in communications infrastructure, or to contain rivalry amongst operators on a categorical basis. Yet the risks which private developers perceive in an uncertain and volatile environment still lead them to call upon the state's power to protect them from excessive or unfair competition. As we have seen, that power was represented in various kinds of industry-specific regulation, but increasingly it means the power of intellectual property law and the power of competition law itself. At the same time, the regulators remain concerned about the conditions on which independent producers and users are to enjoy access to the new media.

So we are reminded that liberalisation does not necessarily mean libertarianism.[19] The OECD report remarked: 'Where there is perfect competition, the regulator may even be put out of a job, but that day has not yet arrived in the communications industry. On the contrary, the job of the regulator seems set to become more involved and more detailed than ever before.'[20] Globalization requires regulators to compare and coordinate national legalities that cut across each other, but they must also mediate between legalities with markedly differing contents. Here, they must finesse the balance between industry-specific regulation, intellectual property and competition policy. We look now at their approaches to intellectual property and competition policy.

INTELLECTUAL PROPERTY REGULATION

This section identifies the key issues which the on-line media present for national intellectual property legalities and considers the efforts of the WTO and other international organizations to mediate them. We might start with a general observation that the intangible and indivisible character of intellectual resources make it difficult for producers to contain them materially. Ideas know no natural physical bounds. As we have suggested, the media which embody these ideas present opportunities to capture their value in various ways. However, the same media can create new ways to gain access and make copies without the need to obtain the producer's authorisation. So intellectual property may be seen as a necessary protection for one's investment when the technical and economic strategies available to do so prove to be inadequate.

At the same time, the innovations in the media expose both conceptual and practical gaps in the coverage of the existing national intellectual property legalities. Attempts to fit the new media to the established categories prove unsatisfactory and modifications have to be considered. Thus Plowman and Hamilton comment: 'Current changes in technology are producing new patterns, with traditional services being combined in unexpected hybrid shapes and uses, in defiance of the established categories.'[21]

Earlier waves of innovation, such as photography and cinematography, have spurred their own law reforms. At each turn, we would not expect national legalities to respond in exactly the same ways. Building on the observations made in chapter two, it is worth mentioning that the responses are not likely to be determined solely along economic utilitarian lines, though where a country fits into an increasingly global structure of producers and users, exporters and importers, this is likely to be influential. The responses will also be shaped by shifting aesthetic and moral judgements. Intellectual property activates a range of views regarding, for instance, what is authored and the value of originality and imitation.[22] Views differ too about what resources should be freely available rather than subject to payment. An example pertinent to our study is the free software movement, represented for instance by the Linux software which is made available on the Internet for experimentation, improvement and use as a collective activity.

Today, national governments are being pressed to adjust their intellectual property legalities in order to catch up with the new media. The requests come from foreign exporters of intellectual value, whether that value is embodied in finished consumer goods, industrial technologies or, as here, on-line transmissions. The home countries of those foreign exporters may take up their claims through bilateral initiatives to obtain better protection. At the same time, we might expect local secondary producers and perhaps end users, especially in countries that predominantly receive intellectual property from elsewhere, to press governments to contain or qualify those protections.

Yet determining a position to take on intellectual property protection can reveal considerable ambivalence. Many producers borrow heavily from existing resources when they invent and originate. The author of a book provides a good example. If the division between perspectives is classically cast as a clash between producer and user, a significant inter-legality today is the difference between the interests of authors, musicians and performers, and their publishers, on the one hand, and, on the other

hand, the industrial firms which are involved in the adaptation, commercialisation and distribution of the works, often in a reconstituted version.

So once again, we find that the claims surrounding copyright law are
much more subtle than a simple dichotomy between straight-out support
or opposition. They deal with such specifics as the scope of the subject
matter to be embraced by the category, the uses which are to be controlled, the freedom with which the rights may be alienated and
acquired, and the provision for non-voluntary licensing and fair dealing.
Consequently, they generate legal pluralism within the national arenas,
even within the countries which are large exporters.

If arbitrating between these conflicting domestic claims is not a hard
enough task, the nation state is faced today with an enormous challenge
in gauging the 'net' consequences of making one kind of regime rather
than another available for the new on-line media. Deterritorialisation and
dematerialisation make it more difficult to devise a policy that can deliver
the benefits of intellectual property to a particular locality. As I have contended in previous chapters, the global carriers provide so many points of
attachment that it is extremely difficult for any one locality to monopolise
jurisdiction. If national laws differ in their substantive content, there is
also competition between locations over whose laws are to apply.

Copyright

Intellectual property has attracted strong philosophical justification. Yet
it does not enjoy the assistance of a unifying principle in the sense of a
core criterion that can determine whether new subject matter and new
uses are entitled to its protection. Again, to do justice to national traditions, we should acknowledge that some countries have striven harder
for a synthesis than others. But, overall, we can say that countries are particularistic in their approaches. So the new intellectual resources must be
matched with the criteria of the established categories. We would find
that a range of categories, such as patents, trade secrets and confidential
information, trademarks and the expanding forms of protection for business reputation, character merchandising and image association are all
relevant to the on-line media. However, for communications media generally, it is safe to say that copyright is the established category. Its substance and legitimacy place it at the centre of the debate again today.
Thus, copyright is the main category for those seeking intellectual property in the new media, whether by way of assimilating the media to the
well recognised copyrightable works and uses or by obtaining copyright
protection for new subject matter and uses.

Copyright has displayed a capacity to adapt to changes in technology.
It has extended its reach, from its initial concern with subject matter such
as musical scores and literary texts, to the new media of films, sound

recordings, wireless broadcasts and computer software. Yet even as it made this progression, divergencies became apparent. In particular, some countries have thought it more appropriate to afford 'neighbouring' or 'related' rights to these modern audiovisual media, usually providing a lesser level of substantive protection.[23] The same has been true of artists' performances. Other new media again have attracted sui generis forms of protection instead. The sui generis form provides more of an opportunity to tailor the protection to the circumstances of the particular media.

In any case, copyright has not conceded every use which the holder might wish to control, whether it be by excluding others from the resource or by licensing subject to conditions of various kinds being met (such as the payment of a fee). Another way in which copyright has been limited is through the bundle of rights which its subsistence attracts. Arguably, the primary right it has been prepared to confer is the right to control the copying or the reproduction of the subject matter. This right makes an issue of the nature of infringement. For example, if it is to be susceptible to reproduction, some countries have said that the subject matter must be fixed in a material form. So to store a poem in one's memory or to read it out aloud has not been an infringement of the copyright, unless the law broadens out the definition of reproduction or adds in further rights that can catch these activities. Some jurisdictions have legislated the rights to control performance in public or the broadcast or communication to the public of certain subject matters. But these extensions reveal variations too.

In this regard, it is useful to think of the on-line media as an activity in which many people are engaged, transforming material, storing it and making it available. The constitution of the on-line media differs from the original materials on which it draws or which, it is sometimes said, underlie it – for example, we can often think of it as a multi-media product. So the law must decide whether its product can be fitted to an existing subject matter of copyright such as a computer program, cinematographic work or wireless broadcast.

However, as it becomes more truly on-line, the media are more of a service activity. Their special value lies in making the existing material accessible in a particularly convenient and useful manner. It is made available to be searched by users, transmitted to them, and modified by them. Thus it is dealing with the existing subject matter in a particular way. We should appreciate here that this activity may involve a number of service providers. There are firms to provide the carriage of the material, to provide the hardware facilities including the personal computers, to provide the operating or systems software, to provide the applications software such as search engines, publishing and processing programs, to provide content in various packages to handle the trans-actions. In these activities, they will seek to be inter-operable. So one question which the law must decide is whether the existing rights allow them to use each other's facilities.

The users are interested in the conditions under which they obtain access to the products and services of the on-line media. They are not necessarily interested in reproducing in hard copy the material which they access on-line. They may be content to browse it on screen or listen to it through speakers. Public access providers such as libraries and schools register an interest here too. Thus the producers of the underly-ing material will be concerned with the new uses which the service providers and the end users are making of their content. The service providers in turn will be concerned to control the uses which the end users make of their services. The law must decide whether the uses attract the control of the existing rights. If the existing subject matter and rights do not cover these aspects of the on-line media, the law must contem-plate making changes.

Software interfaces

By way of illustration, we take a technology which is crucial to making the media functional and attractive. Firms seek copyright protection from those who would pirate their software. We understand pirating to be the direct or literal copying of the whole of the software, without payment of a licence fee to the producer. Some countries have been reluctant to pro-vide copyright protection for computer software even against this kind of copying. But firms also want to build on existing programs so as to pro-duce improvements or enhancements. An issue for software copyright protection is whether the secondary producers may make any derivative use of the original program. Such a use can still involve the reproduction of a part of the original program.

Where countries do offer copyright protection, one way the law resolves this possible infringement of the reproduction right is to look for 'substantial similarity'. Another more searching way to cast the criterion is the level at which the expression is being reproduced. Copy-right is meant to protect the form of expression of a work rather than its underlying ideas and knowledges. If it is possible to write variations on the form in which a code is expressed, we can ask whether the second program performs the same function as that part of the original pro-gram. But would that amount to a protection of the idea behind the pro-gram, the conceptualisation of the problem of function it was to address and its solution to it? Even protection of the expression might do so, if there was only one way feasibly of expressing an underlying idea. The idea/expression distinction has proved difficult to make. Consequently, in key jurisdictions, the courts have oscillated between giving protection to the original producers and allowing freedom for the secondary producers. This jurisprudence has been a significant source of the national divergence in copyright legalities.[24] While actively litigating in a number of jurisdictions, the major international suppliers have not been able to resolve the issue.

A special version of this issue has been the legality of reproducing a copyright holder's software interfaces. Reproducing software interfaces for the purpose of inter-operability may be treated as an infringement of the reproduction right, if the holder is not prepared to license that activity. Even the activity needed to discover these interface specifications, if the holder is not prepared to release the codes, may infringe. The interfacing device might simply be designed to enable circumvention of the original program. We know smart cards are available to activate access without payment, for example to satellite television. But the purpose of the reproduction may rather be to make the particular application work with the core operating facility. The user wants to make its own products or services competitive with the copyright holder's own add-on or plug-in applications. By asserting copyright, the holder may well be seeking to extend its power into related markets.[25]

In the following section of this chapter, we shall see that competition law may be brought into play to discipline such use of the intellectual property right. However, within the body of copyright law, a statutory exception to infringement is a way of recognising the competing interest. Such an exception is a limited instance of the provision for non-voluntary licensing of intellectual property. This instance provides us with a pertinent example of inter-legality. We can refer to two encounters in particular. A major flashpoint was the lobby by the United States Government, along with key producers, to dissuade the European Union from building an exception into its software protection directive which would have allowed reproduction for the purpose of inter-operability.[26] The exception was ultimately confined to the purpose of reverse engineering the software to identify the interface specifications. When the exception was contemplated in Australia, the United States Trade Representative placed the country on its 'watch list'. In 1996, it appears a combination of Microsoft, IBM and Novel was successful in persuading the Australian Government not to adopt a recommendation from an expert committee that an exception be allowed for decompilation.[27]

On-line content

The reproducibility of software interfaces is a very important issue in practical terms, but we shall see that the transmission of content material on-line has created a far bigger conceptual and policy challenge to copyright. We are well aware that material which is copyright in a hard form is being made available for free over the Internet. Sometimes, the transmission is for commercial purposes, sometimes it is styled as emancipatory. Content producers want to ensure that sales of such popular items as books, videos, compact discs, and software programs are not undermined by this practice. The new media are providing more and more effective means to make unauthorised copies and distribute them widely. In some sectors, we can legitimately question whether copying has been at the expense of purchases, for the consumers may very well not be able to afford the authorised version. However, in other areas, such as academic publishing and music recording, the concern is very real and it is feared that the on-line media will aggravate the problem. When digitalisation and bandwidth can deliver recordings with great speed and fidelity, record companies are especially apprehensive.

So the extension of copyright into the on-line media may be needed to provide the original authors and publishers of the underlying content with a means to protect their sales and licence revenues from erosion. In particular, it would give them something with which to bargain for the payment of a royalty or a share of the revenue from on-line custom. Yet it is extremely difficult to enforce the law against the end users of the media, especially of course if they are household rather than commercial users. It may be a better strategy for the content producers to sue those who provide the facilities for the material to be posted and carried to the users, but such legal redress requires an extra step to infringement to be established. If the carriers are not themselves engaging directly in one of the infringing activities, they may instead have to be joined as third parties. Their liability is incurred by their contributing to or authorising an infringement by another.

In the past, such a case has been run against those who provided photocopying machines or video recorders. But the service providers and equipment providers are understandably not enthusiastic about being cast in this responsible role by the content producers. Proposals to stiffen third party liability have for instance met with opposition in the United States. This was said to have held up the passage of the revisions to the Copyright Act.[28] So too, writing on events in the United Kingdom, John thought that the distributors were driving the copyright agenda rather than the authors.[29]

Nonetheless, the service providers seek a legal basis on which they too can charge for their service and control access by those users who do not wish to pay. In appreciating the kind of copyright protection which would suit them, we should understand that the value of the service does not lie simply in its content. Instead, as we noted earlier in the chapter, its speedy, convenient, reliable means of access to information will be part of its attraction. The costs associated with accessing information efficiently are sometimes overlooked; an abundance of information means little without the capacity to use it well. Searchable indexes or abstracts, with follow-up delivery of full copy on-line, are an example of this kind of value-added service. So instead of sales, the provider of an on-line information service may wish to obtain a fee for the information actually used. The use can be measured, for example, by applying a meter to the technology by which it is accessed.

For the providers, the real issue becomes the legal means to control access to a service which is available on-line. For some, it is indeed to prevent the theft of a service.[30] Naturally, the providers are exploring technological measures for securing access to their services. In this regard, the approach is to make it illegal to circumvent those measures by breaking codes, intercepting signals or opening locks. But copyright is also very much under consideration. An approach that makes use of the most established copyright law looks for acts of reproduction within the on-line media. However, we soon discover that there is legal controversy over whether the temporary storage of a work or other subject matter in an electronic medium, such as random access memory or a hard drive, its display ephemerally on the screen, or its relay to other computers in a network, can be regarded as reproduction. Pinpointing the acts of reproduction is crucial to identifying a viable defendant within the network of transmission.

If reproduction is arguable, support may be sought instead in other rights. This strategy shifts the emphasis from protection of the content as such to control over its uses and in particular the ways in which it is distributed. However, so far, a fully fledged distribution right has achieved little acceptance outside the United States. Within existing regimes, those who wish to secure on-line transmission may look to rights over broadcasting or communication to the public, but these rights have often been tied to specific technologies from a previous era. Furthermore, services that are open only to subscribers or services that vary with the user's specifications are seen to strain the concept of a service to the 'public'. The use of the on-line media also involves transmission one to one, closer in form perhaps to 'private' telephone calls or communications by mail than to broadcasting. So the existing rights were likely to prove inadequate. The situation demanded a new technology-neutral right.[31]

Licensing

If the authors of content and their publishers enjoy rights to control the use of their material in the on-line media, the distributors would prefer these rights to be assignable in the marketplace so that they can be mobilised. When works, such as texts, music or images, are reworked and recontextualised in such media, a notable point of friction between legalities centres on the notion of moral rights. Moral rights are meant to retain for the author protection against dealings that undermine the integrity of the work, even though the author has assigned or licensed the work to another. We can also see the moral rights perspective represented in the concern which is expressed about the commercial use of artefacts and folklore that have sacred and cultural significances for indigenous peoples. But, interestingly, it is not only the commercial developers and distributors who are challenging moral rights. Artists with a postmodern sensibility are querying the notions of authorship and originality and welcoming the opportunity to borrow from a diversity of sources and cultures around the world.

If copyright protection finds its way into the on-line media, developers and distributors of multi-media products and information services will need to track down the various authors and make arrangements with them. The industry is working on technological means to obtain clearances. However, in connection with more established media, governments have sometimes stepped in to provide statutory licensing, for example to permit sound recordings to be broadcast on payment of a fee. These schemes have had a troubled history and, in some instances, the content producers have continued to oppose the granting of such licences. National copyright laws also make exception to infringement for certain limited kinds of use. In terms of reproducing content, the most common exception is to allow fair dealing or fair use. This exception permits copies to be made for such purposes as individual research and study, quotation, news reporting, review and criticism, or personal private use.[32] Such allowances start to cause conflict when, for instance, public libraries and educational institutions become involved in making copies for large numbers of researchers. The allowances may also be subject to legal challenge. In particular, it may be argued that they exceed the restricted allowances made to national legislation under the Berne or Rome Conventions.

A crucial issue for the on-line media is whether the new subject matter and the new rights should be qualified by the same kinds of licensing provisions and exceptions from infringement. The suppliers may resist the extension of non-voluntary licensing and fair dealing to the electronic media. Their aim may be to capture value from the provision of a service rather than the sales of hard copies. At the same time, they may feel confident they can extract payments from users of the service on a pay per view or use basis, say by browsing and sampling works on-line. But, equally so, critics are concerned that control of access on-line will present a threat to freedom of information. It will further undermine social goals like general education and social participation. These critics worry that the underlying ideas and information will be just as inaccessible as the on-line forms of expression to those who cannot pay the visitation or user charges. Public libraries and schools have a major stake in the outcome of this debate.[33]

It may remain the case that the information will be made available elsewhere than on-line. Then, it will truly be the way it has been packaged and customised by the on-line service providers which provides its added value. Control of access to such services becomes most critical, then, if it were to come to pass that the on-line media replaced other sources of content completely. Yet, even if those other sources remain in existence, on-line service delivery may create the prospect of a new resource disparity. Select firms and individuals will obtain the advantage of access to information that is reliable, timely and purposeful. Or rather we might anticipate the prospect of a stratification of services distribution, the ordinary user only able to afford basic, undifferentiated services such as popular entertainment, home shopping and electronic gambling. However, it would not do to overstate the contribution which intellectual property might make to the cost of these information-rich services. It may not be content that is costly on-line, but rather the technological facilities which are needed to access and utilise it effectively (see below).

THE TRIPs AGREEMENT

The TRIPs agreement made a major contribution to the international standardisation of copyright law. The agreement did not attempt to specify choice-of-law criteria that would apply in the event of a conflict between national jurisdictions. It has proved difficult, in other fora, to achieve agreement on such criteria. The need for agreement was obviated somewhat by the success of TRIPs in promoting the standardisation of substantive protection across the many member countries. We should further note the trouble it took to ensure that members would make legal facilities available to foreigners to permit effective action against acts of infringement. It seemed determined to see that variations in procedures and sanctions did not defeat its substantive protections. We understand that rights holders still need to localise their protection; they are not provided with an international tribunal to obtain enforcement of the rights the agreement is promoting. But standardisation should make the particular location of less significance.

However, we should concede here once again that the standards remain general and partial. Thus, scope remains for the play of national differences, reined in to some extent by the decisions of the dispute settlement process on complaints of violation. In this chapter, we shall concentrate on the standards relevant to the on-line media. In furthering substantive copyright standards, the primary role of the agreement was to apply the provisions of the Berne Convention. We identified those provisions in chapter six. So TRIPs affirms copyright protection for the subject matter which falls within the Convention's concept of 'works'. It supports the rights which the Convention attaches to copyright such as the right to control reproduction of the work. This application was then a strong case of one international agreement cross-referencing another, drawing on the conceptual groundwork and legitimacy achieved by the older convention and reinforcing the norms of that convention with its own pulling power and capacity to follow through.

In so doing, TRIPs gives copyright recognition to certain of the materials which serve as the underlying content for on-line transmissions. The agreement also extends recognition to other subject matter proving valuable in the on-line environment. To overcome any doubts that surround the coverage of the Convention, TRIPs expressly requires that computer programs, whether in subject or object code, should be protected as literary works under Berne (article 10:1). Members of the WTO are also expressly required to afford protection to compilations of data or other material, whether in machine-readable or other form, which by reason of the selection or arrangement of their contents constitute intellectual creations (article 10:2). This protection is not to extend to the data or material itself, though it is without prejudice to any copyright which otherwise subsists in the data and material. In other words, to attract protection, the underlying content must satisfy the usual requirements for recognition, such as originality. In chapter six, we also noted how the agreement extends recognition, on the basis of neighbouring rights, to performances, sound recordings and broadcasts (article 14).

In applying Berne, the agreement makes the right of reproduction central to its protection of copyright. The preceding discussion in this chapter suggests that the act of transmission on-line is problematic, especially if the content producer wishes to attach one of the parties involved in the transmission of the material rather than the user who prints out hard copies. TRIPs applies the other rights which Berne has itemised. But, thinking in terms of early technologies, these rights did not really anticipate the way material is often communicated on-line. TRIPs is innovative internationally for broaching the matter of distribution rights, nominating rights to control the commercial rental 'at least' of films and software. However, again, it would be stretching the concept to equate rental with on-line transmission. So we can say that TRIPs stopped short of extending copyright protection to rights of control over digital transmissions. The same can be said of the protection it gave to performances, sound recordings and broadcasts.

Where rights are applicable, TRIPs applied a range of specific Berne provisions relating to non-voluntary licensing. Furthermore, in its own express provision for limitations and exceptions, article 13, TRIPs adopts the language of article 9(2) of the Berne Convention. It requires members to confine their limitations or exceptions to exclusive rights, to 'certain special cases which do not conflict with a normal exploitation of the work and do not unreasonably prejudice the legitimate interest of the right holder'. We saw that this language cannot be read too liberally. The allowances to users must respect the commercial interests of the copyright holder. Many on-line uses will undermine those interests. But there are difficult issues ahead in determining whether freedom to cache, display or browse, say for research purposes, cuts across these interests.

WIPO TREATIES

Treaty proposals

The gaps apparent in the coverage of TRIPs revived a long-standing discussion about the need for additions or supplements to the Berne Convention. Early in 1996, WIPO agreed to convene a diplomatic conference in an effort to resolve the discussion. A major interest was the extension of the Convention's copyright protection to new categories of subject matter and rights. Production centres such as the European Union and the United States proposed that the conference return to the question of computer software and deal with the challenges of digital technology.[34] More specifically, the United States proposed that digital transmissions be included within the scope of a distribution right, as it had proposed to do within its own new national model. But such a right would have to be related to the existing Berne rights such as reproduction, communication to the public and public performance. A proposal was also made for an international sui generis protection for non-original databases, along the lines of the European Union Directive, though it was to be additional to other existing protections such as the protection afforded by copyright.[35] But the agenda soon broadened out. Some countries from the South were interested in bringing protection for performers and producers of sound recordings within the embrace of the Convention.

In the previous attempts at scheduling a diplomatic conference, it had proved difficult to reach a consensus on the limitations and exceptions which might attach to such copyright protections. Now there were proposals from the European Union, and, interestingly, from Argentina and Uruguay, to phase out provisions for non-voluntary licensing. The United States Government also showed support for phasing out these provisions, but it was mindful that its own recording, film and broadcasting industries have interests in the facilities of such licensing. On-line services providers in Europe were reported to be sharing this outlook.[36] On the issue of non-voluntary licensing, Oman had earlier counselled the industry in the United States to adopt a consistent line if it hoped to get other countries to agree to rights over electronic transmissions; also if it hoped to win a share of the revenue which is collected in such licensing schemes abroad and especially in the European Union.[37] The lack of national treatment in the distribution of revenues from collective licensing and levy systems was another issue left unresolved by the TRIPs negotiations.

In August 1996, WIPO released a set of proposals for the diplomatic conference which had been drafted by the chairman of its committee of experts.[38] If adopted, the proposals would make clear that the Berne right of reproduction takes in direct and indirect reproduction, whether permanent or temporary, and in any manner or form. This elaboration was intended to catch such acts as the temporary storage of works on a hard disk, together with uploading and downloading whether to or from memory. A right of distribution would be recognised. A sticking point was the reach of such a right, with the draft text providing a choice between national/regional exhaustion and international/global exhaustion of rights. International exhaustion would permit the copyright holder to control importation of copies legally purchased in another jurisdiction. The People's Republic of China is reported to have joined with Uruguay, Canada, the European Union and the United States, in supporting international exhaustion. The proposals also contained a right of rental of originals or copies of works.

The proposals made a major concession to the interests of the authors and publishers of works. The Berne's right to control communication to the public would be strengthened to provide protection in the case of works that are made available by interactive, on-demand acts of communication. This approach seemed to be the preferred option for catching transmissions not covered by the right of reproduction, though some countries had the distribution right in mind too. Argentina, Australia, Canada, Japan and the United States lined up in support of the communication right; Latin American and Caribbean countries favouring recognition of a general right too. At the same time, it was proposed that the allowances in article 9(2) for non-voluntary licensing be explored. Consideration would be given to the status of transitory copies, which were created, for instance, when using public library networks or when downloading from subscriber services.

The proposals also included obligations to abolish certain established types of non-voluntary licensing, specifically the licensing of primary broadcasting for rebroadcasting and the licensing of works for use in sound recording and broadcasting. Here, some Latin American and Caribbean countries joined with Canada and the European Union, but the People's Republic of China and a group of African countries took issue.

Treaty text

Accommodating representation from 130 countries, together with seven inter-governmental organizations and seventy-six NGOs, the WIPO Conference managed to conclude two major treaties, the Copyright Treaty and the Performances and Phonograms Treaty.[39] In terms of copyright protection, both are significant advances on the Berne Convention and the TRIPS agreement.

The Copyright Treaty adds significantly to the rights which may be exercised over copyright works. The Treaty adopts a right of distribution as the exclusive right of authorising the making available to the public of the original or copy of the work through sale or other transfer of ownership (Copyright Treaty article 6). The Conference was not able, however, to settle on an importation right and it leaves countries free to determine the conditions, if any, under which exhaustion of the right applies after the first sale. It institutes a rental right for authors of computer programs, cinematographic works and works embodied in phonograms (CT article 7). A set of agreed statements which accompany the Treaty make it clear that these rights of distribution and rental relate only to fixed copies that can be put into circulation as tangible objects.

The Conference decided ultimately not to extend the right of reproduction explicitly to electronic media. Instead, it leaves the issue to be resolved through reference to the existing international norms. However, the agreed statements did provide that the reproduction right does fully apply in the digital environment, in particular to the use of works in digital form (Agreed Statement Concerning Article 1(4)). They advise that it is to be understood that the storage of a protected work in digital form in an electronic medium constitutes a reproduction within the meaning of article 9 of the Berne Convention. But even this statement proved controversial, some countries apprehensive that it would catch browsing, and it was only adopted on a majority vote.[40]

Perhaps the major initiative of the Treaty is to extend the public communication right into the circumstances of the on-line media. Here, it becomes an exclusive right to authorise any communication to the public of the works by wire or wireless means, including the making available to the public of their works in such a way that members of the public may access these works from a place and at a time individually chosen by them (CT article 8). The act of making available is wider than sending works and could cover, for instance, the connection of a file server containing a work to a public network. It takes in those who put works up on the web rather than those who convey or call them up. So the right is a most expansive one, though it is to be noted that the Copyright Treaty applies it only to literary and artistic works. Thus the Conference did not confer protection on the on-line transmission as such, rather the underlying content which it contains. Instead, the transmission will have to fit one of the recognised categories.

To add to the efficacy of protection, the Treaty also obliges countries to protect against the removal or alteration of rights management information (CT article 12). Furthermore, they must provide adequate legal protection and effective legal remedies against the circumvention of the technological measures which authors use in connection with their rights (CT article 11). Again, this requirement creates a substantial onus, though it was qualified to take account of concerns that technological protections can have the effect of locking up public domain material and obstructing fair dealing access.[41]

At the same time, the Treaty allows countries to provide for limitations of – or exceptions to – the rights under the Treaty (article 10). The agreed statements declare that the Treaty provisions permit the parties 'to carry forward and appropriately extend into the digital environment, limitations and exceptions in their national laws which have been considered acceptable under the Berne Convention' (Agreed Statement Concerning Article 10). Similarly, these provisions should be understood to permit parties to devise new exceptions and limitations that are appropriate to the digital network environment. Yet it should be noted that article 10 adopts the disciplines we found in article 9(2) of Berne.

In the Performances and Phonograms Treaty, performers and producers of phonograms are given similar rights, though the communication and making available to the public rights are here made separate rights. As we have said, previously their rights internationally were limited to neighbouring rights and the rights of performers in particular were severely limited. So again this Treaty is a major advance in terms of protection. Performers are first afforded moral rights (PPT article 5). Then, they are to have the exclusive economic right to authorise the fixation of their unfixed performances, together with the broadcasting or communication to the public of their unfixed performances (PPT article 6). In respect of their performances fixed as phonograms, they also attract rights regarding reproduction, distribution, rental and making available to the public (PPT articles 7–10). Phonogram producers are to enjoy the same rights (PPT articles 11–14).

It can be seen that the Treaty hesitated to afford performers rights to control the use of their fixed performances in audiovisual media such as films and videos. Cresswell suggests that, given its media interests, the

United States was a major opponent.[42] Furthermore, where phonograms have been published for commercial purposes, the right of broadcasting or communication to the public can be confined to schemes of equitable remuneration for non-voluntary use (PPT article 15). Countries were allowed to enter reservations to the right to remuneration, including to national treatment. Provision is also made generally for limitations and exceptions, such as the now common discipline (PPT article 16).

Consideration of the proposal for protection of non-original databases was postponed. The Conference did not have enough time to resolve the difficulties which many countries had with this proposal. The parties agreed to return to this matter at a later date; it has been rumoured that the developing countries want the WIPO model law on the protection of folklore enacted as a trade-off for the protection of databases. But, as we should expect in the case of such very recent negotiations, we shall have to wait for some hard evidence.

Treaty mediation

Negotiations over the WIPO Treaty provide a good example of the way globalization reveals a multi-dimensional pattern to inter-legality. The role of the Treaty is all the more striking then because it was intervening at a time when all countries were shaping their laws. It was able to apply a standard at the formative stage, not just when the 'backward' countries were to be brought into line. Yet in order to achieve anything at all, the Treaty had to leave some sensitive issues to the discretion of policy making and jurisprudence at the national level.

For example, it has been suggested the United States Government saw the WIPO Conference as a way to overcome a clash of legalities within its own community. Internal differences had led to gridlock in Congress over passage of the National Information Infrastructure Copyright Protection Act. Entertainment and publishing companies, the heavyweights of the content industries, were reported to be backing the Government move for the extension of copyright protection.[43] On the other hand, telecommunications companies, together with on-line access and service providers, sought to inform WIPO representatives of their concerns about liability as distributors, while public access organizations such as the Association of Research Libraries and the Digital Future Coalition expressed fears for the freedom to cache, browse or transmit on-line. In addition, computer hardware manufacturers, from Japan and Europe as well, opposed the proposal to outlaw circumvention devices.[44]

Some of these concerns were assuaged by the decision not to translate the reproduction right explicitly into the digital arena.[45] On the sore point of third party liability, a note to the proposals had stressed that they did not attempt to define the nature or extent of liability at the national level; instead, who was to be liable and the extent of liability were for national legislation and case law according to the legal traditions of the contracting party. The agreed statements accompanying the Copyright Treaty declared that: 'It is understood that the mere provision of physical facilities for enabling or making a communication does not in itself amount to communication within the meaning of this Treaty or the Berne Convention' (Agreed Statement Concerning Article 8). We have noted also that the Treaty left the crucial aspect of exceptions unresolved.

In addition, the Conference provoked variations on the accustomed North–South divide. In place of the Group of 77 and the old socialist bloc, more issue-based groupings were evident among the Latin American, Caribbean, African, Asian, Central and Eastern European, and CIS countries. The policies these countries were adopting had become less predictable. For instance, producer groups within certain of the African and South American countries pressed for stronger copyright protection to be given to artists, in particular to musicians and performers. They had in mind the use of their work in videos, films and broadcasts destined for affluent markets in the North. Opposition was also expressed to non-voluntary licensing for musical works. However, these groups encountered resistance, especially from the United States position, and they were only partially successful in their claims.[46] Furthermore, before we signal a sea-change in the attitudes to copyright, we should see how many of these countries actually sign the Treaties.[47]

The Treaty expounds a vital relationship with the TRIPs agreement. WIPO could be said to have stolen a march on the WTO. It has retained its relevance by being able to extend copyright to the on-line media, but in the process it has been able to retain its own style. Just as there were elements of Berne in TRIPs, there are elements of TRIPs in the Copyright Treaty such as the protection for computer software and the rental right. Yet, on the central issue, the on-line media, the Treaty focussed on the authors of underlying works and plumped for its own public communication right over the distribution right. In requiring parties to the Treaty to comply with Berne itself, it has brought moral rights back into the international arena. The companion Treaty extended the reach of copyright, not only to phonograms, but also to performances to some extent.

However, like Berne, the Treaties lack punch. WIPO is still thinking about its own inter-governmental dispute settlement process. A proposal was made to the Conference to include TRIPs-like obligations, making enforcement procedures available at the national level to copyright holders. But it was rebuffed.[48] On the other hand, when TRIPs is reviewed late 1999, early 2000, the agenda is likely to consider application of the provisions of the Treaties. Certainly, the WTO's Work Programme on Electronic Commerce requires attention to intellectual property issues.[49] But once again, we can see that globalization is requiring these international organizations to draw on each other's resources. Such interaction has a tendency to increase the potential of the interface.

COMPETITION REGULATION

In this section, our attention turns to the demands which globalized organization and operation of the on-line media place on national competition policy legalities. It considers whether and with what effect the WTO might mediate these overlapping and conflicting legalities by addressing directly the issue of competition policy standards at the international level. For competition law to be effective in a global field, national differences may generate a demand for mediation. Global flows mean that it is unlikely that the effects of restrictive business practices will be confined to any one country. But competition policy coordination continues to face resistance because individual countries wish to retain the space to exercise discretion and maintain differences.

There are many reasons why countries wish to make unilateral decisions. We might suspect that some countries wish to protect their industries domestically from foreign competition and bolster their strength for participation in export markets. Certainly, we shall see that the authorities are receptive to claims from firms in this field that they would be disadvantaged by the imposition of more stringent competition requirements than their foreign counterparts. But resistance can be more fundamental. Competition law is of course a regulatory legality with its intellectual origins in the market economies of the West. While general economic reforms are making more countries politically susceptible to the adoption of competition law, it can still be considered a major step.[50] Fully fledged, it can have profoundly disturbing implications for existing industry structures and economic relationships across the society.

Furthermore, where competition laws have been introduced, the systems tend to display significant differences. Coordination would require those differences to be submerged to some extent. The differences involve their institutional structures, legislative prescriptions, allowances for exemptions, case jurisprudence and practices of enforcement. Some of these differences reflect historical conditions and the general regulatory cultures of each jurisdiction. But they also reflect the different ways in which national authorities have chosen to grapple with an increasingly complex and sophisticated regulatory task. For instance, the differences reflect attempts to be effective regulators. The drive to be effective has led the authorities into areas which, as we shall see, are less readily amenable to standardised approaches.

Nonetheless, we can observe that the development of competition law tends to move it on from an initial concern with directly and even blatantly anti-competitive practices like collusive price fixing. It begins to take an interest in market structures and the behaviour of firms that occupy dominant positions within the market or enjoy substantial market power. Instead of treating certain practices as illegal per se, the legalities require proof of their purposes and effects. The authorities are drawn into making judgements that turn very much on the characterisation of the conduct in question and an assessment of its impact in a particular situation.

In these more particularistic approaches, economic evaluation interacts with legal criteria in deciding first what is to be regarded as pro-competitive rather than anti-competitive. As we should see, a pertinent example of this issue is whether the aggressive behaviour of market leaders towards their potential rivals just reflects their superior drive and efficiency. Thus, it can be regarded as healthy for competition. The assertion of intellectual property rights presents this issue.

In many systems, a second stage of decision making is then introduced. Provision is made for exemptions and authorisations to be given to anti-competitive conduct. The authorities are entitled to reach the conclusion that the public benefits of the conduct outweigh its anti-competitive costs. A pertinent example is whether integration ought to be allowed because it is considered conducive to technological innovation, especially by a national champion. But even these two approaches do not exhaust the regulatory strategies of the authorities. In this case study, we shall identify a trend towards mandating certain conduct on the part of firms which are seen to control core facilities. For example, they may be required to afford their competitors access to the facilities on reasonable and non-discriminatory terms. Paradoxically, this approach can be reminiscent of the style of the industry-specific regulation which competition law is replacing.

Market power and essential facilities

We use the question of market power and the denial of essential facilities to highlight these issues. Of course, this question is not the only way that competition law has for dealing with the kinds of private control points that may be constructed along the electronic highways, but it represents the trend.

If the question is whether the denial of access to facilities is anti-competitive, we need to think in terms of whether control of the facilities affords a firm power in a market. The first step is the definition or delineation of the relevant market. We can see that the broader the market is defined, the less likely a firm is to be in a dominant position.

The delineation may proceed both by territory and by product. If in terms of geography, the regulator concedes globalization, then one firm is less likely to dominate than it would in a contained national market. In terms of products, acceptance of innovation tends to favour a laissez-faire approach. It proves difficult to say that technologies are not substitutable. Today, should we regard cable television as constituting a separate market to free-to-air broadcasting? What if we add in satellite television from abroad? Is operating systems software to be regarded as a market in its own right or can certain types of wired hardware, applications software or software on the network provide alternatives to the customers? Yet a laissez-faire approach carries a significant risk. In a rapidly developing field, control of a facility in one market may be a springboard to power in a related market, such as a new innovation market. For example, control over the operating software for personal computers may be the way to promote sales in the emerging Internet access and services markets.

A judgement also has to be made about the presence of market power. Broadly speaking, market power might be characterised as freedom to operate without concern for the competitive disciplines of the market, for instance when determining the firm's pricing or product strategies. An indicator of market power might be the market share that a firm enjoys or the number of other firms it faces. However recent 'Chicago School' theory has suggested that even a firm which is alone in a market can still be sensitive to the prospects of competition; its market may be 'contestable'. We should appreciate that other policy analysts are not so sanguine about such prospects. But, Chicago School thinking has been influential in recent years in a number of countries and, on this approach, the attention turns to the level of the barriers to entry into a market, that is, the costs which other firms would have to sink into establishment in order to compete. In this regard, a particular concern lies with the cost of acquiring 'essential facilities', those facilities which rivals need if they are to compete with the incumbent. It may not be practical or reasonable to expect competitors to duplicate those facilities. It is here that economies of scale and scope, together with the capacity to spend on research and development and deploy other assets, may place the incumbent at an advantage. We should note that the rival may not want to compete with the controller of the facilities in its core market. Yet, denial of access to the facilities will still add to the cost of providing ancillary or related services separately, including new types of services.

Again, it may be extremely difficult in a rapidly developing field to judge whether facilities are essential. How ready should the authorities be to accept that alternatives are not feasible? On an optimistic view, innovation may lower entry costs and undermine incumbency advantages. Indeed, the creative destruction wrought by radical innovation may enable new rivals to bypass the facilities. For example satellite-based communications may provide a cost-effective bypass of the facilities controlled by television broadcasters and telecommunications carriers. In such an environment, incumbency can become a disadvantage. In the second phase of a new wave of innovation, when the technology starts to stabilise and standardise, it is these entrants which may consolidate their position and emerge as the new market power. The judgements are all the more difficult to make for new markets which no one presently dominates.

For example, in the computing markets, while competition authorities concentrated on the mainframe giant, IBM, innovations were shifting the fulcrum of power to the personal computer and its operating software. With the limelight now on Microsoft, will those firms pursuing the strategy that 'the network is the computer' take over the field, using the Java computer language in particular to overcome differences in operating software? Or, as News Limited is thinking, will television set-top boxes prove more of a control point for the supply of future media services?

Such uncertainties suggest to the authorities that it would be unwise to concentrate their energies on a single firm. The demarcations between markets are breaking down, and not even the largest firms seem able to sustain a 'stand-alone' position. Still, we should remember that market power may be acquired by forming alliances with firms of a similar size and complementary assets, while at the same time buying into the smaller specialised firms. The independent and alternative producers which remain unaffiliated will be the ones to worry about access.

As we noted earlier in this chapter, the approach taken in industry-specific regulation was to make a priori judgement about the value of vertical or horizontal integration. In return for this government protection from rivals, the incumbents had their spheres of operation limited and their access practices regulated directly. In dealing with powerful firms, competition authorities have shaped the structure of markets too. Blocking mergers and acquisitions is the most common precautionary device. The authorities have also drawn 'lines of business' restrictions around their activities. A prominent instance was the strictures which the United States authorities placed upon AT&T once the regional operating companies were divested. It was bound not to engage in equipment manufacture or in carriage on the local loops. A milder version of this kind of discipline is the requirement for structural and accounting separation of the businesses which operate in related markets. Services are to be unbundled, so the core company deals with its affiliates at arm's length and does not get away with subsidising their competition with other firms.

It is clear though that industry is resisting directives to separate and, certainly, further restrictions on lines of business. Rather, integration should be allowed because it realises the possibilities offered by converging technologies. It achieves the economies necessary to match resources with other major participants in a global market. If, however, the core firms are to be allowed to integrate, the authorities must rely on another regulatory strategy. We may see convergence on 'access regimes'. The firms should be required to grant non-affiliates access to their facilities on reasonable and non-discriminatory terms. We look now at two applications of this regulatory approach: access to make computer platforms inter-operable and access to make telecommunications networks inter-connectable.

Computer platforms

Computer hardware or software may become a core technology. Various strategies can be employed if the controller wants to deny access to those firms which compete with it in related markets, such as peripherals, applications and services markets. The most direct way is to assert the intellectual property rights in order to prevent the competitor's technology from interfacing. We saw that the competitor may have to reproduce the interface specifications to be inter-operable. A related strategy is to license the core technology, but only on condition that the customer take the firm's own peripherals, applications or services or those of its affiliates.

However, the obstacles put in the way of non-affiliates may be more subtle. Now, firms say that they are not trying to build closed, proprietary systems. They are moving to open systems such as the Unix standard. There are varying degrees of openness, nonetheless, and they might be able to put their competitors at a disadvantage by concealing interface code specifications within their systems, changing specifications to stay a step ahead or even to set traps for others, or foreshadowing changes to keep the industry uncertain and deter customers from purchasing alternatives for fear that they will turn out to be incompatible. Perhaps the biggest challenge to the independent producer is the functional integration of technology. The strategy is not to deny competitors access to the core facilities as such but to bundle them up with its own products and services. The facility, speed, reliability and price of the package make it less likely users will be prepared to mix and match and put together their own systems.[51]

Currently, Microsoft is accused of pursuing such a strategy in relation to the on-line media. It is reckoned that Microsoft Windows represents some eighty or more per cent of the operating systems software market for personal computers. Rivals argue that it is leveraging its control over operating software into the related Internet software and services markets. Readers might already be aware that Microsoft is working on a number of fronts. It is building up its own inventory of Internet software and services, partly by making exclusive arrangements with or buying into those other firms which have developed these complementary assets. To make an attractive package, it offers its Internet browser software free with its operating software or tied to the operating software. It engineers the specifications to integrate the browser with the operating software. It begins to do the same with Internet applications software such as web page publishing and home banking software. Windows is also being integrated with Microsoft's central server software and the server software made available free. Microsoft follows up by promoting its own content services like news and travel information on its browser default screen. It forms alliances with or buys up firms with catalogues and repertoires of content.[52] At the same time, it is forming alliances with Internet traffic carriers such as cable and telecommunications companies.

As we noted at the outset, it is not clear whether the technology will permit such control strategies to work. However, a Microsoft strategy aims to meet the possibility that the network will be able to transcend the operating system of the personal computer. The Java computer language may mean that software can be downloaded from the network to any operating system. Microsoft is producing a version of Java which is Windows-specific. More recently, it has started to join up with firms developing set-top box technology.

Will the competition authorities treat Windows as an essential facility and insist that Microsoft grant access to rivals, such as Netscape, on reasonable and non-discriminatory terms? In competition law there are precedents for this approach. In a notable settlement with the European Commission, IBM agreed to release adequate information about its hardware–software interface specifications and its systems network architecture in a timely fashion. Under the Clinton Administration, the Department of Justice was to signal a more robust and questioning approach to the practices of the marketplace. Assistant Attorney-General Ann Bingham advised that it would have little sympathy with the view that near-monopolies must be tolerated for the sake of technical progress. Yet such commitment was missing from the settlement which Microsoft reached with the Department (and the European Commission) in 1994.

When the settlement was presented to the Federal Court, the presiding judge expressed concern that it did not go far enough.[53] When the settlement was eventually approved, the Department undertook to keep Microsoft's Internet access practices under scrutiny. In 1998, the Department took Microsoft to court again. Granting a preliminary injunction, the Federal Court agreed that Microsoft was in breach of the settlement. It could not insist that personal computer manufacturers install its Internet Explorer software if they wanted to license its Windows 95 operating system. But what of Microsoft's plans to integrate the browser with its Windows 98 release? The Department's case dragged on through 1998 and, as the presentations came to a halt, attention began to focus on the kind of remedies which would be sought. The Government was reported to be contemplating some form of structural separation of Microsoft's various operations, particularly the separation of its operating software arm from its net software and services ventures. A more likely request was thought to be the disclosure of the Windows source code.[54]

Microsoft has put up a vigorous opposition to the suit. It responded by arguing that functional integration is only what customers wanted. It could offer manufacturers an operating system with all the browser files removed, but it warned that it would not be able to function as designed. Certainly, the authorities have been receptive to this kind of argument in the past. A private product standard can even be seen as the mark of a firm's efficiency. In contrast, firms will need a competition clearance to collaborate on an industry standard. The competition authorities have been even more reluctant to fix such standards themselves. Thus, while the European Commission sees the value in a single interface decoder system for digital pay-television services, it is not prepared to decide what that system should be.[55]

Microsoft has also warned that the restrictions placed on its market strategies would endanger the United States economy. After all, Microsoft is a major source of export earnings. Similarly, the earlier settlement was met with the claim that it would handicap a national champion at a time when international competition was intense and unfair. The authorities face difficulties responding to such debatable claims. Not only has Microsoft mounted an argument on the merits, it seems it has also threatened to move its headquarters up the road into Canada.[56] We should recall that the anti-trust litigation against IBM ran for thirteen years, only finally to be relinquished by the Reagan administration. But the impact of Microsoft is already worldwide and many countries wait to see whether the United States Government has the resolve to proceed with the case. Despite its awareness of the issues, we cannot expect countries like Australia, for example, to make the running in such cases.

Telecommunications networks

Much more so than the computer industries, telecommunications has been subject to industry-specific regulation as well as generalist competition law. Telecommunications was often a monopoly and, in many countries, the monopoly was held in public ownership. Liberalisation of telecommunications markets began with peripherals equipment, intra-corporate and local area networks, and value-added services such as data transmission. Now it is spreading to basic transport networks and services, as competition is introduced into long-distance and international markets. We saw earlier how the GATS has added a multilateral overlay to the pressures being exerted on countries to liberalise. With liberalisation has come privatisation of the core carriers and the sale of shares to foreign investors, such as the telecommunications companies from Europe and the United States.[57]

The openings made for competitors have brought the access issue alive. Various aspects of the transport networks could be regarded as essential facilities, more so now that the uses made of telecommunications are expanding so rapidly beyond voice telephony. Presently, the existing telephone lines are the main carrier of communications across the Internet. As early as 1983, the anti-trust settlement required AT&T to allow competitors to connect to its local loop distribution facilities. Even in the United States only the most built-up areas, with the most affluent customers, would provide any justification for duplication of the infrastructure. The last line to the home and the office, especially in outlying areas, together with inter-exchange line links, require daunting investments. It remains to be seen whether technologies such as cellular and satellite-based communications can make bypass effective.

The network carriers are concerned, not only to protect their monopolies over local voice telephony, but also to take advantage of their position to provide services in related markets. Again, specification of the technical standards for physical interconnectivity could present an opportunity to practise discrimination. The tendency has been to take this kind of standard setting away from the transport operator. But discrimination against non-affiliates might be practised in more subtle ways. The practice of bundling limits the number of points at which connections can be made into the local loop. If the competitors are riding on the carrier's lines, and the traffic is heavy, the scheduling and queuing of transmissions can affect the speed and ease of service which the competitor is able to offer.

Industry-specific regulatory authorities developed codes of conduct to try to ensure that competitors enjoyed access to those lines. Open network architecture was a goal.[58] But the protections built around the industry are being eroded. A generalist competition law approach is recommended to governments as a more flexible approach. This approach looks at the carrier's practices from the perspective, for instance, of abuse of a dominant position or misuse of market power. But, as experience in the computer industries has shown, it relies heavily on litigation. Yet we know such litigation to be painfully reactive, protracted and expensive. It has not proved possible to jettison the industry-specific regulatory approach. Indeed, the competition authorities have themselves been drawn into the complexities of the industry. They have had to decide which services to declare as essential facilities. They have had to bring the industry participants together in order to produce undertakings on access and to craft interconnection agreements.[59] They have had to arbitrate differences between the carriers, the various entrants into the core and related markets, and the user groups. All of these regulatory tasks recreate a legality that is embedded within the national jurisdiction and which is resistant to standardisation.

At the same time, this approach has required the authorities to attend to the reasons why the national carriers should be allowed to deny access. One reason given is maintenance of the technical integrity and quality of the core network. But a much bigger concern underlies the access issue. Huge and often publicly funded investments have been sunk into the construction of the networks. The public carrier often bears responsibilities for research and development, local employment, domestic equipment purchases, and cross-subsidisation of indigent users. Access might give an advantage to the private competitors who service only the most lucrative customers. So the access regime may be inclined to allow the carrier to exclude services from access if they would undermine the economies of its operation overall or obstruct the performance of its public responsibilities. Where access is allowed, the price should at least reflect something of the capital investment and public outlays of the network.[60]

Yet this focus on the conduct of the incumbent national carrier is increasingly a myopic one. If access is to be truly open and the network become, in the jargon, seamless from end to end, the authorities must consider placing the private competitors under obligations to carry content, services and traffic for all sources. At the very least, the concept of the common carrier must be expanded. Furthermore, because access involves users as well as rival suppliers, the carriers need to be placed under an obligation to contribute to universal service, say by way of payment of a levy into a common fund. Otherwise, the configuration will increasingly become one of privileged closed networks that operate on top of a more amorphous and less resourceful public grid. But this objective is not made any easier by the fact that universal service will need to extend beyond the standard telephone service. It will, as we have argued, have to take in enhanced services such as data transmission and perhaps Internet access.

The fashioning of an effective response is more complicated now because the service providers are not contained within national borders. They operate increasingly within a global network, where communications are switched between lines and between technologies according to the logic of private, commercial considerations. A service that has been rooted in national politics and cultures will be shaped by the economically resourceful around the world. A coordinated approach to regulation will be essential to ensure that commitments to open access and universal service are met on an inter-operator and inter-national basis.

However, before we turn to the role which the WTO will play, we should note that competition policy cannot be neatly confined to rules about access to specific facilities. Indeed, the challenge to regulatory competence lies as much in the complexity of the alliances being fashioned across sectors and across borders. Such alliances combine programming and other content resources with command over distribution channels. To take a recent example from the television sector, we should note that the European Commission ruled in late 1994 against a joint venture to provide technical and administrative services for pay-TV and other television communications services. The venture involved the German telecom, the publishing group Bertelsmann, and a film and television program company Taurus. Rather than persist with a proprietary encryption system, the venturers had indicated their preparedness to provide a common interface for the decoder base which was to be installed in customers' homes. A common interface would allow competitors to plug in their different access control systems. But the Commission felt that the venture would exploit other advantages such as a large subscriber base and knowledge of customer preferences, a catalogue of attractive programs, and the ability to offer a comprehensive service. Even if a common interface was provided, the venture could manipulate access, to delay or bury competitors' programs, citing technical problems or piracy concerns.[61]

The Commission was soon faced with a number of similar 'hard cases'. For instance, it was investigating a joint venture between the German telecom, the same publishing group Bertelsmann, and America Online, one concern about this venture being the access of competing on-line service providers to vital network, services and content. Yet, it is readily appreciated that such alliances offer benefits too. For example, alliances between telecoms might lead to an 'end to end seamless network' which would overcome national incompatibilities. More pragmatically, an alliance among 'European' companies could strengthen their ability to compete in international markets with the giants of Northern America and Japan. Within the ranks of the European Commission, the critical approach of the Competition Directorate was countered with support for the promotion of such European joint ventures.[62]

TRIPs and access regimes

Increasingly, mediation involves the interface between the two legalities of intellectual property and competition policy. We have seen that, while intellectual property is primarily concerned with conferring rights of control, it makes certain limited concessions to competitors. In turn, within national competition policy, intellectual property has often enjoyed a categorical exception. Under such a rule-based approach, the question became whether the use made of the rights was within the scope of the protection which the property had intended to confer. However, latterly, the tendency has been for competition authorities to look at the intellectual property licensing practices much more on the merits. This approach does not make the relationship any easier to manage. For example, while refusals to license are anti-competitive in an immediate sense, the authorities may be receptive to the argument that they contribute in the longer term to investment in innovation. Consideration of such merits requires the authorities to make judgements in specific situations, considering, for example, the degree of market power which the property holder enjoys and the actual impact of the practices on competition.[63]

So far, we have chosen to emphasise access to technological facilities and services as our test of the global competence of competition policy. A brief mention of content is warranted too. Those optimistic about the media anticipate a proliferation of content on the on-line media. But, while we continue to share tastes, we shall see items of popular culture being acquired, and then limited to specific sites, so that they can act as hooks for customers. Presently, sport seems to be a major bait. Specialist streams of hard information such as financial data might also be made available on an exclusive basis. Thus, content could be regarded as an essential facility for competition in trading markets or in the markets for on-line information itself.

Industry-specific legislation has required incumbents to give entrants into such markets as cable television access to essential content. If competition policy was to insist that intellectual property content be licensed to competitors,[64] it would need to respect the provisions of the international copyright acts, the Berne Convention, TRIPs and the new WIPO Treaties. The analysis of all three sources suggests that the main reference point will be the allowance which originates in article 9(2) of the Berne Convention. Of course, this allowance had other objectives in mind than facilitating commercial competitors. Nonetheless, in a decision relevant to the contemporary situation, the European Commission has taken the view that competition law would not contravene article 9(2) if an order was made for essential information to be licensed to a competitor.[65] This view has to be based on a reading of the words of article 9(2). While the WIPO Conventions evince a long history of concern about access to key intellectual resources, it is fair to say that competition policy, in the modern sense, has not been in focus. Our analysis of TRIPs indicates that the drafters were conscious of this particular inter-legality. But, as yet, it makes no determined effort to settle the interface between intellectual property and competition policy. It remains to be seen whether the WTO's new general interest in competition policy will provide greater resolution.

The GATS and access regimes

Earlier analysis identified one area that has already been given attention by the WTO. The Annex on Telecommunications to the GATS agreement takes on some of the issues of access discussed in this chapter. The Annex applies a number of relevant obligations to members, the core obligation being to ensure that service suppliers are accorded access to and use of telecommunications transport networks and services on reasonable and non-discriminatory terms and conditions. The binding, multilateral nature of the Annex makes its provisions worthy of attention.

We can start by identifying the beneficiaries of its obligation. The Annex is said to apply to all measures of a member that affect access to – and use of – public telecommunications transport networks and services. The access obligation is for the benefit of any service supplier of any other member when supplying a service which is included in the member's schedule. So it has been included in the GATS for the benefit of service suppliers generally and not for other telecommunications suppliers. At the same time, access is limited to those services which a member has included in its schedule of commitments. So if telecommunications is inscribed in a schedule, or, for that matter, any other services, such as financial services, audiovisuals, retailing or business services, then their suppliers are to enjoy the benefits of the Annex. It appears that limitations cannot be applied to access or use, except as authorised by the Annex itself or by way of the measures which article XVI of the GATS, the general article on market access, requires to be listed.[66]

To what does the access obligation pertain? Telecommunications are defined broadly to mean the transmission and reception of signals by any electromagnetic means, a definition which can at least encompass the ascending media of fibre optics and wireless satellites (glass and air). The definition of transport networks means the telecommunications infrastructure which permits telecommunications between and among defined network termination points. The definition of transport services states that these services may include telegram, telephone, telex and data transmission typically involving the real-time transmission of customer-supplied information between two or more points without any end-to-end change in the form or content of the customer's information.

Thus, the Annex develops a distinction between such transport networks and services on the one hand and services which attach to them and flow over them on the other. Yet the technology is quite dynamic, and the real power in the future might not lie with the lines but, as we have speculated, with computer software and other systems integration services. The Annex also states that it does not apply to 'measures affecting the cable or broadcast distribution of radio or television programming'. Consequently, it leaves another component of convergence, audiovisual services, to separate negotiations, without the benefit of the definitions and principles of a special annex. Again, technological developments may be making this demarcation problematic.

Within the telecommunications sectors themselves, more conventionally described, the approach is to treat the 'value-added' services sectors increasingly as ordinary commercial sectors subject to liberalisation, but to recognise that many countries still regard the ownership and operation of the basic carriers as a special case. While the negotiations over commitments might lead to liberalisation, for the time being, the access obligation is the trade-off for the retention of state-owned, often monopoly carriers. Nonetheless, privatisation does not necessarily lead to a multiplicity of carriers and access may be just as problematic in the case of private carriers which enjoy market power. The Annex defines public services to be any telecommunication transport service required, explicitly or in effect, by a member to be offered to the public generally. A contrast can be made with intra-corporate or closed user group networks of various kinds. But of course there is pressure for change in this sector too, participation in the two sectors overlaps, and the technology is in fact making it difficult to distinguish between basic and other services functionally.

Much of the access regime can still be explained by the GATS fix on those national public measures which tend to limit the opportunities for global traders and investors to gain access to local markets. Yet, it is important to note that the obligations of the Annex are not confined to public carriers in the sense of state-owned carriers. Nor do they apply only to monopoly or dominant carriers, whether they are state or privately owned. Furthermore, they are not confined to transport networks, they extend to transport services. They include private leased circuits. They run to networks and services offered within or across the borders of members. Thus, the Annex provides the scope to rope in a wider range of carriers. The background note on the WTO negotiations on basic telecommunications begins to develop this picture: 'The specification of terms and conditions of interconnection is just as relevant in respect of dominant private sector suppliers as it is in the case of state-owned suppliers.'[67]

How far does the access obligation reach? To enable access, service suppliers are to be permitted to purchase or lease and attach terminal and other equipment which interfaces with the network, interconnect private leased or owned circuits, and use operating protocols of the supplier's choice. These entitlements are limited, for, to be effective, access might need to extend to customer information and subscriber management systems. The Annex goes on to say that no conditions are to be imposed on the access and use which is embraced, other than is necessary to safeguard public service responsibilities and to protect technical integrity, as well as to limit supply to the commitments made in the member's schedule. The Annex itemises a set of conditions which are to be expected to be associated with these objectives, such as restrictions on resale, requirements for inter-operability, technical requirements relating to attachment of equipment, and restrictions on interconnection of privately leased or owned circuits. In these conditions lies the potential to maintain certain local safeguards. Interestingly, no mention is made of the protection of intellectual property.

The Annex was pursued by the negotiating group on basic telecommunications. It considered whether to promote access by way of a draft model national schedule or a body of general rules and understandings, the former approach being favoured by the beginning of 1996. The group also had to decide whether it would be preferable to do so by means of international rules and regulatory requirements specific to the telecommunications sector or through the applicability of more general competition law principles relating to positions of market dominance. As we have noted, the carry-over negotiations took up the issue of regulatory standards. As a result, the WTO Secretariat drafted a reference paper which fifty-five countries were to incorporate in their schedules.[68] The paper provided definitions and principles regarding the regulatory framework for basic telecommunications services. The issue of interconnection was also addressed. Suppliers of public networks or services were to ensure interconnection at any technically feasible point, and the interconnection would need to be on non-discriminatory terms and terms that are transparent, reasonable and sufficiently unbundled.

The paper went beyond the specific issue of interconnection. The definitions adopted the concept of essential services and identified major suppliers to be those who can materially affect the terms of participation as a result of control over essential facilities or use of a position in the market. Members were to take appropriate measures to prevent major suppliers from engaging in anti-competitive practices and in particular engaging in anti-competitive cross-subsidisation or not making available on a timely basis technical information about essential facilities and commercially relevant information which are necessary for other services suppliers to provide services. At the same time, the paper recognised the right of any member to define the universal service obligations it wished to maintain.

This experience indicates how prepared the WTO is to elaborate re-regulatory requirements when it thinks the cause is justified. This pre-paredness seems highly significant at a time when the WTO is considering taking on competition policy generally. But this broader agenda has spawned competition over the appropriate competition policy to adopt towards international trade, intellectual property and investment.

The WTO agenda for competition regulation

In the post-Uruguay Round world of WTO pre-eminence, much of the intellectual impetus for competition regulation has been coming from experts in the West, some of whom are officials or consultants to the international organizations such as the European Commission, the OECD and the WTO itself, some who are more academically detached. Thus, versions of the proposals which are currently in circulation have appeared in the documents of the organizations as well as in academic journals, though none can be said to have an official imprimatur at this stage.

The proposals concern primarily the type of practices which should be targeted or prioritised by any international policy. So, even within these like-minded policy circles, the proposals involve variations. The choice of each emphasis might be attributed to judgements made about which approaches would 'work' at this level. These judgements are said to be technically minded. Thus, the experts may wish to emphasise those practices which are most amenable to clear, common rules. National systems do proscribe certain practices outright, for instance by deeming them anti-competitive per se, without giving the administrative or judicial authorities the opportunity to make their own characterisation or indeed to apply a rule of reason. In theory, a rule could be devised for any practice, only in some situations it is the case that a blanket proscription does not seem appropriate. To take an example of relevance to our discussion, intellectual property practices rarely, if ever, are the subject of blanket proscriptions, either within the legislative framework or in the guidelines issued by the authorities, such as their various white, grey and black lists. The experts are really making a judgement here about which practices attract the most censure. A worldly version of this approach to international policy making is to say that any international code is going to require the expenditure of political as well as cognitive resources. Therefore, it is advisable for the international forum to confine its efforts to an acceptable core of practices.

This advice begins to recognise that the choice of the contents of the code cannot avoid value preferences. If there are tendencies for competition policies to converge, there are also significant differences. The priorities suggest which practices are considered the most seriously deleterious, here where employed in an international context. Such preferences show through in the examples given by the Director-General of the WTO when he particularised his support for competition regulation. He nominated export cartels, merger controls and cooperative research and development ventures.[69] Then it must be conceded that other perspectives will perceive a different set of practices to be of concern, if they do embrace a competition policy perspective on restrictive trade practices at all. Thus, to cite a few examples, the OECD wish list identified horizontal and vertical agreements, abuse of a dominant position and mergers and acquisitions, but left out intellectual property licensing and consumer protection,[70] while Scherer joined such licensing with export and import cartels and international mergers.[71]

If intelligent competition policy requires much of its regulation to be tailored to the individual situation, then the framework must provide ways to leave as much space as possible to national authorities. Arguably, if the framework is sound enough to attract strong support, then fellow member countries will be prepared to accept and back the judgement of one country's authority, even though the practices have spillover effects to their territories. The framework can involve procedures to be followed in order to ensure that the perspectives of these other members are taken into account. Through its Committee on Competition Policy and Law, the OECD has already worked with such procedures in cases of international mergers.

Ultimately, however, these efforts to allow individualisation may activate the very differences which generated the call for international harmonisation and standardisation in the first place. If individualisation is a necessary part of a competition policy, an international authority might be a better place to invest this discretionary space. Yet, debate over the constitution of such an authority reveals similar problematics as the construction of the legislative framework. A key consultant, Nicolaides, envisages a body more official and binding than the networks of functional national regulators which have gathered in this field as well as other fields of international business regulation such as banking regulation.[72] But he would like to see the authority avoid politicisation: a constitution of neutral experts and government delegates would seem the best way to keep the function technocratic.

As we foreshadowed in chapter three, the constitution of such international regulatory authorities is part of a general contest over the form which global governance is to take. If such authorities are to make sophisticated judgements about the effects on competition of various practices, better perhaps that they are not dominated by any particular theoretical perspective. More so, if they are to weigh the benefits of the practices against their effects on competition, sometimes to the point of allowing the practices to continue, then they will need input from other perspectives, such as producer, employee, consumer and regional interests. They will have to confront a problem that many international organizations are encountering when they make decisions at a remove from local communities, a problem characterised as 'democratic deficit'.

As the power of the WTO is appreciated, its decision making is coming under scrutiny. The opportunities for the smaller member countries to exert a genuine influence over the provisions of its agreements is one issue; another issue is the nature of the involvement of NGOs. But any such democratisation should not allow the nations with the greatest power to discipline the transnationals to pull back from a responsible role. Arguably, the United Nations codes of conduct remained soft law because the major Western powers were not prepared to give complete support to them.[73] If NGOs are to be involved, then it must be appreciated that they will include the representatives of the corporations which are the subjects of the regulation. Already, they have been incorporated in the delegations of some members to the WTO. Again, the efficacy of such regulation may depend on their willingness to comply.

Rather, the NGO question relates to the role for alternative perspectives. It remains to be seen whether, as Reichman speculated when writing for UNCTAD, international competition policy provides an opportunity for small and medium-sized enterprises to form coalitions of interest over national lines.[74] Any such involvement runs the risk of giving legitimacy to a perspective that is basically set against them. One practical consideration is whether they would be able to marshal the resources to participate effectively in what are likely to be very complex and often protracted disputes. Yet, even where competition regulation is working effectively, it tends to make tremendous allowances for imbalances of power and concentrations of interest in the marketplace. Preston suspected that the kind of competition law which treats the globe as the market would show little concern for competitors who wish to operate just within a local part of that market.[75] Larger markets will indeed provide the justification for rationalisations. Specific practices will have to be targeted if opportunities for competition in these localities are to be safeguarded, especially for independent start-up and minor-scale producers. But it is questionable whether competition law can be sufficiently fine tuned to deal with such practices. Paradoxically, competition law begins to take on some of the sector-specific characteristics of industry regulation when it attempts to deal with these practices. The access codes in the telecommunications sector have provided a good illustration.

At the international level, the codes of conduct for multinational enterprises were tailored to the particular practices of concern to importing countries. One of the reasons why these codes might seem more apt is that they explicitly represent a number of economic, cultural and political concerns which go beyond competition policy's focus on allocative efficiency and consumer choice in the marketplace. Rather than creating a set of offences to be avoided, they translate the concerns into positive obligations of fair trading and international corporate citizenship. Industry, labour and tax concerns were among the concerns expressed in the earlier codes; they could now be updated to take account of the growing concerns about the loss of local and indigenous cultures and the damage to the natural environment. I have argued that such an international agenda becomes increasingly important, as trade regulation eliminates many of the protections which have been maintained at the national level and competition law itself sheds the immunities it has allowed within certain sensitive sectors.

In recognition of such concerns, the OECD recently proposed incorporating its own version of these guidelines within the Multilateral Agreement on Investment.[76] But, as evidence that the mood is changing, we should appreciate that one of the grounds of opposition to the agreement was the voluntary nature of the guidelines. Not surprisingly, critics argued for reciprocity when the agreement sought to place legally enforceable obligations on national governments to respect the rights and freedoms of investors. Otherwise, investors would enjoy these rights and freedoms without any compunction to assume the corresponding obligations of citizenship.

The WTO's 1996 Singapore meeting

The competing strands of competition policy surface in the more recent deliberations of the WTO. As we have noted, developing countries had in earlier decades made the running on restrictive business practices, both in the GATT and at the United Nations. At the Singapore Meeting of Ministers, the impetus was to come instead from a European Union proposal. The Union sought to initiate work on four tracks: commitment by all members to effective domestic competition laws, identification of core competition principles and procedures, establishment of instruments of cooperation, and submission of the procedural and material elements of competition law to the WTO dispute settlement process. Other developed countries such as Japan agreed to the work but only if the uses of trade measures such as anti-dumping procedures and safeguards were subject to scrutiny too. There was apprehension among the ASEAN countries that the agenda would aim to break down local monopolies and practices that helped domestic companies maintain market share.[77] But some developing countries supported work on anti-competitive practices (such as transfer pricing and other intra-firm practices) because they thought that the further liberalisation of investment controls would heighten the need for regulation of the restrictive business practices of the transnational corporations. They had in mind the negotiations within the OECD over the MAI and the moves within the WTO itself to negotiate its own code of liberalisation of investment.

After a great deal of discussion, the Singapore meeting agreed to establish a working group to 'study issues raised by members relating to the interaction between trade and competition policy, including anti-competitive practices, in order to identify any areas that may merit further consideration in the WTO framework'.[78] To further this study, a cross-reference was made to the Midrand declaration and the work of UNCTAD.[79] The focus shifted to the framing of the terms of reference of the working party. The developing countries were facing a fight, for the United States representatives made it clear that its sole interest was in the promulgation of anti-monopoly laws which operated at the national level. It saw them as a way to break down cartels and other private anti-competitive behaviour which impeded market access by its exporters.

The working group met for the first time in July 1997. From the many submissions, the chairman drew up a checklist of issues which included the impact of anti-competitive practices of enterprises and associations on international trade, the impact of state monopolies, exclusive rights and regulatory policies on competition and international trade, the relationship between the trade-related aspects of intellectual property rights and competition policy, and the relationship between investment and competition policy. While the checklist represented many of the preoccupations with domestic protection, it also made some concessions to the broader concerns.[80]

At the same time, QUAD countries were promoting a multilateral investment agreement which would establish rules for the liberalisation of direct investment across the board. While the United States preferred to focus its efforts within the OECD, where the campaign began, the European Union, Japan and Canada became prime movers to have the WTO negotiate a broad-based agreement. It should be understood that such an investment agreement would signify a huge advance for the neoliberal agenda at the WTO. It should be appreciated that a fully fledged agreement would swamp the provisions of the most relevant existing agreements, the GATS and the Agreement on Trade-Related Investment Measures (TRIMs), with their in-built controls on liberalisation. It would attack directly the controls many countries place on foreign investment, to limit the level of establishment and equity in sensitive sectors such as agriculture, media and the professions or to attach performance requirements, including requirements of joint venturing, technology transfer and payment of taxation.

We have noted that the GATS recognises investments only obliquely in their capacity as modes of service supply. Furthermore, the listings approach allows countries to withhold whole sectors from the scrutiny of its national treatment and market access norms. Horizontal or sector-specific limitations may preserve existing foreign investment policies in those sectors which are inscribed. Reflecting caution in many quarters, the TRIMs agreement also produced a narrow focus. It relates simply to trade in goods. Members are obliged by the agreement not to apply any TRIMs measures that are inconsistent with the obligations, either of national treatment or the general elimination of quantitative restrictions, which are contained in the GATT 1994. However, the negotiations could only settle on a brief illustrative list of such measures. Essentially, they comprised local product purchasing requirements and import/export balancing requirements.

Much would of course depend on the scope of the particular MAI agreement. If the draft OECD MAI can be regarded as a prototype, that scope would be wide. The MAI is notable for proposing a broad array of rights for foreign investors. Those rights would include most favoured nation and national treatment, which again would have far reaching implications when applied to establishment and operation behind the border. But the rights would extend to protection from expropriation, that is, to government measures that undermine established investments. These measures need not be discriminatory. In furthering such an obligation, the MAI has defined the act of expropriation liberally. It envisages not merely nationalisation in the traditional sense but measures with equivalent effect. Regulatory measures, such as health and environmental measures, could be regarded as having this effect. The exceptions to this obligation have been heavily circumscribed. In addition, it should be noted that the MAI proposes proscribing directly a whole range of performance requirements which governments have attached to foreign investments. Some (but not all) of these requirements would be allowed, if they were joined to the offer of assistance.

At the time of writing, the OECD MAI has run adrift. Negotiations have been suspended on several occasions; in October 1999, the talks reached a stalemate. Members have been unable to agree on key terms and they have sought to enter numerous reservations to the MFN and national treatment requirements. France then decided to withdraw from the negotiations altogether. It is possible the focus will shift back to the WTO and indeed the argument has been made that an OECD agreement would be inconsistent with the MFN obligations under the WTO agreements.[81]

There is disagreement in the WTO too. The initial reaction of developing countries was to oppose the addition of this agenda item. In a manner reminiscent of the early debate over TRIPs, a United Nations body, UNCTAD, was seen as the more appropriate international forum. One view was that investment is not a trade-related issue. But, at the Singapore meeting, several of the developing countries which were included in the informal negotiating groups decided to support a study of the interface between trade and investment. It was to be clear, however, that a study program would not prejudge whether negotiations should be undertaken at a later date. It was also the understanding of these countries that the study would stay within the bounds of the existing WTO provisions and in particular the limits of the TRIMs agreement.

But Khor reports that the European Union (with the seeming approbation of the Director-General) continued to suggest that negotiations on a multilateral investment agreement would be a top priority for the WTO.[82] The Director-General's enthusiasm seemed to spill over and, during the negotiations over the OECD MAI, the WTO was obliged to issue a statement disassociating him from it.[83] We should note that the Singapore declaration carries a safeguard that further negotiations regarding multilateral disciplines on both competition policy and investment policy are to take place only after an explicit consensus decision is taken among WTO members.

The Working Group report

In late 1998, the Working Group issued its first report on competition policy.[84] The general observation to make about the report is how tentative it is, reflecting the lack of consensus within the WTO membership. Its recommendations are confined to educative work and further discussion throughout 1999. The report begins by noting three general views. The first wished to give priority to governmental restraints and distortions, considering that competition 'would be more enhanced by trade liberalization and by competition-oriented reforms of WTO rules rather than by introduction of new WTO rules and standards relating to national competition laws and international cooperation'. The contrasting view preferred a focus on the anti-competitive practices of enterprises that affected international trade, though here the emphasis seemed to remain with the restrictive practices of domestic enterprises and their impact on the market access enjoyed by foreign firms. The third view recommended a balanced approach.

Nevertheless, the survey work done by the Working Group is informative and in particular the section of the report considering the impact of private anti-competitive practices on international trade. The report recognised three categories of practice. The first was practices that affected market access for imports. In this category the report placed such practices as import cartels, vertical restraints, private standard-setting activities, and denial of access to essential facilities. The second was practices affecting different countries in largely the same way. Here the report mentioned international cartels, some mergers and acquisitions, and abuse of a dominant position by firms operating in international markets. The final category was practices which had a differential impact on affected countries, such as export cartels and some mergers. In a special section, the Group noted that exclusive intellectual property rights were not seen as inimical to competition but that competition law was to be applied to the exercise of such rights.

In thinking about possible responses to these problematic practices, the report thought first in terms of government policies and measures that could facilitate harmful anti-competitive practices by enterprises or associations. At the national level, these government policies and measures could include a lack of a well constituted competition law or a failure to enforce existing laws. A specific mention was given to the lack of effective rules governing access to essential facilities, especially in the context of deregulation and privatisation. But we can see the lens opening wider with the report's acknowledgement of lack of jurisdiction to deter anti-competitive conduct originating abroad, lack of rules in the international trading system to deal with the practices, and lack of cooperation between countries to provide appropriate remedies. In particular, it was noted that existing WTO rules do not deal directly with anti-competitive practices by private firms such as international cartels. Presently, there was no alternative but to rely on non-violation complaints.

The Working Group seemed overwhelmed by diversity and the situation-specific or perspective-driven nature of national judgements about such practices. Weakly, it concluded by saying that we cannot expect any more than consultation between countries. 'For a variety of reasons, including different effects in different national markets as well as differing legal standards, it was inevitable that, from time to time, different jurisdictions would reach different conclusions regarding the acceptability of particular arrangements and transactions.'[85] At best, the Group might offer an illustrative list of factors to be considered in the balancing act which occurs at the national level on a case by case basis. The Group might also assist with convergence in procedural requirements.

CONCLUSIONS

This study has been the last and longest of the chapters because it best combines the themes we have developed in this book. The particular case highlights the importance of the digital on-line media to the nature of global networks and their potential to enhance access. Recent developments indicate that the technology is undermining the nation state's ability to apply industry-specific regulation in the audiovisuals and telecommunications sectors. The GATS has added to the pressure on those national measures which were designed to ensure that less powerful and mainstream voices, particularly local ones, enjoyed access to distribution channels. Nevertheless, for the time being, many countries have availed themselves of the opportunities inherent in the GATS itself to maintain limitations on their exposure to the open-trade and free-market norms of the WTO.

If industry-specific regulation is undermined, it is possible that the way will be open for distributors to exploit convergence and assume dominance in a global marketplace. But the technology itself may provide the means to circumvent the bottlenecks on which control has in the past been built. There is doubt whether intellectual property can expect to have much purchase in this environment. Certainly, the emphasis shifts from control over content to a strategic position in the provision of facilities and services. The TRIPs agreement strengthened intellectual property protection globally. But TRIPs fell short of conferring rights squarely over communications on-line. It left a space for another international organization, WIPO, to fill. The 1996 WIPO Treaties have placed intellectual property rights into the on-line environment. But a placatory approach has left room for other concerns to be mediated. The primary beneficiaries of the rights are the authors of works which may be transmitted on-line. Performers and producers of sound recordings have also received support. But the concerns of the on-line intermediaries have been assuaged somewhat by leaving important issues like third party liability to be resolved at each national level. The WIPO Treaties also carried over into the digital environment the established concessions to the interests which end users and public organizations have in maintaining access to informational and educational resources. The scope of these concessions will come under close scrutiny, most particularly I think if the WTO decides to apply the provisions of the Treaties and provide access to its compelling dispute settlement process.

Yet the power of intellectual property, which is limited in its own right, is giving way to command over other assets such as computer platforms and telecommunications networks. As much as qualifications on intellectual property itself, genuine access depends on the coordinated regulation of the acquisition and abuse of market power. This chapter has used the example of the many subtle ways access is denied to essential facilities. At present, we must rely on the variable policy of national competition regulation to deal with this problem. Such potentially global power invites consideration of the institution of competition law standards at the international level. Tentatively, the GATS has acknowledged the issue by developing telecommunications access obligations. These obligations apply in respect of common carriers which are in private hands as well as public sector instrumentalities. But, as we have observed at several points, many countries lack the legal jurisdiction or the political power needed to discipline the restrictive business practices of the transnational corporations. They need help from an international authority.

We saw first in chapter three that competition law continues to hold quite different meanings. A WTO competition policy agenda is just as likely to challenge the industry-specific regulation which survives at the national level as it is to govern the practices of transnational operators. If a narrow view of competition law is to be pursued, it suggests that other, more positive, social obligations will be needed at this level. This is surely the case, if producer access and universal service are to have substance when the on-line media are privately owned and operated on a truly global scale.

CHAPTER 9

CONCLUSIONS AND PROSPECTS

This book has sketched the system which the Uruguay Round has built onto the GATT and institutionalised as the WTO. In exploring the texts of the new GATS and TRIPs agreements, it has pointed up the increasingly influential role which trade law is enabled to play, mediating the reception of foreign legalities by the local legalities of the WTO member countries. We have gone to some trouble to establish why there is a role for a mediating multilateral institution. The WTO agreements have been characterised as mixing the familiar commanding and disciplining role of law with the more seductive role of mediation.

For the GATS, given the potential reach of its norms of national treatment and market access, the bottom-up approach to listing commitments was the most subtle way reservations about liberalisation have been accommodated. However, at this stage, the norms themselves also lack specificity. For instance, we are yet to see what national treatment will demand of members where it reaches beyond formally identical treatment. So too, the real impetus behind market access has related to quantitative limitations, and the agreement acknowledges the place for domestic regulation, especially as regards technical standards and qualification requirements. But what if the next round turns its attention to the so-called qualitative restrictions?

The play in the GATS was seen at work in the case of the legal services sector. Countries took advantage of the listing options, either withholding the whole sector from scrutiny or confining access to advice on home country law. Even the northern countries, which contain strong lobbies for internationalisation, needed to respect the reservations held by their localised professional groups. Where national treatment is fully applied, it remains to be seen whether governments will be allowed to insist on local education and experience, at least for admission to their legal professions proper and thus for access to the reserved areas of practice. But might the momentum of market access override these carefully elaborated schemes of give and take by freeing up business structures? It may be that foreigners will no longer need to become members of the profession if they wish to partner local lawyers or take a controlling equity in a legal services firm. Indeed, investors from outside the sector may be afforded an opening.

The intellectual property rights of TRIPs make a more emphatic statement, but we have been able to discern areas in which this agreement too has remained pliable. Copyright on-line and plant patenting were two such aspects. In regard to copyright generally, TRIPs has relied heavily on the Berne Convention. In stopping short of copyright on-line, it also left space for WIPO to make the running once again. The 1996 WIPO Treaties have advanced copyright for the authors of the traditional works and the producers of sound recordings, while hesitating to assist performers and broadcasters, and sticking with the limited allowance which has been made for non-voluntary licensing. If the WTO now chooses to take the WIPO Treaties on board, it may have to decide how to resolve a number of outstanding questions.

Patent protection was made an international obligation for the first time. Protection was extended to all manner of technology and the rights which accompany the patent are fully fledged too, including the right to control the working of the invention, so significant to the farmer's use of the seed. At the same time, the TRIPs agreement leaves the crucial distinction between a discovery and invention to be resolved at the level of national jurisprudence. It also allows members to take an exception from patentability in respect of plants and animals. That exception is subject to a proviso that plant varieties be protected by an effective sui generis system. But the criteria for identifying such a system were left vague, being notably silent as to whether compliance with another international agreement, UPOV, would suffice. The provision is now due for review. There are increasing demands that private patent rights be somehow reconciled with the aspirations of the Convention on Biodiversity to give states sovereignty over biological resources.

This appreciation of the subtleties was not meant to inflate the capacity of the WTO and its new agreements. We have been ready to acknowledge the many positives involved in opening localities to the cosmopolitan influences of global services supply and intellectual endeavours. But the WTO is yet to prove it can provide independent and alternative producers, performers and users with positive opportunities to gain access to a globalizing economy. In other words, it is yet to demonstrate the gains which flow to those who lack the power of technology and capital to fare for themselves in a laissez-faire global economy. Such gains are needed if the less resource-ful are to lose the national protections, supports and spaces outside the market on which they have relied in the past.

For there is no doubt that this new trade law requires many conventional measures to be relinquished. It is significant enough that the agreements require member countries to accord foreigners no less favourable treatment than they do their own nationals. We have argued that the expanding notion of national treatment means the members cannot simply apply their legalities in such a way as to accord foreigners and locals formal equality before the law. Local legalities will be obliged to grant concessions to the legalities which the foreigners carry with them. In the services and intellectual sectors, 'behind the border', this standard of non-discrimination is all the more significant. After all, the economic protection of locals has not been the sole motive for treating foreigners differently. Special measures have been needed as member countries struggle to retain a semblance of regulatory competence over the progressively more footloose and reflexive operators in a global market.

We have noted how the agreements do make some concessions to the regulatory interests of the locality. They allow for measures that can be justified by certain circumscribed, legitimate objectives of regulation. But, at the same time, they apply disciplines to the member's choice of the instrument by which they would promote those objectives. Essentially, they ask that the most market-friendly approaches be adopted. Moreover, even where the measures do not contravene the agreements, it is apparent that all members will at times find themselves lacking in the necessary legal jurisdiction or political power to make effective use of these small spaces allowed for regulation.

The need to accommodate foreign legalities may generate some impetus for members to search for multilateral agreements on regulatory standards. We have seen that the other component of non-discrimination, most favoured nation treatment, makes it difficult for members to use unilateral or bilateral strategies to influence the level of regulatory standards in other countries. The WTO has held to this position despite the obvious policy spillovers between countries and the insidious effects of regulatory competition. Is this a bad thing? Perhaps the recent radical innovations in technology mean that unilateral and bilateral arrangements could no longer contain the operators anyway.

Nonetheless, the WTO is active itself, making further inroads into local measures. Its goal of expanding market access pushes at the edifice of the members' non-discriminatory regulation of markets. Quantitative limitations, for instance on the number of suppliers given access to a market, might appear to favour local incumbents at the expense of foreign entrants. But again economic protection has not been the sole motive for restrictions on market access. Now, if the GATS proceeds with the liberalisation of qualitative limitations, it will attack regulatory policies which have been adopted for a wide range of non-trade reasons.

If it makes such inroads, the WTO should attract to itself a positive onus to assist member countries with business regulation. In thinking about how that onus might be discharged, we can accept that competition policy is the kind of regulation which a neo-liberal approach will recommend as the best means to check private power. Competition policy is regarded as more market sympathetic than the old fashioned, nationally based legalities of industry-specific and foreign investment regulation. But we have found that the WTO agreements do little more than concede a limited space to the members to operate their own competition laws.

Of course, such a space is needed. Otherwise, reflecting its deregulatory disposition, the general norms of the WTO agreements will view competition regulation as a possible trade barrier, just like any other government measures. Yet allowing a space is not an adequate approach. Our understanding of globalization indicates that liberalisation opens the way for the assumption of market power on a new scale. The exercise of that power must be civilised. And we should appreciate that the WTO's own program for liberalisation has not been fully implemented. As well as further inroads in the service sectors and intellectual fields, the unfinished business includes a fully fledged multilateral agreement on investment. The WTO may now become the focal point for the development of this agreement.

Yet the WTO senses that members are not entirely satisfied with the way the agenda is being cast. Increasingly too, pressure will be brought to bear by the NGOs which are finding voice at the global level. It seems doubtful that the WTO's carefully crafted let-out clauses and procedural exits can manage this tension. It seems also from our analysis that the general doctrines of the past, like nullification and impairment, will not provide the platform from which re-regulation can be launched.

The WTO is an impressive achievement in institution building. On business regulation, however, it seems to be stuck in a groove like the playing of an old record. It is in need of conceptual and political 'circuit-breakers'. Help is needed to move it on and make a go of reconciling its version of a desirable global economy with the cultural and social stabilities which cannot be protected at the national level anymore. Perhaps, this progression will take time. After all, the pattern in industrialising countries like Britain, and more recently regional free-trade compacts like the European Community, was for social regulation to come after market liberalisation.

Yet is a positive role in re-regulation so hard for the WTO to attain? We have given over a lot of our discussion to the TRIPs agreement. This commitment was justified not simply because TRIPs operates in a field so important to globalization. TRIPs is an emphatic innovation in multilateral re-regulation. In its light, we can be forgiven for asking whether it really is such a conceptual challenge for the WTO to extend support to positive re-regulation. Intellectual property regulation was given support with no apparent danger to the purity and consistency of the traditional focus on barriers to trade. Intellectual property protection seems very much concerned with the regulation of unfair trade practices by private competitors. So why not other programs of re-regulation too? Has our institutional learning advanced so little that we are destined to experience another period of turmoil and injustice, where some reap windfall profits and others suffer devastating losses?

Looking forward to the Millennium Round, what issues might we nominate as providing a test of the WTO's mettle? Within the GATS, one such issue is the potential of the WTO to foster multilateral standards for the conduct of liberalised professional services. The innovations which come with liberalisation have various beneficial aspects. Yet, increasingly, multilateral standards will have to assume the role which national measures have served in the past, encouraging global operators to learn about local lore and to respect local practices. Within TRIPs, a key issue is the development of sui generis intellectual property systems that can give recognition to local, indigenous contributions to biological resources. Another important initiative would be the institution of intellectual property rights for performers which were of equal strength to those enjoyed by others who are taking advantage of the new on-line media. Both these achievements would help the WTO live up to its promise that liberalisation benefits producers across the board. They would have symbolic as well as material benefits. Undoing the straitjacket of article 9(2) and legislating clear conditions of access to content resources would also be a responsible thing to do. Extending the telecommunications access obligations to the facilities of the other converging media is vital too to the WTO's legitimacy. These initiatives would offer ways in which, within intellectual property and competition law, the global power of the core operators could be offset.

Prospects post-Seattle

These suggestions build on potential which was already present in the two agreements – without the need to agree on a new agenda. Seattle has shown that the wider agenda is too ambitious a goal at this stage. We know that the GATS contains an in-built requirement for members to commence a new round of negotiations for commitments to national treatment and market access. Prior to Seattle, an agenda had already been fashioned for negotiations to proceed. Nevertheless, it may be hard to build momentum into these negotiations without the opportunity to trade off concessions in other sectors. Negotiations on agriculture are also part of the in-built agenda. In other sectors, however, the denouement in Seattle has postponed fresh negotiations. The next two years will prove interesting.

The GATS must also deal with some matters of substance. The work program for electronic commerce has raised the question whether Internet transactions should properly be dealt with under the aegis of a services agreement. For the majority of transactions, most countries favour the GATS, but some are unhappy. The GATS approach to listing commitments will afford countries scope to maintain limitations on national treatment and market access.

At the same time, there is interest in how the access obligations of the Telecommunications Annex (see chapter eight) should relate to Internet services. The Annex gives Internet service providers the benefit of access to public telecommunications networks, but some members are now asking whether the Internet service providers should themselves be obliged to offer access to others. In the lead-up to Seattle, the Council for Trade-Related Aspects of Intellectual Property Rights had identified some issues for discussion. It is likely the work on geographical appellations (see chapter six) will proceed, the European Union wishing to strengthen the protection for foodstuffs such as cheeses, and attracting some interesting allies including India, which has attachments to spices and basmati rice.

Part of the in-built agenda of TRIPs is to revisit the terms of the exception to patentability for plants, animals and biological processes. Information gathering has begun, but important questions of substance remain to be resolved. On a related issue, some members pushed hard at Seattle for the World Health Organization's list of essential drugs to be made exempt from patentability. A proposed alternative was to permit compulsory licensing of patented brands. But this allowance would backtrack on obligations fixed in the Uruguay Round.

By Seattle, there was also a strong campaign to give developing countries more time again to implement their obligations under TRIPs, particularly in relation to patents and copyright. The collapse of the Conference meant that these allowances were not granted and some other interesting issues did not get on to the agenda. They included: ensuring the agreement responds effectively and neutrally to new technologies; incorporating new trade-related treaties adopted outside the WTO (such as the WIPO Copyright Treaty); and streamlining administrative aspects such as harmonising aspects of the way governments process patent applications.

With developing countries now obliged to implement the substantive protections, much of the action on TRIPs may revolve around disputes about complying. The disputes will primarily concern violations of the text. It is of interest, nonetheless, that it is time for members to reconsider the place for non-violation complaints.

At Seattle, another proposal was a review of the Dispute Settlement Understanding. The preparations identified implementation of rulings as a pressing issue. The review sought a clearer delineation of the procedures for dealing with disagreements over whether a member who was found in breach had correctly implemented the ruling of the panel or Appellate Body. This clarification affects the circumstances in which the complainant country may take unilateral retaliatory action.

Another issue, symptomatic of the wider concerns about WTO accessibility and democracy, concerns the openness of the dispute settlement process. Some members had reached the view that the credibility of the system would be enhanced if it were opened to parties other than the member governments. But there is also a view that the WTO is exclusively and properly inter-governmental in nature. If, for example, NGOs wish to make an argument to a panel, they should have to convince a government to present it for them.

This review is also in limbo because of Seattle. It is worth noting that, in the Shrimp Products/Sea Turtle dispute (see chapter three) the Appellate Body did allow the United States Government to put in submissions that had been prepared by environmental NGOs. It further upheld the right of the panel to accept submissions from sources other than government, even if the panel had not itself requested those submissions to be made.

If the rate of disputes is to increase again, the capacity of some smaller countries to participate will be tested. One of the messages from Seattle is the increasing assertiveness of the developing countries. But the dispute settlement system is very demanding of resources; an important consideration is the quality of legal representation. It seems the WTO Secretariat has been providing some smaller countries with legal assistance.

Apart from any openings which may be found within the established agenda, such as through the GATS and TRIPs, competition policy is also on hold after Seattle. A variety of countries were sceptical of the European Union's initiative in this regard. However, competition policy may receive a fillip if the liberalisation of investment measures attracts further consideration. Another possible linkage is the reform of anti-dumping rules.

Beyond these recognised concerns lie the very thorny issues of labour and environmental standards. We have said that competition policy would provide only one component of a code of conduct for global citizens. Clearly, there was a demand at Seattle for the WTO to give positive support to such standards, rather than simply to view them as possible trade barriers. This role depends too on further institutional innovations, including cooperation with other established international organizations.

It is apparent again that any consensus on the content of these standards is a long way off. At Seattle, the United States proposed that the WTO establish a committee to work on biotechnology issues, such as government approval processes for genetically modified products. However, many member countries preferred this matter to be left to an agreement in Montreal in early 2000 for a United Nations Biosafety Protocol.

Labour standards were to be one of the issues that broke the back of the Seattle Conference. The prospect of the WTO becoming involved may have injected new life into the international organization that is well established in this field, the International Labour Organization. But if countries want the ILO to remain the main focus for this kind of international social regulation, they should start to take some of its key conventions and recommendations seriously within their own jurisdictions.

There is no room in this book to address these issues squarely, as important as they now appear to the future legitimacy of the WTO. But, if Seattle has set them back considerably, they will surely receive treatment at some time in the future. The WTO will remain an institution crucial to the progress of globalization. The Seattle experience reinforces the message of this book, the need for institutions that are able to mediate the effects of globalization, and especially the current trend in economic globalization.

NOTES

1 TRADE LAW AS A GLOBAL MEDIATOR

1 The WTO legal documents are generally available through electronic media and in hard copy. The texts of the Uruguay Round agreements, including the GATS and TRIPs, can be accessed at the WTO's web site: <http://www.wto.org>. In hard copy, they are available in the publication: WTO, *The Results of the Uruguay Round: The Legal Texts* (Geneva: WTO, 1994). They are also available from the WTO on CD-ROM.

2 The Final Act Embodying the Results of the Uruguay Round of Multilateral Trade Negotiations was adopted at a meeting of government representatives in Marrakesh on 15 April 1994. The head agreement is the Agreement Establishing the World Trade Organization. By the Final Act, the representatives agreed that the WTO Agreement would come into force by 1 January 1995. Participants in the negotiations were given two years to accept the Agreement individually. See WTO, *Legal Texts*.

3 As well as various collections of papers, there have been many articles in the journals. *The Journal of World Trade*, *World Competition*, and *The World Economy* are good sources for this perspective.

4 See for example P. Alston and M. Chiam (eds) *Treaty-Making and Australia: Globalisation versus Sovereignty?* (Sydney: Federation Press, 1995); J. Kelsey, 'Global Economic Policy-Making: A New Constitutionalism?', *Otago Law Review* 9 (1999), 535.

5 For extended analyses, see M. Trebilcock and R. Howse, *The Regulation of International Trade* (London and New York: Routledge, 1995); M. Kahler, *International Institutions and the Political Economy of Integration* (Washington: The Brookings Institution, 1995); and B. Hoekman and M. Kostecki, *The Political Economy of the World Trading System: From GATT to WTO* (Oxford University Press, 1996).

6 For example, R. Nader et al., *The Case Against Free Trade: GATT, NAFTA and the Globalization of Corporate Power* (San Francisco: Earth Island Books, 1993); G. Dunkley, *The Free Trade Adventure* (Melbourne University Press, 1997).

7 Such as C. Raghavan, *Recolonisation: GATT, the Uruguay Round and the Third World* (London: Zed Books, 1990); V. Shiva, *Monocultures of the Mind: Perspectives on Biodiversity and Biotechnology* (London: Zed Books, 1995). The web site of the Third World Network is a good source of critical commentary: <http://www.twnside.org.sg>.

8 I owe this idea to S. Ostry, 'The Domestic Domain: The New International Policy Arena', *Transnational Corporations* 1(1) (1992), p. 7. Ostry forecast that: 'Most of the policies which will be the subject of the new international initiative are in the domestic domain: the new international policy arena.'

9 See B. da Sousa Santos, 'Law: A Map of Misreading: Towards a Postmodern Conception of Law', *Journal of Law and Society* 14 (1987), 279.

10 Yves Dezalay and Bryant Garth have been perhaps the most perceptive students of this phenomenon; see for example Y. Dezalay and B. Garth, *Dealing In Virtue: International Commercial Arbitration and the Construction of a Transnational Order* (University of Chicago Press, 1996). Of course, there have been versions in the past too, such as the law merchant of the trade fairs, the ecclesiastical law of the churches and the law of the international sports associations.

11 This concept has already been employed by the renowned trade lawyer, John Jackson, in relation to the GATT agreements; see J. Jackson, *The World Trading System: Law and Policy of International Economic Relations* (Cambridge: MIT Press, 1989).

12 An insider's view of this objective is provided by Kawamoto who is with the OECD Trade Directorate; see A. Kawamoto, 'Regulatory Reform on the International Trade Agenda', *Journal of World Trade* 37(3) (1997), 81. My emphasis will be on the content of this 'efficient' regulation. Some commentators prefer to emphasise the national character of this legality, suggesting in particular that trade law is exporting a peculiarly European or American type of legality.

13 In devoting all this attention to the WTO, I might seem to favour its agenda. My position is one of a detached and sceptical observer. I am sure the WTO should be taken seriously, but my interest lies in seeing whether it can live up to its promise to create opportunities for all kinds of producers or whether it can assume responsibility for the regulation of the market power it is helping to create.

14 The restriction on government regulation would be substantial, as expropriation runs to any measures having equivalent effect.

15 For an articulation of this concept, see A. Giddens, *Beyond Left and Right: The Future of Radical Politics* (Cambridge: Polity Press, 1994).

2 A GLOBAL CONTEXT

1 For a perceptive and early formulation, see R. Nimmer and P. Krauthaus, 'Globalisation of Law in Intellectual Property and Related Commercial Law Contexts', *Law In Context* 10(2) (1992), 80.

2 A phrase used by Joel Handler in his insightful address as President of the Law and Society Association; see J. Handler, 'Postmodernism, Protest and the New Social Movements', *Law and Society Review* 26 (1992), 697.

3 Y. Dezalay, 'Introduction: Professional Competition and the Social Construction of Transnational Markets', in Y. Dezalay and D. Sugarman (eds) *Professional Competition and Professional Power: Lawyers, Accountants and the Social Construction of Markets* (London: Routledge, 1995).

4 V. Gessner, 'Global Approaches in the Sociology of Law: Problems and Challenges', *Journal of Law and Society* 22 (1995), p. 93.

5 J. Trachtman, 'Unilateralism, Bilateralism, Regionalism and Functionalism: A Comparison with Reference to Securities Regulation', *Transnational Law and Contemporary Problems* 4 (1994), p. 117.

6 For a version of this, see U. Mattei, 'Efficiency in Legal Transplants: An Essay in Comparative Law and Economics', *International Review of Law and Economics* 14 (1994), 3.

7 In her Presidential Address to the Law and Society Association, Susan Silbey wonders whether the narrative of reason might here be subordinated to the narrative of desire. She hopes that the narrative of justice will also find a place in this world. S. Silbey, '"Let Them Eat Cake": Globalisation, Postmodern Colonialism and the Possibilities of Justice', *Law and Society Review* 31 (1997), 207.

8 Upendra Baxi's writing on law and society allows us the benefit of a non-Western perspective; see for instance U. Baxi, 'Life of Law Among Globalization' in C. Arup and L. Marks (eds) *Cross-Currents: Internationalism, National Identity and Law* (Melbourne: La Trobe University Press, 1996).

9 Axford's is one of a number of recent theorisations which see opportunities in globalization; B. Axford, *The Global System: Economics, Politics and Culture* (Cambridge: Polity Press, 1995).

10 'Life world' is a term employed by Jurgen Habermas to indicate the world which has not yet been commodified or politicised; it can be aesthetic, personal, cultural, etc. See J. Habermas, *Between Facts and Norms: Contributions to a Discourse Theory of Law and Democracy* (Cambridge: MIT Press, 1996).

11 Sassen provides a rich empirical account; S. Sassen, *The Global City: New York, London, Tokyo* (Princeton University Press, 1991).

12 The implications are neatly captured in W. Mitchell, *City of Bits: Space, Place and the Infobahn* (Cambridge: MIT Press, 1995).

13 J. Ruggie, 'Territoriality and Beyond: Problematizing Modernity in International Relations', *International Organization* 47 (1993), 139.

14 Dezalay, 'Professional Competition', p. 4.

15 A point made very clearly by a colleague of mine; see V. Goldwasser, 'Current Issues in the Internationalisation of Securities Markets', *Companies and Securities Law Journal* 16 (1998), 464. Braithwaite and Drahos see countries filling different niches in the market for regulation; J. Braithwaite and P. Drahos, 'Globalisation of Corporate Regulation and Corporate Citizenship', *Flinders Journal of Law Reform* 3(1) (1999), 33.

16 For example, in a commentary on the Russian experience, see T. Waelde and J. Gunderson, 'Legislative Transplants in Transition Economies: Western Transplants – A Short-Cut to Social Market Economy Status?', *International and Comparative Law Quarterly* 43 (1994), 347.

17 Hirst and Thompson have striven to show the possibilities here; P. Hirst and G. Thompson, *Globalization in Question: The International Economy and the Possibilities of Governance* (Cambridge: Polity Press, 1996).

18 Though, thinking positively, globalization may provide the impetus for these standards to be pursued; see D. Vogel, *Trading Up: Consumer and Environmental Regulation in a Global Economy* (Cambridge: Harvard University Press, 1995).

19 M. Waters, *Globalisation* (London: Routledge, 1995), p. 9.

20 For example, W. Hutton, *The State We're In* (London: Jonathan Cape, 1994).

21 See for example D. Harvey, *The Condition of Post-modernity: An Inquiry into the Origins of Cultural Change* (Oxford: Blackwell, 1989).

22 For illustrations in the fields under study here, see S. Lash and J. Urry, *The Economies of Signs and Space* (London: Sage, 1994).

23 Dezalay, 'Professional Competition'.

24 G. Teubner, '"Global Bukowina": Legal Pluralism in the World Society', in G. Teubner (ed.) *Global Law Without A State* (Aldershot: Dartmouth, 1997).

25 The work of Sol Picciotto has been most painstaking in appraising these complexities; see for example S. Picciotto, *International Business Taxation: A Study in the Internationalization of Business Regulation* (London: Weidenfeld and Nicolson, 1992).

26 A realistic treatment of conflicts is F. Juenger, *Choice of Law and Multistate Justice* (Dordrecht: Martinus Nijhoff, 1993).

27 From J. Werner, 'Application of Competition Law by Arbitrators: The Step Too Far', *Journal of International Arbitration* 12(1) (1995), 21.

28 Offering us an Italian example, V. Olgiati, 'Process and Policy of Legal Professionalization in Europe: The Deconstruction of a Normative Order', in Dezalay and Sugarman, *Professional Competition.*

29 As my colleague, Christoph Antons, shows in reference to certain Asian countries; see C. Antons, 'Analysing Asian Law: The Need for a General Concept', *Law In Context* 13(1) (1995), 106.

30 See for example D. Saunders, *Authorship and Copyright* (London: Routledge, 1992).

31 For an indication, see P. Geller, 'Conflicts of Laws in Cyberspace: International Copyright', *Copyright Bulletin* XXXI(1) (1997), 3.

32 Ably explained by J. Ginsburg, 'Global Use/Territorial Rights: Private International Law Questions of the Global Information Infrastructure', *Journal of the Copyright Society of the USA* 42 (1995), 318.

33 G. Teubner, 'Piercing the Contractual Veil: The Social Responsibility of Contractual Networks', in T. Wilhelmsson (ed.) *Perspectives of Critical Contract Law* (Aldershot: Dartmouth, 1993). Here again, 'networks' are an appropriate metaphor. See more generally M. Castells, *The Rise of the Network Society* (Oxford: Blackwell, 1996).

34 For a very good treatment, see P. Blumberg, *The Multinational Challenge to Corporation Law: The Search for a New Corporate Personality* (New York: Oxford University Press, 1993).

35 For a very helpful review, see S. Merry, 'Review Essay: Law and Colonialism', *Law and Society Review* 25 (1991), 889.

36 For example, R. Coombe, 'The Properties of Cultures and the Possession of Identity: Postcolonial Struggle and the Legal Imagination', in B. Ziff and P. Rao (eds) *Borrowed Power: Essays on Cultural Appropriation* (New Brunswick: Rutgers University Press, 1997).

37 B. da Sousa Santos, 'Law: A Map of Misreading: Towards a Postmodern Conception of Law', *Journal of Law and Society* 14 (1987), 279.

38 Nimmer and Krauthaus, 'Globalisation of Law'. See further J. Braithwaite, 'Sovereignty and Globalisation of Business Regulation', in P. Alston and M.

Chiam (eds) *Treaty-Making and Australia: Globalisation versus Sovereignty?* (Sydney: Federation Press, 1995).

39 For example, A. Watson, *Legal Transplants: An Approach to Comparative Law* (Edinburgh: Scottish Academic Press, 1974).

40 The search is most obviously for models of business law, but a more general movement towards legal 'constitutionalism' has also come under notice. Societies in transition adopt constitutions, often with bills of rights, which to a certain extent 'judicialise' politics. There are recent instances in Eastern Europe, Latin America and South Africa.

41 For an application to the WTO, see M. Kahler, *International Institutions and the Political Economy of Integration* (Washington: The Brookings Institution, 1995). More generally, see J. Ruggie, *Constructing the World Polity: Essays on International Institutionalization* (London: Routledge, 1998), especially chapters 2 and 4.

42 G. Garrett, 'The Politics of Legal Integration in the European Union', *International Organization* 49 (1995), 171.

43 W. Mattli and A. Slaughter, 'Law and Politics in the European Union: A Reply to Garrett', *International Organization* 49 (1995), 183.

44 P. Davies, 'Market Integration and Social Policy in the Court of Justice', *Industrial Law Journal* 24 (1995), 49.

45 For example, P. Nichols, 'Realism, Liberalism, Values, and the World Trade Organization', *University of Pennsylvania Journal of International Economic Law* 17(3) (1996).

46 S. Charnovitz, 'Participation of Non-Governmental Organizations in the World Trade Organization', *University of Pennsylvania Journal of International Economic Law* 17 (1996), 331.

47 For an evaluation of copyright policy, see C. Lury, *Cultural Rights: Technology, Legality and Personality* (London: Routledge, 1993).

3 THE WORLD TRADE ORGANIZATION

1 Address by Renato Ruggiero to the XII Meeting of the Common Market Council at the MERCOSUR Heads of State Summit in Asuncion; see WTO Press Release PRESS/74, 19 June 1997. These press releases are available for a time at the WTO web site, <http://www.wto.org>, or from the Information and Media Relations Division in Geneva.

2 Address to the Herbert Quandt Foundation, Bonn; see WTO Press Release PRESS/15, 22 June 1995.

3 Ruggiero, MERCOSUR.

4 For a short history, see S. Reisman, 'The Birth of a World Trading System: ITO and GATT', in O. Kirshner (ed.) *The Bretton Wood–GATT System: Retrospect and Prospect After Fifty Years* (Armonk: ME Sharpe, 1997).

5 For background, see B. Hoekman and M. Kostecki, *The Political Economy of the World Trading System: From GATT to WTO* (Oxford University Press, 1996).

6 For the relevant texts, see WTO, *The Results of the Uruguay Round: The Legal Texts* (Geneva: WTO, 1994). I shall cite articles from the agreements in the text, nominating the particular agreement only when it is not evident from the text.

7 The making of the commitments is discussed in chapter four. For a record of the commitments, see WTO, *Legal Instruments Embodying the Results of the Uruguay Round of Multilateral Trade Negotiations* (Geneva: WTO), vols 28–30. Available from the WTO in hard copy or on CD-ROM.

8 One special inter-legality is a constitutional one – between the national government's obligations as a signatory to the WTO agreements and its obligations under its own domestic constitutional arrangements to obtain authorisation to enter into such treaties and to implement them locally. Domestic authorisation is not just a legal issue, of course. A number of governments have run into domestic difficulties because they treated agreement as a matter for the officials rather than an issue on which they needed to obtain broad political and public consensus; see J. Kelsey, 'Global Economic Policy-Making: A New Constitutionalism?', *Otago Law Review* 9 (1999), 535.

9 These declarations and decisions are also set out in WTO, *Legal Instruments*.

10 For insights from an insider, see H. Broadman, 'The Uruguay Round Accord on International Trade and Investment in Services', *The World Economy* 17 (1994), 283. Broadman was Assistant United States Trade Representative for Services, Investment and Science and Technology.

11 For a graphic portrayal of that process, see P. Drahos, 'Global Property Rights in Information: The Story of TRIPs at the GATT', *Prometheus* 13 (1995), 6.

12 See the report by Peter Drahos, 'Thinking Strategically About Intellectual Property Rights', *Telecommunications Policy* 21 (1997), 201.

13 For discussion of the process, see E. Petersmann (ed.) *The GATT/WTO Dispute Settlement System: International Law, International Organizations, and Dispute Settlement* (London: Kluwer, 1997). See also the articles in two journal issues: *International Lawyer* 32(3) (1998) and *Law and Policy in International Business* 30(2) (1999).

14 GATT, *Analytical Index: Guide to GATT Law and Practice*, sixth edition (Geneva: GATT/WTO, 1994). There is a body of expert commentary in the secondary literature; see for instance J. Jackson, *The World Trading System: Law and Policy of International Economic Relations* (Cambridge: MIT Press, 1989), E. McGovern, *International Trade Regulation: GATT, the United States and the European Union*, second edition (Exeter: Globefield Press, 1986); and R. Hudec, *The GATT Legal System and World Trade Diplomacy*, second edition (Salem: Butterworths, 1990), plus the many works by Ernst-Ullrich Petersmann.

15 See in particular T. Stewart (ed.) *The GATT Uruguay Round: A Negotiating History (1986–1992) Volume II: Commentary* (Boston: Kluwer, 1994) and J. Croome, *Reshaping the World Trade System: A History of the Uruguay Round* (Geneva: WTO Publications, 1995).

16 There are now Working Procedures for the Appellate Body, which can be consulted at the WTO web site.

17 The statistics are available from the WTO web site – click on Dispute Settlement. Information about the status of disputes is also made available in the WTO's regular newsletter, *WTO Focus*, which is published by the Information and Media Relations Division.

18 See Appellate Body Report, European Communities – Measures Affecting Meat and Meat Products (Hormones) – complaint by the United States,

WT/DS26, adopted by the DSB, 13 February 1998. Reports are available from the WTO web site if you have the technology to download them. A private London firm, Cameron May Ltd, publishes the International Trade Law Reports (ITLR) for the World Trade Law Association. The Association also publishes a Yearbook. Some reports are reproduced in the series *International Legal Materials*.

19 Appellate Body Report, India – Patent Protection for Pharmaceutical and Agricultural Chemical Products – complaint by the United States, WT/DS50, adopted 16 January 1998.

20 Hence a real headache for the WTO has been the banana dispute. The United States insists that the European Union be sanctioned for favouring banana imports from ex-colonies in the Caribbean. See European Communities – Regime for the Importation, Sale and Distribution of Bananas, complaints by Ecuador, Guatemala, Honduras, Mexico and the United States, WT/DS27. The WTO finally authorised the United States to impose sanctions on European imports.

21 See United States – Sections 301–310 of the Trade Act 1974, complaint by the European Communities, WT/DS 152/1.

22 See S. Charnovitz, 'Participation of Non-Governmental Organizations in the World Trade Organization', *University of Pennsylvania Journal of International Economic Law* 17 (1996), 331.

23 See a report of his speech, 'Preparing the WTO for the 21st Century', Speech at the commemoration of the 50th anniversary of the multilateral trading system, in *WTO Focus*, no. 31, June 1998.

24 See the report in R. Martha, 'Representation of Parties in World Trade Disputes', *Journal of World Trade* 31(2) (1997), 83.

25 See Panel Discussion, 'Is the WTO Dispute Settlement Mechanism Responsive to the Needs of Traders? Would a System of Direct Action by Private Parties Yield Better Results?', *Journal of World Trade* 32(2) (1998), 147.

26 Article I:1 of the GATT 1947 reads in part: 'any advantage, favour, privilege or immunity granted by any contracting party to any product originating in or destined for any other country shall be accorded immediately and unconditionally to the like product originating in or destined for the territories of all other contracting parties'.

27 Article III:4 of the GATT 1947 reads in part: 'The products of the territory of any contracting party imported into the territory of any other contracting party shall be accorded treatment no less favourable than that accorded to like products of national origin in respect of all laws, regulations and requirements affecting their internal sale, offering for sale, purchase, transportation, distribution or use.'

28 A criticism made by Geller; see P. Geller, 'Conflicts of Laws in Cyberspace: International Copyright', *Copyright Bulletin* XXXI(1) (1997), 3.

29 On this point, see the new Appellate Body Report, Japan – Taxes on Alcoholic Beverages – complaints by the European Communities, Canada and the United States, WT/DS8, adopted 1 November 1996, comparing Japanese *shochu* with whisky, cognac and vodka.

30 A useful review is provided by F. Roessler, 'Diverging Domestic Policies and Multilateral Trade Integration', in J. Bhagwati and R. Hudec (eds) *Fair Trade*

and Harmonization: Prerequisites for Free Trade?, 2 vols (Cambridge: MIT Press, 1996), vol. 2.

31 See the journal article by Mattoo (1997), who is with the Trade in Services Division of the WTO; A. Mattoo, 'National Treatment in the GATS – Corner-Stone or Pandora's Box', *Journal of World Trade* 31(1) (1997), 107.

32 Drake and Nicolaidis relate how this idea caught on; W. Drake and K. Nico-laidis, 'Ideas, Interests and Institutionalisation: "Trade in Services" and the Uruguay Round', *International Organization* 46 (1992), 37.

33 Analysing NAFTA, Stoyer provides a handy typology; A. Stoyer, 'Market Access and the North American Free Trade Association', *Transnational Law and Contemporary Problems* 4 (1994), 133.

34 An observation made early on in the Round by H. Ullrich, 'Industrial Prop-erty Protection: Fair Trade and Development', in F. Beier and G. Schricker (eds) *GATT or WIPO?: New Ways in the International Protection of Intellectual Prop-erty* (Munich: Max Planck Institute, 1989).

35 See Panel Report, Canada – Administration of the Foreign Investment Review Act, DS23/R, adopted 19 June 1992, BISD 30S/40. GATT panel reports are also available from the WTO web site: click on Dispute Settle-ment. They are reprinted in the supplements of the GATT series, *Basic Instru-ments and Selected Documents* (BISD).

36 Note the interesting discussion in C. Jones, 'Capitalism, Globalization and the Rule of Law: An Alternative Trajectory of Legal Change', *Social and Legal Studies* 3 (1994), 195. It remains to be seen whether the new 'constitutional-ism' will alter this.

37 Panel Report, India – Patent Protection for Pharmaceutical and Agricultural Chemical Products, WT/DS50, adopted 16 January 1998.

38 Interestingly, the administrative approach resulted because the Indian Par-liament was blocking the amendments to patent legislation necessary to enact the TRIPs provisions; see Kelsey, 'Global Policy-Making'.

39 WTO, Report of the Appellate Body, India – Patent Protection for Pharma-ceutical and Agricultural Chemical Products, WT/DS50/AB/R, 19 Decem-ber 1997, available at the WTO's web site.

40 The jurisprudence is analysed by A. Chua, 'Reasonable Expectations and Non-Violation Complaints in GATT/WTO Jurisprudence', *Journal of World Trade* 32(2) (1998), 27.

41 For a summary, see GATT, *Analytical Index*, from p. 609.

42 WTO, Appellate Body, India – Patent Protection for Pharmaceutical and Agricultural Chemical Products, p. 18.

43 On matters of procedure and proof, see C. Thomas, 'Litigation Process Under the GATT Dispute Settlement System: Lessons for the World Trade Organization', *Journal of World Trade* 30(2) (1996), 53.

44 Panel report, Japan – Measures Affecting Consumer Photographic Film and Paper, complaint by the United States, WT/DS44, adopted 22 April 1998.

45 A close account is provided by F. Upham, 'Retail Convergence: The Struc-tural Impediments Initiative and the Regulation of the Japanese Retail Indus-try', in S. Berger and R. Dore (eds) *National Diversity and Global Capitalism* (Ithaca: Cornell University Press, 1996).

46 Panel report, at p. 436. The complaint against the measures regulating promotions also failed to establish causality.

47 WTO, Appellate Body, India – Patent Protection for Pharmaceutical and Agricultural Chemical Products, p. 15.

48 An accusation levelled against the Japanese patents system in the past; see A. Wineberg, 'The Japanese Patent System: A Non-Tariff Barrier to Foreign Business?', *Journal of World Trade Law* 22 (1988), 11.

49 See for example, the GATT Panel Report, Thailand – Restrictions on Importation of and Internal Taxes on Cigarettes, DS10/R, adopted 7 November 1990, which is discussed in GATT, *Analytical Index*, from p. 522. See also WTO Panel Report, United States – Standards for Reformulated and Conventional Gasoline, complaints by Venezuela and Brazil, WT/DS2, adopted 20 May 1996.

50 The ban was said to breach the GATT provision against quantitative restrictions and prohibitions on imports (GATT 1947, article XI).

51 GATT Panel Report, United States – Restrictions on Imports of Tuna, DS21/R, unadopted, BISD 29S/91. The text of the report is reproduced in *International Legal Materials* 30 (1991), 1594. It is discussed in GATT, *Analytical Index*, from p. 525.

52 GATT Panel report, United States – Restrictions on Imports of Tuna DS29. The text of the report is reproduced in *International Legal Materials* 33 (1994), 839.

53 United States – Import Prohibition of Certain Shrimp and Shrimp Products – complaint by India, Malaysia, Pakistan and Thailand, WT/DS58, adopted 13 February 1998. The report is reproduced in *International Legal Materials* 37 (1998), 834.

54 See Appellate Body Report, United States – Import Prohibition of Certain Shrimp and Shrimp Products, WT/DS58, 12 October 1998, reproduced in *International Legal Materials* 38 (1999), 118.

55 For arguments to this effect, see J. Braithwaite, 'Transnational Regulation of the Pharmaceutical Industry', *Annals of the American Political Science Society* 525 (1993), 12.

56. For commentary, see S. Picciotto, 'The Regulatory Criss-Cross: Interaction Between Jurisdictions and Global Regulatory Networks', in W. Bratton et al. (eds) *Regulatory Competition and Co-ordination* (Oxford: Clarendon Press, 1996).

57 Another version of this approach is the European Union principle of 'subsidiarity'.

58 For a discussion of the relationship between multilateral trade and environmental agreements, see J. Thompson, 'The Impact of GATT and the Proposed MAI on Multilateral Enviroment Agreements', *Environmental and Planning Law Journal* 15 (1998), 307.

59 For the criticism, see L. Wallach, 'Hidden Dangers of GATT and NAFTA', in R. Nader et al., *The Case Against Free Trade: GATT, NAFTA and the Globalization of Corporate Power* (San Francisco: Earth Island Books, 1993). By the same token, the standards would be higher than those of some other countries.

60 Appellate Body Report, European Communities – Measures Affecting Meat and Meat Products (Hormones) – complaint by the United States, WT/DS26, adopted 13 February 1998.

61 Furthermore, by March, 1999, the United States was pushing for the go-ahead to place retaliatory sanctions on European Union products if the Union did not comply with the ruling and lift the restrictions. More disputes about this trade are likely; note W. Kerr, 'International Trade in Transgenic Food Products: A New Focus for Agricultural Trade Disputes', *The World Economy* 22 (1999), 245.

62 For a version of this characterisation, see S. Charnovitz, 'The World Trade Organization and Social Issues', *Journal of World Trade* 28(5) (1994), 17.

63 D. Vogel, *Trading Up: Consumer and Environmental Regulation in a Global Economy* (Cambridge, Mass.: Harvard University Press, 1995). Vogel has in mind the United States here and the Clinton Administration has latterly been arguing for labour and environmental standards to be given recognition in various ways, at the WTO as well as APEC and in relation to the OECD MAI.

64 See *Guardian Weekly*, 28 February 1999. The United States has also been reported as opposing the move in the Codex Alimentarius Commission for the labelling of foodstuffs containing genetically modified organisms; see the *Australian*, 29 April 1999. Yet labelling would seem to be a market-friendly approach because it helps inform consumers' choices. The Commission has also responded to safety concerns about milk produced by dairy cows injected with growth hormones, *Guardian Weekly*, 29 July 1999.

65 David Held is one of the most energetic proponents of this concept; for instance D. Held, *Democracy and the Global Order: From the Modern State to Cosmopolitan Governance* (Cambridge: Polity Press, 1994).

66 See WTO Press Release PRESS/107, 16 July 1998.

67 See Third World Network web site report: 'Democracy, transparency don't exist at WTO', 27 August 1997.

68 For example, Drahos, 'Property Rights'.

69 The Declaration is reproduced in *WTO Focus*, No. 15, January 1997.

70 B. Hawk, 'Antitrust Policy and Market Access', *OECD Observer* 201 (1997), 10.

71 M. Malaguti, 'Restrictive Business Practices in International Trade and the Role of the World Trade Organization', *Journal of World Trade* 32(3) (1998), 117.

72 See the survey by B. Hoekman, 'Competition Policy and the Global Trading System', *The World Economy* 20 (1997), 383. But also note the findings of S. Sell, 'Intellectual Property and Antitrust in a Developing World: Crisis, Coercion, and Choice', *International Organization* 49 (1995), 315.

73 F. Scherer, *Competition Policies for an Integrated World Economy* (Washington: The Brookings Institution, 1994).

74 Nicolaides, a consultant to the OECD; see P. Nicolaides, 'For a World Competition Authority', *Journal of World Trade* 30(4) (1996), 131.

75 From within the Trade Directorate of the OECD secretariat; see C. Falconer and P. Sauve, 'Globalisation, Trade and Competition', *OECD Observer* 201 (1997), 6.

76 C. Raghavan, *Recolonisation: GATT, the Uruguay Round and the Third World* (London: Zed Books, 1990), p. 157.
77 For background on these codes, see C. Cabanellas, *Antitrust and Direct Regulation of International Transfer of Technology Transactions*, IIC Studies in Industrial Property and Copyright Law (Munich: Max Planck, 1984) and M. Blakeney, *Legal Aspects of the Transfer of Technology to Developing Countries* (Oxford: ESC Publishing, 1989).
78 A problem for the United Nations codes; see F. Nixson, 'Controlling the Multinationals?: Political Economy and the United Nations Code of Conduct', *International Journal of the Sociology of Law* 11 (1983), 83.
79 Ruggiero, The Fourteenth Paul-Henri Spaak Lecture, Harvard University; see WTO Press Release PRESS/25, 16 October 1995.
80 V. Shiva, *Monocultures of the Mind: Perspectives on Biodiversity and Biotechnology* (London: Zed Books, 1995).

4 THE GENERAL AGREEMENT ON TRADE IN SERVICES

1 For a good pre-GATS survey, see R. Grey, *The Services Agenda* (Halifax: The Institute for Research on Public Policy, 1990).
2 B. Hoekman, 'Services and Intellectual Property Rights', in S. Collins and B. Bosworth (eds) *The New GATT: Implications for the United States* (Washington: The Brookings Institution, 1994). A prolific writer on trade regulation, Bernard Hoekman is from the World Bank.
3 WTO, *Legal Instruments Embodying the Results of the Uruguay Round of Multilateral Trade Negotiations* (Geneva: WTO), vols 28–30. Available from the WTO in hard copy or on CD-ROM. The schedules are set out in tabular form country by country. The columns run through the sectors or sub-sectors which the country has inscribed, listing the limitations on market access and national treatment under each mode of supply, with an extra column for additional commitments. The schedule may also include 'horizontal' commitments, which apply in every sector included in the schedule.
4 WTO, Services Sectoral Classification List, MTN.GNS/W/120.
5 In current jargon, it is called a bottom-up rather than top-down approach. See H. Tuselmann, 'The Multilateral Agreement on Investment: the case for a multi-speed convergence liberalization', *Transnational Corporations* 6(3) (1996), 87. Exceptions and reservations bedevilled the negotiations over the MAI, leading to the observation that the draft had 'more holes than cheese'.
6 See Guide to Reading the Schedules of Specific Commitments and the Lists of Article II (MFN) Exemptions, *Legal Instruments*, vol. 28, Introduction, p. ii.
7 Guides, *Legal Instruments*, vol. 28, Introduction, p. iii.
8 Early appraisals were made in H. Broadman, 'The Uruguay Round Accord on International Trade and Investment in Services', *The World Economy* 17 (1994), 283; also B. Hoekman, 'Market Access through Multilateral Agreement: From Goods to Services', *The World Economy* 17 (1994), 707; and P. Sauve, 'Assessing the General Agreement on Trade in Services: Half-Full or Half-Empty?', *Journal of World Trade* 29(4) (1995), 125. A more systematic analysis is to be found in L. Altinger and A. Endes, 'The Scope and Depth of GATS Commitments', *The World Economy* 19 (1996), 307.

9　The WTO has made a table available at its web site. For each member country, it shows in which of twelve broad service sectors they made specific commitments. See <http://www.wto.org/services/websum.htm>. A country-by-country breakdown according to a list of 149 service 'activities' can be found in Altinger and Endes, 'GATS Commitments'.

10　W. Goode, 'Services', in K. Anderson (ed.) *Strengthening the Global Trading System: From GATT to WTO* (Centre for International Economic Studies, University of Adelaide, 1996). Walter Goode was a senior official with the Australian Department of Foreign Affairs and Trade.

11　See Altinger and Endes, 'GATS Commitments' for a catalogue.

12　In this regard, note the concerns expressed by the Director-General, Renato Ruggiero, Address to the Business Council, Williamsburg, WTO Press Release PRESS/24, 13 October 1995: 'bilateralism politicizes trade. Negotiations emphasize power-based relations over rules-based relations … Commitment to international cooperation is weakened, and international agreements become less stable.' The Director-General was hinting at United States approaches to the carry-over negotiations on financial services and basic telecommunications.

13　For such a critique, see G. Dunkley, *The Free Trade Adventure* (Melbourne University Press, 1997).

14　According to the report on the negotiations in T. Stewart (ed.) *The GATT Uruguay Round: A Negotiating History (1986–1992) Volume II: Commentary* (Boston: Kluwer, 1994) and J. Croome, *Reshaping the World Trade System: A History of the Uruguay Round* (Geneva: WTO Publications, 1995).

15　Sauve, 'Half-Full'. Here again, because the negotiations were not made public, it is necessary to rely on insiders for insights.

16　Broadman, 'Uruguay Round', p. 285.

17　Guide, *Legal Instruments*, vol. 28, Introduction, p. iv.

18　M. Trebilcock and R. Howse, *The Regulation of International Trade* (London and New York: Routledge, 1995).

19　For a helpful technical analysis in the European context, see P. Eeckhout, *The European Internal Market and International Trade: A Legal Analysis* (Oxford: Clarendon Press, 1994).

20　See A. Mattoo, 'National Treatment in the GATS – Corner-Stone or Pandora's Box', *Journal of World Trade* 31(1) (1997), 107.

21　Hoekman, 'Services', pp. 87–8.

22　See R. Burnett, *The Law of International Trade* (Sydney: Federation Press, 1994).

23　Guide, *Legal Instruments*, vol. 28, Introduction, p. iii.

24　Mattoo, 'Pandora's Box', p. 109.

25　The various annexes form part of the GATS and are included in the WTO publications, *The Results of the Uruguay Round: The Legal Texts* (Geneva: WTO, 1994) and *Legal Instruments* (see details in note 3 above).

26　The Understanding was adopted at Marrakesh, see WTO, *Legal Instruments*, for the text.

27　See Stewart, *A Negotiating History*.

28　An argument put by the renowned trade theorist, J. Bhagwati, 'Comment on Hoekman', in Collins and Bosworth (eds), *New GATT*.

29 For insight into the European experience, see Lord Wedderburn, *Labour Law and Freedom: Further Essays in Labour Law* (London: Lawrence and Wishart, 1995).

30 See WTO, *Legal Instruments*, vol. 1.

31 These commitments comprise a Third GATS Protocol: Schedules of Specific Commitments relating to Movement of Natural Persons. These country schedules are available from the WTO in a separate publication.

32 WTO, Committee on Trade and Environment, Report, WT/CTE/1 (Geneva: WTO, 1996).

33 See WTO Press Release PRESS/51, 1 July 1996.

34 As reported by Sauve, 'Half-Full'.

35 See WTO Press Release PRESS/18, 26 July 1995; also *WTO Focus*, no. 5, August–September 1995.

36 Second GATS Protocol: Revised Schedules of Commitments on Financial Services, available from the WTO as a separate publication.

37 See Second GATS Protocol.

38 See *WTO Focus*, no. 3, May–June, 1995.

39 *Australian Financial Review*, 28 July 1995.

40 See Ruggiero, Address to the Business Council, Williamsburg, WTO Press Release PRESS/24, 13 October 1995.

41 Fifth GATS Protocol: Schedules of Specific Commitments and Lists of Exemptions from Article II concerning Financial Services, available from the WTO as a separate publication.

42 See *WTO Focus*, no. 25, December 1997. A summary of commitments, country by country, was made available at the WTO web site: <http://www.wto.org/wto/new/sumfin.htm>.

43 The Chair of the WTO Council for Trade in Services has suggested this; see R. De Sola Sauvel, 'Proposals Advancing Liberalization Through Regulatory Reform', in OECD, *International Trade in Professional Services: Assessing Barriers and Encouraging Reform* (Paris: OECD, 1997).

44 Japan – Measures Affecting Distribution Services, complaint by the United States, WT/DS45. The current status of the dispute is still pending consultations.

45 Grey, *Services Agenda*.

46 See for example the recent report by the OECD, *Harmful Tax Competition: An Emerging Global Issue* (Paris: OECD, 1998).

5 THE CASE OF LEGAL SERVICES

1 Y. Dezalay and B. Garth, *Dealing In Virtue: International Commercial Arbitration and the Construction of a Transnational Order* (University of Chicago Press, 1996).

2 For an exploration of this theme, see M. Cain and C. Harrington (eds) *Lawyers in a Postmodern World: Translation and Transgression* (Buckingham: Open University Press, 1994).

3 See for example the study of corporate takeover work in M. Powell, 'Professional Innovation: Corporate Lawyers and Private Lawmaking', *Law and Social Inquiry* 18 (1993), 423.

4 I owe this rounded view to Terry Halliday, 'The State of Art on the Art of State: Politics and the Craft of Legal Professions', paper presented to the Annual Meeting of the Research Committee on the Sociology of Law, International Sociological Association, University of Tokyo, August 1995.

5 See for example the experience with privatisation law; M. Moran and T. Prosser, *Privatization and Regulatory Change in Europe* (Buckingham: Open University Press, 1994).

6 See P. Lewis (ed.) *Law and Technology in the Pacific Community* (Boulder: Westview Press, 1994).

7 For such comments on the Eastern European experience, see M. Krygier, 'The Constitution of the Heart', *Law and Social Inquiry* 20 (1995), 1033.

8 See for instance M. Kessler, 'Review Essay: Lawyers and Social Change in the Postmodern World', *Law and Society Review* 29 (1995), 769.

9 T. Waelde and J. Gunderson, 'Legislative Transplants in Transition Economies: Western Transplants – A Short-Cut to Social Market Economy Status?', *International and Comparative Law Quarterly* 43 (1994), 347.

10 C. Whelan and D. McBarnet, 'Lawyers in the Market: Delivering Legal Services in Europe', *Journal of Law and Society* 19 (1992), 49.

11 U. Baxi, 'Life of Law Among Globalization', in C. Arup and L. Marks (eds) *Cross-Currents: Internationalism, National Identity and Law* (Melbourne: La Trobe University Press, 1996).

12 S. Sassen, *The Global City: New York, London, Tokyo* (Princeton University Press, 1991).

13 J. Shapland, 'How Do Lawyers Accomplish Trans-National Lawyering?', paper presented to the Joint Meeting of the Law and Society Association and the Research Committee on the Sociology of Law, University of Strathclyde, Glasgow, July 1996.

14 See *Japan Law Journal*, February 1995.

15 See generally OECD, *International Trade in Professional Services: Assessing Barriers and Encouraging Reform* (Paris: OECD, 1997).

16 However, we would expect countries to argue that 'service providers' involved in the administration of justice, such as judges and state advocates, are excludable.

17 For a summary, see WTO, Council for Trade in Services, *Legal Services*, Background Note by the Secretariat, S/C/W/43, 6 July 1998. The note was made available at the WTO's web site in early 1999.

18 See chapter four for an explanation of the architecture of the GATS and the meaning of these terms.

19 WTO, *Legal Services*, p. 18.

20 Again, to some extent, I have to rely on insiders' accounts, see S. Kigawa, 'Gaikoku Bengoshi Ho, Foreign Lawyers In Japan: The Dynamics Behind Law no. 66', *Southern California Law Review* 62 (1989), 1489.

21 See the report by R. Grondine, 'Foreign Law Firms in Japan Thwarted', *International Financial Law Review* 13(7) (1994), 11.

22 See WTO, *Legal Instruments Embodying the Results of the Uruguay Round of Multilateral Trade Negotiations* (Geneva: WTO), vol. 29, pp. 24040–5.

23 A good history is provided by R. Goebel, 'Lawyers in the European Community: Progress Towards Community-Wide Rights of Practice', in M. Daly and

R. Goebel (eds) *Rights, Liability and Ethics in International Legal Practice* (New York: Transnational Juris Publications, 1995).

24 My source is I. Jacobs, 'The Theory and the Practice of Implementation of the Mutual Recognition of Diplomas Directive', *New Law Journal*, 3 June 1994.

25 See WTO, *Legal Instruments*, vol. 28, pp. 23568–9.

26 Grondine, 'Foreign Law Firms in Japan'.

27 EC Directive 98/5/EC to facilitate practice of the profession of lawyer on a permanent basis in a member state other than that in which a qualification was obtained [1998] O.J. L077, 14.03.98.

28 For the rule, see American Bar Association, 'Model Rule for the Licensing of Legal Consultants', *International Lawyer* 28 (1994), 207.

29 T. Stewart (ed.) *The GATT Uruguay Round: A Negotiating History (1986–1992) Volume II: Commentary* (Boston: Kluwer, 1994).

30 See the outline by a member of the US delegation, R. Self, 'Legal Services and the Emergence of a Service Economy: Practical and Theoretical Considerations', in B. Garth et al. (eds) Issues of Transnational Legal Practice, *Michigan Yearbook of International Legal Studies* 7 (1985), 269.

31 See WTO, *Legal Instruments*, vol. 30, pp. 25269–88.

32 See the report by L. Wayne, 'Asia-Pacific: The Regulation of Foreign Lawyers and Law Firms', *Asia Law*, September 1993, p. 7.

33 Whelan and McBarnet, 'Lawyers in the Market'.

34 S. Nelson, 'Legal Services', in OECD, *Professional Services*, p. 47.

35 R. De Sola Sauvel, 'Proposals Advancing Liberalization Through Regulatory Reform', in OECD, *Professional Services*, p. 111.

36 In an upbeat report for UNCTAD, see J. Reichman, 'The "TRIPs" Agreement and the Developing Countries', *UNCTAD Bulletin* 23 (1993), 8.

37 See WTO, *Legal Services*, p. 14.

38 The incident is reported in a history of one of the law firms involved in the litigation; see M. Cannon, *That Disreputable Firm ... The Inside Story of Slater and Gordon* (Melbourne University Press, 1998).

39 See WTO Press Release PRESS/73, 29 May 1997. The Release appended the Guidelines.

40 De Sola Sauvel, 'Proposals', p. 111.

41 WTO, Council for Trade in Services, Disciplines on Domestic Regulation in the Accountancy Sector, see *WTO Focus* no. 36, December 1998, or available at the WTO's web site.

6 THE AGREEMENT ON TRADE-RELATED INTELLECTUAL PROPERTY RIGHTS

1 United States – Imports of Certain Automotive Spring Assemblies, adopted 26 May 1983, reproduced in *Basic Instruments and Selected Documents*, Supplement 30, p. 107.

2 United States – Section 337 of the Tariff Act of 1930, The Case of Certain Aramid Fibre, adopted 7 November 1989, BISD 36S/345.

3 For a catalogue of action taken, see for example A. Gutterman, 'The North-South Debate Regarding the Protection of Intellectual Property Rights', *Wake Forest Law Review* 28 (1993), 29.

4 The 'legislative history' comes from T. Stewart (ed.) *The GATT Uruguay Round: A Negotiating History (1986–1992) Volume II: Commentary* (Boston: Kluwer, 1994); see also D. Gervais, *The TRIPs Agreement: Drafting History and Analysis* (London: Sweet and Maxwell, 1998).

5 A figure often cited at the time; see for instance an article by an official with the OECD Trade Directorate, E. Dohlman, 'International Piracy and Intellectual Property', *OECD Observer* 154 (1988), 33.

6 See P. Drahos, 'Global Property Rights in Information: The Story of TRIPs at the GATT', *Prometheus* 13 (1995), 6; also G. Evans, 'Intellectual Property as a Trade Issue in the Making of the Agreement on TRIPs', *World Competition* 18(2) (1996).

7 As set out in S. Golt, *The GATT Negotiations 1986–90: Origins, Issues and Prospects* (London: British–North American Committee, 1988).

8 See the GATT's own report in *GATT Activities 1991* (Geneva: GATT, 1992).

9 As nominated by the United States Federal Trade Commission, The Effects of Greater Economic Integration within the European Community and the United States, Third Follow-up Report, reproduced in K. Simmonds and B. Hill (eds) *Law and Practice Under the GATT*, loose-leaf updated (Dobbs Ferry: Oceana Publications, 1991).

10 See for example the report by the OECD, *Biotechnology and Patent Protection* (Paris: OECD, 1985).

11 See for example the article by a senior official, J. De Miramon, 'The International Interest in Intellectual Property', *OECD Observer* 163 (1990), 4.

12 See the papers published at the time; UNCTAD, *Uruguay Round: Further Papers on Selected Issues* (New York: United Nations, 1990) and UNCTNC, *New Issues in the Uruguay Round of Multilateral Trade Negotiations* (New York: United Nations, 1990).

13 'Review of Developments in International Trade Law', in the Attorney-General's Department publication, *Eighteenth International Trade Law Conference* (Canberra: AGPS, 1991).

14 The proper names being the Paris Convention for the Protection of Industrial Property, the Berne Convention for the Protection of Literary and Artistic Works, the International Convention for the Protection of Performers, Producers of Phonograms and Broadcasting Organisations, and the Treaty on Intellectual Property in respect of Integrated Circuits. The text of these conventions can be accessed at the WIPO web site: <http://www.wipo.org>. They are also available in hard copy as WIPO publications, available from the WIPO headquarters in Geneva.

15 For a useful analysis, see G. Evans, 'The Principle of National Treatment and the International Protection of Industrial Property', *European Intellectual Property Review* 18 (1996), 149.

16 Evans, 'The Principle of National Treatment'.

17 In particular, S. Ricketson, *The Berne Convention for the Protection of Literary and Artistic Works 1886–1986* (Deventer: Kluwer, 1987).

18 For a discussion of national variations, see Note, 'Global Limits on "Look and Feel": Defining the Scope of Software Copyright Protection by International Agreements', *Columbia Journal of Transnational Law* 34 (1996), 503.

19 See the evaluation by J. Reichman, 'Universal Minimum Standards of Intellectual Property Protection under the TRIPs Component of the WTO Agreement', *International Lawyer* 29 (1995), 345.

20 It is complemented by the Patent Cooperation Treaty, which WIPO administers as well.

21 Patent protection has been the subject of dispute at the WTO already. A focal point has been 'pipeline' protection. But an important dispute is looming between the European Union and Canada. The European Union has challenged the permission Canada gives to local manufacturers to work inventions, trialling and stockpiling generic drugs, in anticipation of the patent running out on the brand name drug.

22 According to H. Wegner, 'The Many Faces of Patent Harmonization', *European Intellectual Property Review* 15 (1993), 3.

23 For a survey, see V. Suthersanen, 'A Brief Tour of "Utility Model" Law', *European Intellectual Property Review* 20 (1998), 51.

24 Again, a WIPO administered treaty.

25 See *WTO Focus*, no. 17, March 1997. More recently, members have begun to discuss a proposal for a registration system; see *WTO Focus*, no. 36, December 1998.

26 The issue is canvassed in J. Lahore, 'The Herschel Smith Lecture: Intellectual Property Rights and Unfair Copying: Old Concepts, New Ideas', *European Intellectual Property Review* 14 (1992), 428.

27 For a discussion, see C. Arup, *Innovation, Policy and Law* (Cambridge University Press, 1993).

28 A point well made by Michael Blakeney, *Trade Related Aspects of Intellectual Property Rights: A Concise Guide to the TRIPs Agreement* (London: Sweet and Maxwell, 1996), appendix.

29 R. Dhanjee and L. de Chazournes, 'Trade-Related Aspects of Intellectual Property Rights (TRIPs): Objectives, Approaches and Basic Principles of the GATT and Intellectual Property Conventions', *Journal of World Trade* 24(5) (1990), p. 10.

30 So for these (seventy so) countries, the deadline is the year 2000.

31 For this suggestion, see F. Abbott, 'Commentary: The International Intellectual Property Order Enters the 21st Century', *Vanderbilt Journal of Transnational Law* 29 (1996), p. 474.

32 C. Raghavan, *Recolonisation: GATT, the Uruguay Round and the Third World* (London: Zed Books, 1990).

33 My own work has examined this regulation, see Arup, *Innovation.*

34 J. Reichman, 'Beyond the Historical Lines of Demarcation: Competition Law, Intellectual Property Rights, and International Trade After the GATT's Uruguay Round', *Brooklyn Journal of International Law* XX (1993), 75.

7 THE CASE OF GENETIC CODES

1 A useful analysis of trends was provided by Margaret Sharp, from the prestigious Science Policy Research Unit at Sussex University; see M. Sharp, 'David, Goliath and the Biotechnology Business', *OECD Observer* 164 (1990), 22.

2 OECD, *Agricultural Policies, Markets and Trade: Monitoring and Outlook 1994* (Paris, OECD, 1994).

3 See for example the appraisal by P. McMichael, 'World Food Restructuring under a GATT Regime', *Political Geography* 12 (1993), 198.

4 These are recognised in the work of Geoff Lawrence, 'Genetic Engineering and Australian Agriculture: Agenda for Corporate Control', *Journal of Australian Political Economy* 25 (1989), 1.

5 Lawrence, 'Genetic Engineering'.

6 Venda Shiva (1993) has issued this warning about developments in India; see *Cultivating Diversity: Biodiversity, Conservation and the Politics of the Seed* (Dehra Dun: Research Foundation for Science, Technology and Natural Resources Policy, 1993).

7 A point stressed in my earlier work; see C. Arup, *Innovation, Policy and Law* (Cambridge University Press, 1993).

8 K. Pavitt, 'Introduction', in G. Bertin and S. Wyatt, *Multinationals and Intellectual Property: the Control of the World's Technology* (Hemel Hempstead: Harvester Wheatsheaf, 1988), p. xii.

9 McMichael, 'World Food'. The WTO banana dispute has epitomised how trade brings different farming methods and established social allegiances into conflict. The United States complained of European favouritism for the small-scale producers of their old Caribbean colonies.

10 A good overview is to be found in the paper by two officials of the OECD's Science, Technology and Industry Directorate; see L. Auriol and F. Pham, 'What Pattern to Patents?' *OECD Observer* 179 (1992–3), 15. WIPO publishes figures for patents, broken down for instance by country of origin and country of destination; see WIPO, *Industrial Property Statistics*, an annual publication in two parts, abridged and final. These statistics can also be downloaded from WIPO's web site: <http://www.wipo.org>.

11 The OECD produces useful industry surveys; see for example OECD, *Biotechnology, Agriculture and Food* (Paris: OECD, 1992).

12 See J. Kloppenburg, *First the Seed: The Political Economy of Plant Biotechnology 1492–2000* (Cambridge University Press, 1988). This trend is confirmed by a recent Christian Aid report, outlined in the *Guardian Weekly*, 16 May 1999.

13 See the business periodical, *India Today*, 15 January 1994.

14 Michael Blakeney (1998) notes that it has become a standard bearer for regional trade agreements; see M. Blakeney, 'The Role of Intellectual Property Law in Regional Commercial Unions in Europe and Asia', *Prometheus* 16 (1998), 341.

15 For a record of the experience prior to TRIPs, see A. Rotstein, 'Intellectual Property and the Canada–United States Free Trade Agreements: The Case of Pharmaceuticals', *Intellectual Property Journal* 8 (1993), 121; also A. Gutterman, 'The North-South Debate Regarding the Protection of Intellectual Property Rights', *Wake Forest Law Review* 28 (1993), 29.

16 OECD, *Biotechnology*.

17 For a spirited defence of patenting, see S. Crespi, 'The Wicked Animal Must Defend Itself', *European Intellectual Property Review* 17 (1995), 431.

18 S. Sell, 'Intellectual Property and Antitrust in a Developing World: Crisis, Coercion, and Choice', *International Organization* 49 (1995), 315.

19 See C. Antons, 'Analysing Asian Law: The Need for a General Concept', *Law In Context* 13(1) (1995), 106.

20 For a recent survey, see OECD, *Intellectual Property Practices in the Field of Biotechnology* (Paris: OECD, 1999).

21 These examples are drawn from S. Bent et al., *Intellectual Property Rights in Biotechnology Worldwide* (New York: Macmillan Stockton Press, 1987).

22 The notes are set out in D. Nichol, 'Should Human Genes be Patentable Inventions under Australian Patent Law?', *Journal of Law and Medicine* 3 (1995–1996), 231.

23 Genetech v Wellcome Foundation [1989] *RPC* (*Reports of Patent, Design and Trade Mark Cases*) 147.

24 Chiron v Murex (Hepatitis C Virus) [1995] *FSR* (*Fleet Street Reports of Patent Cases*) 4.

25 Biogen v Medeva [1995] *RPC* 25.

26 [1995] *EPOR* (*European Patent Office Reports*) 1.

27 Biogen v Medeva (1996) 30 *IPR* (*Intellectual Property Reports Australia*) 438.

28 Amgen v Chugai Pharmaceutical, 18 *USPQ* (*United States Patents Quarterly*) 2d 1016 (Fed. Cir., 1991).

29 In re Deuel, 34 *USPQ* 2d 1210 (Fed. Cir., 1995).

30 B. Looney, 'Should Genes Be Patented? The Gene Patenting Controversy: Legal, Ethical and Policy Foundations of an International Agreement', *Law and Policy in International Business* 26 (1995), p. 23.

31 P. Ducor, 'In re Deuel: Biotechnology Industry v Patent Law?', *European Intellectual Property Review* 18 (1996), 35.

32 I. Karet, 'Priority and Sufficiency, Inventions and Obviousness: UK Court of Appeal Decision in Biogen v Medeva', *European Intellectual Property Review* 17 (1995), pp. 45–6.

33 Ducor, 'Biotechnology Industry'.

34 P. Crespi, 'Opinion: Biotechnology, Broad Claims and the EPC', *European Intellectual Property Review* 17 (1995), p. 268.

35 For reports, see R. Eisenberg, 'Genes, Patents, and Product Development', *Science* 257 (1992), 903. A good illustration of the variations in standpoints on intellectual property is the international group of scientists who have decided to publish information about the human genome on the Internet before it can be patented; see *Guardian Weekly*, 9 December 1999.

36 See J. Strauss, 'Patenting Human Genes in Europe – Past Developments and Prospects for the Future', *International Review of Industrial Property and Copyright* 26 (1995), 920.

37 Diamond v Chakrabarty, 447 *US* (*United States Reports*) 303 (1980).

38 For a summary, see Strauss, 'Human Genes'.

39 Patents Act 1990 (Cth), section 19(2).

40 W. Lesser, *Equitable Plant Protection in the Developing World: Issues and Approaches* (Christchurch: Eubios Ethics Institute, 1991).

41 [1995] *EPOR* 357. For discussion, see M. Llewelyn, 'Article 53 Revisited: Greenpeace v Plant Genetic Systems NV', *European Intellectual Property Review* 17 (1995), 506.

42 For a report, see [1996] 3 EIPR D-90, the news section of the *European Intellectual Property Review.*

43 See *New Scientist,* 4 March 1995, p. 5.

44 See *New Scientist,* 11 March 1995.

45 Legal Protection of Biotechnological Inventions – Directive 98/44 [1998] *Official Journal of the European Communities* (O.J.) C108/6. The Directive is to be implemented by 30 July 2000.

46 C. Correa, 'The GATT Agreement on Trade-Related Aspects of Intellectual Property Rights: New Standards for Patent Protection', *European Intellectual Property Review* 16 (1994), 327.

47 B. Greengrass, 'The 1991 Act of the UPOV Convention', *European Intellectual Property Review* 13 (1991), p. 468.

48 R. Jarvis, 'Plant Patent, Plant Variety Right or Both?', *Australian Intellectual Property Journal* 4 (1993), 211. Presumably, the 'activities' would have to be more assertive.

49 C. Correa, 'Biological Resources and Intellectual Property Rights', *European Intellectual Property Review* 14 (1992), 154.

50 I rely on Greengrass, '1991 Act', for these insights.

51 Ibid., p. 469.

52 Lesser, *Equitable Protection.*

53 Including the United States and the People's Republic of China. These country-by-country developments are noted in the *World Intellectual Property Report* and the *European Intellectual Property Review.* WIPO lists states which are party to the various acts of the Convention in its monthly publication: *Intellectual Property Laws and Treaties.*

54 D. Scalise and D. Nugent, 'International Intellectual Property Protection for Living Matter: Biotechnology, Multinational Conventions and the Exception for Agriculture', *Case Western Reserve Journal of International Law* 27 (1995), 83.

55 The history is in T. Stewart (ed.) *The GATT Uruguay Round: A Negotiating History (1986–1992) Volume II: Commentary* (Boston: Kluwer, 1994).

56 Interview with Mr Matthijs Geuze, Legal Affairs Officer, at GATT Secretariat, July 1993.

57 Again, see regular reports in the *World Intellectual Property Report* and the *European Intellectual Property Review.*

58 C. Correa, 'Implementation of the TRIPs Agreement in Latin America and the Caribbean', *European Intellectual Property Review* 19 (1997), 435.

59 J. Carlson, 'Strengthening the Property-Rights Regime for Plant Genetic Resources: The Role of the World Bank', *Transnational Law and Contemporary Problems* 6 (1996), 91.

60 First formulated in Rio de Janeiro in 1995. The Convention is administered by a secretariat associated with the United Nations Environment Program (UNEP).

61 V. Shiva, *Monocultures of the Mind: Perspectives on Biodiversity and Biotechnology* (London: Zed Books, 1995).

62 Confirmed at the fourth implementation conference in Bratislava, 4–15 May 1998.

63 See *World Intellectual Property Report* 1996(11), 20. Earlier, the WTO Committee on Trade and Environment had assisted the Secretariat of the

Convention in the preparation of a document entitled Biological Diversity and Trade-Related Intellectual Property Rights: Synergies and Relationship. It is available from the WTO Secretariat. The Convention's Executive Secretary has observer status in the Committee on Trade and Environment.

64 United Nations Environment Program, Convention on Biological Diversity, Note by Executive Secretary, Workshop on Traditional Knowledge and Biological Diversity, Madrid 24–28 November 1997, UNEP/CBD/TKBD/1/2.

65 The TRIPs Council has begun to make preparations for the review. Members are being asked to provide information on how they are applying the provisions, particularly through use of alternative sui generis systems; see *WTO Focus* no. 36, December 1998. The Convention on Biodiversity will also be invited to supply information.

8 THE CASE OF COMMUNICATIONS MEDIA

1 See the *Age* (Melbourne), 5 September 1996.

2 There are variations between countries as well as within countries. For figures relating to the relatively affluent OECD countries, see for example OECD, *Information Technology Outlook 1997* (Paris, OECD, 1997); more widely, World Bank, *World Development Report 1998–99* (New York: World Bank, 1999).

3 A particular enthusiast is G. Gilder, *Life After Television: The Coming Transformation of Media and American Life* (New York: Norton, 1994). Also see F. Cairncross, *The Death of Distance* (London: Orion Business Books, 1998).

4 Quoted in the *Guardian Weekly*, 17 April 1996.

5 For a sympathetic critique, see H. Rheingold, *The Virtual Community: Homesteading on the Electronic Frontier* (New York: Addison-Wesley, 1993).

6 *Guardian Weekly*, 22 May 1994.

7 A concept borrowed from a colleague of mine, Peter White, 'On-Line Services: The Emerging Battle for Transactional Space', *Media Information Australia* 79 (1996), 3. An earlier work I found particularly helpful was N. Garnham, *Capitalism and Communication: Global Culture and the Economics of Information* (London: Sage, 1990).

8 E. Dyson, 'Intellectual value and the Net', *Wired* 3.07 (1995), 136.

9 For a useful analysis, see the report by the OECD, *Telecommunications and Broadcasting: Convergence or Collision?* (Paris: OECD, 1992).

10 For some survey and analysis of the field, see R. Mansell, 'Strategic Issues in Telecommunications: Unbundling the Information Infrastructure', *Telecommunications Policy* 18 (1994), 588. Mansell is with SPRU.

11 For an account of these negotiations, see I. Shefrin, 'The North American Free Trade Agreement: Telecommunications in Perspective', *Telecommunications Policy* 17 (1993), 14.

12 See the report by H. Ungerer, 'EC Competition Law in the Telecommunications, Media, and Information Technology Sectors', *Fordham International Law Journal* 19 (1996), 1111. Ungerer is with the European Commission Competition Directorate.

13 According to a report by P. Drahos and R. Joseph, 'Telecommunications and Investment in the Great Supranational Regulatory Game', *Telecommunications Policy* 19 (1995), 619.

14 See *WTO Focus*, no. 6, October–November 1995.

15 Director-General Renato Ruggiero, Address to the Business Council, Williamsburg, WTO Press Release PRESS/24, 13 October 1995.

16 See WTO Press Release PRESS/48, 1 May 1996.

17 See *WTO Focus*, no. 16, February 1997.

18 Fourth GATS Protocol: Schedules of Specific Commitments concerning Basic Telecommunications, available from the WTO as a separate publication. The Protocol, together with the Decision on Commitments in Basic Telecommunications, is reproduced in *International Legal Materials* 36 (1997), from p. 354.

19 An observation made by E. Noam, 'Beyond Liberalization: From the Network of Networks to the System of Systems', *Telecommunications Policy* 18 (1994), 286.

20 OECD, *Convergence or Collision*, p. 101.

21 E. Plowman and L. Hamilton, *Copyright: Intellectual Property in the Information Age* (London: Routledge and Kegan Paul, 1991), p. 149.

22 For an intriguing study of cultural difference, see W. Alford, *To Steal a Book is an Elegant Offence: Intellectual Property in Chinese Civilization* (Stanford University Press, 1995).

23 S. Stewart, *International Copyright and Neighbouring Rights*, second edition, 2 vols (London: Butterworths, 1993) has brought together many examples.

24 For some discussion, see Note, 'Global Limits on "Look and Feel": Defining the Scope of Software Copyright Protection by International Agreements', *Columbia Journal of Transnational Law* 34 (1996), 503. Unfortunately, there is not space to expound all the national differences. As we shall see, the approach to protection adopted by TRIPs now starts to channel these issues, but it still leaves scope for differences.

25 For a lively account of the industry disputes, see J. Band and M. Katoh, *Interfaces on Trial: Intellectual Property and Interoperability in the Global Software Industry* (Boulder: Westview Press, 1995).

26 The events are set out in P. Waters and P. Leonard, 'The Lessons of Recent EC and US Developments for the Protection of Computer Software under Australian Law', *European Intellectual Property Review* 13 (1991), 124. See Legal Protection of Computer Programs – Directive 91/250 [1991] O.J. L122/42 for the outcome.

27 See the report in the *Age* (Melbourne), 23 April 1996. The recommendation came from Australian Attorney-General's Department, Copyright Law Review Committee, *Computer Software Protection* (Canberra, 1995). In April 1999, a subsequent Government introduced into Parliament a Bill to amend the Copyright Act 1968 (Cth) and provide a decompilation right.

28 See the item in *World Intellectual Property Report* 1996(10), 259.

29 S. John, 'What Rights Do Record Companies Have on the Information Superhighway?', *European Intellectual Property Review* 18 (1996), 74.

30 A characterisation ventured by Oman (1993), who had been Register of Copyright in the United States; see R. Oman, 'Berne Revision: The Continuing Drama', *World Intellectual Property Report* 1993(7), 160.

31 A number of jurisdictions have been discussing and developing an approach. See in particular the European Union: Copyright and Related Rights in the

Information Society – Proposal for Directive [1998] O.J. C108/6; and the United States: Digital Millennium Copyright Act 17 U.S.C. #1201 (1998).

32 A comparative survey of such provisions can be found in Australian Copyright Council, *Fair Dealing in the Digital Age*, Bulletin no. 92 (Sydney: ACC, 1996).

33 From Australia, see for instance A. Mason, 'Developments in the Law of Copyright and Public Access to Information', *European Intellectual Property Review* 19 (1997), 636.

34 See *World Intellectual Property Report*, 1996(10), 82.

35 See Legal Protection of Databases – Directive 96/9 [1996] O.J. L77/20.

36 Ungerer, 'EC Competition Law'.

37 Oman, 'Berne Revision'.

38 WIPO, Diplomatic Conference on Certain Copyright and Neighbouring Rights Questions, Basic Proposal for the Substantive Provisions of the Treaty on Certain Questions Concerning the Protection of Literary and Artistic Works to be Considered by the Diplomatic Conference, WIPO, Geneva, CRNR/DC/4, 30 August 1996. Made available at the WIPO web site: <http://www.wipo.org>.

39 The texts of the Treaties can be consulted at the WIPO web site. They are reproduced in *International Legal Materials* 36 (1997), from p. 67.

40 The insider's account comes from Cresswell (1997) who was head of the Australian Government delegation to the Conference; see C. Cresswell, 'Copyright Protection Enters the Digital Age: the New WIPO Treaties on Copyright and on Performances and Sound Recordings', *Copyright Reporter* 15(1) (1997), 4.

41 For a useful discussion of these points, see J. Cohen, 'WIPO Copyright Treaty Implementation in the United States: Will Fair Use Survive?', *European Intellectual Property Review* 21 (1999), 236.

42 Cresswell, 'Copyright Protection'.

43 See the *Australian*, 24 December 1996.

44 See *World Intellectual Property Report* 1996(11), 31.

45 See *Australian Financial Review*, 6 February 1997.

46 Within WIPO, discussions have been held subsequently in relation to the rights of performers and broadcasters, but key WIPO members are so far resisting the convening of a diplomatic conference on audiovisual rights; see *World Intellectual Property Report* 1999(6), 198. The main sticking point was said to be the readiness with which rights in audiovisual performances should be transferable. The data protection proposal has also made slow progress.

47 For updates on signatories, see WIPO, *Intellectual Property Laws and Treaties*.

48 For this report, I rely on A. Dixon and M. Hansen, 'The Berne Convention Enters the Digital Age', *European Intellectual Property Review* 18 (1996), 604.

49 See *WTO Focus*, no. 33, August–September 1998. Further, WTO Secretariat, *Electronic Commerce and the Role of the WTO* (Geneva, 1998).

50 See the country survey by B. Hoekman, 'Competition Policy and the Global Trading System', *The World Economy* 20 (1997), 383.

51 These possibilities were well recognised by the United States Federal Trade Commission, *Anticipating the 21st Century: Competition Policy in the New High Tech, Global Marketplace: A Report by FTC Staff* (Washington, 1996).

52 One acquisition was the catalogue of Ansel Adams photographs.

53 For reports of this case, see the articles by A. Page, 'Microsoft: A Case Study in International Competitiveness, High Technology and the Future of Antitrust Law', *Federal Communications Journal* 47 (1995), 99 and L. Anderson, 'US v Microsoft, Antitrust, Consent Decrees, and the Need for a Proper Scope of Judicial Review', *Antitrust Law Journal* 65 (1996), 1.

54 The Federal Trade Commission had had success obtaining Intel's consent to an order prohibiting it from withholding technical information which is vital to companies developing systems that use or work with Intel's microchip processors; see *Australian Financial Review*, 19 March 1999.

55 A good account of this vacillation is provided in D. Levy, 'The Regulation of Digital Conditional Access Systems', *Telecommunications Policy* 21 (1997), 661.

56 The *Age* (Melbourne), 23 February 1999.

57 These investments assume interesting patterns, the Spanish telecom being active for example in Latin America.

58 For a resume of these codes, see OECD, *Telecommunications and Broadcasting: Convergence or Collision?* (Paris: OECD, 1992).

59 Some examples come from the European Commission, *Competition Aspects of Interconnection Agreements in the Telecommunications Sector*, Final Report to the European Commission (DG IV) (Brussels: EC, 1995).

60 OECD, Committee for Information, Computer and Communications Policy, *Information Infrastructure Convergence and Pricing* (Paris: OECD, 1996).

61 See the European Commission Decision, MSG Media Service [1994] O.J. L364/1.

62 Ungerer, 'EC Competition Law'.

63 Consequently, the policies are both particular and tentative; see for example United States Department of Justice and Federal Trade Commission, 'Antitrust Guidelines for the Licensing of Intellectual Property', reproduced in *European Intellectual Property Review* 17(7) (1995), supplement 3.

64 Intellectual property would just be one source of 'content' control. In the United Kingdom, the Monopolies Commission barred News Ltd from acquiring the Manchester United soccer club.

65 I have relied on Vinje (1995) for a report of the outcome of this case, the Magill case. In this case, television stations were using copyright to deny access to the program information needed to make a rival magazine competitive. See T. Vinje, 'The Final Word on Magill', *European Intellectual Property Review* 17 (1995), 297.

66 This latter proviso is not self-evident but is one of several elucidations offered in a paper by Tuthill from the WTO Secretariat; see L. Tuthill, 'Users' Rights: The Multilateral Rules on Access to Telecommunications', *Telecommunications Policy* 20 (1996), 89.

67 The Background Note was made available at the WTO web site.

68 The paper is reproduced in *International Legal Materials* 36 (1997), 367.

69 Ruggiero, Economic Globalization Increases Impact of National Competition Policies on International Trade, WTO Press Release PRESS/30, 30 November 1995.

70 See P. Lloyd and G. Sampson, 'Competition and Trade Policy: Identifying the Issues After the Uruguay Round', *The World Economy* 18 (1995), 681.

71 F. Scherer, *Competition Policies for an Integrated World Economy* (Washington: The Brookings Institution, 1994).

72 P. Nicolaides, 'For a World Competition Authority', *Journal of World Trade* 30(4) (1996), 131.

73 For this interpretation, see F. Nixson, 'Controlling the Multinationals?: Political Economy and the United Nations Code of Conduct', *International Journal of the Sociology of Law* 11 (1983), 83.

74 J. Reichman, 'The "TRIPs" Agreement and the Developing Countries', *UNCTAD Bulletin* 23 (1993), 8.

75 P. Preston, 'Competition in the Telecommunications Infrastructure: Implications for the Peripheral Regions and Small Countries of Europe', *Telecommunications Policy* 19 (1995), 253.

76 For the experience with the Guidelines, see R. Blainpain, 'Guidelines for Multinational Enterprises' in R. Blainpain (ed.) *Comparative Labour Law: Law and Industrial Relations in Industrialized Market Economies*, fifth and revised edition (Deventer: Kluwer, 1993).

77 See the report by Martin Khor, 'Competing views on "competition policy"', at the Third World Network web site: <http://www.twnside.org.sg>.

78 *WTO Focus*, no. 15, January 1997.

79 For insight into UNCTAD's recent views about competition policy, see UNCTAD, *World Investment Report 1997: Transnational Corporations, Market Structure and Competition Policy* (New York: United Nations, 1997).

80 See W. Rothnie, 'Trade, Competition and Intellectual Property', *Prometheus* 16 (1998), pp. 355–6. Also see the discussion of competition policy in WTO, *Third Annual Report* (Geneva: WTO Publications, 1997), vol. 1.

81 See A. Wimmer, 'The Impact of the General Agreement on Trade in Services on the OECD Multilateral Agreement on Investment', *World Competition* 19(4) (1996), 109.

82 M. Khor, 'Trade and investment: Fighting over investors' rights at the WTO', published at the Third World Network web site.

83 'WTO Denies Claim by Special Interests Linking Ruggiero to MAI', WTO Press Release PRESS/91, 17 February 1998.

84 WTO, Report (1998) of the Working Group on the Interaction Between Trade and Competition Policy to the General Council, WT/WGTCP/2, 8 December 1998 (available at the WTO's web site).

85 Ibid., p. 39.

INDEX

bilateralism, 33–4, 179–80

codes of conduct
  communications media and, 288,
    303
  legal services and, 170–2
  OECD and, 297
  plant genetic resources and, 247
  transnational business practices
    and, 14, 90, 296–7
  United Nations and, 89, 296
Codex Alimentarius Commission, 81,
  83
competition regulation
  access codes, 141, 288–93
  computer platforms and, 284–6
  essential facilities and, 281–8
  GATS and, 138–41, 291–3
  market access and, 87–9
  Microsoft case, 284–6
  national differences, 280–1
  nullification or impairment and, 88
  Seattle meeting and, 310
  Singapore meeting and, 297–300
  telecommunications networks and,
    141, 286–9
  trade barrier as, 85–7
  transnational business practices
    and, 89–91
  TRIPs and, 210–11, 289–90, 240–2
  WTO agenda for, 294–300
  WTO Working Group report,
    300–1
communications media
  access to, 256–9
  competition regulation and,
    262–3, 280–9
  convergence of, 258–9, 289

copyright and, 263–72
  GATS and, 260–3, 291–3, 309
  globalization and, 255–9
  national regulation and, 259–60
  TRIPs and, 272–4, 289–90
  WIPO treaties and, 274–80
conflict of laws, 29–32, 90
copyright
  Berne Convention and, 187–8
  communication right of, 270,
    275–7
  exceptions to, 207–9, 271, 277
  licensing practices, 189, 270–2
  national differences and, 264–5
  non-voluntary licensing and,
    207–9, 271, 290
  on-line content and, 267, 268–70,
    276–8
  performances and, 190, 277–8, 279
  related rights, 190
  reproduction right of, 270, 276
  software interfaces and, 188,
    267–8, 273
  sound recordings and, 190, 277
  TRIPs and, 187–91, 272–4
  works and, 188, 276
  WIPO treaties and, 274–80

developing nations
  GATS and, 108–9
  TRIPs and, 179, 201–3
  WIPO treaties and, 279
  WTO decision making and, 49–50,
    310
dispute settlement
  access to, 54, 310
  Dispute Settlement
    Understanding, 50, 310

dispute settlement *contd.*
  disputes, pattern of, 52–3, 309
  GATS and, 132–4
  GATT and, 78–9
  jurisprudence of, 50–1
  non-violation complaints and, 75,
    133, 205
  nullification or impairment in,
    70–5
  process of, 50–2
  reform of, 54, 310
  TRIPs and, 203–6

environmental standards, 78–9, 83,
  128–9, 310–11

foreign investment
  GATS and, 122, 127–8
  MAI and, 12, 297–300
  national regulation of, 127
  Singapore meeting and, 297–300
  TRIMs and, 298–9

GATS
  audiovisual services and, 260–1
  commitments by member
    countries, 106–10
  competition regulation and,
    139–141, 291–3
  dispute resolution and, 132–4
  exceptions to, 75–6, 128–32, 142
  financial services and, 134–8
  foreign investment and, 122, 127–8
  law as, 68–9, 100–4
  legal services and, 158–61, 167–72
  listings approach, 75, 103–6, 121
  market access and, 62–3, 117–21
  MFN in, 56–7, 107, 110–13, 135–8
  modes of service supply, 122–8
  movement of natural persons and,
    124–6
  national measures and, 66, 115,
    119–21
  national treatment in, 61–2,
    113–17
  non-violation complaints and, 75,
    133

Seattle meeting and, 308–9
services nature of, 97–8, 101–2
telecommunications services and,
  141, 261–3, 291–3
transparency and, 132
Uruguay Round and, 106–10
GATT
  dispute settlement, 51
  environmental measures and,
    77–9, 81
  jurisprudence of, 51
  MFN in, 55
  national measures and, 66
  national treatment in, 58
  nullification or impairment in, 71–4
globalization
  carriers of, 4, 14–15
  communications media and, 255–9
  conceptualisations of, 19–21
  convergence and divergence in,
    22–7
  culture and, 25–7
  economics of, 22–3
  genetic codes and, 215–19
  law and, 22, 27–32, 215–19
  legal services and, 146–55
  localism and, 22–7
  research into, 18–19

interface, concept of, 8–10, 16–18,
  32–8
inter-legality, concept of, 5–8, 32–4, 43

law
  GATS and, 68–70
  globalization and, 27–9
  mediation as, 17–18, 36–7,
  multilateral institutions and, 34–7,
    44–5
  TRIPs and, 68–70
labour standards, 82, 84, 310–11
legal pluralism, concept of, 5–8,
  27–32
legal services
  business structures for, 168–70
  competition regulation and, 169
  European Union and, 164–6

GATS and, 158–61
globalization and, 146–55, 167–72
Japan and, 161–4
locations for, 151–4
multidisciplinary practices and, 169
national regulation of, 150–1, 154–8
professional standards for, 170–2
styles of service supply and, 146–8
United States and, 166–7
lex mercatoria, 7, 27–8, 148

market access
competition regulation and, 87–9
GATS and, 61–3, 117–21
legal services and, 118–19, 159–60
national regulation and, 63, 120–1
nature of, 11–12, 62–3, 117–21
non-discrimination and, 63, 119
MFN
environmental measures and, 57, 78–9
exceptions to, 56–7, 100, 111–12
GATS and, 56–7, 110–13
GATT and, 55
legal services and, 158–9
national measures and, 77–9
nature of, 10–11, 55, 109–10
regional agreements and, 112–13
TRIPs and, 56–7, 186–7
multilateralism, 34–6, 183
mutual recognition, 80, 131

national treatment
GATS and, 61–2, 113–17
GATT and, 58
legal services and, 159
mutual recognition and, 80, 131
national measures and, 58–9, 115–6
nature of, 10–11, 57–61, 114–16, 300
regulatory competence and, 59, 109
TRIPs and, 61–2, 184–6
neo-liberalism, 9, 14, 59, 63, 76, 91, 119

OECD, 222, 247, 297, 299

patents
attitudes to, 220–3, 230–3
competition regulation and, 209–11, 242
compulsory licensing of, 193, 209–11, 231–4, 241–3
discovery/invention distinction, 224–9
European exceptions to, 230–3
genetic codes and, 224–30
indigenous property rights and, 222–4, 242–7
national differences, 223–8
Paris Convention and, 191
role of, 218–22
TRIPS and, 191–4, 238–42, 309
UPOV and, 237
plant genetic codes
agriculture and, 216–19
Convention on Biodiversity and, 245–7
genetically modified products and, 81–3, 311
globalization and, 215–19
indigenous peoples and, 219, 242–7
patents and, 224–30, 233
science and technology of, 215–17
TRIPs and, 238–42
UPOV and, 234–8

regulatory competition, 24–5, 79–83

transnational business practices
codes of conduct and, 14, 90, 296–7
competition regulation and, 89–91
GATS and, 131–2
MAI and, 297
TRIPs and, 211
WTO and, 13, 41, 141–2, 307
TRIPs
competition regulation and, 210–11, 240–2, 289–90
Convention on Biodiversity and, 247
copyright, 187–91, 272–4
dispute settlement and, 203–6

TRIPs *contd.*
  enforcement provision for, 199–201
  exceptions, 77, 192, 207–10, 239–40, 274
  geographical indications, 196, 309
  information, 198–9
  law, as, 68–70, 203–4
  MFN in, 56–7, 186–7
  national treatment in, 61–2, 184–6
  non-violation complaints and, 74, 205
  patents, 191–4, 238–42, 309
  re-regulation, as, 13
  Seattle meeting and, 309
  trademarks protection for, 194–5
  trade regulation, as, 11–13, 64–5, 95, 179
  transparency, 203
  UPOV and, 240
  Uruguay Round and, 178–83

UNCTAD, 84, 182, 221, 298–9
United States
  financial services and, 135–8
  legal services and, 166–7
  MFN and, 100, 135–8
  TRIPs and, 179–83
  WIPO treaties and, 275–9
  WTO disputes and, 53, 54

WIPO
  Copyright Treaty, 274–80
  Performances and Phonograms Treaty, 274–80
  WTO and, 82, 84, 205, 279, 309
WTO
  agenda for, 9, 294–300, 307–8
  constitution of, 47–9, 307, 310
  decision making in, 49–55, 310
  dispute settlement by, 49–55, 310
  interface as, 8–10, 37–8, 41
  international organizations and, 82–5
  NGOs and, 83–4, 296, 310
  Seattle meeting, 308–11
  Singapore meeting, 297–300
  SPS Agreement, 81–2